# Reading Primary Sourc

MW00356251

'*Reading Primary Sources* is at once a bold and useful book . . . With felicity and insight, the authors of this volume show us how modern historians now read primary sources . . . A wonderful volume for teachers and students alike.' – Helmut Walser Smith, *Vanderbilt University, USA*.

Primary sources are not only the very basis of historical research, but are also widely used in undergraduate teaching as a way to introduce students to voices from the past. The contributors to this book explore various traditions in source-criticism, explain the different ways documents can be read, and use exciting examples from their own research to suggest the insights (and also difficulties) texts might offer.

Taking into account the huge expansion in the range of primary sources used by historians, the volume includes chapters on opinion polls, surveillance reports, testimony and court files, in addition to more traditional genres such as letters, memoranda, diaries, novels, newspapers, political speeches and autobiography. To aid the reader's understanding of source criticism, the chapters in the first part of this unique volume give an overview of both traditional and new methodological approaches to the use of primary documents. In addition, the introduction offers an accessible checklist suggesting some of the most important steps for interpreting historical sources.

Taking examples of sources from many European countries and the USA, and providing up-to-date information on the most widely used textual sources, this is the perfect companion for every student of history who wants to engage with primary sources.

**Miriam Dobson** is Lecturer in Modern History at the University of Sheffield. Her forthcoming monograph explores popular responses to the reforms of the Khrushchev era.

**Benjamin Ziemann** is Reader in Modern History at the University of Sheffield. His recent publications include: *War Experiences in Rural Germany 1914–1923* (2007); (ed.), *Peace Movements in Western Europe, Japan and the USA during the Cold War* (2007).

# Routledge guides to using historical sources

Routledge Guides to Using Historical Sources is a series of books designed to introduce students to different sources and illustrate how they are used by historians. Each volume explores one type of primary source from a broad spectrum and, using specific examples from around the globe, examines their historical context, and the different approaches that can be used to interpret these sources.

**Reading Primary Sources**
*Miriam Dobson and Benjamin Ziemann*

**History Beyond the Text**
*Sarah Barber and Corinna Penniston-Bird* (forthcoming)

**Using Material Sources** (forthcoming)

# Reading Primary Sources

The interpretation of texts from nineteenth- and twentieth-century history

**Edited by Miriam Dobson and Benjamin Ziemann**

Routledge
Taylor & Francis Group

LONDON AND NEW YORK

First published 2009 by Routledge
2 Park Square, Milton Park, Abingdon, Oxon OX14 4RN

Simultaneously published in the USA and Canada
by Routledge
711 Third Ave, New York, NY 10017

*Routledge is an imprint of the Taylor & Francis Group, an informa business*

Typeset in Times New Roman
by Swales and Willis Ltd, Exeter, Devon

*British Library Cataloguing in Publication Data*
A catalogue record for this book is available from the British Library

*Library of Congress Cataloging in Publication Data*
Reading primary sources: the interpretation of texts from 19th and 20th
century history/edited by Miriam Dobson and Benjamin Ziemann.
    p. cm — (Routledge guides to using historical sources)
1. History—Methodology.   2. History, Modern—
19th century——Sources.   3. History, Modern—20th century——Sources.
I. Dobson, Miriam.   II. Ziemann, Benjamin.
D16.R23 2008
909.8072—dc22

ISBN 10: 0–415–42956–0 (hbk)
ISBN 10: 0–415–42957–9 (pbk)
ISBN 10: 0–203–89221–6 (ebk)

ISBN13: 978–0–415–42956–6 (hbk)
ISBN13: 978–0–415–42957–3 (pbk)
ISBN13: 978–0–203–89221–3 (ebk)

# Contents

vi  *Contents*

# Acknowledgments

The idea for this volume grew out of the experience of teaching source-based modules to history undergraduates at the University of Sheffield. We found no proper guidance on source interpretation reflecting recent theoretical developments, nor any up-to-date introduction to some of the most important source genres used in the writing of modern history. Our attempt to fill this void owes a lot to the help and encouragement of many people. First and foremost, the authors, an interdisciplinary team of younger scholars from the USA, the UK and the European continent, brought their expertise and their reflexivity to this venture. We are most grateful for their efforts and their readiness to share ideas on textual interpretation. Many other colleagues in England, across the Channel and the Atlantic offered help and advice, or commented on a draft version of our introduction. In particular, we would like to thank Henk de Berg, Caroline Bland, Rüdiger Graf, Caroline Hoefferle, Daniel Morat, Helmut Walser Smith, Martin Heale, Daniel Scroop and Matt Houlbrook. In addition, Benjamin Ziemann would like to thank Christoph Reinfandt and Christiane Eifert, Willibald Steinmetz and Thomas Welskopp, who invited him to discuss the topic of this volume in their research seminars in Tübingen and Bielefeld, and those who asked pertinent questions at these occasions. He would also like to thank Thomas Kühne and Thomas Mergel, friends and permanent interlocutors.

At Routledge, Eve Setch was enthusiastic about our project from the beginning. Her support has made this book possible, and her help during the early stages was invaluable. We would also like to thank the anonymous reviewers she solicited for their suggestions. Annamarie Kino, who took over from Eve as our editor, was equally cheerful and guided us safely into and through the production process. Thanks go also to Christine Brocks for her professional work in compiling the index. We gratefully acknowledge the permission to print excerpts from the diaries of Therese Lindenberg, published by the Böhlau Verlag in Vienna, and to print excerpts from the *Meldungen aus dem Reich*, granted by Heinz Boberach. The University of Sheffield kindly granted permission to use documents from the university archive as a cover illustration. Our thanks go to the University of Sheffield and to Anthea Stevenson in particular who helped select appropriate images.

Miriam Dobson and Benjamin Ziemann, Sheffield, February 2008

# Contributors

**David Carlson** is Associate Professor of English Literature at the California State University, San Bernardino.

**Miriam Dobson** is Lecturer in Modern History at the University of Sheffield.

**Moritz Föllmer** is Senior Lecturer in Modern European History at the University of Leeds.

**Christa Hämmerle** is Professor of Modern History at the University of Vienna.

**Anja Kruke** is Research Associate at the Historical Research Centre of the Friedrich Ebert Foundation, Bonn.

**Philipp Müller** is Assistant Professor at the Department of History, Humboldt University, Berlin.

**Devin O. Pendas** is Associate Professor of History at Boston College.

**Stephen Vella** is Assistant Professor of British History at Wake Forest University, Winston-Salem, NC.

**Paul Readman** is Lecturer in Modern British History at King's College London.

**Julia Reid** is Lecturer in Victorian Literature at the University of Leeds.

**Christoph Reinfandt** is Professor of Modern English Literature at the University of Tübingen.

**Kristina Spohr Readman** is Lecturer in International History at the London School of Economics and Political Science.

**Claudia Verhoeven** is Assistant Professor of Modern European History at George Mason University, Fairfax, VA.

**Benjamin Ziemann** is Reader in Modern History at the University of Sheffield.

# Abbreviations

| | |
|---|---|
| AHR | American Historical Review |
| CSH | Cultural and Social History |
| CWH | Cold War History |
| D&S | Diplomacy and Statecraft |
| DH | Diplomatic History |
| EHR | English Historical Review |
| H&T | History and Theory |
| HJ | Historical Journal |
| HRes | Historical Research |
| HWJ | History Workshop Journal |
| JCWS | Journal of Cold War Studies |
| P&P | Past and Present |

# Introduction

*Benjamin Ziemann and Miriam Dobson*

Since the late 1980s, heated debates about the nature of historical knowledge have at times unsettled our profession. As in every controversy, this is in part a conflict about reputations and material resources, situated in the context of an ever more specialised, differentiated and ultimately also fragmented academic discipline. On the surface, however, the issue is presented as a conflict about the 'truth' historians can expect to establish about the past. In the United States and in Great Britain (less so actually on the European continent, where different and more diverse intellectual traditions come into play), it is labelled as the opposition between postmodernism and its critics. Proponents of the former declare their interest as being to liberate the engagement with the past from what they call 'empiricist' notions of knowledge and truth, i.e. the notion that the truth can be easily established through a focus on the empirical facts without any further theoretical or conceptual ado.[1] Advocates of the latter rush to the 'defence of history' as they understand it. They refer to the seemingly both pivotal and eternal 'rules of verification' which have been come down to us unscathed from the 1820s, when they were first laid down by the German historian Leopold von Ranke. These saviours of history have no doubt that the postmodernists are 'simply . . . unrealistic', and that their assertions are 'self-evidently' wrong.[2]

Strong language indeed in both camps, an indication that the stakes are big and emotions are running high. And language is actually at the core of this controversy. It is basically an epistemological conflict (from the Greek word *episteme*=knowledge) over the nature and the possibilities of knowledge about the meaning of language and of written texts in particular. The debate between postmodernists and the defenders of a 'realist' conception of historical research is largely focused on the way primary sources or historical texts should be handled, read and interpreted in order to make true assertions about the past. As one would expect from the fever-pitch nature of this controversy, it has led to a veritable theory industry which has no precedent in Anglophone historical scholarship. In recent years, a growing number of monographs have attempted to outline the epistemological foundations of the study of history and the possibilities of knowledge about the past. Most of these books can be fairly labelled as belonging to the 'realist' camp. They engage with what they perceive as postmodernism and its twin, literary criticism, acknowledge some of its questions but hardly any of its answers. Ultimately, these books defend the position that history is based on the proper reading and weighing of sources. Altogether, they explain the rules of a methodological toolkit that amounts, in the words of John Tosh, 'to little more than the obvious lessons of common sense'.[3] Moreover, none of these books provide a detailed example of the actual practice of textual interpretation for the purposes of the historian.[4]

The rather abstract nature of declarations regarding historical study is the point of departure for this volume. In presenting these chapters, we are guided by the idea that the distinction between realist and 'postmodern' positions outlined above also determines the way we handle primary sources. The chapters of this volume aim to introduce the peculiarities and possible interpretations of different source genres, in a combination of methodological reflection and practical example. The contributors to this volume share the assumption that controversies about the nature of textual interpretation are at the core of the debate on postmodernism in the historical profession, and that these controversies can be solved not by abstract deliberations, but only by a serious effort to reflect theoretical differences in the light of the actual empirical work of the historian. Whatever their individual take on these issues is, they agree that at the heart of an historian's work is her reading and interpretation of texts, and that any theoretical assumptions must make a tangible difference to these interpretations to be at all relevant.

This is the aim of this book: to introduce anyone who is interested in the interpretation of primary documents from the nineteenth and twentieth centuries to some of the most important textual source genres, their history, forms, implications and possibilities, and thus to inform, expand and differentiate the interpretation of these texts. After we have explained the scope and organisation of this volume, the following section of this introduction intends to provide a comprehensible checklist with some general rules and practical hints for the interpretation of sources. In doing so, the chapter also highlights the plurality of possible reading strategies historians can pursue nowadays, without necessarily subscribing to the assertion that such a position has to be labelled as 'postmodernist'.

## Organisation and scope of this volume

The first part of this volume will explore different approaches to the interpretation of texts. In the first chapter, Philipp Müller demonstrates how the interpretation of primary sources became the very basis of historical research as professional standards for scholarship in this discipline were developed from the late eighteenth century onwards. Here the focus is usually on Leopold von Ranke, whose image as the inventor of the 'historical-critical method' of source criticism seems to be set in stone. In fact he did not actually invent the repertoire of techniques for the verification, collation and documentation of sources. Rather, he refined and summed up a tradition of textual criticism dating back to sixteenth-century humanism.[5] More important, source criticism in nineteenth-century German historicism, which set the standards for professional historical scholarship, was bound up with the notion of understanding (*Verstehen*) as the means to access the meaning of texts from the past. And in this respect, not Ranke, but Johann Gustav Droysen (1808–1884) was the key figure.[6] Droysen carefully distinguished between the rather technical aspects of 'source-criticism', and the more substantial 'interpretation' of past ideas and meanings. In making this distinction, the idea of understanding through interpretation and thus the concept of hermeneutics (from the Greek *hermeneuein*=to interpret) was central, and became pivotal for the 'elevation of history to the rank of a science'.[7]

For Droysen, verifying the authenticity of a source or its exact date was only the first, preparatory step. His core interest was to decipher the meaning of utterances from the past through hermeneutical means, famously stating that 'the essence of historical method is *understanding* by means of *research*'.[8] One of the problems of this approach, however, was that the possibility of understanding was only partly provided by appropriate techniques of textual interpretation. It rested rather on the ability of the historian to empathise with past actors or to 'feel into' (*Einfühlen*) their mindset. Droysen thus imagined that the historian would feel a certain empathy towards the aspirations and fears of historical actors. He argued that this ability was ultimately guaranteed by the overarching continuity of Western civilisation since Greek antiquity. This rather questionable assertion reveals the deeply ethnocentric nature of classical historicist scholarship, and is one of the reasons why recent cultural historians, often dealing with premodern or non-Western cultures, have stressed the opaque and alien nature of past utterances. In order to gain access to these cultures, they often rely on the cultural anthropology of Clifford Geertz, who has described the starting point for his reflections on a new, semiotic hermeneutics succinctly in the question: 'What happens to *verstehen* when *einfühlen* disappears?'[9] Geertz is thus questioning whether we really have the necessary bonds or shared heritage with people from the distant past (or indeed distant lands in the present) to make this kind of instinctive understanding possible.

As an alternative to hermeneutics, a growing number of historians have shown an interest in theories of discourse since the 1970s.[10] With both the older, historicist and the more recent, anthropological hermeneutics these approaches share the idea that historical research is based on the interpretation of meaningful utterances from the past. But they disagree with regard to the idea that understanding can be based on empathy, and that it is possible to unearth the 'true' intentions of the author. Based on various and sometimes diverse semiotic and linguistic theories, discourse analysis seeks to interpret a text not with regard to the meaning an author has invested in it, but rather as a result of the interplay of the various linguistic elements within the text. In the second chapter, Christoph Reinfandt provides an accessible account of the 'linguistic turn' and some of the myths and controversies which tend to cloud its significance. From the perspective of a literary scholar, he reflects on the connections between theories of textual interpretation and practices of reading, and gives a state-of-the-art introduction to recent debates on these issues.

In the second part of the volume, each chapter provides an in-depth discussion of one particular source genre. After an introduction to the definition and history of the particular genre, the contributors explore the ways historians have used and interpreted these sources, using examples. The authors of these chapters are experts in modern European and North American history, and will introduce the reader to the tradition and usage of documents in various countries, including Austria, France, Germany, Russia, the United Kingdom and the United States. Each chapter discusses at least one example in detail, and explains if and how recent theoretical debates have affected the actual interpretative strategy with regard to a particular type of primary source.

In our selection of genres, we do not aim for a comprehensive coverage of all widely used textual sources. Rather, we have decided to present a mixture of traditionally and more recently used genres. Some of them, for example newspapers, memoranda, speeches and also autobiographies, have been part of the staple diet of both political and social historians for quite a long time. Others, for example opinion polls, court files or surveillance reports have been widely used only in the past two decades. Some of these genres have been particularly important in motivating historians to expand the boundaries of textual interpretation and to experiment with more sophisticated reading techniques. But all of these genres can be approached with a variety of different strategies, as the chapters in this part demonstrate in detail.

Some crucial omissions should at least be mentioned, though.[11] One of them is petitions, in which subjects appeal or complain to their rulers or political representatives and voice their individual and collective grievances. They are essentially an early modern genre, situated in the context of a hierarchical society and political representation through estates, as the most prominent example, the *Cahiers de Doléances* which were presented to the French Estates General in 1789, indicates. But as hierarchical patterns of deference faded away only gradually, petitions were filed also in many nineteenth- and even twentieth-century contexts, and they offer crucial insights into the political languages and the experiences of ordinary people.[12] Another more recently used type of documentation about the past is patient records. Since the 1980s, historians of medicine have used these sources in order to get a more vivid picture of the social relations within hospitals and asylums and to analyse the experiences of patients. Beyond their context of origin, these sources have also a bearing on the wider cultural history of modern societies.[13]

This volume focuses on textual sources (bearing in mind that before technology allowed for the easy recording of sound, speeches and testimony – although oral sources – only survived when turned into text). Such a focus may seem obsolete when we consider the massive expansion of the foundations of historical research since the beginning of the twentieth century. Marc Bloch, the co-founder of the French history journal *Annales* in 1929, was one of the first historians to massively expand the repertoire of sources on which historical research is based. In his main field of expertise, medieval agricultural history, he investigated evidence from field-names, maps of settlements, technical artefacts and even aerial photos, as well as more traditional documents. These efforts were a deliberate challenge to the dominant position of philology (the discipline for the interpretation of texts) that at the time forced historians to focus on written texts.[14] Since then, historians of the modern era have also discovered and used a variety of non-textual source genres such as films, photos and cartoons, but also uniforms, architecture and material culture more generally.[15]

We have chosen to focus on written documents in order to give coherence to this volume. Firstly, it can be argued that the bulk of the primary evidence used in current research on European and American history since 1800 still falls under the categories tackled in this volume, despite the diversification of historical sub-disciplines in the last three decades and the subsequent pluralism in the definition of what constitutes legitimate sources. Secondly, the issues raised here can be of relevance when working with other kinds of sources. It is not true that 'tools of lit-erary analysis are of little use' for historians because they use genres which cannot be put under the scrutiny of these approaches. Even sources such as 'statistical series' of criminal offences which, Richard Evans argues, 'bear little resemblance to any form of literature', can, we argue, qualify for a textual reading.[16] Discourse theory has transformed our understanding of what constitutes a text. From this per-spective a list of criminal statistics can be read as a text. Such a reading is not pri-marily interested in the actual figures it contains, but rather in the categories and distinctions it uses, and in the set of meaningful assertions criminal statistics allow about the social 'reality' of a society.[17]

Finally, it should not be forgotten that the idea of 'facts' to be found in archival sources is in itself fictitious, since the management and storage of information in archives has an important bearing on the selection of those texts which can actually come under the scrutiny of the historian. From 1800, the individual subject has been constituted through records about his or her employment, marriage, tax returns and so on, meaning that knowledge about the people who make up the 'nation' is recorded and preserved in archival collections of state papers. In the nineteenth century, the formalisation and differentiation of administrative techniques came together with the preservation of certain documents in newly established national archives, on which the historical profession mostly relied. Although these struc-tures could accommodate new types of documents, provided they were of concern for the nation – for example after the First World War, many national archives started to collect war letters of their citizen soldiers – they favoured a strictly state-centred canon of documents. Only in recent years, along with the expansion of their interpretative techniques and interests, have historians tried to build up or identify alternative archives that give us access to neglected or even suppressed documents, such as the diaries of ordinary people or the testimony of survivors of genocides.[18]

## How to interpret primary sources – a basic checklist

How do all these ideas and theories affect the way we read and interpret a particu-lar primary source, one that we might encounter in the context of a history module at university or in private reading? Are there some rules of thumb which render a service to those who need to come to grips with texts from the past? The following section aims to offer some practical guidance. It does not provide a 'catechism' for the analysis of sources, comparable to one the late Arthur Marwick has suggested.[19] Firstly, the plurality of possible readings renders problematic the idea of a fixed set of rules to be memorised and heeded, suggested by religious connotations of the term 'catechism'. Secondly, the following list of possible approaches is not concerned with the verification of sources, with issues of authenticity and veracity, but focuses instead on the interpretation of the meanings a text carries. Thirdly, this list does not focus on the intentions and interests the author might have possibly had, as a hermeneutical reading would encourage. Rather, it builds on the insights of a variety of more recent approaches to the interpretation of texts, and tries to explain and apply their potential with reference to practical examples.

## 1  What are the key concepts of the source and their connotations?

This analytical strategy follows the idea of a history of concepts, developed by J.G.A. Pocock, Quentin Skinner and Reinhart Koselleck in slightly different ways.[20] The common denominator of these approaches is the assumption that every time a person speaks or writes they use terms that carry a complex set of meanings (called semantics), developed over a long period of time. For example, politicians may talk about the role of the state and about the liberty of the people they represent. The use of these terms is pragmatic and unique, specific to the current context in which it is used. But 'state' and 'liberty' are not only words or technical terms with a single meaning. They are also concepts, nouns which aggregate and accumulate different meanings over time. 'Welfare state' or 'nation state' are key connotations of the state in recent times, whereas 'liberty' could refer to the liberties (in plural) of early modern estates, but also to a modern catalogue of human rights. Every pragmatic usage of concepts is embedded in these historical semantics. In order to capture the richness of a text, we should analyse not only how meanings have evolved over time (called a diachronic perspective), but also the different and often competing connotations a term can carry at any given historical moment (synchronic perspective).

Concepts are not only indicators or reflections of historical change, but can also be factors causing change. An example from a period of accelerated change might illustrate this. In 1970, the Catholic Church in West Germany organised an opinion poll among its members. The analysis of 21 million questionnaires, distributed to all adult Catholics, was meant to reflect the attitudes and expectations of the laity. But it was also intended as an outlet for the growing discontent among many progressive Catholics, frustrated with the snail's pace at which the reforms promised by the Second Vatican Council from 1962 to 1965 were being implemented. The wording of the questionnaire, however, proved controversial – and highly revealing. Throughout the 14 questions of the survey, the term 'Church' was synonymous with church officials and the church hierarchy and thus reflected a very traditional conception of the hierarchical nature of the Catholic Church. These semantics stood in a stark contrast to the constitutions of the Vatican Council, which had just promulgated the concept of the church as the 'people of God', implying that the hierarchical offices had only a servant role and that all church members would have a call to holiness.[21]

A focus on the concepts of the questionnaire can thus reveal important reasons for the inner strife in the Catholic Church during these years, when the meaning of the term 'church' was the object of intense conflict. Within this one institution, we find significant differences in the way this key concept was being used, and this tells us something significant about the reforms and the uneven, contested nature of their implementation.

## 2 Does the text use imbalanced binary distinctions?

The analysis of historical semantics is a key avenue to reconstruct the meaning of primary sources. There is, however, a separate category of concepts that deserves special attention: binary concepts which distinguish between social groups or collectives in an imbalanced manner.[22] The distinction between Gentiles and Jews is perhaps the best example for the exclusionary consequences of binary concepts, and the study of antisemitic discourse has indeed been a trailblazer for this line of enquiry. When nineteenth-century antisemites talked about the differences between the French or German people and the Jews, they implied an imbalance and indeed a strong preference. Gentiles and Jews did not simply represent two different poles, as North and South Pole, where no one would indicate a preference for either of the two. Antisemitic texts used the concept 'Jews' and its connotations rather to portray them in a derogatory manner as the very opposite of French and Germans, and as the most dangerous enemy of French and German national identity. These texts had a clear preference for the national in-group, bearing in mind that most of the Jews they scorned were also French or German passport-holders.

The Jews were, for example, characterised as lazy idlers who generated income only through speculation and money-lending, whereas Germans were portrayed as hardworking, industrious and honest people, to such an extent that just the mention of the lack of these qualities could be read as allusions to 'Jewish' people even without naming them explicitly. With the accumulation and repetition of a whole catalogue of differences between the two groups, the semantics of antisemitism cemented the asymmetry between Gentiles and Jews, but also the internal coherence of both groups. A vocabulary of prejudice thus relied on asymmetrical binary distinctions, which prepared the ground first for exclusionary legislation and later for violent action against Jews.[23] Sometimes, then, a text in fact includes commentary or reflection on concepts (or groups) that are not even mentioned. Condemnation of the Jewish 'other' tells us also something about the identity and values of their binary opposite (e.g. the French, German etc.), even if there is no reference to the dominant group. This can also work for other kinds of binary pairs. By defining women in certain ways (for example, as hysterical and neurotic), texts also tell us something about men in a patriarchal society, namely that they are the polar opposite (rational and controlled) – and as such, they are of course worthy of political, social and economic power.

## 3 Does the text employ metaphors, and what is their specific function for the argument of the text?

Metaphors are the most widely used and important tropes in various textual genres. They do what the term (from the Greek *meta-pherein*=carrying over) literally indicates: they carry meaning from one semantic field to another, help to express meaning that could not easily be articulated with other textual means, and thus create resonance in the receiving field. For example, a prime minister might be described as the 'helmsman of the state'; Stalin liked to see himself as a gardener, Mussolini as a sculptor.[24] In each case, the metaphor used reveals something about how political power is imagined: the helmsman takes over responsibility for directing the course of the nation (seen as a vessel), where in contrast Stalin had a far more seminal, indeed intrusive role, for he must plant seeds, nurture the small saplings (i.e. shape and educate the future citizens) and pull out the 'weeds' that endangered the wellbeing of the nursery. (Weeding was a metaphor used in Soviet rhetoric and referred to the arrest, banishment, death of allegedly 'unhealthy elements'.) Of course metaphoric language is not limited to the political domain. Some of the most intriguing and innovative studies on the uses of metaphors have focused on the history of the humanities and sciences. They make clear that the distinction between concept and metaphor is not absolute, but dependent on the situation. Even in the sciences, the metaphorical use of language is inevitable. It does not simply add something to the 'true', proper meaning of a text, but is rather part and parcel of the terrain on which the significance of social action is constituted.[25]

Metaphors should not be interpreted with respect to the alleged intentions of the author of the text, not least because we cannot determine these intentions from the source itself. Rather, they have to be situated in the semantic repertoire of a given thematic field, and their functional effects need to be deciphered. Let's take the memorandum written by Sir Eyre Crowe in 1907 as an example (for background on it, see the more detailed discussion in the chapter on memoranda). The text displays two key metaphors. The first is the description of the international system as a 'balance of power'. This metaphor refers to Newton's mechanics, and has been traditionally used to justify the necessity of adequate measures to maintain an 'equilibrium' between the European nation-states.[26] The second and perhaps more important metaphor describes Germany as a 'professional blackmailer'. Crowe introduces the metaphor as such, as an 'analogy and illustration'. But the function of this metaphor is not merely illustrative, but rather heuristic (from the Greek verb *heuriskein*=to find, i.e. allowing to develop and pursue a new perspective on a known topic).[27] By portraying Imperial Germany as a 'professional' – and not only an occasional! – crook, the metaphor offers a substantially new perspective on the already established topic of Anglo-German antagonism, and floated this idea among the British foreign policy elites. As a criminal, Crowe concluded, Germany would need to be treated with 'determination', and this pivotal conclusion to the memorandum is reached by associating Germany with utterly unlawful activity. Whether or not Crowe hated Germany, the use of this metaphor raised the stakes and injected a sense of urgency into the British perception of German power ambitions. As with every trope, it was not only a stylistic ornament, but a persuasive rhetoric device.

### 4   Does the source include references to the narrator and the reader?

Historians usually try to establish the author of a source not only in order to determine his identity, but also because they want to extrapolate possible motives, interests or prejudices which may have affected or biased the source. We suggest an alternative strategy, one that focuses on the position of the narrator and the reader in the text itself.[28] The best way to grasp the implications of this strategy is to think about your own undergraduate essays. Usually, the seminar tutor will advise you to write in the third person and to avoid the 'I'-form. This narrative technique is meant to create an air of scientific objectivity, since the individual subject is perceived as the very opposite of objectivity. Also, you would usually not use a phrase like 'About this topic, dear reader, I am going to tell you more in a moment' (though many nineteenth-century novels do address the reader directly in this way). Read as a source by historians in the twenty-second century, what would your essays tell them about you as an author? Almost nothing, even though your name appears on the title page. What they do reveal, however, is the prevalence of an epistemological discourse in early twenty-first century university teaching that understood objectivity as the erasure of narrative subjectivity – in other words, the disappearance of the 'I'. In the 1970s, the situation was rather different; in the aftermath of the rebellion of 1968 and when feminism declared that 'the personal is political', student essays and even academic books often had a very personal narrative, and feminist authors declared: 'All I want is my voice.'[29]

While reading a source, check to see what kind of presence the narrator has: what is her function for the text? Does she erase herself, act as story-teller or offer more generalised commentary on it? Or does she perform a reflective function, i.e. comment on her own narration? These are not only narrative strategies you might find in genres such as novels, autobiographies, diaries or newspaper reports. The author of a memorandum could stress her own experiences and expertise with the subject matter, or refer to the topic in an impersonal tone (as Crowe for example did, even though he had extensive first-hand knowledge of Imperial Germany). In all belligerent nations, soldiers of the two World Wars have often reflected on the difficulty they encountered telling their gruesome experiences in the letters to their friends and relatives, rather then recounting them directly.

Connected to such issues is the status of the reader and her relationship with the text's narrator. The reader often seems to be beyond the reach of the historian. We often struggle with the question of how the texts we study were read and received at the time because the act of reading is after all a silent – or at best spoken – one and escapes the historical record. Yet writers can be deeply curious about the impact of their text, and narrators often comment on what they hope or imagine the reader's response to be. When the importance of the reader is flagged in the narrative itself, this needs special attention. A good example are again letters from the two World Wars, in which many soldiers directly addressed their wives, tried to anticipate their reactions, and to embed these reactions into their account of life at the front. Such a narrative strategy helped to foster a fictitious consensus between the spouses, and possibly helped them to reassure one another of the continuing relevance of their marital relation even over extended periods of separation. Not only their content, but also the narrative form of these letters was an important part of their communicative function.[30]

## 5  *In which mode of emplotment is the text couched?*

Over recent decades, 'narrative' has become a contested topic amongst historians. This was in part prompted by Hayden White's work which cautioned readers that historical writings are stories, and as such they do not simply contain lists of certain items of information but in fact present them as a sequence with a certain order, with a clearly defined beginning and end, and a structured form for the bulk of the content material in between. This structure distinguishes, for example, a story about the past from a chronicle, where a sequence of events is recorded without a characteristic form and without any 'culminations or resolutions'. In his book *Metahistory*, published in 1973, White called the specific kind of story a text tells, or the form of its narrative, the mode of 'emplotment'.[31]

What has been overlooked in the stormy debates that have surrounded White's work is the fact that the concept of emplotment can be applied to primary sources as well. Many historical sources, if not most of them, tell a story. This is quite obvious for genres such as testimony, autobiography and speeches, but also valid for opinion polls.[32] White posited Romance, Tragedy, Comedy and Satire as four basic modes of emplotment, and he also linked them, in a rather speculative move, to ideological orientations of, respectively, an anarchist, radical, conservative and liberal nature.[33] When reading a primary source, it is necessary to focus on the way the encounter between the hero of the story and the wider world is cast, and on the moral judgements and conclusions the plot suggests at least implicitly. Let's take a source from the French rebellion of 1968 as an example. 'The students at Flins', an article in a student newspaper published in August 1968, gives a retrospective account of the encounter between Parisian students and the workers at the Renault car plant at Flins in early June 1968. At the height of a massive general strike, the workers 'asked for help' in their confrontation with the riot police CRS. One student was driven to Flins by a young worker in order to examine the situation. During the journey, he was asked about the effects of tear gas grenades, since the students 'already knew the score'. A pub-owner offered his telephone for a token charge, allowing him to call his fellow-students at the Art School in Paris, who then produced a leaflet. Next day, students and workers managed to bar the morning shift from entering the plant, and remained calm in their collective stand-off with the police. At a subsequent rally, students were allowed to speak despite the attempts of the functionaries of the Communist trade union CGT to hinder them. So Alain Geismar, one of the figureheads of the student rebellion, was able to reassure the workers to a 'storm of applause', that the students had only come to their 'service'.[34]

This is not a straightforward chronicle of what happened at Flins, but rather a plot with the characteristic elements of a romance. It displays the students as heroes in a drama of 'self-identification' and self-discovery, celebrates the triumph of the good after trials and tribulations, and shows 'final liberation' in this fairy tale of mutual solidarity between workers and students. Hayden White has linked the romantic mode of emplotment with an anarchistic ideology, and this was indeed the prevalent political orientation of the Parisian students in 1968.[35] The narrative elements of this text stress the students' longing for the recognition of their revolutionary sincerity. But it is also the story of their missionary zeal to teach the workers how to conduct a serious uprising, and can be paralleled with the reports of Christian missionaries about their encounter with the natives.

It is perhaps not convincing for historians to subsume all possible forms of narrative in this structuralist fashion under four basic types of emplotment. Nonetheless, the mode of emplotment is crucial for the interpretation of primary sources.[36] It is worth looking out for the way the setting and the main characters contribute to the story, for the form of the beginning and ending of the story (the proverbial 'happy ending' being only one of the possible solutions), and analysing if the overall setting of the characters in the story-world implies certain moral conclusions or dichotomies.

## 6  What is the reality effect of the source?

Steps one to five of this checklist should help to gather information on some of the most important features of the source. Many other linguistic elements of the text could be analysed as well and will shed further light on its microstructure.[37] But these efforts have only a preparatory function. They should ultimately serve to decipher the meaning of the primary source under scrutiny. All the strategies for reading mentioned above assume that the language of a text is not only an instrument to express the author's intention, but also imply that the language of the text itself creates a reality of its own. In an article on the language of historiography, the French semiologist Roland Barthes has called this the 'reality effect' of a text.[38] Concepts, binary distinctions, metaphors, the position of the narrator and the mode of emplotment are key features of any given text, and they can all be analysed in their own right. In the end, they all contribute to the reality effect of a particular source genre, and it is perhaps with regard to these different genres that this notion is best understood.

A study of opinion polls, for example, might focus on the concepts used, and their connotations and implications. It might also investigate the metaphors and the narrative employed by the accompanying report or media coverage. All these textual elements have a bearing on the political meaning of a poll, irrespective of the particular quantitative evidence and percentage figures it produces. But in addition, polls as a genre have a more general function. Their 'reality effect' is to ensure that politicians, academics, media commentators, and indeed ordinary citizens are aware that the 'people' is sovereign, and that popular opinion matters. In the pie-charts of polls we can see a graphic description of the people as the powerful, but also invisible, sovereign of a democracy, as well as the actual breakdown of the views held with regard to a certain issue. An interpretation of opinion-polls would ultimately lead to an analysis of this reality effect, and would try to establish how the practice of polling and disseminating the results from polls contributes to specific forms of political representation in a parliamentary democracy.

Another way to think about the 'effect' of a text is to think about its relationship to existing discourses. We have been tending to think about the way in which existing discursive patterns influence and shape the production of the texts we study: for example, we have considered the way in which a speaker or writer uses metaphors or narrative structures that depend on certain prevailing interpretations of the world and her position within it. Discourses are not unchanging, however, and in some texts we find the seeds of these shifts. Let us examine texts from court files to illustrate this point. During an interrogation and in the verdict the defendant is described in certain ways, perhaps as a person with inferior moral qualities, and thus within the categories of a moralistic discourse. In the nineteenth century, however, courts increasingly relied on the expertise of psychiatrists to explore the soundness of mind of the defendant. These medical reports were used to determine if he or she was a 'person' who could be held responsible for his or her deeds. Since roughly the 1880s, these reports began to search for hereditary strains in the family history of the defendant, relying on concepts from social Darwinism. With such language, court files were part and parcel of a racist discourse that construed the reality of a biologically inferior person.[39] The court files thus demonstrate a shift in the way deviant behaviours were understood. The fact that this shift came as a result of the intervention of prosecutors, judges, psychiatrists and doctors suggests it is those with power in a society who bring into being new practices and discourses: here the calling of expert witnesses and the articulation of new 'scientific' explanations of criminality as hereditary.

These discourses, however powerful, are not set in stone though. Court files can also tell us something about how contemporaries, including the poor and powerless, responded to prevailing discourses. Prisoners' appeals and the statements given at trial provide evidence of their attempt to negotiate the terrain laid out by the legal system. In the Soviet Union, for example, petitions seem to suggest that some prisoners recognised official discourses that blamed criminality on a bad upbringing. Although the regime primarily had in mind a pre-revolutionary, capitalist childhood when it blamed the family for deviant behaviour, some criminals drew on this concept to talk about their own difficult times as children during war, with one complaining that the death of his parents as a result of the Nazi invasion in 1941 left him 'without the supervision of family or friends who could have put me on the true path in life, so that I could have lived and through work been useful to the Fatherland'. Although he bought into the official notion that a good upbringing was the key to a successful path in life, this petitioner was also subversive for he challenged another of the regime's cherished myths, that of the 'happy childhood' provided by Stalin. Such texts – and they were not uncommon – demonstrate that powerful discourses may shape ordinary people's understanding of the world, but their 'effect' does not go uncontested. In turn, the alternative readings developed by those without power were themselves not without consequence. In the Soviet Union we find political figures at the highest levels intervening in legal cases and offering their own interpretation and their own response to prisoners' accounts of their life.[40] Texts may try to impose a single meaning, yet they are never definitive. The effect of a text may seem to contribute to new sets of beliefs, but these rarely go unchallenged. This in effect brings us back full circle to the point where we started: the changing and unfixed nature of concepts, terms, and ideas over time and space.

## 7 How far is the context important for the interpretation of the text?

Historians, and history teachers, tend to insist on the importance of context for understanding sources. By this they often simply mean the importance of understanding the world in which the author produced the source in question; perhaps they have in mind the social and economic standing of the author and the reader, issues of literacy, censorship and publishing opportunities, the political matters of the day. Very often, contextualisation thus becomes 'an end itself'.[41] But this kind of approach is ultimately flawed. For how do we know about this so-called 'context'? We only know something of the economic, political, social milieu in which a text was produced by reading *other* texts. There is no way to know the past prior to reading texts.

A slightly different approach to context recognises this conundrum, but still insists that an awareness of the circumstances in which the text was produced is important. After all, as historians our interest in texts is not for their aesthetic value (as perhaps with some strands of literary criticism), but for what they tell us about people and societies in the past. We should, therefore, do our utmost to learn about the material circumstances in which a text was produced and disseminated in order to pinpoint as carefully as possible the milieu in which it was written and read.

Four different levels of contextual analysis can be distinguished.[42] The first is the situational context: what was the place and time – parliament or open field? – in which a speech was delivered, and in front of whom? Was the news on the declaration of war reported in the morning or in the evening issue of a newspaper? – a crucial question not only with regard to 2 August 1914. The second is the media context: was a specific speech held in parliament covered in a front-page article or buried in the miscellaneous section? Was it accompanied by a photo or not? Media (not in the sense of dissemination media such as radio or television, but in the wider meaning of media that provide forms for communication)[43] are not only neutral instruments of mediation, but they structure and determine signification, and hence this contextualisation is important. Thirdly, the institutional context needs consideration. Most source genres emerge either in the context of an organisation (a court, a party, a parliament) or of an interactive encounter (a family or an army platoon, looming large in the diaries of a housewife or soldier's letters). The social and normative rules of these institutions have a bearing on sources. For example the editorial policy and the organisation of the newsroom will affect the coverage of a newspaper and will determine whether a speech in parliament is at all covered, fully reprinted, or only available in specialist libraries in the massive volumes of Hansard. In a rather different setting, the comings and goings, interjections and idiosyncrasies of family members may likewise shape what is said and not said in personal correspondence.

Finally, the wider historical context needs to be acknowledged. Any articles printed in the *Morgenpost* or the *Berliner Tageblatt*, only two of the many widely read newspapers published in Berlin around 1900, need to be contextualised in the bustling and vibrant German capital city of that time. But these newspapers themselves were also part and parcel of metropolitan identities, and constituted what Peter Fritzsche has called a 'word city', in which the newspaper was 'a perfect metonym for the city itself'.[44] Berlin around 1900 was not only an agglomeration of brick buildings, streets and trams, but also 'Berlin', a complex of images, perceptions and collective sensibilities laid out in and affirmed by newspaper articles. This is a good example of the interplay between text and context, the fact that every text also changes its own context. Thus, it serves as a helpful reminder that the distinction between text and context is, in the end, always a relative one. The consideration of contexts should not be used as a substitute for an appropriate interpretation of the text. Rather, it should help to find answers to the current line of historical enquiry. Ultimately, both the interpretation of texts and the consideration of their contexts is limited by constraints of time.

Sources rarely come alone, and thus the collation of different texts remains an important business for the historian. But each step of this checklist can also be applied to a single primary source. By now, it should be clear that the careful elimination of 'bias' in order to restore the clarity and proper meaning of a text is not only problematic, but also impossible. The concept of bias is very often presented as a core element of source interpretation.[45] In fact it should be scrapped because it is impossible to get round the structural patterns and material elements of texts which every source genre imposes in a different way. Rather than trying to unearth the hidden but distorted meaning the author has invested in a text, historians should aim to focus on the specific mediality and the inherent structure which are provided by every genre of text.

## Conclusion

After 1800 the romantic idea that the true, spiritual meaning of a text could only be found after the husk of the letter had been removed gained currency and became deeply engrained in nineteenth-century hermeneutics.[46] The romantics scorned the notion of a poet who focused on the materiality of the text, ridiculing him as a mere 'typesetter'. The letters on the page were dead, only the idea was alive.[47] Historicist historians further contributed to this notion that interpretation needs to distinguish between the pure meaning and an element of clouding. Conjuring up images of pure water from a wellspring, the very term 'source' itself served as an important metaphor to support this idea. Subsequently, Droysen shifted the metaphor to optics, and posited that 'even the very best' sources would give the historian only 'polarised light'.[48] However, the idealistic notions of this concept can no longer be sustained. Sources do not flow easily like water from a wellspring, but must be carefully excavated by the historian equipped with sophisticated technical and analytical skills.[49] The focus on the surface of a text and on the patterns of speech does not say farewell to the idea that historians should search for the truth, though. Quite to the contrary. By applying the checklist outlined above, it will be possible to distinguish true from less plausible or even false interpretations. As Frank Ankersmit has rightly stated, the linguistic turn 'can never be construed as an attack on truth'.[50] What is irrevocably lost, though, is the belief of Ranke and other historicist historians that the work of textual interpretation is ultimately grounded and confirmed by a religious world order, objectivity hence the result of a 'history religion'.[51] In these secular times, we are looking for different kinds of truth: about how words allow relationships – of power, of community, of love or hate – to be created and sustained in different ways and at different times. In examining the ways in which these communications work, we can reveal something significant about the changing nature of social and political interactions and experience over time.

## Notes

1 K. Jenkins, *Re-thinking History* (1991), London: Routledge, 2003, pp. 30, 45.
2 R.J. Evans, *In Defence of History*, London: Granta, 1997, pp. 127, 106, 109.
3 J. Tosh with S. Lang, *The Pursuit of History. Aims, Methods and New Directions in the Study of Modern History*, Harlow: Pearson Longman, 2006, p. 110. Compare M. Fulbrook, *Historical Theory*, London: Routledge, 2002; C. Brown, *Postmodernism for Historians*, Harlow: Longman, 2004.
4 Compare Fulbrook, *Theory*, pp. 98–121; Evans, *Defence*, pp. 103–128; Tosh and Lang, *Pursuit*, pp. 88–113, 193–198; Brown, *Postmodernism*, pp. 48, 72; M. Howell and W. Prevenier, *From Reliable Sources. An Introduction into Historical Methods*, Ithaca and London: Cornell University Press, 2001.
5 A. Grafton, *The Footnote. A Curious History*, London: Faber and Faber, 2003.
6 It should be noted that Johann Christoph Gatterer and Johann Martin Chladenius, two main proponents of the eighteenth-century Göttingen-school of historians, had already provided important reflections on the connections between historical research and hermeneutics. See P.H. Reill, 'History and Hermeneutics in the Aufklärung: The Thought of Johann Christoph Gatterer', *JMH* 45, 1973, 24–51; P. Szondi, *Introduction to Literary Hermeneutics*, Cambridge: Cambridge University Press, 1995, pp. 14–66.
7 J.G. Droysen, *Outline of the Principles of History* (1858/1868), Boston: Ginn & Company, 1893, pp. 21–32, 61. For background, see H. White, 'Historik', *H&T* 19, 1980, 73–93, who notes on p. 75 that according to Droysen, Ranke had betrayed the hermeneutic ideal of interpretation in favour of source 'criticism'.
8 Droysen, *Outline*, p. 12 (italics in original, translation amended).
9 C. Geertz, '"From the Native's Point of View": On the Nature of Anthropological Understanding', in R.A. Shweder and R.A. LeVine (eds), *Culture Theory. Essays on Mind, Self and Emotion*, Cambridge: Cambridge University Press, 1984, pp. 123–136, p. 124.
10 As an excellent overview, see P. Schöttler, 'Historians and Discourse Analysis', *HWJ* 27, 1989, 37–65.
11 For a wide-ranging and thoughtful assessment of source materials in a particular field of research compare R. Hilberg, *Sources of Holocaust Research. An Analysis*, Chicago: I.R. Dee, 2001.
12 See L.H. van Voss (ed.), *Petitions in Social History*, Cambridge: Cambridge University Press, 2002 (International Review of Social History, Supplement 9).
13 G.B. Risse and J.H. Warner, 'Reconstructing Clinical Activities: Patient Records in Medical History', *Social History of Medicine* 5, 1992, 183–205.
14 See U. Raulff, *Ein Historiker im 20. Jahrhundert: Marc Bloch*, Frankfurt/M.: S. Fischer, 1995.
15 See S. Barber and C. Peniston-Bird (eds), *History Beyond the Text*, London: Routledge, 2008.
16 Evans, *Defence*, p. 111.
17 R.F. Wetzell, *Inventing the Criminal: A History of German Criminology, 1880–1945*, Chapel Hill: University of North Carolina Press, 2000, pp. 21–25. According to Adam Tooze, statistics 'should be treated like other cultural artefacts, texts or images'. J.A. Tooze, *Statistics and the German State, 1900–1945. The Making of Modern Economic Knowledge*, Cambridge: Cambridge University Press, 2001, p. 3.

18   A. Burton (ed.), *Archive Stories: Facts, Fictions, and the Writing of History*, Durham, NC: Duke University Press, 2005.

19   A. Marwick, *The New Nature of History*, London: Palgrave, 2001, pp. 179–185.

20   See M. Richter, *The History of Political and Social Concepts. A Critical Introduction*, Oxford: Oxford University Press, 1995; Richter, 'Reconstructing the History of Political Languages: Pocock, Skinner, and the Geschichtliche Grundbegriffe', *H&T* 29, 1990, 38–70. See also the online journal *Contributions to the History of Concepts* at <http://contributions.iuperj.br/> (accessed 18 April 2007).

21   B. Ziemann, 'Opinion Polls and the Dynamics of the Public Sphere. The Catholic Church in the Federal Republic after 1968', *German History* 24, 2006, 562–586, 573f.

22   Reinhart Koselleck has labelled them as 'asymmetrical counter-concepts'. This is a clunky term that could be replaced by the simpler and equally precise word 'code', at least when it is meant, as in sociological systems theory, to denote any asymmetrical binary distinction. See R. Koselleck, 'The Historical-Political Semantics of Asymmetric Counterconcepts', in his *Futures Past. On the Semantics of Historical Time*, New York: Columbia University Press, 2004, pp. 155–191; B. Ziemann, '"Linguistische Wende" und "kultureller Code" in der Geschichtsschreibung zum modernen Antisemitismus', *Jahrbuch für Antisemitismusforschung* 14, 2005, 301–322.

23   In a landmark article, Shulamit Volkov has described this distinction as a 'cultural code'. See her 'Antisemitism as a Cultural Code. Reflections on the History and Historiography of Antisemitism in Imperial Germany', *Yearbook of the Leo Baeck Institute* 23, 1978, 25–45, reprinted in B. Ziemann and T. Mergel (eds), *European Political History 1870–1913*, Aldershot: Ashgate 2007, pp. 243–265; see also Volkov, *Germans, Jews, and Antisemites. Trials in Emancipation*, Cambridge: Cambridge University Press, 2006, pp. 91–155.

24   R.C. Tucker, 'The Rise of Stalin's Personality Cult', *AHR* 84, 1979, 347–366, 365; S. Falasca-Zamponi, *Fascist Spectacle: The Aesthetics of Power in Mussolini's Italy*, Berkeley: University of California Press, 1997, pp. 21–26. There is an abundance of both historical and linguistic literature on metaphors. Still useful is G. Lakoff and M. Johnson, *Metaphors We Live By*, Chicago: University of Chicago Press, 1980.

25   B. Latour, *The Pasteurization of France*, Cambridge: Harvard University Press, 1993; P. Sarasin, *Anthrax. Bioterror as Fact and Fantasy*, Cambridge, Mass.: Harvard University Press, 2006; P. Sarasin, *Geschichtswissenschaft und Diskursanalyse*, Frankfurt: Suhrkamp, 2003. See also the remarks on the power of antisemitic metaphors in Volkov, *Germans*, pp. 82–90.

26   C. Schäffner, 'The "Balance" Metaphor in Relation to Peace', in Schäffner and A.L. Wenden (eds), *Language and Peace*, Aldershot: Ashgate, 1995, pp. 75–91.

27   For this distinction see S. Maasen, E. Mendelsohn, P. Weingart, 'Metaphors: Is There a Bridge over Troubled Waters?', in their *Biology as Society, Society as Biology: Metaphors*, Dordrecht: Kluwer, 1995, p. 2.

28   See R. Barthes, *Image, Music, Text*, London: Fontana 1977, pp. 79–124.

29   A. Leclerc, 'Woman's Word' (1974), in E. Marks and I. de Courtivron (eds), *New French Feminisms. An Anthology*, New York: Schocken Books, 1981, pp. 58–63, p. 58.

30   See R. Earle (ed.), *Epistolary Selves. Letters and Letter-Writers, 1600–1945*, Aldershot: Ashgate, 1999. For another example for the narrative position of narrator and reader, see the remarks about the 'autobiographical pact' in the chapter on autobiographies.

31   H. White, *Metahistory. The Historical Imagination in Nineteenth-Century Europe*, Baltimore and London: Johns Hopkins University Press, 1973, p. 6.

32   The plot of opinion polls is presented in the accompanying media reports. Polls on church attendance and issues of faith, for example, appear to be regularly cast in the satiric mode. The data are presented in a way that allows the churches to be mocked for apparent secularisation, and they portray an image of meaningless change in which every kind of attitude towards belief is possible. With regard to the following, it should

be noted that polls on the decline of organised religion are usually of a liberal ideological nature. For an example see Ziemann, 'Polls', p. 575.

33 White, *Metahistory*, pp. 11–31.

34 'The Students at Flins' (1968) in A. Feenberg and J. Freedman, *When Poetry Ruled the Streets. The French May Events of 1968*, Albany: SUNY Press, 2001, pp. 132, 137.

35 White, *Metahistory*, p. 8.

36 For further guidance on categories of narrative analysis, see S. Rimmon-Kenan, *Narrative Fiction: Contemporary Poetics*, London and New York: Routledge, 2001.

37 For further guidance, compare R. Wodak and M. Meyer (eds), *Methods of Critical Discourse Analysis*, London: Sage, 2001; D. Schiffrin, *Approaches to Discourse*, Oxford: Blackwell, 1994.

38 R. Barthes, 'History and Discourse', in M. Lane (ed.), *Structuralism: A Reader*, London: Jonathan Cape, 1970, pp. 145–155, p. 154. It should be noted that the history of concepts departs at this point from the more radical stance of French poststructuralism. In a famous formulation, Reinhart Koselleck stated that concepts should be analysed as 'factors', but also as mere 'indicators' of historical change. See his introduction to the multi-volume encyclopaedia of basic political concepts, in O. Brunner, W. Conze and R. Koselleck (eds), *Geschichtliche Grundbegriffe*, vol. 1, Stuttgart: Klett, 1972, p. xiv.

39 R. Harris, *Murders and Madness. Medicine, Law and Society in the Fin de Siècle*, Oxford: Clarendon, 1989, pp. 138–154. As an example, see the medical expert report in a German court-martial file from 1916: <http://germanhistorydocs.ghi-dc.org/pdf/eng/706_A%20(134).pdf> (accessed 16 April 2007).

40 See M. Dobson, *Khrushchev's Cold Summer: Citizens, Zeks, and the Soviet Community after Stalin*, forthcoming. For another example of a multi-layered and complex interpretation of discourses in court files see R. Schulte, *The Village in Court. Arson, Infanticide, and Poaching in the Court Records of Upper Bavaria, 1848–1910*, Cambridge: Cambridge University Press, 1994.

41 J.G. Gunnell, 'Time and Interpretation. Understanding Concepts and Conceptual Change', *History of Political Thought* 19, 1998, 641–658, 656.

42 See A. Landwehr, *Geschichte des Sagbaren. Einführung in die Historische Diskursanalyse*, Tübingen: edition diskord, 2001, pp. 108–111.

43 For this distinction, see Niklas Luhmann, *The Reality of the Mass Media*, Oxford: Polity, 2000.

44 See his brilliant *Reading Berlin 1900*, Cambridge, Mass.: Harvard University Press, 1996, pp. 10, 23.

45 Compare for example Marwick, *Nature*, p. 183, or G.R. Elton, *The Practice of History*, London: Collins, 1969, p. 104.

46 Literally this is described as the 'slag of the letter'. Due to the polysemic nature of language, a major point we hint at in this introduction, we have used a different expression.

47 See, quoting from the *Kleine Nachschule* by Jean Paul from 1825, T. Hoinkis, *Lektüre. Ironie. Erlebnis. System- und medientheoretische Analysen zur literarischen Ästhetik der Romantik*, doctoral thesis, University of Bochum, 1997, p. 72.

48 See M. Zimmermann, 'Quelle als Metapher', *Historische Anthropologie* 5, 1997, 268–87; Droysen, *Outline*, § 25, p. 20.

49 For exemplary insights into the necessary techniques and possible problems compare Hilberg, *Sources*.

50 F.R. Ankersmit, *Historical Representation*, Stanford: Stanford University Press, 2001, p. 36.

51 See the pathbreaking interpretation by W. Hardtwig, 'Geschichtsreligion – Wissenschaft als Arbeit – Objektivität: Der Historismus in neuer Sicht', *Historische Zeitschrift* 252, 1991, 1–32.

## Select bibliography

Clark, E.A., *History, Theory, Text. Historians and the Linguistic Turn*, Cambridge, Mass.: Harvard University Press, 2004.

Droysen, J.G., *Outline of the Principles of History* (1858/1868), Boston: Ginn & Company, 1893.

Iggers, G., *The German Conception of History. The National Tradition of Historical Thought from Herder to the Present*, Middletown, Conn.: Wesleyan University Press, 1983.

Iggers, G., 'The History and Meaning of the Term "Historicism"', *Journal of the History of Ideas* 56, 1995, 129–152.

Koselleck, R., *The Practice of Conceptual History. Timing History, Spacing Concepts*, Stanford: Stanford University Press, 2002.

Koselleck, R., *Futures Past: On the Semantics of Historical Time*, New York: Columbia University Press, 2004.

Lakoff, G. and Johnson, M., *Metaphors We Live By*, Chicago: University of Chicago Press, 1980.

Richter, M., *The History of Political and Social Concepts. A Critical Introduction,* Oxford: OUP, 1995.

Schiffrin, D., *Approaches to Discourse,* Oxford: Blackwell, 1994.

Schöttler, P., 'Historians and Discourse Analysis', *HWJ* 27, 1989, 37–65.

White, H., 'Historik', *H&T* 19, 1980, 73–93.

# Part I
# Reading primary sources
Contexts and approaches

# 1   Understanding history

## Hermeneutics and source-criticism in historical scholarship

*Philipp Müller*

In his private correspondence the German historian Johann Gustav Droysen did not hesitate to call a spade a spade. Reflecting on the achievements of Leopold Ranke who was already considered one of the most important founders of modern historical scholarship Droysen declared: 'Unfortunately . . . because of Ranke and his school we have become lost in what is called source-criticism whose entire feat consists in asking whether a poor devil of an annalist has copied from another.'[1] Because of Ranke's influence Droysen felt he had a hard time convincing his fellow historians that the decisive part in studying history was not the verification but the interpretation of the sources. In his letter he continued: 'It has caused some shaking of heads when I happily contended that the historian's task was understanding or, if one prefers, interpreting.'[2] By emphasizing the significance of interpretation Droysen did not intend to neglect the merits of critical source-reading. As a matter of fact, his 'Historik', a series of lectures where he explained the scholarly principles of history, includes one of the most detailed accounts of the methods to establish the credibility of historical documents that was ever written. But at the same time, Droysen believed that history had to go beyond the mere collection of true facts about the past and, in his eyes, this was exactly where his predecessors had failed to develop a proper explanation of scholarly procedures. He especially held Ranke responsible for a simplified image of history that did not recognize that one could only gain historical knowledge through interpreting historical records. As far as Droysen was concerned, Ranke's search in the dust of the archives was only the first step to be taken in order to reconstruct the past.[3]

This picture in which Droysen advances a more sophisticated outlook on history while Ranke personifies the daily drudge of historical research by providing the tools of source-criticism, however, neither does justice to the tradition of classical scholarship and its techniques of textual criticism, nor does it correspond with the actual practice of Ranke's historical writing.[4] Even if Ranke has often been credited for having invented the critical methods of professional historical research his originality in that respect has been much exaggerated.[5] What really distinguishes both Ranke and Droysen is their treatment of historical facts as evidence of an object that could only be grasped by a specific mental act which has become known as '*Verstehen*' (understanding). Rather than just representing another technical issue, understanding history took shape in the theory of hermeneutics and became the core procedure of the historian's work not only in Germany but also in European and North American historiography. In the following chapter, Ranke (1795–1886), Droysen (1808–1884) and Wilhelm Dilthey (1833–1911), three main proponents of hermeneutics in historical scholarship, will be discussed in order to give a picture of the development of its basic structures in the nineteenth century.[6] Although their efforts differed considerably, each one of them contributed to the emergence of a modern approach to interpreting historical sources with lasting effects far into the 1960s and beyond.

## Humanism and textual criticism

In order to fully appreciate the idea of understanding and its meaning it is first necessary to outline the development of critical source-reading before the nineteenth century. The techniques of historical criticism were imported from other disciplines which developed the need to verify and secure information much earlier than did historiography. Historians of the early modern period were more interested in moral and rhetorical questions than in knowledge of the past for its own sake. Classical philology, biblical criticism and modern jurisprudence, on the other hand, were drawn into a sense of scholarship that forced them to base their knowledge on reliable sources.

The humanists of the fifteenth and sixteenth centuries began to consider the established picture of the classical authors of antiquity as distorted. Until then the tradition of the classics had been based on generations of handwritten copies which had altered the texts either because their content did not correspond with the religious and moral beliefs of the copyists or because of mistakes in the process of reproduction. As a consequence, humanists understood antiquity as a lost world that had to be recovered from its remnants. Anything that was thought to belong to the age of the Roman Empire or the Greek city-state (*polis*) was now considered to be worthy of conservation. The humanists started to search for old manuscripts all over Europe in order to retrieve the original form of Latin and Greek texts by comparing different copies to each other. They stressed that it was important to master the old languages as an instrument to differentiate between original sections and later changes.[7] Although their inquiries were aimed at resurrecting an idealized picture of antiquity which, in itself, was not submitted to historical scrutiny, humanists developed a new sense of tradition that worked its way through to sources without accepting the form and content of the documents they found as given.

Even before these forms of criticism were introduced into the study of history they were adopted in theology. Clerics of the seventeenth century published collections of records and documents concerning the history of the church and began to take an historical interest in Christian traditions. The critical reading of sources led to new conclusions concerning the transmission of the texts of the Bible. For example, in his 'Histoire critique du vieux testament' of 1678 Richard Simon, a French clergyman, identified different layers of language in the Old Testament. He pointed out that the sections which recounted the history of the flight of the people of Israel from Egypt did not show a coherent structure. Arguing that the text included knowledge on events after Moses' death Simon rejected the traditional view which still took Moses to be the author. He concluded that instead of an original account the Bible contained only a mangled version that was composed long after the events had taken place and was produced by writers from different times and backgrounds.[8]

In addition to philology and theology, textual criticism also made its way into jurisprudence before it came to be regarded as a distinctive feature of historical scholarship. In the sixteenth and seventeenth centuries the status of the traditional corpus of Roman law as a collection of texts that should govern contemporary jurisdiction was challenged. French critics like Guillaume Budé and Jean Bodin were convinced that the original Roman law within the 'Corpus iuris' was buried under medieval glosses and commentaries which had misunderstood the meaning of ancient notions because they had not bothered to study the change of judicial institutions and terms.[9] Again, the humanist tradition of textual criticism emphasized the significance of primary sources and encouraged systematic vigilance for possible distortion. In order to detect mistakes of tradition, different versions of texts had to be compared to each other, the verisimilitude of the textual content had to be examined and the style and language checked.[10]

In Germany, historians adopted the practices of textual criticism in the late eighteenth century. Scholars like Johann Christoph Gatterer and August Ludwig Schlözer conceived of history as an immanent process that reflected the course and development of mankind. Academic historical studies increasingly began to define themselves as a scientific discipline that was concerned with true knowledge of the past that could be gained by reconstructing and studying primary sources. Especially at the reform-minded universities of Göttingen and Halle the methods of source-criticism were spelled out in systematic guidelines for historical research and became a cornerstone of academic training.[11] As a consequence, professional historiography changed its character: rather than simply rewriting the accounts of their predecessors historians were now supposed to produce historical knowledge that was justified by verified information. While philology had used textual criticism to restore the original wording of documents, history used the techniques of restoration of texts to establish reliable knowledge of the past itself.[12]

Therefore, when Ranke famously proclaimed, that he wanted to show history 'as it actually was', basing his historiography on the strict practice of textual criticism, he was not a methodological revolutionary in source-reading.[13] Rather, he followed an already established path which had been prepared by classical philology, the historians of the late enlightenment and recent historians of antiquity like Barthold Georg Niebuhr.[14] Ranke was familiar with the practices of textual criticism because he was trained as a classical philologist. When he wrote the *Histories of the Romanic and Germanic Peoples* in 1824, he included a critique of renaissance historians in the appendix to his book. He aptly demonstrated that much of the historiography on early modern Europe had been led astray because it relied on traditional authorities instead of primary sources.[15] Although this was considered an astonishing piece of work at the time – and earned Ranke an associate professorship at the University of Berlin in 1825 – his real historiographical achievements lie elsewhere. For Ranke, source-criticism in itself could not reveal the meaning of history: this could be achieved only when the historian went beyond the collection of true facts about the past. In this respect, Ranke's conception of historical studies relied on a form of understanding which was not taken into consideration by critics like Droysen.

## Ranke and the claim to be objective

The historians of the enlightenment had not only transformed history into a discipline that based its claims on empirical evidence, but had also reflected on the connections between the sources and historical knowledge. In this respect, Gatterer and Schlözer developed an approach that has been summarized as 'pragmatic' historiography. They thought that professional historians should comprehend the historical development as an effect that had to be explained by identifying appropriate causes. The course of historical events was supposed to show a system of causal connections that allowed the historian to form an account according to the notion of rational progress.[16] But in the early nineteenth century widespread doubts concerning the ability of the human mind to discover the essence of reality made this conception increasingly unacceptable. Ranke held that subsuming particular facts under a general rule of rational progress did not lead to historical knowledge, but was rather mere philosophical speculation.[17] He agreed with the enlightenment historians that history rested on a unified structure, but insisted that this structure could not be reconstructed by notions of progress and reason. As he explained in one of his lectures in the early 1830s, the historian had to develop a sense that was able to see a whole emerging from the particular elements of past reality without reducing it to formulas of abstract reasoning. The solution Ranke found already contained many of the elements that were later conceptualized by Droysen as '*Verstehen*' (understanding). In Ranke's conception, however, understanding was closely tied to his philosophical, religious and aesthetic convictions.[18]

Ranke's outlook on history was originally shaped by philosophical and religious studies during his student years. He was imbued with concerns that arose from his reading of Johann Gottlieb Fichte, Friedrich Schlegel and Friedrich Schleiermacher (among others), who contributed to the philosophical underpinnings of Idealism and Romanticism.[19] Ranke translated romantic concepts into the epistemology of history and, thereby, combined the empirical techniques of source-reading with an idealist point of view. According to the beliefs diffused by the romantic school, the mundane structures of the human mind were not capable of knowing the core of reality, since reality was thought of as being constituted by the eternal creativity of God. As a consequence, rather than apprehending it in a straightforward manner, the historian could deduce the divine origin of the past only when he established a common thread between historical phenomena. Thus for Ranke particular facts by themselves did not constitute historical knowledge because their hidden nature was only revealed in their relationship to others.

The attempt to find the overall connection between events was meant to provide access to the inner essence of history. In Ranke's opinion, the historian would decipher the historical truth hidden within sources only when he recognized that facts which appeared to be unconnected were in reality harmoniously connected elements of general spiritual tendencies. He conceived the general content of the past as the work of spiritual forces which could be discovered indirectly by inferring from singular elements of historical reality to their common deeper ground. This conception presupposed the unique mental capacity of the historian. Ranke believed that one could develop mental capacities within oneself which reflected the spiritual essence behind historical events. He declared:

> Since the character of all unity is spiritual, it can only be known by spiritual perception. This is based on the correspondence of the rules according to which the observing spirit proceeds, with those rules according to which the perceived object shows itself.[20]

The concordance between knowing subject (the scholar) and the object to be known (the subject of study) was based on the idea of developing an approach specifically designed for historical studies. In order to discover the meaning of history, Ranke suggested combining the principles of philosophy and poetry. Although he agreed with its aims, Ranke blamed philosophy for constructing abstract categories that ignored the limits of the human mind and, therefore, only pretended to show the spiritual unity of reality. Poetry, on the other hand, was not concerned with the real aspects of life and nature, but adopting its procedures could prove fruitful. Ranke held that a poetic sense of synthesis could integrate the particular facts of the past into a whole that did not represent an abstract notion but a unity of its own kind.[21] The poetic formation of an image of past reality presupposed a mental creativity within the historian and this corresponded with the hidden spiritual creativity he thought lay within historical phenomena. For Ranke, expressing the particular elements of history in an aesthetic form could reveal the hidden general content of the past because it reflected the spiritual principle of historical reality. Accordingly, science and art did not exclude each other, but were rather constructed as complementary elements of historical knowledge.[22] Ranke explained:

> One could be inclined to think that the beauty of form is only achievable at the cost of truth. If this was the case the idea of combining science and art would have to be abandoned as wrong. I am convinced of the opposite ... A free and great form can only arise out of that which has been completely apprehended by the mind.[23]

Of course he maintained the emphasis on documentary discrimination of facts and stressed the importance of a critical assessment of historical sources. But for Ranke, the meaning of historical facts could only emerge from what the historian's sense of poetic synthesis had in common with the spiritual essence of reality.

From Ranke's point of view, historical knowledge was thus the result of an interplay between subjective and objective forces. The historian should use his own creative capacities to seek what Ranke designated as the 'ideas' behind events. But rather than rendering historical knowledge subjective, Ranke asserted that the sense of poetic synthesis was influenced by the spiritual content it was supposed to reconstruct. For him, disclosing the historical ideas behind past events enabled one to develop a sense of the general structure of history. By producing a coherent image of the past the historian would purge himself from the mere subjective elements of his perception and form his mind according to the general truth he was discovering. As Ranke's conviction of the spiritual content of history rested on his belief in the divine origin of reality, he conceived of historical research as a way to harmonize the self and the world as it was created by God.[24] 'When we remove the shell from things and turn out what is essential in them, it happens that in our own being, essence, spiritual life, soul and the breath of god take wing.'[25] Conceiving history from that point of view led Ranke to believe in the objectivity of historiography. For him, historical knowledge was achieved if the historian transformed his subjective point of view into an objective reverberation of ideas hidden underneath the appearances of historical changes. According to his religious and philosophical convictions he was convinced of the possibility of submerging the subject into the object by the means of historical understanding:

> My happiness is to observe the world, past and present, from this point on which I stand, and to absorb it into myself, insofar as it is congruent with me ... Often one is hardly aware of having a personality any more. One no longer has an ego. The eternal father of all things, who gives life to all, draws us to Him without resistance.[26]

Ranke's rejection of abstract definitions prevented him from casting his reflections into an elaborated theory of historical knowledge. Apart from occasional statements in essays and letters he developed his practice of source-reading and understanding within his empirical historical writing. Droysen's distorted picture of Ranke as being uniquely concerned with source-criticism can partly be explained by Ranke's reluctance to spell out his theoretical assumptions. But more important than his silence in this respect are the differences between Ranke's and Droysen's historical approaches themselves.

## Droysen and the theory of historical understanding

Droysen conceived of academic historiography as having a social task that consisted in forming a subject capable of taking on the responsibilities of a modern citizen.[27] He was convinced that the study of history could change the habits of his contemporaries if it was not left to antiquarians who were only concerned with collecting records from a distant past. For Droysen, the sources themselves could not yield historical knowledge; they stood for the past rather than what he conceptualized as history in its full meaning:

> Those who consider it to be the highest task of the historian that he does not add anything of his own thinking, but simply lets the facts speak for themselves, do

not see that the facts themselves do not speak except through the words of someone who has seized and understood them.[28]

Droysen considered sources to be the indispensable basis of history; but in his eyes, they only revealed their significance if they were interpreted by the historian.

Droysen pointed out that historical knowledge had to be based on traces of the past that were still accessible in the contemporary world.[29] He proposed classifying these traces according to the character of their relation to the present. In his conception, the term 'remains' (*Überreste*) encompassed all kinds of traces of human actions that had not been intended to make the past known to the future. 'Remains' had been originally part of the daily life of the past without being designed for the purpose of historical tradition. According to Droysen, institutions and works of art, for example, could deliver historical information, but their existence did not depend on the intention of letting people in the future know what had happened in the past. 'Sources' (*Quellen*) in the proper sense, on the contrary, were the result of an effort to constitute historical memory. Any kind of writing on contemporary or recent affairs, from saga to chronicle, originated from the intention of recording events for times to come. 'Sources' in Droysen's usage of the term did not accidentally reflect the past, but already translated it into some kind of a meaningful story that was supposed to be transmitted to future generations.[30]

In both cases, however, the records required further work:

> The result of critical source-reading by itself would not be anything like living reality; the bricks of a building put side by side are only the bricks not the building . . . they are only particular elements which do not give an image of the whole.[31]

Both have their difficulties: 'remains' reflect the purpose for which they were made but reveal nothing about their function and influence within a larger context, while 'sources' – though designed to establish clear meaning – are construed from a specific point of view, one that is entangled in the beliefs and aims of the writer of the past. Only when brought into an interpretative frame-work set up from a retrospective, historical point of view can 'remains' and 'sources' be turned into what Droysen understood to be historical information. He believed that the perspective of the present on the past enabled the historian to overcome the limits of the sources by integrating them into an interpretation of history.[32]

According to Droysen, rather than restricting themselves to the literal meaning of the sources, historians should seek to uncover the mental content embodied in the facts and events documented by written texts, monuments and so on. In his conception, history was interested in aspects of reality which had been shaped by the human mind. Historians, therefore, should be concerned with the results of thoughts and plans of the past which had found expression in historical actions.[33] Despite this interest in the way historical actors thought, Droysen distinguished between historical interpretation and psychological interpretation. Whereas the latter focused on the personal motives of individuals, historical interpretation was concerned with larger historical forces. Understanding actions psychologically meant tracing them back to the character and personality of individuals; historical understanding, as Droysen explained, was based on the belief that the human will depends on the world of which it is part and, therefore, has to be perceived as something beyond the mere outcome of psychological motives. Droysen was convinced that historical epistemology could be based on the existence of a chain of general ideas behind individual thinking, which gave particular thoughts and motives their meaning.[34] This concept was the key to the hermeneutic character of Droysen's theory of history and reading sources. Understanding history meant interpreting particular phenomena as part of a whole, a whole that was constructed by the historian in order to determine their historical significance.[35]

Droysen asked himself whether presupposing a general connection of ideas within history could be methodologically justified. In his eyes, the present had to be perceived as the current result of the historical development of the past. For that reason, he did not accept the charge that the historian's assumption of a general spiritual content behind individual historical phenomena rested on mere subjective imagination. Rather, he argued that the capacities the historian employed to reconstruct the past could not be alien to their subject since they were as much conditioned by the process of history as anything else. Indeed, the idea of a general spiritual development buried within the traces of the past, which historians formed during the process of interpretation, was itself the consequence of historical tradition. 'The historian's question is the result of the entire mental content that we have unconsciously collected within ourselves and transformed into our own subjective world.'[36] Since studying history meant using mental capacities which were the result of history, historical knowledge could rely on a tacit connection between the historian's perspective and history itself.

This conception of understanding also affected the aim of historical studies. If historiography was unconsciously shaped by history, historical scholarship was not only the discovery of the past as it 'essentially' had been. It was also an effort to deepen the capacity for historical knowledge by revealing its relation with historical development.[37] In this respect, Droysen's endeavour departed significantly from Ranke. Whereas Ranke had proposed reconstructing history according to an eternal divine principle, Droysen wanted to establish an evolutionary principle of history that could make progress possible.[38] The historical ideas behind the individual phenomena of the past were for him expressions of 'ethical powers' (*sittliche Mächte*) embodied in the form of language, art, religion, law and the state. While interpreting the records of the past, the historian was supposed to follow their progressive development:

> The interpretation of ideas . . . demands . . . one not only to see: this is how the idea of the state, the church, the law etc. has been perceived at a certain point but also: this is how they progressed until then, this is the point they reached within the overall movement of ideas, because only within this continuity they can be understood.[39]

Whereas Ranke denied the possibility of discerning the spiritual tendency within historical phenomena as a progressive development, for Droysen this was a decisive part of his effort to reveal the hidden relationship between the subject (the scholar) and object of historical knowledge (the topic being studied).

Droysen's determination to study the development of ethical powers was closely tied to what he conceived as the purpose of historical scholarship. If the mind of the present was constituted by the development of historical ideas over time, and if those ideas were by nature progressive, historical knowledge was meant to reveal a wider principle of historical evolution: it was not only significant for knowing the past, but it could also offer orientation within the contemporary world. By revealing the historical nature of one's own thinking, Droysen hoped to give the individual who studied the past a sense of his place in his own time, and to stimulate historical development through the enhancement of social and collective powers. The wider goal of historical inquiry was to make the subject of historical knowledge aware of the historical meaning of his thoughts and ideas, in order to develop a sense of his position and function within a historical continuum stretching into the future.[40] For Droysen, understanding history meant recognizing that selfhood was constituted by an evolutionary principle of history which – once it was fully grasped – enabled the individual to transcend his current situation in order to carry on the tradition of progress. Historical studies were meant to highlight this continuity as the essence of history, with the purpose of ensuring its further development: 'The idea itself strives to an ever new expression, its existence is to become and to grow ... Its deployment is the becoming and growing of history, history is the progressing ... growth of the ideas.'[41] By revealing the presence of the past within the contemporary way of studying history, Droysen thus claimed that the acquisition of historical knowledge was ultimately driven by the same notion of progress as historical development itself. As a consequence, from Droysen's point of view, understanding history was synonymous with eventually fulfilling the task of advancing the cause of mankind.[42]

For that reason, Droysen severely criticized the proposal of historians like Henry Thomas Buckle who wanted to model historical knowledge on the natural sciences.[43] According to Droysen, the general content within particular historical phenomena could not be cast into a law of history that resembled its counterparts in physics or chemistry. Rather than causing the reproduction of a fixed set of occurrences, he conceived general ideas as being constituted by a constant evolution and which, as a result, could not be comprehended as a permanent structure. Droysen believed that understanding history would help the task of revealing both true knowledge of the past and self-knowledge by fusing them within a human science. In that respect, ideas similar to Droysen's were enlarged and systematized by Wilhelm Dilthey.

## Dilthey and understanding as the core of the human sciences

Dilthey combined a strongly developed sense for philosophical questions with extensive research on the history of literature, historiography and general intellectual history. His main interest was to develop a scientific foundation for the humanities, coining the term '*Geisteswissenschaften*' (literally translated as: 'sciences of spirit') with his *Introduction to the Human Sciences* in 1883.[44] Throughout his work he relied on notions of the German concept of *Bildung* which were already present in the approaches Ranke and Droysen developed. The meaning of *Bildung* is not covered by literal translations like 'education'. Rather than describing a process of acquiring a pre-given catalogue of knowledge or skills, *Bildung* aimed at the combination of knowledge and personal self-formation that was expressed by the notion of understanding.[45] Accordingly, Ranke did not simply want to establish objective knowledge of the past, but believed that historical studies changed the mental capacities of individuals. Droysen held that history had an educational responsibility which surpassed the discovery of the truth about the past, because it aimed to orient his fellow citizens in the contemporary world. In both of these approaches, gaining historical knowledge was linked with self-formation because it developed the individual's capacity for self-determined thinking and acting. As such, along with neo-humanist intellectuals like Wilhelm von Humboldt, key proponents of German history turned *Bildung* into an ideal conduct of life that was independent from external constraints because it followed an internally motivated concordance with the principles of reality.[46]

Dilthey elaborated on these characteristics of historical studies in a theory of the humanities which was supposed to justify their independent existence as a 'science'. He argued that the natural sciences constructed an object by abstracting from their own perspective, whereas the human sciences focused on the subjective dimensions of the experience of objects. Dilthey thus made a distinction between 'understanding', which was the appropriate method for the human sciences, and 'explanation', a method used in the natural sciences:

> We explain nature, but we understand the life of the soul . . . This determines a huge difference in the methods we use when we study . . . history and society from the methods which have led to the knowledge of nature.[47]

For Dilthey, understanding could rely on a mental relationship inherent in the experience of living itself. Whereas the natural sciences approached their objects from the outside, the human sciences focused on the idea that every experience rested on the existence of a mental frame inside the human subject.[48] Having an experience presupposed a web of beliefs, ideas, sentiments which gave each particular instance of experience its meaning. The method of understanding used this idea in two ways. First, the interpretation of the historical world was itself an experience which relied on the mental frame of the interpreting subject. Second, understanding treated the traces of the past as the 'objectification' of particular experiences of others which were themselves related to an inner mental frame.[49] The process of understanding was designed to show that the two forms of mental composition were connected.

Dilthey differentiated between different forms of *Verstehen*: elementary understanding read the expressions of mental life backwards from the outcome to its source; re-experiencing, on the other hand, constituted a higher form of understanding. His explanation of re-experiencing relied on a circular form of reasoning: according to Dilthey, any mental experience represented a part of the psychological whole of a subject. Every particular experience derived its meaning from the overall composition of a mind and, in turn, every instance of experience had significance for the whole. Since the historian had no direct access to the mental composition of those he studied, he had to start by taking his own life-experience as a point of comparison. From there, the meaning of an expression of experience of others could then be inferred by way of analogy. Using one's own ideas, convictions and sentiments as a starting-point, re-experiencing meant reconstructing the web of experience of others by enforcing or weakening the elements of one's own inner being and by critically comparing the other person's expression of mental experience with one's own manner of expressing a supposedly similar experience.[50] Although this process was not supposed to ever accomplish an actual re-creation of another person's mind, Dilthey held that it enabled one to understand the historical traces of the human world.

For Dilthey, the circle of reasoning in understanding and re-experiencing was not a vicious circle one had to get out of. Rather, he argued that the mental origin of historical life should be treated as a part of the tradition which had eventually formed the historian's own contemporary situation including his perspective on other minds. Consequently, as in Ranke's and in Droysen's conceptions, the subject of historical knowledge and inquiry was not to be construed as external or separated from its object of study. Rather, understanding meant recognizing that subject and object were internally connected through history. Understanding particular historical expressions of the soul was supposed to activate the common features of the human mind within oneself. Eventually, this would lead to the comprehension of a general structure of historical continuity which Dilthey summarized as the 'objective spirit'. Because subject and object appertained to the same sphere of human activity (*Wirkungszusammenhang*) within the 'objective spirit', the effort of understanding was already a part of what was to be understood.[51] Dilthey declared:

> From this world of objective spirit the self receives sustenance from the earliest childhood, it is the medium in which the understanding of other people and their expressions take place. For everything in which the mind has objectified itself contains something held in common by the I and the Thou.[52]

Accordingly, the circle of understanding, for Dilthey, constituted the possibility of becoming aware of the interrelationship between the present and the past which determined the meaning of one's own thinking. Instead of trying to recognize the presence of God in one's own soul (as Ranke) or to proof the tradition of historical progress (as Droysen), Dilthey wanted to develop a system of the human sciences in order to show the historicity of the human mind.

## Conclusion

Within nineteenth-century history, the notion of *Verstehen* brought together two different attitudes towards history which had long been separated in earlier historiographical traditions. Antiquarians had been concerned with collecting remnants of past times, while philosophical historians had dealt with the general sense of historical development.[53] Around 1800, scholars began to combine the quest for the meaning of history with a need for reliable documents which could back up their arguments. Historians adopted the techniques of textual criticism from other disciplines to base their accounts on verifiable facts, and they developed new ways of integrating them into a coherent account of the past.

As a consequence, historiography increasingly had to sustain its claims by documentary research. And at the same time, leading scholars like Ranke and Droysen conceptualized history as the embodiment of spiritual forces beneath the particular historical facts. The spiritual content of history was not concerned with individual psychological motives, but rather with the historical ideas which dominated the thoughts and beliefs of an age. It was the business of historians to find the common mental ground which was taken as the origin of past events, by relying on their capacity to detect connections between the facts as they were documented in the historical record. In the eyes of Ranke, Droysen and Dilthey, the historian's endeavour was justified because the subjective mental forms used when constructing historical ideas were themselves determined by the tradition of the past that was under scrutiny. The emphasis on *Verstehen* in the historical thought of the nineteenth century has often been denounced as embodying a naïve theory of empathy which supposed that historians could feel themselves into the past by effacing their own subjectivity. Yet, the aim of historical understanding – as it was conceived by their main proponents – was not mental contemporaneity or self-forgetfulness, but rather to combine the acquisition of factual knowledge with a way of deepening and forming the scholar's selfhood.

Understanding and source-criticism had formed the backbone of historical scholarship in European and North American historiography since the beginning of its academic institutionalization in the second half of the nineteenth century.[54] One of the most famous theoretical reflections on the issues involved in interpreting historical documents was presented in the 1930s by Robin G. Collingwood, who developed his concept of re-enacting the thoughts of the past by carefully reviewing his predecessors of the nineteenth century.[55] From the early 1960s onward, however, concerted efforts to transform academic historiography into a historical social science struck a serious blow to the notion of understanding as the core of historical studies. Reform-minded social historians were critical of the way in which the concept of *Verstehen* had prompted generations of scholars to be uniquely concerned with highbrow intellectual history, and had barred them from taking the social contexts of ideas properly into account.

Critics like Arthur Danto, Louis Mink and Hayden White on the other hand insisted that historical studies should be independent of the theoretical efforts advanced in the social sciences and recast 'understanding' as the inescapable narrative dimension of historical accounts.[56] Even though today only few historians would claim to interpret historical records in the tradition of Ranke, Droysen and Dilthey, many of their ideas either survived or have recently been reinvented by historians who adopt and practise anthropological and micro-historical approaches. The methodological call to reconstruct past events from the perspective of historical actors, and to deduce the meaning of their particular practices from the whole of their culture (rather than assuming a social structure of which contemporaries were not aware) still points back to the concept of combining source-criticism and hermeneutics as it was developed within the historical studies of the nineteenth century.

## Notes

1  Johann Gustav Droysen to Wilhelm Arendt, 20 March 1857, in *Briefwechsel*, ed. Rudolf Hübner, vol. 2 1851–1884, Berlin. Leipzig: Deutsche Verlagsanstalt, 1929, p. 442.
2  Ibid.
3  A critical and complete edition of Droysen's *Historik*, his key text on the theory of history, was first published only in 1977. Even then it might be useful to consult the English translation of an earlier version, published as J.G. Droysen, *Outline of the Principles of History*, trans. E.B. Andrews, Boston: Ginn, 1897. All quotes in this chapter are from the critical edition: J.G. Droysen, *Historik. Rekonstruktion der ersten vollständigen Fassung der Vorlesungen (1857). Grundriß der Historik in der ersten handschriftlichen (1857/1858) und in der letzten gedruckten Fassung (1882)*, (ed.) Peter Ley, Stuttgart-Bad Cannstatt: Fromann-Holzboog, 1977, pp. 11f.
4  See A. Grafton, *The Footnote. A Curious History*, Cambridge, Mass.: Harvard University Press, 1997, pp. 73ff.
5  Lord Acton called Ranke 'the real originator of the heroic study of records'. Lord Acton, 'Inaugural Lecture on the Study of History', in J.E.E.D. Acton, *Lectures on Modern History*, London and Glasgow: Collins, 1960, p. 22.
6  Another important author in the foundation of the hermeneutic tradition was Wilhelm von Humboldt, who inspired especially Droysen. See among others T. Prüfer, 'Wilhelm von Humboldts "Rhetorische Hermeneutik"', in Prüfer and D. Fulda (eds), *Faktenglaube und fiktionales Wissen. Zum Verhältnis von Wissenschaft und Kunst in der Moderne*, Frankfurt/Main: Peter Lang, 1996, pp. 127–166.
7  See U. Muhlack, *Geschichtswissenschaft im Humanismus und in der Aufklärung. Die Vorgeschichte des Historismus*, Munich: C.H. Beck, 1991, pp. 351–352.
8  See in general B. Neveu, 'L'érudition ecclésiastique du XVIIe siècle et la nostalgie de l'Antiquité chrétienne', in his *Érudition et religion aux XVIIe et XVIIIe siècles*, Paris: Michel, 1994, pp. 333–363.
9  See Muhlack, *Vorgeschichte*, pp. 371–373.
10  For a more detailed account of the development of source-criticism as a reaction to the systematic doubt against historical knowledge see M. Völkel, *'Pyrrhonismus' und 'fides historica'. Die Entwicklung der deutschen Methodologie unter dem Gesichtspunkt der historischen Skepsis*, Frankfurt/Main: Peter Lang, 1987.
11  See H.W. Blanke, *Historiographiegeschichte als Historik*, Stuttgart-Bad Cannstatt: Fromann-Holzboog, 1991, pp. 156–163.
12  See U. Muhlack, 'Historie und Philologie', in H.E. Bödecker (ed.), *Aufklärung und Geschichte*, Göttingen: Vandenhoeck & Ruprecht, 1986, p. 67.
13  Ranke says (in the second edition of his book): 'Man hat der Historie das Amt, die Vergangenheit zu richten, die Mitwelt zum Nutzen zukünftiger Jahre zu belehren, beigemessen: so hoher Aemter unterwindet sich gegenwärtiger Versuch nicht: er will blos zeigen, wie es eigentlich gewesen.' L. v. Ranke, *Geschichten der romanischen und germanischen Völker von 1494 bis 1514*, 2nd edn, Leipzig: Duncker & Humblot, 1874, p. vii. The English translation is taken from the extract in F. Stern (ed.), *The Varieties of History. From Voltaire to the Present*, London: Macmillan, 1970, pp. 55–62.
14  On Niebuhr see G. Walter, *Niebuhrs Forschung*, Stuttgart: Steiner, 1993.

15  Comparing different accounts to each other Ranke especially showed that Guicciardini's *History of Italy* of 1508 which had been taken as a reliable source consisted for the most part not only of copies from other authors, but that Guicciardini had also changed and invented historical facts. See Ranke, 'Zur Kritik neuerer Geschichtsschreiber', in Ranke, *Geschichten*, pp. 1–39.

16  See T. Prüfer, *Die Bildung der Geschichte. Friedrich Schiller und die Anfänge der modernen Geschichtswissenschaft*, Cologne: Böhlau, 2003, pp. 267ff.

17  See L. Krieger, *Ranke. The Meaning of History*, Chicago: University of Chicago Press, 1977, p. 15.

18  As he declared in one of his letters of the time against his critics: 'That I am supposed to lack philosophical and religious interest is ridiculous since this is just . . . what drove me to historical research.' Ranke to Heinrich Ritter, 6 August 1830, in Ranke, *Das Briefwerk*, Hamburg: Hoffmann & Campe, 1949, p. 216.

19  See especially C. Hinrichs, *Ranke und die Geschichtstheologie der Goethezeit*, Göttingen: Musterschmidt, 1954, pp. 119–120, 146–147; S. Backs, *Dialektisches Denken in Rankes Geschichtsschreibung bis 1854*, Cologne and Vienna: Böhlau, 1985, pp. 43ff.

20  L. v. Ranke, 'Idee der Universalhistorie', in Ranke, *Vorlesungseinleitungen*, ed. V. Dotterweich and W.P. Fuchs, Munich and Vienna: Oldenbourg, 1975, p. 78.

21  Ibid., pp. 72–83.

22  See D. Fulda, *Wissenschaft aus Kunst. Die Entstehung der modernen Geschichtsschreibung 1760–1860*, Berlin and New York: de Gruyter, 1996, p. 407; J. Süssmann, *Geschichtsschreibung oder Roman? Zur Konstitutionslogik von Geschichtserzählungen zwischen Schiller und Ranke (1780–1824)*, Stuttgart: Steiner, 2000, pp. 215f.; P. Müller, 'Wissenspoesie und Historie. Rankes Literaturgeschichte Italiens als Rekonfiguration ästhetischer Geschichtsphilosophie', *German Studies Review* 29 (2006), 1–20.

23  L. Ranke, *Französische Geschichte, vornehmlich im sechzehnten und siebzehnten Jahrhundert*, 4th edn, vol. 5, Leipzig: Duncker & Humblot, 1877, p. 6.

24  See W. Hardtwig, 'Geschichtsreligion – Wissenschaft als Arbeit – Objektivität. Der Historismus in neuer Sicht', *Historische Zeitschrift* 252 (1991), 8–12.

25  Ranke to Anton Richter, 13 April 1823, in Leopold von Ranke, *Gesamtausgabe des Briefwechsels: vol. 1, 1813–1825*, (eds) U. Muhlack and O. Ramonat, Munich: R. Oldenbourg, 2007, p. 337; see Krieger, *Meaning*, p. 10.

26  Ranke to Heinrich Ranke, 30 November 1832, in Ranke, *Das Briefwerk*, pp. 252f. In an earlier letter to his brother Ranke stated: 'Real joy is to forget oneself, to give oneself, to become more conscious of oneself in the larger whole'. Ranke to Heinrich Ranke, 20 and 21 November 1828, in ibid., p. 175; see Krieger, *Meaning*, p. 14.

27  See H. White, 'Droysen's Historik. Historical Writing as a Bourgeois Science', in White, *The Content of the Form. Narrative Discourse and Historical Representation*, Baltimore and London: Johns Hopkins University Press, 1987, pp. 83–103.

28  Droysen, *Historik*, p. 218.

29  Ibid., pp. 9f., 67.

30  See J.G. Droysen, 'Zur Quellenkritik', in his *Texte zur Geschichtstheorie. Mit ungedruckten Materialien zur 'Historik'*, (ed.) G. Birtsch and J. Rüsen, Göttingen: Vandenhoeck & Ruprecht, 1972, pp. 60–66; Droysen, *Historik*, pp. 71–100. Droysen established a third category that designated all the traces of the past which expressed the intention of preserving events but, at the same time, had a practical function within the contemporary affairs of their origin. Droysen called them 'monuments', a category that comprised for example legal documents and diplomatic reports.

31  Droysen, *Historik*, p. 166.

32  Ibid., pp. 103–104.

33  Ibid., pp. 12–13.

34  See ibid., pp. 187–194.

35 See H.G. Gadamer, *Wahrheit und Methode. Grundzüge der philosophischen Hermeneutik*, 6th edn, Tübingen: Mohr, 1990, pp. 216–222.
36 Droysen, *Historik*, p. 107. Compare also the later remark: 'I would not be able to think an idea that has not already won expression . . . We have within ourselves all the ideas that are thinkable, since they are thinkable only insofar they have become, as they are the result of history.' Ibid., p. 206.
37 See J. Rüsen, *Konfigurationen des Historismus. Studien zur deutschen Wissenschaftskultur*, Frankfurt/Main: Suhrkamp, 1993, pp. 254–255.
38 This side of Droysen's conception of history was strongly influenced by the philosophy of Georg Wilhelm Friedrich Hegel. See Rüsen, *Konfigurationen*, pp. 254–255.
39 Droysen, *Historik*, pp. 211–212.
40 See White, *Droysen's Historik*, pp. 95–96.
41 Droysen, *Historik*, p. 201.
42 See ibid., pp. 363–366.
43 See the introduction of H.T. Buckle, *History of Civilization in England*, 2 vols, London: J.W. Parker, 1857.
44 In the following I do not discuss whether different stages in Dilthey's intellectual career should be distinguished. For the purpose of this essay I follow the arguments of R.A. Makreel, *Dilthey. Philosopher of the Human Studies*, Princeton: Princeton University Press, 1975, pp. 7–8.
45 See R. Koselleck, 'On the Anthropological and Semantic Structure of Bildung', in Koselleck, *The Practice of Conceptual History. Timing History, Spacing Concepts*, Stanford: Stanford University Press, 2002, p. 170.
46 See R. Vierhaus, 'Bildung', in O. Brunner, W. Conze, R. Koselleck (eds), *Geschichtliche Grundbegriffe. Historisches Lexikon zur politisch-sozialen Sprache in Deutschland*, Stuttgart: Ernst Klett Verlag, 1972, vol. 1, p. 529.
47 W. Dilthey, 'Ideen über eine beschreibende und zergliedernde Psychologie', in Dilthey, *Die geistige Welt. Einleitung in die Philosophie des Lebens*, Leipzig and Berlin: Teubner, 1924, p. 144.
48 See ibid., pp. 140–142.
49 See W. Dilthey, 'Die Entstehung der Hermeneutik', in his *Die geistige Welt*, p. 236.
50 See W. Dilthey, *Der Aufbau der geschichtlichen Welt in den Geisteswissenschaften*, Leipzig: Teubner, 1927, pp. 214–215.
51 See Makreel, *Dilthey*, p. 314–322.
52 Dilthey, *Aufbau*, p. 208. Compare C.R. Bambach, *Heidegger, Dilthey, and the Crisis of Historicism*, Ithaca, N.Y.: Cornell University Press, 1995, p. 162.
53 See A. Momigliano, 'Ancient History and the Antiquarian', in Momigliano, *Contributo alla storia degli studi classici*, Rome: Edizioni di storia e letteratura, 1955, pp. 67–106.
54 For the significance of Ranke's methodology for historians in the USA see Peter Novick, *That Noble Dream. The 'Objectivity Question' and the American Historical Profession*, Cambridge: Cambridge University Press, 1988, pp. 21–46.
55 Collingwood's theory of re-enactment should not be confused with Dilthey's concept of re-experiencing. In opposition to Dilthey Collingwood restricted understanding on the re-enactment of acts of thought which he defined as separate from the overall composition of the mind. It bears some resemblance with Dilthey's definition of a notional expression of life. For Collingwood's judgement on Dilthey see R.G. Collingwood, *The Idea of History*, rev. edn, ed. J. van der Dussen, Oxford: Clarendon Press, 1993, pp. 171–176.
56 See for example White, *Content*.

## Select bibliography

Bambach, C.R., *Heidegger, Dilthey, and the Crisis of Historicism*, Ithaca: Cornell University Press, 1995.

Grafton, A., *The Footnote. A Curious History*, Cambridge, Mass.: Harvard University Press, 1997.

Harrington, A., 'Dilthey, Empathy and Verstehen. A Contemporary Reappraisal', *European Journal of Social Theory* 4, 2001, 311–329.

Iggers, G.G., *The German Conception of History. The National Tradition of History Thought from Herder to the Present*, rev. edn, Middletown, Conn.: Wesleyan University Press, 1983.

Iggers, G.G. and Powell, J.M. (eds), *Leopold von Ranke and the Shaping of the Historical Discipline*, Syracuse: Syracuse UP, 1990.

Krieger, L., *Ranke. The Meaning of History*, Chicago: University of Chicago Press, 1977.

Makreel, R.A., *Dilthey. Philosopher of the Human Studies*, Princeton: Princeton University Press, 1975.

Schnädelbach, H., *Philosophy in Germany 1831–1933*, Cambridge: Cambridge University Press, 1984.

Toews, J.E., *Becoming Historical. Cultural Reformation and Public Memory in Early Nineteenth-Century Berlin*, Cambridge: Cambridge University Press, 2004.

White, H., 'Droysen's Historik. Historical Writing as a Bourgeois Science', in H. White, *The Content of the Form. Narrative Discourse and Historical Representation*, Baltimore: Johns Hopkins University Press, 1987, pp. 83–103.

# 2 Reading texts after the linguistic turn

## Approaches from literary studies and their implications

*Christoph Reinfandt*

'Who's afraid of the "linguistic turn"?' the German historian Peter Schöttler asked in 1997, some eight years after his excellent survey of what he perceived to be historians' new interest in the analysis of language and discourse in the 1980s.[1] His answer was that, plainly, many historians still were. Apparently, the discipline's misgivings about the implications of addressing the linguistic and discursive parameters of both history and historiography were not easily dispelled. To this day, the uncertainty and instability going along with a focus on language and discourse is perceived as a threat to the institutional standards and foundations of historiography. History, conceived in this way, seems to lose its factuality and to evaporate into fiction, irrationality or merely discourse itself; any 'grand' or 'master narratives' of modernity are scattered into 'little narratives', and the unity of history itself appears to have been abandoned.[2] Accordingly, beyond the programmatic but strangely half-hearted 'Defense of History' by writers such as, most prominently, Richard J. Evans,[3] constructive engagements with the challenge are few and far between and do not always come from the heart of the profession.[4]

What strikes the outsider such as the present writer with a background in literary studies, literary theory and sociological systems theory as slightly odd, however, is the persistence of the catchphrase 'the linguistic turn' in the context of this particular debate. To be sure, the 'turn' taken by philosophy and other disciplines at the beginning of the twentieth century – identified retrospectively as 'the linguistic turn' by the philosopher Richard Rorty only in 1967 – is of fundamental importance.[5] But then there has been so much going on since then that the – from the historian's point of view – apparently widely accepted equation linguistic turn = literary theory = postmodernism surely merits closer scrutiny.[6] This seems particularly necessary in view of the fact that in the fields of literary and cultural studies there has been a proliferation of subsequent 'turns' of all kinds since the 1980s, and this development makes the epithet 'linguistic' surely look old-fashioned and not 'postmodern' at all.[7]

So how does it all hang together? In the present chapter, the broader context of theoretical positions in literary studies will be outlined with an eye to their viability in realms beyond literature, and particularly history. Theory itself will be conceived of as springing from the renegotiations of objectivity that are characteristic of modernity. From the eighteenth century onwards at the latest, traditional notions of objective truth had to face the emergence of subjectivity as a core ingredient of modern culture. Once truth became potentially subjective and thus relative, all truth claims had to be justified in new ways, and this function was taken over by theory in a specifically modern sense. Ultimately, however, the emergence of modern theory inaugurated an increasing awareness of the pervasiveness of reflexivity in modern culture at large. This fundamental importance of reflexivity was finally acknowledged with the linguistic turn in the early twentieth century, which later fed into the apotheosis of literary theory in the 1980s[8] marked by its 'postmodern' ambition of taking the decisive step from being a theory of something towards being just 'plain "theory"' – with seemingly unlimited reach in explaining the world in terms of textuality and representation.[9]

The first section will address theories of textual meaning before the linguistic turn. In contrast to the assertion occasionally put forward in primers of literary theory in the English-speaking world that before literary theory there was only the ideology of liberal humanism,[10] earlier theories about 'textual meaning and how to get at it in the case of literature' will be traced. From the eighteenth century onwards, the theory of interpretation called hermeneutics has tried to preserve the ideal of stable and unequivocal ('objective') textual meaning in spite of its increasing awareness of the fact that meaning can only be realized in subjective acts of interpretation. In the nineteenth century, on the other hand, the competitive projects of positivism and Marxism tried to establish extra-textual (i.e. social and historical) frames of objectivity from which textual meaning was to be derived. It is against theoretical orientations such as these that the early twentieth century emancipation of literary theory proper positioned itself by taking its inspiration from linguistics.

Accordingly, the second section will begin with a discussion of the internal ideological contradictions of the Anglo-American varieties of formalism ('Practical Criticism', 'New Criticism'), which are, in spite of their a- and transhistorical aspirations and their longevity, seen as transitional movements caught between the old paradigm of liberal humanism on the one hand and the emerging new paradigm of critical theory on the other.[11] This emergence of critical theory is then traced from Russian Formalism through Structuralism into Poststructuralism and Deconstruction, with the last two dominating the emerging self-descriptions of late twentieth-century Western culture as 'postmodern' between, say, 1968 and the early 1980s for better or worse. It is the stringency of this twentieth-century success story with its focus on language and textuality that makes the equation linguistic turn = postmodernism so attractive a target for its opponents. However, as the third section will then show, there has been a re-orientation towards history after the heyday of 'theory' in the 1980s, and fruitful ideas for the interpretation of texts from modern history can be drawn from this context. The chapter will accordingly end with an attempt to map the various components of the checklist outlined in the introduction to this volume onto recent theoretical and methodological positions in the fields of literary, cultural and media studies.[12]

## Theory before theory

In an influential survey of the history of Western aesthetics, the literary critic M.H. Abrams suggests that approaches to reading texts can be grouped according to how they understand the relation of a text to the world.[13] Since antiquity, the most widely held assumption is that a work of art imitates reality. Theories with this focus can be classified as 'mimetic theories' (from Greek *mimesis*, meaning 'imitation'), and they are often combined with 'pragmatic theories' focusing on the question as to why and how this imitation of reality should be accomplished and what effects it has (or should have) on an audience. While these theoretical orientations are still very much with us, a radically new orientation emerged at the end of the eighteenth century when 'expressive theories' focused on the mind and genius of the writer as the origin and sole frame of reference for the work. This Romantic emancipation of the work from the constraints of imitation and moral edification led in turn to a new type of 'objective theories' largely concerned with the work as an object in itself which was fully realized in the modernist movement at the beginning of the twentieth century and in formalist schools of literary criticism emerging at that time.

Broadly, then, one can distinguish between traditional, 'old-European' positions predicated on notions of objective truth on the one hand and specifically modern positions predicated on subjectivity and reflexivity on the other. While mimetic and pragmatic theories rest on the assumption that meaning and truth are basically residing in the world and function as eternal and objective norms of beauty and moral behaviour, this frame of reference no longer holds for expressive and subjective theories. As specifically modern theories they acknowledge the loss of ontological certainty characteristic of the modern age and try to compensate for this loss through an insistence on the autonomy of art as prefigured in notions of the artist as genius.

For the present purposes of reading texts from modern history the latter positions are obviously crucial, but it is important to note that the outline presented above does not indicate a linear sequence with each new position replacing the preceding one. Instead it is based on a cumulative principle: to this day, the ideal of objective truth has not vanished, although ever since the eighteenth century all truth claims have had to come to terms with the fundamental instability introduced by subjectivity and reflexivity. Accordingly, textual meaning under modern conditions unfolds in a three-dimensional sphere in which objective, subjective and reflexive orientations of meaning are simultaneously present. However, the bias of the rules of reading shifted only slowly from a nostalgic longing for objectivity to an acknowledgement of culturally domesticated forms of subjectivity and finally to a full-blown engagement with the cultural reflexivity induced by – well, not language as the phrase 'the linguistic turn' suggests, but rather, as will be seen later in this chapter, writing, printing and, of late, the electronic media. And the beginning of this trajectory is marked by the emergence of a theory of interpretation which tries to balance the ideal of stable, unified meanings as part of objective truth with the subjective implications of all acts of reading (and writing, for that matter).

The beginnings of hermeneutics (from Greek *hermeneutikos* 'an expert in inter-pretation') can be traced to the aftermath of the Reformation, which, in its rejection of the monopolizing of the interpretation of scripture by Catholic dogma, posed the problem of how to legitimize the newly democratized readings of the Bible.[14] The basic principle established here was that of the hermeneutic circle, i.e. the assump-tion that the understanding of parts of the Bible as read by the individual reader is framed by the meaning of the whole and vice versa, while the meaningfulness of the whole can be taken for granted because of its status as 'God's word'. As soon as this idea is applied to texts beyond the realm of Holy Scripture, however, the problem of whether the meaningfulness of the whole (what whole?) can be presupposed sur-faces, and it is exacerbated by the problem of historical distance. Generally, this problem is solved in hermeneutics by assuming a continuity of cultural expression since antiquity which creates a link between all texts. As late as 1960 Hans-Georg Gadamer (1900–2002) suggested in his seminal *Wahrheit und Methode* (Truth and Method) that the problem of subjectivity can be overcome by accepting tradition as a normative element which helps to avoid arbitrary subjective readings.[15] Still, the problem of the potential subjectivism of all reading (and writing) acts resurfaced again and again in the hermeneutic tradition, and it found its seminal expression in Wilhelm Dilthey's (1833–1911) project of establishing the human sciences (*Geisteswissenschaften*) as an alternative to the increasingly successful objectivist paradigm of the natural sciences. In this context, Johann Gustav Droysen (1808–1884) insisted that when writing history the distinction between (objective) 'source criticism' on the one hand and (inevitably subjective) 'interpretation' on the other must be maintained, while the subjective implications of the latter should be reined in by the overarching continuity of Western civilization.

As opposed to this direct engagement with the cultural dimension of subjectiv-ity, the nineteenth century also saw a redoubled attempt at preserving the unity of an objective world view. In France, the mathematician and philosopher Auguste Comte (1798–1857) laid out the programme for what he called positivism and which ultimately evolved into the discipline of sociology.[16] In keeping with the French connotations of the word *positive*, this scientific programme for dealing with social problems strictly focused on what is real (as opposed to imagined), use-ful (as opposed to meaningless), certain (as opposed to uncertain) and constructive (as opposed to destructive). Following the anti-metaphysical tradition of the European enlightenment, positivism restricts itself to the observation and exami-nation of given facts which are then classified in order to find out and establish the unchangeable laws of the world. On these premises, Comte develops his 'Encyclopaedic Law of the Classification of the Sciences' culminating in the his-torical method of sociology and integrates this into a larger world-historical scheme with clear political implications: Comte envisages a hierarchical model of society in which spiritual authority resides with an elite of sociologists while secu-lar authority resides with bankers and businessmen.

At this point the ideological framing of scientific objectivity under modern con-ditions becomes obvious: while the observation and examination of facts may be undertaken for its own sake, there is, behind its back, as it were, a larger agenda resting on a firm belief in the interconnectedness of scientific, economic, and social progress, i.e. the master narrative of modernity. From here it is only a small step to an outright materialistic philosophy of history as introduced by Karl Marx (1818–1883). While in many respects related to positivism, Marxism replaces the emphasis on knowledge as something arrived at through science with a radically new emphasis on a theoretical model of the material basis of a society as manifested in stages and states of its economy.[17] This move provided the basis for the most powerful counter-narrative of modernity. It also made it clear once and for all that under modern conditions everything can be viewed from (at least) two angles, thus preparing the ground for all kinds of fundamentally critical projects in the twentieth and twenty-first centuries, such as, for example, some of the positions subsumed under the heading of 'postmodernism'.

With regard to the reading of texts from modern history, however, this implies that since Comte and Marx there have been two objectivities, as it were. Both positivistic and Marxist approaches to literature, taking a decidedly anti-hermeneutical stance, regard literary texts as social and historical facts which should be explained without drawing upon fuzzy Romantic concepts like 'genius' or 'creative freedom', but nevertheless they part company with regard to their respective evaluations of texts. In the case of positivism, the basic assumption is that society determines the life of the author who in turn determines the shape of the work. This leads to an author-centred approach which searches for traces of biographical facts in the works.[18] In spite of its anti-hermeneutical origins this mode of inquiry is not completely incompatible with the hermeneutical project of finding out what the author really meant, and to this day the combined power of these two positions, plus experiences drawn from everyday life as well as the conventions of school teaching and encyclopaedias, governs the attitude of many a normal reader or novice student of literature in spite of the fact that all kinds of epistemological problems could be identified (What are biographical 'facts'? How do we get at them? What happens to them in the poet's mind?). Similarly, the time-honoured, 'old-European' notion that literature mirrors reality (cf. Abrams's 'mimetic theories') is perpetuated in a fairly naïve way, notwithstanding the Marxist insight that literary texts do not necessarily mirror reality, because they might as well distort it. And finally, the seemingly straightforward analysis of 'objective' textual features turns out to be heavily influenced by subjective interpretive strategies.

Marxist thinkers, on the other hand, address some of these problems by somewhat paradoxically placing literature on the fairly inaccessible level of 'superstructure' (i.e. as part of the ideas and institutions which mediate between material existence of human beings and their consciousness) whilst acknowledging that the material basis of society is laid by its economic structure. According to these thinkers, literature in a class society is an ideological phenomenon caught up in the necessarily wrong or limited consciousness brought forth and controlled by the power structures of capitalism, though it does have, to a certain extent, the potential for transcending these conditions through its limited independence from the restraints of material production. Obviously, this framework offers a more sophisticated account of the social determination of textual meaning than positivism by acknowledging that there need not be a one-to-one mirroring of reality. At the same time, however, this step opens up texts for alternative readings in the light of the version of modern progress that Marxism envisages. And with the benefit of hindsight one can see from today's vantage point that objectivity under modern conditions seems to be an ideological construct anyway, be it of bourgeois-capitalist persuasion as in positivism or opposed to this as in Marxism.

Theories of textual meaning before the emergence of literary theory, then, were very much preoccupied with staking claims for objectivity by linking textual meaning to something 'objectively' given outside of the text. Within the frameworks of positivism and Marxism, meaning is determined and unequivocally unified by society and history, while their wholesale and largely uncritical adoption of mimetic and pragmatic theories of art and literature manifests the ongoing longing for objectivity which is characteristic of modern culture to this day. The problem is, alas, that the alternative master narratives of modern progress projected by positivism and Marxism themselves undermine their aspiration to perpetuate objectivity, and one can assume that this fundamental relativity contributed massively to the explicitly reflexive turn modern culture took finally at the beginning of the twentieth century.

There was, however, another sphere increasingly claiming its own objectivity, as it were, in the course of the nineteenth century. In the Romantic period, a modern understanding of art and literature as imaginative and autonomous fields of cultural practice established itself. Just like the tradition of hermeneutics, this new aesthetic and literary paradigm tried to acknowledge the fundamental importance of subjectivity in all acts of reading and writing on the one hand and to salvage the possibility of unified meaning as guaranteed by the ideal of objectivity on the other. For all practical artistic purposes, the hermeneutic projection of objectivity into an idealized realm of 'culture' was translated into an emphatic insistence on the unity and totality of works of art (cf. Abrams's 'objective theories'), and at this point hermeneutics feeds into the momentous formation of what has come to be known as the Romantic ideology.[19] As will be seen in the next section, reading practices in the fields of literature and education were heavily influenced by this ideological formation.[20] Before the linguistic turn, then, there were at least three objectivities available in modern culture: the master narrative of progress as envisaged in positivism on the one hand, and the two counter-narratives of Marxism and aesthetic autonomy on the other.[21]

## The linguistic turn and beyond: modernity coming into its own

Objectivity, this brief survey suggests, became a highly problematic and contested category towards the end of the nineteenth century. Just like many other dimensions of modern culture, it was subject to differentiation, and an important effect of this development can be found in the proliferation of academic disciplines, each successfully negotiating its own highly specialized truth claims and objectivities but finding only limited acceptance beyond its own sphere. Obviously, this fragmentation contributed massively to the overall emergence of reflexivity as a signature of modern culture in the early twentieth century. Against this background, the emergence of professional standards for the discipline of history in the course of the nineteenth century can be described in terms of the combination of hermeneutical and positivistic procedures outlined above, albeit with a strong bias towards objectivity as the ultimate yardstick of professionalism and defining quality of good practice. To this day, the conviction that 'things really did happen in the past and that historians can often find out what they were' is at the heart of the historical profession, and justly so as long as it goes hand in hand with the new sense of 'acute methodological self-consciousness' recently described by Keith Thomas.[22] Or, as another observer puts it:

> We did not need postmodernism to tell us that objectivity was always a chimera, that individual historians, their lives, loves and beliefs, are always there, in choice of subject and argument and in the very words they write. History never was just facts; it was always the interpretation of them. Before the historian, the first person who told stories about the past, history didn't exist. Facts existed, and the past, but not history.[23]

Here, however, we are obviously back to square one in terms of the nineteenth-century schism between 'source criticism' and interpretation, and the question is: on what grounds can an *objectivity* not only *of evidence and induction,* but ultimately *of interpretation* be established as the defining quality of good practice within the discipline, and how can it accommodate the standards of postmodern epistemology without undermining the foundations of historians' professionalism?

One possible answer may lie in acknowledging the fundamental twentieth century shift from objectivity to reflexivity as a regulative idea of academic practice.[24] Interestingly, this shift was addressed earlier in literary studies than in history, presumably because of literature's lack of 'objective' and factual credentials. As the new discipline of literary studies emerged it had to come up with notions of 'literariness' in order to justify its existence, and a turn to language as literature's core ingredient seemed the logical next step, especially as linguistics was also emerging as a new discipline at the same time – and one with strong 'scientific' leanings and aspirations. This step was, however, taken only half-heartedly in the English-speaking world. Beginning with I.A. Richards's (1893–1979) and C.K. Ogden's (1889–1957) attempt at transferring methods of linguistic analysis to the reading of literary texts in *The Meaning of Meaning* (1923), the emergent approach of 'Practical Criticism' rejected subjectivist and impressionist modes of literary criticism as well as positivistic approaches.[25] All non-literary factors (author, context, reality) were relegated to their new status as 'background knowledge', and the literary text was emphatically conceived of as an organic unity in the face of an increasingly fragmented modern reality. Here it becomes obvious that the new objectivity of the approach oscillated precariously between scientific aspirations on the one hand and the ideological underpinnings of the object of study on the other, i.e. an a priori understanding of the literary text as a 'great', 'timeless' and unified work of art.[26] Nevertheless, the codification of this new 'intrinsic approach' with its exclusive emphasis on 'close reading' under the banner of the 'New Criticism' in the United States of the 1940s established a new focus on the literary text itself as the sole origin of its meaning. And what is more, the truth-value of poetic language with its connotative and metaphorical levels of meaning and its toleration of ambiguity was for the first time explicitly emancipated from the understanding of truth in 'normal' (and scientific) language with its one-to-one denotations of the most literal and limited meaning of a word and its seemingly clear-cut reference to the world.[27] Accordingly, time-honoured notions of linguistic truth as rooted in language's correspondence to reality were supplemented by the notion that truth might equally reside in the coherence and acceptability of works of art or, by extension, language, texts or discourses in general. While this idea was at first exclusively limited to literature, the twentieth century saw its gradual expansion and, inversely, an erosion of referential, ontological notions of truth.

Meanwhile, on the other side of the world, an emerging group of Russian formalists was less encumbered by ideological burdens.[28] In Moscow and St Petersburg, a number of scholars tried to get rid of the unsystematic, subjective and impressionistic ways of dealing with literature inherited from the nineteenth century by focusing on 'how' instead of 'what' a text means. Just like the New Criticism, the first steps in this direction were heavily influenced by the aestheticist and avantgardistic poetic movements of the day with their programmatic insistence on aesthetic autonomy. Focusing on the distinction between 'normal' language based on habitual, automatic responses, mechanical recognition and reference to reality on the one hand, and self-referential poetic language which provokes a new awareness and intensity of perception in the reader on the other, the Russian formalists envisaged a dialectics of automatization and defamiliarization based on concrete acts of reception.[29] As opposed to the New Critics' insistence on 'timelessness', this dynamic model introduced the possibility of describing literary history in terms of an evolution of literary forms. Later stages of Russian formalism then moved beyond notions of form by introducing the concept of structure in which textual unity is not achieved by a combination and merging of elements, but rather by their dynamic interaction.[30] And finally, this development culminated in the so-called 'Structuralist Manifesto' (1928), which marked the final transformation of Russian formalism into structuralism.[31] The shift from 'form' (with its firm link to the individual text at hand) to 'structure' (with its greater appreciation of the internal dynamics of texts) marked a decisive step in spelling out the implications of the linguistic turn. While for all practical purposes, structuralist readings of literary texts in the English-speaking world frequently remained strictly within the confines of terminologically upgraded close readings modelled on work by Roman Jakobson and Claude Levi-Strauss,[32] the term structure continuously implied larger contexts in that the meaning of textual elements such as binary oppositions was conceived of as being embedded within larger structures, such as society understood as a structure of structures conditioning each other in no particular hierarchical order.[33]

According to such approaches, meaning, then, takes its origin in structures, and the basic patterns of structures are prefigured in language itself. The modern linguistics of Ferdinand de Saussure (1857–1913) was hugely influential, in particular his examination of binary oppositions. De Saussure's *Cours de linguistique générale* as transcribed by one of his students and published posthumously in 1916 describes language as a system or structure of elements whose relation to each other is governed by codes. Its most revolutionary and ground-breaking idea is that meaning emerges from these relations and oppositions rather than from a sign's reference to the world.[34] In other words: the relationship between the materially graspable side of a linguistic sign, the 'signifier', and its meaning, the 'signified', is governed by conventional aspects internal to the language system and thus arbitrary. Accordingly, meaning is a purely linguistic phenomenon basically independent from reference, though for all practical purposes the assumption of a reference implied by the apparent unity of the sign is of course helpful.

At any rate, this emancipation of meaning from reference and the idea that the principle of codes as binary oppositions could be transferred from the realm of language to the realm of culture at large were put to good use in structuralism's wide coverage of cultural phenomena. This coverage ranged from the analysis of poems to the question of how the aesthetic can be described as a social phenomenon, from investigations of the anthropological significance of distinguishing raw food from cooked food to the workings of narrative and the mythologies of everyday life in popular culture.[35] This in turn inaugurated the fully fledged cultural dispersion of the linguistic turn's implications, which were now refashioned in terms of semiotics, i.e. in terms of the systematic study of all factors involved in the production and interpretation of signs or in processes of signification. And it was in this realm that the final steps from structuralism into the much more radical claims of poststructuralism evolved.

Roland Barthes (1915–1980) suggested as early as 1964 that meaning is not dependent on the structure of the language system alone, but also on socially and culturally embedded secondary systems of signification such as politics, science, literature or whatever.[36] In the contexts of these secondary systems, every linguistic sign in de Saussure's sense, with its arbitrary but fairly stable denotative relation between signifier and signified, functions in its entirety as a new signifier. The signifieds of this new signifier unfold in a field of connotations particular to a given secondary system, and it surely does make a difference whether you talk about a tree in a linguistics class, in a nature poem, in the contexts of 'green' or conservative politics, or in terms of its economic potential. What is more, the plurality of secondary systems in modern culture suggests that their interaction might actually even create tertiary systems of signification in which signs taken in their entirety from one secondary system may stimulate ever-new connotations in another system which thus shifts into a tertiary position. Accordingly, the process of meaning production (semiosis) cannot be delimited, and the potential signifieds of a given signifier proliferate. It is this basic instability of meaning that is finally and notoriously addressed by the 'postmodern' theories of poststructuralism and deconstruction, and it should by now be clear in the light of the preceding survey that this position is the outcome of the linguistic turn at the beginning of the twentieth century. It is, in other words, not just the spleen of some particularly inventive French theorists in the 1970s, but rather the eventual surfacing of a broader reflexive turn taken by modern culture at large, marked by a shift from 'old-European' ontology with its concomitant essentialism predicated on identity to an all-pervasive constructivism predicated on difference.[37]

While structuralism and poststructuralism share the assumption that language is constitutive of human dealings with reality and that the world is a world of arbitrary signs, their understanding of the sign differs significantly. Where structuralism insists on the unity of the sign – *within* which meaning resides with its implied reference to the world – poststructuralism acknowledges that only the material dimension of the sign (the signifier) is accessible while its possible signifieds evolve unfixably from never-ending processes of semiosis. Accordingly, there is, in principle, a gap rather than a link between signifier and signified, the sign is not a unit, but rather an access point to a cultural practice which does not point towards anything beyond itself. As the French philosopher Jacques Derrida (1930–2004) argued, there is no 'transcendental signified' which is somehow present without any discursive mediation and can thus stop the endless play of signifiers.[38]

In the light of these ideas, the structuralist project of providing a scientific basis for the human sciences by describing the laws and constants of the symbolic activity of the human mind finally had to be abandoned as the poststructuralist insistence on the fundamental openness and instability of meaning undermined the belief in the possibility of final explanations of all kind. Accordingly, Derrida suggested that the Western belief in final explanations is a 'logocentric' illusion brought about by the ontological self-deceptions of a culture grounding its world view on a 'metaphysics of presence', i.e. the idea, based on the primacy of spoken language in Western thought, that reality is represented in language through a direct correspondence between word and referent within an essentially whole thinking subject. Instead, reality is, in the context of Western culture, rather represented in language through writing (*écriture*) and the accumulation of information and ideas enabled by the storage function of written texts. Under these conditions, meaning is subject to what Derrida calls *différance*: it is never given and stable, but rather the effect of a never-ending dynamics of signifiers pointing at each other ('to defer') and mutually defining each other in a structure without a centre ('to differ'). Thus, signs neither mean anything 'in themselves' nor do they refer to anything beyond the ongoing process of *dissémination*.[39] Every decoding is also another encoding,[40] or, as Derrida notoriously put it: 'There is nothing outside of the text.'[41] From a deconstructionist point of view, all readings predicated on 'transcendental signifieds' such as truth or reality are 'weak readings' while only readings which are deconstructing these truths by laying open their linguistic foundations can be considered 'strong'.

Clearly, in the light of these ideas, meaning can no longer be determined, criticized or evaluated by reference to facts or objects in reality, and accordingly the question of what historians are supposed to do indeed becomes pressing. But then, even if we accept that we cannot get at reality as such in its totality and ultimate meaningfulness (and the present writer for one does), this does not necessarily imply that reality does not exist, and even historians' belief in historical truth can survive the onslaught of deconstruction if one acknowledges that interpretations are all we have. For most if not all practical purposes, however, we will have to distinguish between acceptable ('true') and unacceptable ('false') interpretations, especially in view of the power texts can wield in the world, and here the problem of referentiality cannot be evaded. Historians, for example, will insist that it all depends on evidence: if you get your evidence (sources, facts, events) wrong, your interpretation will turn out to be unacceptable, and this insistence on evidence is indispensable in view of the reality-constituting effects of historical interpretations and, most notoriously, in view of the disturbing implications of relativist positions with regard to the holocaust.[42] However, a deconstructionist would say, the *meaning* of evidence accrues *exclusively* in the realm of (inter-)textuality made up of source texts with their *implied* reference to things, facts and events; it does not originate in things, facts and events themselves. And to this, a constructivist would add: even if we accept that things, facts and events have no historical meaning in their mere existence, it is nevertheless quite clear that they acquire their status as historical facts if a majority of sources *and* interpretations concurs in positing their existence.

It is this concurrence of sources and interpretations which provides an opening for a puncturing, as it were, of the theoretically impenetrable realm of textuality by referentiality. This opening transforms the implicit but ultimately untenable referentiality of statements about the world into a textually and discursively *constructed* explicit reference. Similarly, deconstruction's revolutionary gesture of demonstrating that all aspirations for reference, origins, totality, identity and truth are ultimately untenable because of the fundamentally unstable and non-referential character of language has to be countered with further questions: How can it be that genuinely unstable systems of signification acquire the power of reality principles nevertheless? Or, to put it differently: How do stable patterns of communication emerge? And why (and how) does culture work? These questions have been addressed by many recent approaches in literary, cultural and media studies in a shift from formalism through the heyday of pure theory towards a new, fully reflexive functionalism on a deconstructive basis, which is perhaps the most obvious sign of modernity having finally come into its own, albeit paradoxically under the label of 'postmodernity'.[43]

## Reading texts after the linguistic turn

The trajectory of approaches to reading in the main strand of literary studies in the twentieth century can be described as a sequence of decentring moves from work to text and beyond into realms of (inter-)textuality and, ultimately, towards an inquiry into the media conditions that restrict and empower cultural practices around texts of all kinds.[44] Starting with a focus on the literary text as a unified work of art, formalist and structuralist approaches soon shifted their attention to the more general linguistic underpinnings of texts, which in turn fed into notions of an overarching textuality of culture.[45] The cultural continuity of (inter-)textuality, however, cannot be adequately understood without addressing its indispensable prerequisite in terms of media conditions, i.e. the dissemination of texts. It is Jacques Derrida's lasting achievement to have put this dimension with all its implications on the theoretical agenda. Under the auspices of writing, language can no longer be seen in terms of the difference between world and representation. Instead, it introduces a new difference between writing and voice which reproduces the difference between reference and sign (which 'transcends' the boundaries of language) within the confines of (written) language. In written language, this difference turns up ('immanently', as it were) as the difference between signifier and signified, from then on constituting its own reality in the realm of (inter-)textuality as described above.[46] At the same time, it is also clear that writing alone cannot account for the proliferation of this second-order 'reality', and here the specifically modern convergence of cultural differentiation and printing comes into play: the distributional power of printing supplements the storage and accumulation potential provided by writing and inaugurates a cultural dynamics unheard of before and eventually boosted by the even stronger distributional prowess of electronic media and digitalization.[47]

What does this historical sketch entail for the practice of reading texts from modern history in order to write (about) modern history? It suggests, for example, that the mandate of reflexivity first articulated in the linguistic turn and then generalized in 'postmodern' theory and philosophy can be answered by paying attention to shifts in the history of different media with their implications for literacy (with all its ideological ramifications)[48] and historical semantics.[49] What affects the practice of reading texts from modern history most crucially, however, is the consequences of media-historical conditions for the availability of the historical record in terms of sources.[50] In this respect, the deconstructive slant on evidence introduced above can be put to good use. While there is, in principle, an ongoing process of semiosis and dissemination which amounts, ultimately, to a circulation of social energy (as Stephen Greenblatt put it memorably and metaphorically[51]), the material access point to these processes is provided by texts, and texts are always produced, circulated and received under social and media-specific conditions of accessibility and availability which in turn govern their availability as historical sources. It should be profitable, therefore, to supplement the venerable and highly successful tradition of historical 'source criticism' with deconstructive and media-historical ideas in order to bridge the unproductive schism between historical criticism on the one hand and literary criticism on the other.[52] There can be no doubt that there are pragmatic differences between 'speakers' and 'voices' in literary/poetic/fictional texts on the one hand – which are, under modern conditions, often predicated on staging or framing subjectivity and, in the course of modern literary history, increasingly aware of their own textuality and mediality – and non-literary/historical/non-fictional texts on the other, which frequently insist on straightforward, transparent and seemingly objective referentiality. But it is also clear in the light of the preceding theoretical reflections that there is, even for the historian, nothing outside of the text at hand in terms of evidence, as the 'outside' can only be constructed and verified through a concurrence and convergence of sources *and* interpretations. Accordingly, and this is the link between source criticism and deconstructive approaches, the apparent unity of a text or source can only be taken as a merely superficial and pragmatic one which has to be decentred in critical readings. It is the task of the historian as critic to analyse how a text creates its apparent unity and what historical tensions, rifts and aporias are elided in the process of this particular construction with its media- and genre-related as well as institutional and social constraints and opportunities.[53]

Basically, then, texts are not so much 'carrying' meaning from a source to a recipient but rather bearing traces of meanings intentionally 'inscribed' as well as medially, socially and institutionally 'framed'. These meanings are then supplemented by all the meanings which are constructed in interpretations by various recipients under similarly complex conditions – and the latter are not at all limited to 'intended' meanings. The interpretation of texts from modern history should therefore be concerned with how the text functions rather than its origins. These functions can be mapped onto the three dimensions of meaning simultaneously present in modern culture, i.e. objectivity, subjectivity and reflexivity.[54] With regard to objective dimensions of meaning, the transformation of implied referentiality into constructed reference as introduced above has to be read against the background of Western traditions of mimesis on the one hand and in terms of the 'reality effect' created by intertextual as well as intermedial relations to existing discourses on the other.[55] Only in such a concurrence and convergence of discourses and texts can key concepts and binary distinctions, metaphors and modes of emplotment be 'naturalized' as objective representations of the world, and this effect is strongly supported by the implementation of neutral and impersonal modes of presentation. Nevertheless, given Western culture's strong bias towards spoken language with its concomitant tendency to think of writing in terms of transcribing a 'voice', subjective dimensions of meaning can frequently be found in texts, either implicitly in oblique allusions to subjective experience or explicitly through references to the 'speaker', 'narrator', writer or author of a text as well as by hints at its assumed or implied addressee or reader. And finally, reflexive dimensions of meaning can be analysed in terms of a text's acknowledgement, implicit or explicit, of its situational and institutional contexts, of its medial set-up including questions of genre and structure, and of its self-conscious and/or self-confident positioning in a wider historical context.[56]

Reading texts in an academic context after the linguistic turn should critically question both the text under scrutiny and the act of reading itself as instalments in an ongoing process of acting in and making sense of the world. Against the background of the historical overview provided in this chapter, current readings should acknowledge the fact that the materiality of the world can be approached from various angles (such as language, semiosis, textuality, discourse, media conditions or communication) but never reached or, in its meaning(s), fully controlled.[57] In the end, then, it is important to realize that the theoretical turn taken by the humanities following on from the linguistic turn does not imply allegiance to a fixed body of work or to this or that school or approach. Instead, it requires an awareness of the contingency of one's own and other people's practice of ascribing meaning to texts. Theory in this sense is, first and foremost, a mode of persistent questioning always in danger of 'tipping over' into a self-confirmatory practice by letting its *provisional* answers 'harden' into dogma. However, oversimplifications of abstract theoretical thought will always find their limits in the resistance of texts with their precarious, complex and contingent relation to material history in its inaccessible totality. And it is this complex interrelation between the human and material dimensions of history in an increasingly mediatized and globalized world that can be addressed through reflexive strategies of reading texts after the linguistic turn.[58]

## Notes

1  Cf. P. Schöttler, 'Wer hat Angst vor dem "Lingustic Turn"?', *Geschichte und Gesellschaft: Zeitschrift für historische Sozialwissenschaft* 23, 1997, 134–151; idem, 'Historians and Discourse Analysis', *History Workshop Journal* 27, 1989, 37–65. For a more recent overview cf. J.E. Toews, 'Linguistic Turn and Discourse Analysis in History', in *International Encyclopedia of the Social and Behavioral Sciences*, Amsterdam: Elsevier, 2001, vol. 13, pp. 8916–8922.

2  Cf. K. Jenkins, *Re-Thinking History*, London: Routledge, 1991 and B. Skordili, 'Little Narratives', in V.E. Taylor and C.E. Winquist (eds), *Encyclopedia of Postmodernism*, London: Routledge, 2001, pp. 230–232.

3  Cf. R.J. Evans, *In Defense of History* [1997], New York/London: Norton, 2000, p. 7f. The debate, of course, is not confined to questions of history, but implicates the foundations of scientific and philosophical truth in general. See, for example, from a philosophical perspective P. Boghossian, *Fear of Knowledge: Against Relativism and Constructivism*, Oxford: Clarendon, 2006, and, from a journalistic perspective, O. Benson and J. Stangroom, *Why Truth Matters*, New York/London: Continuum, 2006.

4  Cf., for example, G.M. Spiegel (ed.), *Practicing History: New Directions in Historical Writing after the Linguistic Turn*, New York/London: Routledge, 2005, in which only five out of 13 contributors hold positions in history while the remaining eight have backgrounds in political science, sociology, anthropology, psychoanalysis, philosophy and English studies.

5  Cf. R. Rorty (ed.), *The Linguistic Turn: Recent Essays in Philosophical Method*, Chicago: University of Chicago Press, 1967.

6  For a programmatic textbook cf. C.G. Brown, *Postmodernism for Historians*. Harlow: Pearson, 2005, and with regard to the tacit linguistic turn=postmodernism equation esp. pp. 33–48.

7  A recent survey study in German (D. Bachmann-Medick, *Cultural Turns: Neuorientierung in den Kulturwissenschaften*, Reinbek: Rowohlt, 2006) identifies no less than seven turns under the general heading of 'Cultural Turns': the interpretive turn, the performative turn, the reflexive or literary turn, the postcolonial turn, the translational turn, the spatial turn, and the iconic turn.

8  Cf. J. Hillis Miller, 'Presidential Address 1986: The Triumph of Theory, the Resistance to Reading, and the Question of the Material Base', *PMLA – Publications of the Modern Language Association* 102.3, 1987, 281–291.

9  Cf. J. Culler, *Literary Theory: A Very Short Introduction*, Oxford: Oxford University Press, 1997, p. 1.

10  Cf. P. Barry, *Beginning Theory: An Introduction to Literary and Cultural Theory*, Manchester: Manchester University Press, pp. 11–32.

11  Barry, *Beginning Theory*, pp. 32–36.

12  Needless to say, the condensation of this huge field of theorizing about reading and meaning within the confines of just one chapter will necessarily be reductive, but it is to be hoped that these very restrictions will facilitate the emergence of a map, the functional point of which, if it is to serve its purpose of orientation, is its reductiveness.

13  Cf. M.H. Abrams, 'Types and Orientations of Critical Theories', in: idem, *Doing Things With Texts*, New York: Norton, 1989, pp. 3–30.

14  On the seminal importance of the Reformation for the emergence of modernity cf. Alan Sinfield, 'Protestantism: Questions of Subjectivity and Control', in idem, *Faultlines: Cultural Materialism and the Politics of Dissident Reading*, Oxford: Clarendon, 1992, pp. 143–180.

15  Cf. Hans-Georg Gadamer, *Truth and Method*, New York: Seabury, 1975.

16  For an extensive overview in English cf. *The Positive Philosophy of Auguste Comte, Freely Translated and Condensed by Harriet Martineau* [1896], Kitchener: Batoche Books, 2000. Available from the McMaster Archive for the History of Economic Thought: <http://socserv2.mcmaster.ca/~econ/ugcm/3ll3/index.html> (accessed 10 January, 2008).

17  For a concise introduction to Marxist thought cf. Peter Singer, *Marx: A Very Short Introduction* [1980], Oxford: Oxford University Press, 2000.

18  Ordered, for example, according to Hippolyte Taine's (1828–93) famous triad *race/milieu/moment* or Wilhelm Scherer's (1841–1886) version *das Erlernte/Ererbte/Erlebte* ('education'/'inheritance'/'experience').

19  Cf. J. McGann, *The Romantic Ideology: A Critical Investigation*, Chicago: University of Chicago Press, 1983, who explicitly draws upon Marx's and Engels's *The German Ideology* (1845).

20  Cf. A. Richardson, *Literature, Education and Romanticism: Reading as a Social Practice, 1780–1832*, Cambridge/New York: Cambridge University Press, 2004.

21  It is this affinity between two critical counter-narratives that might explain why (neo-) Marxists succumbed so easily to the charms of aesthetic autonomy, as in Adorno's clinging to the notion of true and authentic art which somehow resists commodification or in Althusser's conviction that art is not among the ideologies (cf. McGann, *The Romantic Ideology*, p. 66).

22  K. Thomas, 'New Ways Revisited: How History's Border's Have Expanded in the Past Forty Years', *Times Literary Supplement* October 13, 2006, 3f., 4.

23  S. Tillyard, 'All Our Pasts: The Rise of Popular History', *Times Literary Supplement* October 13, 2006, 7–9, 9.

24  On a larger scale this development can be described in terms of a shift from ontological and essentialist conceptions of scientific truth to constructivist conceptions of scientific truth. See, for example, N. Luhmann, 'The Modernity of Science', *New German Critique* 61, 1994, 9–23. Again, it is important to point out that both dimensions were present in modern culture from fairly early on. Cf., for example, Kant's concept of an all-pervasive critique as indicated in the 1781 preface to his *Critique of Pure Reason* ('Our age is, in especial degree, the age of criticism, and to criticism everything must submit.' Quoted from <http://www.hkbu.edu.hk/~ppp/cpr/prefs.html> P 009n, accessed on Jan. 14, 2008) as opposed to the longing for objectivity underlying his work at large.

25  Cf. I.A. Richards, *Practical Criticism* [1929], London: Routledge and Kegan Paul, 1964.

26  Cf. Abrams's 'objective theories' and the hermeneutic and Romantic heritage in notions of aesthetic autonomy as well as the larger frame of liberal humanism as indicated in the preceding sections of this chapter.

27  Cf. J.C. Ransom, *The New Criticism* [1941], Westport, Conn.: Greenwood, 1979.

28  Cf. E.M. Thompson, *Russian Formalism and Anglo-American New Criticism*, The Hague: Mouton, 1971.

29  V. Shklovsky, 'Art as Technique', in D. Lodge (ed.) *Modern Criticism and Theory: A Reader*, Harlow: Longman, 1988, pp. 15–30.

30  I. Tynianov, *The Problem of Verse Language* [1924], Ann Arbor: Ardis, 1981.

31  I. Tynianov and R. Jakobson, 'Problems in the Study of Literature and Language' [1928], in Matejka and Pomorska, *Readings in Russian Poetics*, pp. 79–81.

32  R. Jakobson and C. Levi-Strauss, '*Les Chats* of Charles Baudelaire' [1962], in R. Jacobson, *Selected Writings*, Vol. 3, The Hague: Mouton, 1981, pp. 447–464.

33  For a brief and accessible introduction to Structuralism cf. Barry, *Beginning Theory*, pp. 39–60.
34  Cf. F. de Saussure, *Course in General Linguistics*, London: Duckworth, 1983.
35  Cf., for example, J. Mukařovský, *Aesthetic Function, Norm and Value as Social Facts* [1936], Ann Arbor: Michigan Slavic Publications, 1970; C. Levi-Strauss, *The Raw and the Cooked* [1964], New York: Harper and Row, 1969; R. Barthes, 'Introduction to the Structural Analysis of Narrative' [1966], *New Literary History* 6, 1975, 237–262 and *Mythologies* [1957], New York: Hill and Wang, 1972.
36  R. Barthes, *Elements of Semiology* [1964], New York: Hill and Wang, 1968.
37  For the philosophy-linguistics-interface in this process and its recent shift towards history and culture cf. M. Currie, *Difference, The New Critical Idiom*, London: Routledge, 2004.
38  For an accessible and concise introduction to Poststructuralism and Deconstruction cf. Barry, *Beginning Theory*, pp. 61–80. The by now classic introduction in English is J. Culler, *On Deconstruction: Theory and Criticism after Structuralism*, Ithaca: Cornell University Press, 1982.
39  Cf. J. Derrida, 'Structure, Sign and Play in the Discourse of the Human Sciences' [1966], in D. Lodge (ed.) *Modern Criticism and Theory*, pp. 107–123 and *Of Grammatology* [1967], Baltimore: Johns Hopkins University Press, 1976.
40  The most instructive illustration of this principle is probably the analogy to second language learners who are only allowed a monolingual dictionary for a written exam: every word that they look up is encoded in new words, a certain percentage of which would have to be looked up again etc. ad infinitum.
41  Derrida, *Of Grammatology*, p. 158.
42  See, for example, the assessment in Evans, *In Defense of History*, pp. 106–108, 206–210 and the broad overview in R. Eaglestone, *The Holocaust and the Postmodern*, Oxford: Oxford University Press, 2004.
43  Cf. N. Luhmann, 'Why Does Society Describe Itself as Postmodern?', *Cultural Critique* 30, 1995, 171–186.
44  For some basic contours see also R. Barthes's influential essay 'From Work to Text' [1971], in J.V. Harari (ed.), *Textual Strategies*, Ithaca: Cornell University Press, 1979, pp. 73–81 (also in R. Barthes, *The Rustle of Language*, New York: Hill and Wang, 1989, pp. 56–64). For a concise overview of the implications of this development in terms of a widened scope beyond literary texts cf. P. Childs, *Texts: Contemporary Cultural Texts and Critical Approaches*, Edinburgh: Edinburgh University Press, 2006, pp. 1–10 and passim.
45  Cf. S. Greenblatt's notion of a 'poetics of culture' at the heart of the New Historicism as introduced in S. Greenblatt, 'Towards a Poetics of Culture', in H. Aram Veeser (ed.), *The New Historicism*, New York: Routledge, 1989, pp. 1–14. Interestingly, the earlier Positivism/Marxism-divide resurfaced in the new, textual dispensation of the 1980s in the form of a political alternative between the largely U.S.-based New Historicism and an explicitly left-wing Cultural Materialism in the U.K. as well as in discussions about the relation between postmodernism and postcolonialism.
46  Typical literary examples of this transformation are the invention of the individualized, subjective 'speaker' in lyrical poetry in early modern times (in the English context particularly in sonnets by Wyatt, Surrey, Spenser, Sidney and then, of course, Shakespeare) as well as the invention of an omniscient authorial voice for the emergent genre of the modern novel by Henry Fielding in the 1740s.
47  It is probably the shift towards a fully fledged digital society which enables us to see the mediality of the age of print more clearly than ever while we are already on our way into the 'next society' (Peter Drucker) under the auspices of the computer. On the theoretical implications of this shift cf. C. Huck and C. Schinko, 'The Medial Limits of Culture: Culture as Text vs. Text as Culture', in G. Sebald and J. Weyand (eds), *GrenzGänge – BorderCrossings: Kulturtheoretische Perspektiven*, Münster: LIT, 2006, pp. 57–71.

48 Cf., for example, B.V. Street, *Literacy in Theory and Practice* [1984], Cambridge: Cambridge University Press, 1999 and 'What's New in New Literacy Studies? Critical Approaches to Literacy in Theory and Practice', *Current Issues in Comparative Education* 5.2, 2003, 77–91 as well as, with a stronger historical focus, Gerd Baumann (ed.), *The Written Word: Literacy in Transition*, Oxford: Clarendon, 1986.
49 Cf. R. Koselleck, *The Practice of Conceptual History: Timing History, Spacing Concepts*, Stanford: Stanford University Press, 2002.
50 The profession's awareness of this crucial factor is marked by the inclusion of an article addressing this dimension in the *TLS New Ways of History Revisited* issue. Cf. Alex Burghart, 'Web Works', *Times Literary Supplement* October 13, 2006, 16–17.
51 S. Greenblatt, *Shakespearean Negotiations: The Circulation of Social Energy in Renaissance England*, Berkeley: University of California Press, 1988.
52 Cf. D.B. Mathewson, 'A Critical Binarism: Source Criticism and Deconstructive Criticism', *Journal for the Study of the Old Testament* 98, 2002, 3–28 who argues that the approaches are not antagonistic in a theological context but can rather be taken to mark various stages in a continuing modern/postmodern engagement with the problem of truth under modern conditions.
53 Cf. Stephen Greenblatt's influential analysis of the doubling of enabling and restricting functions in culture as summed up in S. Greenblatt, 'Culture', in Lentricchia and McLaughlin (eds), *Critical Terms*, pp. 225–223.
54 On the narratological implications of this threefold frame cf. C. Reinfandt, 'Dimensions of Meaning in Modern Narrative: A Systems-Theoretical Approach to Narratology', in S. Tötösy de Zepetnek and I. Sywenky (eds), *The Systemic and Empirical Approach to Literature and Culture as Theory and Application*, Edmonton/Siegen: LUMIS publications, 1997, pp. 83–90 and 'A Matter of Perspective: The Social Framing of Narrative Meaning', in B. Reitz and S. Rieuwerts (eds), *Anglistentag 1999 Mainz: Proceedings*, Trier: WVT, 2000, pp. 389–402.
55 Cf. R. Barthes, 'The Discourse of History' and 'The Reality Effect' in *The Rustle of Language*, New York: Hill and Wang, 1989, pp. 127–140, 141–148 and F.R. Ankersmit, *The Reality Effect in the Writing of History: The Dynamics of Historiographical Topology*, Amsterdam: Noord-Hollandsche, 1989.
56 See also the 'Basic Checklist' of 'How to Interpret Primary Sources' in the introduction to the present volume, pp. 5–14.
57 On the implications of a shift from the language/text/discourse-paradigm of the main strand of 'postmodern' theory to an alternative paradigm focused on non-foundationalist notions of observation, mediality, and communication cf. N. Luhmann, 'Deconstruction as Second-Order Observing', *New Literary History* 24, 1993, 763–782.
58 Cf. a recent German introduction to historiography 'in global perspective' (Markus Völkel, *Geschichtsschreibung: Eine Einführung in globaler Perspektive*, Wien: Böhlau, 2006) as reviewed by Simon Ditchfield, 'Noted Down', *Times Literary Supplement* November 9, 2007, p. 7.

## Select bibliography

Barry, P., *Beginning Theory: An Introduction to Literary and Cultural Theory*, 2nd edn., Manchester: Manchester University Press, 2002.
Benson, O. and J. Stangroom, *Why Truth Matters*, London/New York: Continuum, 2006.
Childs, P., *Texts: Contemporary Cultural Texts and Critical Approaches*, Edinburgh: Edinburgh University Press, 2006.
Clark, E.A., *History, Theory, Text: Historians and the Linguistic Turn*, Cambridge/Mass.: Harvard University Press, 2004.

Culler, J., *Literary Theory: A Very Short Introduction*, 2nd edn., Oxford: Oxford University Press, 2000.

Curry, M., *Difference, The New Critical Idiom*, London: Routledge, 2004.

Eagleton, T., *Literary Theory: An Introduction*, 2nd edn., Oxford: Blackwell, 1996.

Lentricchia, F. and T. McLaughlin, eds., *Critical Terms for Literary Studies*, 2nd edn., Chicago: University of Chicago Press, 1995.

Spiegel, G.M., ed., *Practicing History: New Directions in Historical Writing after the Linguistic Turn*, New York/London: Routledge, 2005.

Waugh, P., *Literary Theory and Criticism: An Oxford Guide*, Oxford: Oxford University Press, 2006.

# Part II

# Varieties of primary sources and their interpretation

# 3    Letters

*Miriam Dobson*

Even if we cast it as a 'thirst for knowledge', the historian's search for new documents and artefacts from the past stems at least in part from curiosity, even nosiness; there is a desire for secret, perhaps salacious, information about people who lived long ago. In this quest, a heavy file bulging with letters perhaps represents a particularly good haul. Re-opening an envelope dried with time, inching out a crisp letter, and gazing down at a page of crabbed handwriting, the researcher feels she might be experiencing the same emotions felt by the first recipient, however many years ago. Addressed to a named reader (or readers), we feel we are breaking the ties of confidentiality and unlocking the mysteries of a past age. Letters seem to promise the personal, the familiar, the intimate: as such they represent a hugely exciting source for the historian.

Despite their apparent appeal, however, letters represent a troublesome genre. Firstly, there are many different kinds of writing that come under the heading of 'letter': business correspondence, petitions to the government, letters to newspaper editors, intellectual dialogue between thinkers, writers, and politicians, and of course the more everyday exchange of news between friends and family geographically separated from one another. Secondly, the letter's apparently personal nature is rather deceptive. Very often, letters though ostensibly for a single reader have been used in a wider context: in the past many were read aloud, at home or in the coffee-shop, some were re-copied and forwarded to additional readers, while others even made it into print.[1] Cécile Dauphin has suggested that letters should be considered 'an experimental form', 'a meeting place between the social and the inner being, between conventions and their use in practice, between the private and political'.[2] Issues to be addressed in this chapter therefore include: What kind of letters can be of interest to the historian, and what kind of information can we hope to acquire through reading them? How does the presence of an intended reader, or even unnamed readers, shape the text? How do we go about extracting information from the text? Why have the letters been preserved, and does this affect the way we read them? And can the mere fact that this correspondence took place – regardless of its content – tell us something about the function of written communication in the past?

The chapter will begin by tracing the way in which broader historiographical developments have driven the expansion of the epistolary corpus used by historians: in particular, we shall examine how a focus on the correspondence of 'eminent men of the age' has, with the rise of social history, given way to an increasing endeavour to study the writings of 'ordinary' men and women. The chapter will then examine how philosophical trends have also impacted on historians' use of epistolary evidence: in particular, we shall consider the way cultural historians and those responsive to the implications of the 'linguistic turn' have interpreted letters. This long middle part of the chapter will focus on how the letter can become a site for creating different kinds of selfhood, community, and citizenship. Finally, and in light of the above, a letter written in 1953 by a Moscow tramdriver and sent to Viacheslav Molotov, then Minister of Foreign Affairs and a leading member of the Communist Party of the Soviet Union, will be analysed in detail.

## The epistolary corpus

Great revolutionary to some, monstrous dictator to others, V.I. Lenin seems to represent one of the great enigmas of the twentieth century, and historians have made extensive use of his letters to try to uncover the real essence of the man. When the Soviet authorities authorized a new edition of Lenin's correspondence in the mid-1960s, John Keep was quick to recognize the new collection's appeal:

> The correspondence of the great has always exercised a powerful fascination for the historian or the biographer. Ideally, it ought to reveal the hidden aspects of a man's psyche, his secret motivations and objectives; at the least it may cast light upon his personal relationships with others in a way that would not be apparent from more formal documents.[3]

In using Lenin's personal correspondence alongside his other writings and speeches, Robert Service's biography added new dimensions to what we already knew of Lenin. In particular, letters to his mother, wife, and sisters reveal moments of fragility, of despondency and fatigue, as well as insight into the development of his political thought and his reflections on the progress of the revolutionary underground.[4] At the other end of the twentieth century, biographers of another 'great man', Nelson Mandela, have again used personal correspondence to probe the private life of their subject. Mandela's tender, sometimes remorseful prison letters to his wife Winnie have been used extensively and are, according to one biographer, evidence of the complex passions that animated his 'domestic world'.[5] In both cases, private letters allow the historian to complicate the image their subject sought to present in public life.

The fact that correspondence has been used as means to conduct political and scholarly discussions also means that intellectual historians have drawn extensively on epistolary sources. This is particularly the case for historians of the early modern period, when limited publishing meant that networks of correspondence fulfilled a unique forum for sharing ideas amongst a group of like-minded people, with letters regularly copied and forwarded on to interested parties.[6] In the nineteenth and twentieth centuries, intellectuals have been more likely to publish their ideas in newspapers, journals books, or lately, the internet, but correspondence has retained its appeal for historians. As with political biographies, letters seem to promise a glimpse into the personal life of philosophers, artists, and scientists.

In political and intellectual history, therefore, private correspondence has always been respected as an important source both for tracing the development of ideas and ideology and for unmasking personal characteristics. Over the course of the twentieth century, however, the profession has seen increasing attempts to write histories that are not only about 'eminent men' – powerful politicians and great thinkers – but also accounts of how ordinary men and women lived in the past. The rise of social history led historians to search for new kinds of sources that would allow them to explore the lives of much wider sectors of the population. In the USA, these trends began in the first half of the twentieth century but became entrenched with the development of 'New Social History' in the 1960s and 1970s, an approach that sought to challenge the 'traditional political master narrative of American history, with its elite, Anglo-Saxon, and male perspective'.[7] Letters sent home by new immigrants to the United States, for example, became an important source for examining the history of a social group that had previously been excluded from many historical accounts. Scholars of slavery were also keen to use letters. Explicitly influenced by W.E.B. DuBois's call for historians to write about 'the common run of human beings' instead of their rulers, Robert Starobin studied the letters of house-servants and drivers in the early 1970s. Using the letters of 'privileged bondsmen', Starobin explored aspects of slaves' lives such as their relationships with masters and fellow slaves, as well as controversial issues such as the nature of discipline and resistance on slave plantations.[8]

As the two above examples suggest, historians of the nineteenth and twentieth centuries in particular have been drawn to letters as a means to explore the lives of the poor and powerless within society – and for obvious reasons. Although literacy figures are disputed, it is clear that over the course of the seventeenth and eighteenth centuries, the ability to read spread to growing sectors of the population in Europe and North America, while in the nineteenth century, the expansion of compulsory elementary education ensured an ever-growing number of citizens who could themselves write.[9] Over the same period, postage systems became more accessible. The invention of the 'penny post' – a cheap flat-rate for sending a letter – was introduced in Britain in 1840 and soon adopted in many other European countries. With the creation of the Universal Postal Union (UPU) in 1875, inhabitants of the member countries – which included not only countries of Western Europe, but also Russia, Greece, Egypt, and the USA – were linked in a common system of flat-rate postage. The establishment of the UPU meant the number of letters sent and received could be assiduously counted: the statistics produced show a rise in epistolary activity towards the end of the nineteenth century and the years running up to the First World War, an event that itself caused an unprecedented wave of graphomania.[10] Four million letters made their way from or to the French front every day, while in the German Empire, about 9.9 million items of post were sent home from the front daily, and 6.8 million came the other way, with free postage in both directions.[11] Ordinary lives were thus leaving a written record as never before.

Yet recognition of the richness of ordinary people's letters was rather slower than might have been expected, despite the pioneering work of social historians such as Starobin. One reason might have been social historians' preference for statistical 'hard' evidence.[12] Another might be that on close examination the actual content is not necessarily as path-breaking as the historian might hope. With reference to love letters, Roland Barthes summarized their key message as being: 'I've got nothing to say to you, but it's to you I want to say this nothing.'[13] Private letters are often full of 'nothingness': descriptions of ill-health, family gossip, the passing on of greetings – all about people of whom little other record is left, and whose lives still remain opaque. The moment of finding and opening a letter is exciting for the historian, but the content does not always match expectation. It might perhaps appear odd, then, that the study of family correspondence has undergone a boom over the last decade or so. Ironically, it is in fact the rather humdrum nature of many letters that has been drawing scholarly attention. Increasingly historians have become interested to know why people exerted such effort – and letter-writing *was* an effort for those whose literacy was still basic and budget constrained – to articulate what was sometimes fairly mundane information. The philosophical roots of this development are examined below.

## Private correspondence and identity

One approach to family or private letters is to assume that as correspondents have a close emotional tie they essentially tell 'the truth' about their lives. Following this logic, their letters should therefore give us a window onto the private experiences and inner thoughts of the author. Letters are often praised for the 'human dimension' they bring to history, allowing the scholar to capture the raw experiences and emotions of actors in the past.[14] Yet are historical subjects really so transparent? Can we really hope to capture 'hidden aspects of a man's psyche' and 'his secret motivations and objectives' (to return to Keep's terms)?

More recently scholars have begun to question the assumption that letters are the true record of the writer's inner world. Instead, letter-writing is seen to be part of an individual's attempt to *establish* the meaning of their life (rather than just reflect or communicate existing truths). A clear example of this kind of construction can be found in cases where an individual devotes significant energy to preserving, and perhaps doctoring, their collection of personal correspondence. In his study of the utopian feminist and polemical journalist, Céline Renooz (1849–1928), James Smith Allen argues that the attention she paid to the careful collection and reconstruction of her letters represented a 'sustained effort to shape a stable discursive identity'. Renooz, who wrote articles and speeches on evolutionary embryology, scientific epistemology and visionary feminism, corresponded with nearly every intellectual leader in France (though they did not always respond) and in her will she arranged for her papers to be turned over to an established archival collection on French feminism. A total of 7,400 letters were preserved, though it transpires that many of them are in fact copies and re-creations that she made long after the originals were sent.[15] In creating her own personal archive, Renooz was acutely aware that her correspondence was one of the prime ways that future generations would know of her and her ideas, and for Renooz it was desperately important that she personally crafted the story of her life.

Not all letter-writers are quite as concerned with their posthumous reputation as Renooz, of course. Often the preservation of correspondence is far more haphazard. In the case of immigrants' letters, for example, their survival depends primarily on the recipients filing them away, and then on future descendants eventually deciding to deposit them in an archive.[16] Yet even if the letters are not intended for preservation, the act of corresponding itself helps to shape certain forms of identity. The acquisition of literacy changes the way people think about themselves and their lives. The ability to write provides a forum in which the individual reflects on his or her life in a distinct manner; in the case of letters, in the form of a solitary written reflection which is also part of a dialogue with the reader or readers.[17] To be able to write a letter requires the author to be able to narrate and order their experiences. Reading is an essential part of this process, for the texts a person reads – be they newspapers, novels, or indeed other people's letters – shape their thoughts and suggest to them the appropriate way to express their feelings.[18] As theorists such as Michel Foucault have persuasively argued, self-reflection does not happen in a vacuum, but is prompted, guided, and directed by powerful discourses within a given society.[19] The survival of written sources (such as letters) is therefore not just a handy means to access people's experiences, but rather the record of a new kind of cognition. New theoretical approaches thus suggest highly productive ways of reading letters: first we shall examine letter-writing as opportunity for self-reflection through dialogue; second, we shall explore how reading other texts shape and condition this introspective act.

As we see in David Carlson's chapter on autobiography in this volume, scholars from a range of disciplines including neuropsychology, sociology, and literary criticism, as well as history, increasingly stress the role that memory and narrative play in shaping a person's identity. To make sense of who they are at the present moment, human beings tell stories about their past. For those who are physically separated from close ones, the act of letter-writing can provide a medium for reconciling past and present and fashioning a workable sense of self.

Such ideas shape David Gerber's study of the letters Protestant immigrants to the USA and Canada sent back home to England, Scotland and Ireland in the nineteenth century. For immigrants there was a particular need to reflect on the nature of their community and their place within it.[20] In part this was to do with ethnic identity, for arrival in the new world brought them into contact with people unlike themselves and into a new kind of public culture, but, Gerber argues, this was not the primary feature of their letters. Reflection on identity was more the result of a fundamental need to shore up an imperilled sense of self, for immigrants risk 'a radical rupture of the self, a break in their understanding of who they are'.[21] For example, even a man whose new life in America was materially successful admitted he was 'starving' for letters from back home, while those emigrant men who seemed to embrace a formless and chaotic existence, moving from place to place and repeatedly deserting wives and children, often chose to re-establish contact with relatives even after a break of several years; while the transitory nature of their lives implied a refusal to build for a stable future, they nonetheless felt the psychological need to nurture a link with their past.[22] Gerber's study of letters has important implications for the history of immigration, for he is arguing that this desire for continuity with the past challenges the significance scholars often attach to group identity. Neither assimilation to the new American nation nor membership of an ethnic community proved sufficient to heal the internal rupture experienced in leaving the homeland behind.

The study of epistolary exchanges thus remind us that modern identity is not, as sometimes assumed, overwhelmingly individualistic, nor solely about identification with 'imagined communities' such as ethnic group or nation.[23] Recent work on the First World War letters suggests that the maintenance of family values became increasingly important during war. Arguing not only that French soldiers' letters were disarmingly honest about their experiences, Martha Hanna has claimed that as the war worsened and exhaustion reduced soldiers' letter-writing time, so their circle of correspondents narrowed. She suggests it was 'the ultimate irony' that letter-writing sustained intimacy within the immediate family and created greater alienation beyond it, thus unsettling the common assumption that war incites passionate patriotism and a strong sense of belonging to the 'nation'.[24] Letters often seem to suggest that family or local ties are at least as important in shaping an individual's sense of self as collective forms such as nationalism or ethnicity.

Whilst this first approach focuses primarily on the existence and meaning of correspondence networks, a second method instead concentrates on the text of the letter itself. Influenced by the 'linguistic turn' this scholarship examines the power of existing discourses and their reproduction in personal writings. If we stay with First World War letters for a moment, we can see why such issues are important. Scholars of front-line correspondence have often disagreed about the efficacy of wartime censorship, and the extent to which it inhibited soldiers' freedom of expression.[25] At the very least, it seems certain that soldiers would not have written about every aspect of life at the front, and their letters at best give a partial life in the trenches.[26] However, a discursive approach to these letters suggests that the fact that they do not give an entirely 'truthful' or total account of the author's experience does not mean such letters are useless. In fact where they remain silent on a certain topic, or chose what might seem like clichéd formulations, letters tell us something of how the individual author responded to society's expectations.

European culture has a long tradition of letter-writing manuals which seek to educate people about the correct way to correspond, meaning that letter-writers rarely sit down to a truly blank sheet.[27] In the First World War the authorities were particularly keen to ensure that troops were not left without guidance in their correspondence, and published collections of letters became a flourishing sub-genre of wartime literature. In producing model forms for such letters, the authorities crafted a socially acceptable version of combat that suggested to soldiers the correct way of interpreting their experiences. The question is: how far did soldiers follow these models?

According to John Horne's work, the letters that appeared in French published collections in the first year of the war were – unsurprisingly – rich with heroism and bravura, drawing on notions of chivalry that had been central to the canon of national literature developed in the nineteenth century.[28] As the suffering of the war intensified over coming years, the published correspondence evolved: although the heroics did not disappear, a discourse of 'sacrifice' emerged, relying on the resonance of this concept in a predominantly Catholic country. Soldiers who wrote letters home were certainly influenced by these models. Even in the spring of 1917, amidst a severe political crisis exemplified by the mutinies of French troops that followed the failed Nivelle offensive, ordinary letters depicted the Germans as barbarians and criminals, the French as chivalrous heroes. Yet as the losses piled up, it was the concept of sacrifice that was called into question. The sacrifice trope suggested death had meaning, but soldiers explicitly and repeatedly wrote that the war of attrition, and the huge body-count it created, was without meaning.[29] Horne's work alerts us to the fact that letter-writers are in dialogue not only with the actual recipient of their letter, but also with imagined readers. The soldier was aware of what was expected from a soldier's letter, but rebelled, implicitly rebuking the imagined reader for expecting his ready sacrifice.[30] This suggests the power, but also limits, of nationalistic, heroic, discourse in First World War France.

At the same time not only German and Austrian soldiers but also their wives at home were instructed in the art of patriotic letter-writing. Women were told they must send upbeat and positive letters, for they bore responsibility for maintaining morale at the front. They were not to speak of suffering, despite worsening food shortages at home. Christa Hämmerle's close study of one Austrian couple's correspondence again suggests that although the idealism trumpeted in published correspondence shaped how soldiers and their wives wrote to one another, it ultimately fractured under the ongoing pressure of war and separation.[31] Leopold and Christl Wolf, a young bourgeois couple whose fledgling courtship was interrupted by the outbreak of war, used their correspondence to nurture their sense of a shared identity, referring constantly to everyday matters rather than the atrocities of war. Initially Christl's letters fitted with the models provided: she created a picture of the marital bliss to which she hoped Leopold would eventually return. Yet increasingly war encroached on this comfortable life. According to Hämmerle, Christl reacted to this change with two contradictory narrative strategies: she condemned any changes to the class system (from which she benefited), while at the same time often expressing sympathy for the burdens carried by working-class women. Christl's letters suggest that the idealized domestic hearth propagated in the media continued to appeal to her, but she also criticized aspects of a social system she had previously accepted unthinkingly. For this young Viennese woman, war produced confusion about what the ideal 'married woman' from her background should be like, and, according to Hämmerle, female identity became more 'contradictory' as a result of war.

To conclude this section: it would be naïve to think that letters allow us to know the thought-patterns immigrants, soldiers, their wives back home or any other letter-writer pursued inside their heads when entirely alone, for the way they articulated their thoughts on paper was shaped by what they thought the reader expected and the conventions of letter-writing. Yet human beings also create identity through this kind of interaction with others. As Paul John Eakin and others have convincingly argued, identity is relational, even if Western culture's cult of the individual sometimes blinds us to this.[32] Narrative forms (such as autobiography) have often been associated with the existence of an autonomous author, but the practice of letter-writing shows that life-stories can also be created through dialogue with others. The study of private correspondence thus allows the historian to examine how people in the past have used the epistolary form to establish images of themselves through their relations with others. With close attention to the text, moreover, the historian can examine how a particular culture imposed certain interpretative models or social ideals onto its subjects. Letter-writing manuals, published letters, and (on occasion) censorship, help to set certain parameters to the epistolary dialogue and to the writer's conceptualization of his or her self. However, historical studies show that these parameters can also be challenged or fragmented. The study of letters therefore enriches our understanding of past mentalities, allowing us to understand more fully the way in which individuals create their own place in the world, influenced by – but not perhaps prisoner to – existing discourses.[33]

## Public letters and the writing of citizenship

Some people choose to write to figures they have never met: to political leaders, or to the editors of newspapers. Letters to figures in authority can act as a forum for 'self-analysis and self-exploration' just as much as the private correspondence examined above, yet here the letter-writer is reflecting not only on their place in the community or family, but also their role in the wider world.[34] Through the act of writing, the author establishes their status as a citizen, inscribing themselves into the political system he or she inhabits.

In the Soviet Union the authorities were particularly keen to encourage their citizens to compose letters. Although accused of being 'faceless' and inhuman – and of course in many ways it was – the Soviet system was also an oddly personalized one: the right to housing, release from prison, membership of the party, a stint in a holiday home and many other benefits were all dependent upon writing the correct 'petition' letter.[35] Moreover, the regime also encouraged its citizens to write letters to leading members of the Communist Party or to newspaper editors, on topics ranging from key political events in the country's political life to local affairs.[36] In part this was to do with surveillance: paranoid about possible dissent, the Soviet state was desperate to find any clues that might lead them to detect possible enemies.[37] Yet this was not the only reason, for by writing, it was hoped, workers and peasants would also become active participants in the life of the Soviet polity. Encouraged by the state to take up their pens, thousands of citizens dispatched letters, some simply addressed to 'The Kremlin, Moscow', and the state bodies to whom they were sent carefully packed them away, ensuring that today every archive in the former Soviet Union contains hundreds of files of handwritten letters. For historians this is, of course, an incredibly rich find. Without the results of democratic elections or the kind of writings found in countries with a free press, scholars of the Soviet Union have always lacked the kind of evidence that would allow them to explore the crucial question: what did people *think* about Soviet power? The letters that were uncovered when the doors of the archives opened in the late 1980s and early 1990s seemed to offer some way around this, apparently offering the means for historians to trace 'popular opinion'.

Yet many of the questions raised above in relation to wartime correspondence are significant here too: how free were people to express their views? To what extent did the existence of the censor and fear of the secret police distort the way in which letter-writers expressed themselves? Certainly, when citizens articulated their views about Soviet life in a letter meant for the eyes of a high-ranking party or government figure, or the editor of a party-run newspaper, they chose different words and expressions than they might when speaking to their husband in the privacy of their bedroom, or after a beer with close friends. Writers would be deeply influenced by what they knew to be expected of them. Soviet citizens had to adopt the language of the regime, or, as Stephen Kotkin has put it, learn the 'rules of the game'. Kotkin's term 'speaking Bolshevik' has been widely adopted in the literature on Soviet mentalities, for it seems to neatly convey the widespread pervasion of official rhetoric into all kinds of unofficial and personal writings.[38] His approach has serious implications, though. If we accept that letter-writers are merely game-playing, what use are their texts? Kotkin argues that what is significant is that this process of acquiring political literacy happened at all; in other words, the very fact that an ordinary worker could now produce a letter in Bolshevik language indicates the state's success in shaping the minds of its citizens.

Can we go further than this? Can we hope to unpick something of the letter-writer's mindset? The approach taken in the example given below recognizes that these sources are artefacts purposefully created and intended for a specific audience, but suggests that we can nonetheless glimpse into the author's worldview through a close reading of the text. Soviet citizens' letters are clearly shaped by the textual world they inhabited, for they reproduced the language they read in newspapers or heard at party meetings. However, they do not always get it quite right. Their ability to 'speak Bolshevik' was rarely perfect, and this makes their letters all the more interesting. Firstly, we get a sense of these letter-writers' understanding of the discursive boundaries of the system in which they operated: we have a record of what ordinary people *felt* was an acceptable interpretation or commentary on their lives and on political events occurring. Secondly, we can, by reading between the lines, get a sense of how their own ideas and beliefs departed from the official script. In seeking to adopt the Bolshevik-speak they found in the newspapers, citizens often went wrong, but these transgressions and re-workings of the authoritative text allow us important insight into their worldview. In their written texts, Soviet citizens displayed a broad range of dialects and idiosyncrasies as they tried to 'speak Bolshevik'.

The concept of 'speaking Bolshevik' can of course be thought-provoking for countries and periods other than the Soviet Union. In essence 'speaking Bolshevik' is simply a short-hand for the terms and concepts that prevail in a given culture. The important – and disputed – question here is the extent to which these are authoritative. When individuals speak or think, can they use alternative concepts or terms? Or can they perhaps use established ones in original or innovative ways? How far are we bound by the semantic web in which we live?

## A letter to Molotov

The source to be interpreted in this chapter was located in the Russian State Archive of Social and Political History in Moscow, in the personal *fond* of the Soviet statesman Molotov. Here, file upon file of handwritten letters from ordinary citizens – many anonymous – have been preserved. The example below dates from the spring of 1953, just a few weeks after Stalin's death on 5 March 1953.

> Deeply respected Viacheslav Mikhailovich [Molotov], Forgive my audacity in daring to write to you, but I can't hold myself back any more. I ask you to defend us simple people from the persecution and terror of thieves. They go about stealing in the broad light of day, they walk about with knives and razor blades, and if anyone tries to stand up to them, they start on him. This happened to tram conductor Grigor'eva from the Krasnaia Presnia district. You go to work, and you don't know if you're going to make it home OK or not. The police are powerless, and when you call for help – for example on the train – all the passengers keep quiet because they're scared of being stabbed. Such disgraceful horrors happen in Moscow, without even speaking about the Moscow suburbs, where the bandits reign, especially with their lairs in Nikitovka and Obiralovka, stations on the Gor'kii railway line.
>
> Indeed this dirty water, these Russian 'gangsters' are without conscience or honour. We conquered Germany when she was armed to the teeth, can it really be that our state is without the strength to conquer these parasites?
>
> We beg you to write a law which says that any thief who is caught has five fingers chopped off his left hand and is branded, so that everyone knows that he is a thief and keeps away from him. Merciless and strict measures must be taken. We've had enough of being 'humane' with these weeds. Only the grave corrects the hunchback. Only then will us honest workers get the peace and security, knowing that they'll make it home safe each night.
>
> Take any tram conductor from the Krasnaia Presniia district, and they'll be able to tell you a lot. It is impossible to bear this situation any longer.
>
> Yours sincerely,
> Antonova.[39]

What then can we learn from this letter? The first temptation is to assume that this source can tell us something about crime-levels in the Soviet Union. According to this Moscow tram-driver, the spring of 1953 had experienced an unprecedented crime-wave with ordinary people living in daily fear of violent assault. But is she right? She might, after all, be nothing more than a hysterical scare-monger, perhaps frightened by the death of Stalin and the political uncertainties that followed. In fact, other sources, such as government reports on crime, seem to corroborate her perceptions about increased criminality. Three weeks after Stalin's death an extensive amnesty had been decreed, and over a million prisoners released over the coming months. In the spring and summer of 1953 the number of thefts, rapes, and murders had increased significantly in comparison with the previous year.[40] However, by itself the letter only tells us of an *anxiety* regarding law and order.

A close reading of the text can tell us something more about Antonova's identity and beliefs, however. Antonova is keen to present herself as a respectable Soviet citizen: she claims to write on behalf of us 'simple people' and us 'honest workers' and she invokes their collective heroism against Germany in the Second World War. Appealing to Molotov, a long-standing member of the Soviet government, she wants to convince him that she is a reliable spokesperson for the Soviet people. Yet in several places inconsistencies or idiosyncrasies in her letter suggest that she has experienced problems in finding the words to articulate her views effectively. In discussing this problem, it was not easy for her to 'speak Bolshevik', however much she might be trying.

In the Soviet Union, the first years after the 1917 revolution had seen almost obsessive discussion of crime, but since the mid-1930s, the official media had largely drawn a veil of silence over this social ill, with relatively few references to crime and punishment in the press. Faced with this dearth of terminology, Antonova draws on foreign, early Soviet, and even pre-revolutionary sources. Let us take the first line of the second paragraph: 'Indeed this dirty water, these Russian "gangsters" are without conscience or honour.' This odd sentence mixes its metaphors – referring both to nature and American films – as if the author is struggling to find a coherent way to approach the problem. In labelling them as 'dirty water', Antonova picks up on earlier tropes in Soviet culture which had identified criminal offenders as sources of contagion: these had been common currency in the 1920s, but largely dropped out of official texts since.[41] With the term 'Russian gangster' (*russkii gangster*), however, she obviously takes inspiration not from the Soviet lexicon, but from overseas, for the word 'gangster' was an American borrowing and still had the feel of a foreign word in the 1950s.[42] Antonova thus cast these criminals not as citizens of the Soviet Union, but as dangerous outsiders. (It is also significant that she denotes them as Russian and not the contemporary term Soviet: in the old Russian past there had indeed been thieves and bandits, she implies, but these should not be part of the new Soviet world.) In the final paragraph, her solution to the crime problem draws on a third source. In begging for a law that 'says that any thief who is caught has five fingers chopped off his left hand and is branded' her text suggests pre-revolutionary concepts of crime and justice.[43] These three figures of speech thus tell us something about Antonova's feelings towards criminals: she fears they are contagious, she wants them repudiated as outsiders to the Soviet community, and she readily proposes corporal punishment.

Drawing on metaphors from the early 1920s, American words and even pre-revolutionary concepts, her language is varied, pointing to the failure of Stalinist culture to provide an effective language with which to discuss this problem – a problem the leadership claimed did not exist.

In the first months following Stalin's death, the new leadership had already begun to break this silence, however. Following the amnesty decree of 27 March 1953, a newspaper editorial written by the Minister of Justice, Gorshenin, encouraged *Pravda* readers to view the amnesty decree, and the promises of further criminal justice reform that accompanied it, as evidence of 'Soviet humanity'.[44] Gorshenin also argued that the amnesty decree was evidence of the fact that Soviet laws helped those who committed errors 'to correct themselves' and then return to the 'path of honest labour', ideas that had once been important themes in discussions of criminal justice, but like other terms relating to crime and punishment disappeared from official texts from the mid-1930s onwards. Antonova is clearly aware of these new developments, yet explicitly rejects them, writing 'we've had enough of being "humane" with these weeds'. Her brash assertion that 'only the grave corrects the hunchback' also rejects Gorshenin's claim that beneficiaries of the amnesty had been 'corrected' by their time in the Gulag. Her use of this old Russian proverb again demonstrates the survival of traditional beliefs to rival Soviet concepts. What is interesting is that she uses this alongside established Soviet terms, suggesting that her attempt to 'speak Bolshevik' was a blend of the old and the new.

Before summarizing what this study of Antonova's language can tell us, let us think a little more about the significance of this act of letter-writing in itself. Antonova begins her letter with an apology: 'Forgive my audacity in daring to write to you, but I can't hold myself back any more.' Using such a convention, Antonova demonstrates to her reader she is aware that in addressing Molotov she is appealing to someone at the very apex of the hierarchy of power. Yet she also believes that the government should be interested in what ordinary people think: 'Take any tram conductor from the Krasnaia Presnia district, and they'll be able to tell you a lot.' Whether or not this is the case, her letter suggests she believed that the Kremlin leaders cared about the views of the ordinary citizen and would revise policy in light of their views.

Several conclusions can therefore be reached. In the spring of 1953 Antonova was highly concerned about law and order and believed that government policy was failing to deal with the problem. She was distressed and confused. She sought to present herself as a loyal citizen, but found the Stalinist lexicon did not provide effective ways to express her concerns about crime. She also rejected the post-Stalinist solutions as inconsistent with other views she held dear, and which – even though they might in fact draw from pre-revolutionary sources – she did not consider at odds with her identity as a good Soviet worker. Her letter points to some of the difficulties following Stalin's death: it alerts us not only to the social issues resulting from new policies such as the release of prisoners, but also to the state's difficulty in imposing new ways of conceptualizing such issues. This text suggests that in 1953 there was no fixed or authoritative 'Bolshevik-speak' – or at least not one that was meaningful to Antonova or that she could reproduce effectively. This led her to criticize the failings of the police, though it did not push her towards outright rebellion. The very act of writing a letter to a Soviet leader suggests her faith that the government, if correctly informed, was indeed willing and able to remedy the situation.

Finally, we cannot assume that Antonova was 'typical'. Although the archives contain many similar letters, this only tells us that other people were also sufficiently anxious about crime to compose a letter: it does not mean that such worries were universal, or even widespread.[45] Here again the key is to look to other sources. At a plenum of the party's Central Committee held in July 1953 several high-ranking party members discussed the sudden tide of letters regarding crime received by official bodies.[46] The letter therefore has a 'reality effect' (as described in the introductory chapter). The letter is not only of interest because of what it tells us about Antonova's concerns, but also because letter-writing was a phenomenon that had serious political implications, creating the sense of a 'moral panic' and at least indirectly feeding into the elaboration of new criminal justice policies in August 1953.[47]

## Conclusion

This chapter has focused particularly on two different kinds of letter: first, personal correspondence sent between family members; second, texts written by citizens intended either for publication or for consideration by the country's political leaders. They clearly serve quite different purposes, and have distinct effects. What, then, makes them a genre in their own right? The feature that distinguishes letters from other texts is that they identify not just the author, but also the intended audience. Whether a petition, business correspondence, a weekly letter to a relative, or an appeal to Molotov, they all begin 'Dear so-and-so'; they all have a reader (or readers) in mind. This encourages us to think about texts in terms of dialogue, and to remember that the act of writing can never be a fully solitary act, for the writer is always responding to previous interactions and earlier exchanges. In addition to the specific reader addressed moreover, the letter-writer is aware of what society *expects* from a letter both in terms of the form and the content, expectations that were aided by letter-writing manuals, education, the press, and in some contexts censorship. Letters can therefore help us to explore both social conformity and – when the norms are broken or distorted – individual inventiveness. As such, they do not offer a transparent window into the mindset of the author, but they do allow the careful historian to examine the complex web of relationships between individual, family, and society that shapes a person's sense of self and their understanding of the world they inhabit.

## Notes

1 In eighteenth-century America, for example, correspondence between merchants might be read loud or excerpts pinned on bulletin boards in the coffee houses where they liked

to gather. In the following century, the letters written by emigrants to the New World back to relatives in the British Isles would often be circulated through the extended family and local community. In many societies, even romantic correspondence which might seem the most intimate of exchanges would be approved by a parent first, as Martin Lyons's study of two fiancés in the late nineteenth century demonstrates. T.L. Ditz, 'Formative Ventures: Eighteenth-Century Commercial Letters and the Articulation of Experience', in R. Earle (ed.) *Epistolary Selves: Letters and Letter-writers, 1600–1945*, Aldershot: Ashgate, 1999, pp. 59–78, p. 70; D. Fitzpatrick, *Oceans of Consolation: Personal Accounts of Irish Migration to Australia*, Cork: Cork University Press, 1994, p. 478; M. Lyons, 'Love Letters and Writing Practices: On Ecritures Intimes in the Nineteenth Century', *Journal of Family History* 24, 1999, 232–239.

2  C. Dauphin, 'Les Correspondances comme objet historique: un travail sur les limites', *Sociétés et représentations* 13, 2002, 43–50, 44.

3  J. Keep, 'Lenin's Letters as a Historical Source', *Russian Review* 30, 1971, 33–42, 33.

4  R. Conquest, *Lenin: A Biography*, London: Macmillan, 2000.

5  T. Lodge, *Mandela: A Critical Life*, Oxford: Oxford University Press, 2006, pp. 78–79.

6  For an example of a work of intellectual history based almost entirely on correspondence, see T. Leng, *Benjamin Worsley (1618–77) Trade, Interest and the Spirit in Revolutionary England*, Woodbridge: The Boydell Press, 2008.

7  D. Gerber, 'The Immigrant Letter between Positivism and Populism: American Historians' Uses of Personal Correspondence,' in Earle (ed.), *Epistolary Selves*, pp. 37–55.

8  R.S. Starobin, 'Privileged Bondsmen and the Process of Accommodation: The Role of Houseservants and Drivers as Seen in Their Own Letters', *Journal of Social History* 5, 1971, 46–70. See also his edited collection of slave correspondence: R.S. Starobin (ed.), *Blacks in Bondage: Letters of American Slaves*, New York: New Viewpoints, 1974.

9  E.T. Bannet, *Empire of Letters: Letter Manuals and Transatlantic Correspondence, 1688–1820*, Cambridge: Cambridge University Press, 2005, pp. 13–14; D. Vincent, *The Rise of Mass Literacy: Reading and Writing in Modern Europe*, Cambridge: Polity, 2000, pp. 1–26.

10  Vincent, *Mass Literacy*, pp. 1–26.

11  M. Hanna, 'A Republic of Letters: The Epistolary Tradition in France during WWI', *American Historical Review* 108, 2003, 1338–1361; C. Hämmerle, '"You Let a Weeping Woman Call You Home?": Private Correspondences during the First World War in Austria and Germany', in Earle (ed.), *Epistolary Selves*, pp. 152–182.

12  T. Welskopp, 'Social History', in S. Berger, H. Heldner, K. Passmore (eds), *Writing History: Theory and Practice*, London: Arnold, 2003, pp. 203–222, p. 204.

13  Cited in C. Dauphin, P. Lebrun-Pezerat, and D. Poublan, *Ces bonnes lettres: Une correspondance familiale au XIXe siècle*, Paris: Bibliothèque Albin Michel Histoire, 1995, p. 135.

14  See David Gerber's description of American historians' use of letters, particularly his discussion of Lloyd Husvedt's work. D.A. Gerber, *Authors of Their Lives: The Personal Correspondence of British Immigrants to North America in the Nineteenth Century*, New York: New York University Press, 2006, pp. 44–45.

15  J.S. Allen, 'The Gendered Politics of Correspondence: the Curious Case of Céline Renooz, 1849–1928', in C. Bland and M. Cross (eds), *Gender and Politics in the Age of Letter-Writing, 1750–2000*, Aldershot: Ashgate, 2004, pp. 161–172.

16  Gerber, *Authors*, pp. 8–9.

17  For references and a clear explanation of this line of argument, see Gerber, *Authors*, pp. 74–75. For an excellent article on autobiographies and letters that examines 'the relationship between literacy and the formation of modern forms of selfhood', see S.E. Rowe, 'Writing Modern Selves: Literacy and the French Working-class in the Early Nineteenth Century', *Journal of Social History* 40, 2006, 55–83.

18  In her study of one adulterous couple's letters from 1824–1849, Paula Cossart shows how notions of love found in romantic literature (in particular the idea of love as an

elemental force that fights against society's conventions) shaped the narrative of their affair developed in their voluminous correspondence. See P. Cossart, 'Usages de la rhétorique romantique. L'expression epistolaire du sentiment amoureux adultère (1824–1849)', *Sociétés et représentations* 13, 2002, 151–164.

19  An excellent introduction to Foucault's works is P. Rabinow (ed.), *The Foucault Reader: An Introduction to Foucault Thought*, Harmondsworth: Penguin, 1991. See also M. Foucault, 'About the Beginning of the Hermeneutics of the Self: Two Lectures at Dartmouth', *Political Theory* 21, 1993, 198–227.

20  Gerber, *Authors*, pp. 19–28.

21  Gerber, *Authors*, p. 3.

22  Gerber, *Authors*, pp. 57–58 and 68.

23  The term 'imagined community' is taken from B. Anderson, *Imagined Communities: Reflections on the Origin and Spread of Nationalism*, London: Verso, 1991.

24  Hanna, 'A Republic of Letters'.

25  Martin Lyons for example stresses the reticence of French soldiers' letters, while Martha Hanna finds them surprisingly honest about their feelings of suicidal despondency. M. Lyons, 'French Soldiers and Their Correspondence: Towards a History of Writing Practices in the First World War', *French History* 17, 2003, 79–95 and Hanna, 'A Republic of Letters'.

26  As Benjamin Ziemann has argued, historians looking for information about the mistreatment of civilians in France and Belgium will have little luck with the letters of German soldiers; extra-marital affairs are unlikely to feature in letters home to the wife. B. Ziemann, *War Experiences in Rural Germany 1914–1923*, Oxford: Berg, 2007, pp. 12–13.

27  On the development of letter-writing manuals for a wide audience during the long eighteenth century, see Bannet, *Empire of Letters*. For an excellent study of letter-writing manuals in the nineteenth century, see Cécile Dauphin's chapter in R. Chartier, A. Boureau and C. Dauphin (eds), *Correspondence: Models of Letter-Writing from the Middle Ages to the Nineteenth Century*, trans. Christopher Woodall, Princeton: Princeton University Press, 1997, pp. 112–157.

28  J. Horne, 'Soldiers, Civilians and the Warfare of Attrition: Representations of Combat in France, 1914–18', in F. Coetzee and M. Shevin-Coetzee (eds), *Authority, Identity and the Social History of the Great War*, Providence and Oxford: Berghahn, 1995, pp. 223–250, p. 226.

29  J. Horne, 'Soldiers', p. 240.

30  For an excellent study of Second World War letters that focuses on the concepts and beliefs that allowed German soldiers to legitimate their actions, see Klaus Latzel, 'German Soldiers in Victory, 1940', P. Liddle, J. Bourne, I. Whitehead (eds), *The Great World War 1914–45: Lightning Strikes Twice*, London: Collins, 2000, 264–277.

31  Hämmerle, '"Weeping"'.

32  P.J. Eakin, *How Our Lives Become Stories: Making Selves*, Ithaca: Cornell University Press, 1999, pp. 43–98.

33  Regenia Gagnier's work offers a thoughtful challenge to what she calls the 'post-structural conception of subjectivity' in which 'the I, the apparent seat of consciousness, is not the integral centre of thought but a contradictory, discursive category constituted by ideological discourse itself'. In the early 1990s, Gagnier argued that more work needed to be done to explore the way in which individuals mediate, or transform, those discourses in everyday lives. R. Gagnier, *Subjectivities: A History of Self-Representation in Britain, 1832–1920*, New York and Oxford: Oxford University Press, 1991, pp. 9–11.

34  S. Fitzpatrick, 'Editor's Introduction: Petitions and Denunciations in Russian and Soviet History', *Russian History/Histoire Russe* 24, 1997, 1–9, 7.

35  On Soviet petition-writing, see L.H. Siegelbaum, 'Narratives of Appeal and Appeal of Narratives: Labor Discipline and its Contestation in the Early Soviet Period', *Russian*

*History/Histoire Russe* 24, 1997, 65–87; G. Alexopoulos, *Stalin's Outcasts: Aliens, Citizens, and the Soviet State, 1926–1936*, Ithaca: Cornell University Press, 2003; and on Soviet letter-writing more broadly, S. Fitzpatrick, 'Supplicants and Citizens: Public Letter-Writing in Soviet Russia in the 1930s', *Slavic Review* 55, 1996, 78–105.

36  The editorial offices not only published occasional letters to encourage further correspondence, but also responded to a significant proportion of these letters, thanking the writer for corresponding and offering advice. See S. Fitzpatrick, 'Readers' Letters to *Krest'ianskaia Gazeta* 1938', *Russian History/Histoire Russe* 24, 1997, 149–170 and M.E. Lenoe, 'Letter-writing and the State: Reader Correspondence with Newspapers as a Source for Early Soviet History', *Cahiers du Monde russe* 40, 1999, 139–170.

37  On Soviet surveillance, see M. Föllmer's chapter in this volume, and P. Holquist, '"Information Is the Alpha and Omega of Our Work": Bolshevik Surveillance in Its Pan-European Context', *Journal of Modern History* 69, 1997, 415–450.

38  S. Kotkin, *Magnetic Mountain: Stalinism as a Civilization*, Berkeley: University of California Press, 1995, 198–237. For a very useful discussion of his work, see I. Halfin and J. Hellbeck, 'Rethinking the Stalinist Subject: Stephen Kotkin's "Magnetic Mountain" and the State of Soviet Historical Studies', *Jahrbücher für Geschichte Osteuropas* 44 (1996), 456–463.

39  'Letter to Molotov from Antonova', 2 May 1953, RGASPI (Rossiiskii gosudarstvennyi arkhiv sotsial'no- politicheskoi) f. 82, op. 2, d. 1440, l. 78.

40  M. Dobson, '"Show the Bandits No Mercy!": Amnesty, Criminality and Public Response in 1953', in P.A. Jones (ed.), *The Dilemmas of De-Stalinisation: Negotiating Cultural and Social Change in the Khrushchev Era*, Oxon: Routledge, 2006, pp. 21–40.

41  D. Beer, '"The Hygiene of Souls": Languages of Illness and Contagion in Late Imperial and Early Soviet Russia', PhD diss., University of Cambridge, 2001, pp. 163–165.

42  According to N.M. Shanskii's *Etymological Dictionary of the Russian Language* of 1965, this borrowing came from the USA in the twentieth century. He notes that it appeared for the first time in the *Dictionary of Foreign Words* in 1942.

43  Abby Shrader writes that in nineteenth-century Russia a combination of corporal punishment, physical mutilation, and Siberian exile 'served as a mechanism by which autocrats constructed social boundaries by marking those who transgressed the parameters of social behaviour'. A.M. Shrader, 'Branding the Exile as "Other": Corporal Punishment and the Construction of Boundaries in mid-19th Century Russia', in D.L. Hoffmann and Y. Kotsonis (eds), *Russian Modernity: Politics, Knowledge, Practices*, Basingstoke: Macmillan, 2000, pp. 19–40, pp. 21–22.

44  'Sotsialisticheskaia zakonnost' na strazhe interesov naroda', *Pravda*, 17 April 1953, p. 2.

45  See Chapter I and VI of M. Dobson, *Khrushchev's Cold Summer: Citizens, Zeks, and the Soviet Community after Stalin*, Ithaca: Cornell University Press, 2009, forthcoming.

46  RGANI (Rossiiskii gosudarstvennyi arkhiv noveishchei istorii) f. 2, op. 1, d. 42, l. 12.

47  See Chapter V of Dobson, *Khrushchev's Cold Summer*.

## Select bibliography

Bland, C. and Cross, M. (eds), *Gender and Politics in the Age of Letter-Writing, 1750–2000*, Aldershot: Ashgate, 2004.

Chartier, R., Boureau, A. and Dauphin C. (eds), *Correspondence: Models of Letter-Writing from the Middle Ages to the Nineteenth Century*, trans. Christopher Woodall, Princeton: Princeton University Press, 1997.

Earle, R. (ed.) *Epistolary Selves: Letters and Letter-writers, 1600–1945*, Aldershot: Ashgate, 1999.

Fitzpatrick, D., *Oceans of Consolation: Personal Accounts of Irish Migration to Australia*, Cork: Cork University Press, 1994.

Fitzpatrick, S., 'Supplicants and Citizens: Public Letter-Writing in Soviet Russia in the 1930s', *Slavic Review* 55, 1996, 78–105.

Gerber, D.A., *Authors of Their Lives: The Personal Correspondence of British Immigrants to North America in the Nineteenth Century*, New York: New York University Press, 2006.

Hanna, M., 'A Republic of Letters: The Epistolary Tradition in France during WWI', *American Historical Review* 108, 2003, 1338–1361.

Horne, J., 'Soldiers, Civilians and the Warfare of Attrition: Representations of Combat in France, 1914–18', in F. Coetzee and M. Shevin-Coetzee (eds), *Authority, Identity and the Social History of the Great War*, Providence and Oxford: Berghahn, 1995, pp. 223–250.

Kotkin, S., *Magnetic Mountain: Stalinism as a Civilization*, Berkeley: University of California Press, 1995.

Starobin, R.S., 'Privileged Bondsmen and the Process of Accommodation: The Role of Houseservants and Drivers as Seen in Their Own Letters', *Journal of Social History* 5, 1971, 46–70.

# 4    Surveillance reports

*Moritz Föllmer*

European states have been producing surveillance reports since the early modern period. In the nineteenth century, they increasingly standardised the methods of compiling and summarising relevant information. The surveillance of attitudes was significantly expanded during the First World War and became part of the modern state's efforts to transform the hearts and minds of the populace. The dictatorships of the twentieth century continued these existing surveillance practices while creating new agencies and ideological perspectives. What insights can we derive from these reports? Can they tell us something about popular opinion or rather about the mindsets of their authors and the shifting contexts of state surveillance? Historians have given different answers to this question. For their interpretation of surveillance reports, Nazi Germany and Bolshevik Russia have been particularly important testing grounds.

## In search of popular opinion in Nazi Germany and Stalinist Russia

Surveillance reports rose to prominence as a historical source in the 1970s. By that time, totalitarianism had begun to lose sway as an interpretation of the Nazi and Stalinist regimes. Particularly in its cruder versions, this theory had taken a top-down view of how the two dictatorships worked. Orders from above were applied to the very bottom of society. Citizens were in reality subjects who lacked any latitude in controlling their lives. Coerced and manipulated, deprived of any independent source of information, they ultimately lost control of their own hearts and minds. Only a small minority managed to preserve a realm of private conscience, and an even smaller, heroic group of people took it upon themselves to resist.

From the 1960s, some historians of the 'Third Reich' and of Stalinist Russia began to question the framework of this theory whose plausibility had owed much to the political context of the early Cold War.[1] At first, they focused on different institutions and groups, pointing out that the workings of government and the dynamics of society were more complex than the totalitarianist interpretation had acknowledged. Careful archival research revealed conflicts of interest between institutions, groups and individuals that had remained invisible to an essentially pre-empirical theory. These were now connected to the radicalisation of both dictatorships and integrated into a new interpretive framework dubbed 'functionalist' or 'structuralist' for Nazism and 'revisionist' for Stalinism.[2]

The historiographical trend to view the 'Third Reich' and Stalinist Russia no longer as regimes organised from the top down and as strictly controlled societies prompted further questions that went beyond government institutions and socio-economic groups. For if there was no such thing as 'total' supervision and manipulation, then it was not at all clear that Germans and Russians were coerced by the respective dictatorships into adopting the official viewpoint. They appeared less malleable, more independent of propagandistic influence, potentially more rooted in pre-Nazi or pre-Stalinist beliefs. What, really, did people think in both societies? How did they react to the worldviews presented to them and the policy initiatives directed at them? And to what extent did the answer to these questions depend on social, political and cultural differences?

Popular opinion in dictatorships thus became an exciting field of historical enquiry. But finding relevant information was no small challenge. Questioning the impact of official propaganda was one thing, reconstructing an alternative 'public' another. There was no free press in the two dictatorships and thus little critical reporting, discussion of different viewpoints and expression of popular grievances. Memoirs and diaries are mostly written by members of an educated minority; for both the 'Third Reich' and Stalinist Russia, self-justifying leading actors on the one hand and people who were persecuted for political or racial reasons on the other are over-represented among the authors. A wide array of letters only became available later and could primarily serve to elucidate the experiences of soldiers in the Second World War.[3] Given the difficulty of finding adequate sources, it was of particular interest that both dictatorships, ever anxious about the mood of their populaces, went to considerable lengths to gather information about them. They established networks of informers and routines of writing, collecting and systematising reports. It is on these sources that the emerging historiography of popular opinion under the two regimes was based.

The historians of the 'Third Reich' took the lead since in contrast to their colleagues working on Stalinist Russia they enjoyed access to surveillance reports early on. Though Nazi institutions such as the German Labour Front as well as the pre-existing 'general' or political administration reported on popular opinion as well, the Sicherheitsdienst (Security Service, SD) left the most relevant sources. Unlike the Gestapo (Secret State Police), the SD did not merely observe political, religious or racial foes of the regime. From 1938, it also assembled information on the economy, society and culture with a focus on how far they were influenced by the Nazi ideology. Moreover, the SD found out how the populace felt about these realms of life through local volunteer informants who eavesdropped on conversations. For instance, the unit in the town of Koblenz consisted of one doctor, four public sector employees, four policemen, a teacher and a veterinarian. On the federal level, staff in the SD headquarters compiled systematic reports from the local material several times a week, comprising sections on 'general mood and situation', 'cultural areas', 'law and administration', 'the economy' and, from April 1940, '"folkdom" and public health'. The first section included popular reactions to political events, such as military operations or speeches by Nazi leaders; later, the SD also attempted more generally to identify trends in German opinion.[4]

In the absence of free speech and opinion-polling, such a systematic picture of public opinion was of significant value for propaganda minister Joseph Goebbels, who used it to target his efforts more efficiently (even though he preferred to draw on reports from his own apparatus). However, when the SD reports highlighted an increasingly pessimistic mood in the second half of the war, Goebbels, SS leader Heinrich Himmler, and others increasingly dismissed them as defeatist and kept them from Hitler's view. In retrospect, this critical edge makes the SD reports appear relatively unbiased, an assessment that prompted the emerging historiography of German popular opinion in times of dictatorship and war to draw heavily from them. Complemented by the aforementioned reports by other institutions, they formed Marlis Steinert's source basis for studying 'public mood and attitude during the Second World War'.[5] The findings of her research were that Germans reacted perceptively to military fortunes, food supply, church politics and the realities of one-party rule. In the second half of the war, the majority of them turned moderately critical, notwithstanding Goebbels's efforts. Propaganda could reinforce but mostly not alter existing views, which were modified at least as much by personal experience.

Thus there emerged a picture of a popular, semi-public and partly critical opinion in the 'Third Reich' derived from surveillance reports. In a classic monograph on Bavaria, Ian Kershaw elaborated this picture.[6] His regional focus allowed for a more detailed treatment than in Steinert's book. A wide array of reports by different agencies of the Nazi regime in Bavaria had survived, including general, aggregated assessments as well as unrefined accounts of local events. Kershaw was careful to eliminate the biases of individual informants by comparing different sources. Given the prevailing atmosphere of intimidation and denunciation, he regarded the critical comments emerging from the surveillance reports as 'but the tip of the iceberg'.[7] Moreover, he was able to draw on a different kind of source: the Social Democratic Party organisation in exile had set up an underground network of informants who regularly reported on popular opinion. Adding newspaper accounts (which, when read between the lines, offered glimpses of conflict), institutional correspondence and court records, Kershaw concluded that there could be 'little mistaking the broad lines of mood and opinion'.[8]

What did these 'broad lines' look like? In this largely rural German state, peasants were disgruntled about a coercive regime that interfered in production and marketing and prevented them from dividing their estates. Workers were alienated by bad conditions, low wages and political repression. Small businessmen, civil servants and teachers who had disproportionately supported the Nazis were now frequently complaining about downward mobility and stormtrooper rowdyism. Shifting the focus from socio-economic to confessional identities, Catholics in particular but also Protestants resented the anti-clerical measures of party and state such as the abolishment of religious schooling, the elimination of crucifixes in the classroom and the killing of the mentally disabled, forcing the regime to backtrack at several points. Christians cared much less about the fate of the persecuted Jewish minority. A combination of grumbling about street violence, self-centredness and latent anti-Semitic prejudice led them to accept legal and less visible forms of exclusion.[9]

The prevailing mood of passivity, dissatisfaction and complaint did not improve when the war imposed severe additional strains on the populace, which increasingly dismissed the *Volksgemeinschaft* (national community) as a fraud. But this also meant that dissent was overwhelmingly confined to personal grievances, that indifference towards the fate of the Jewish minority continued and that there was little basis for political resistance. Moreover, in a companion volume Kershaw has pointed to a nexus between dissatisfaction about economic hardships, bureaucratic absurdities and the behaviour of local party members on the one hand and the widespread popularity of Adolf Hitler on the other. As the same surveillance reports reveal, the Führer was seen as a morally pure individual with exceptional abilities whose foreign policy 'accomplishments' were admired precisely because everyday life often looked so grim. This myth could be sustained until the military disaster became obvious after the defeat in Stalingrad and the ever-increasing bombings.[10]

Some years after Kershaw's books appeared, historians of Stalinism found themselves in a position to pursue a similar research strategy. Due to the climate change in Gorbachev's Russia, they enjoyed unexpected access to reports on popular opinion that had long been hidden in secret archives. In the 1930s, these reports were assembled by the secret police, the NKVD, the Communist Party and the youth organisation the Komsomol. Informants recorded conversations or jokes; these notes were then summarised and handed to a couple of select party leaders. While acknowledging that the majority of the populace had reacted well to a particular policy or event, the reports listed a number of 'backward' or 'counter-revolutionary' statements, with shifts in focus depending on what the party line was. In an important book, Sarah Davies used these newly available texts to test assumptions about coercion and consent in the Stalinist dictatorship that had previously lacked a reliable source basis. She concluded that there were constant signs of critical popular opinion throughout the 1930s and, following Kershaw, assumed that the recorded instances of dissent were just the 'tip of the iceberg'.[11]

According to Davies, Russians frequently voiced disappointment. Despite the propaganda about life having become 'better' and 'merrier', workers were angry about the shortage of food and other consumer goods which amounted to a decrease in real wages. Peasants complained that opportunities to preserve private land fell short of their expectations. People disapproved of the campaigns against the Orthodox Church and continued to celebrate religious holidays. Moreover, they voiced considerable ethnic hostility, including prejudices against Jews. As for political matters, the reports reveal a previously underrated popular awareness of constitutional rights. While some people supported Soviet foreign policy, others expressed admiration for Adolf Hitler. The Great Terror seems mostly to have been received with indifference. But it also enjoyed some support, since Russians' social identities revolved around the opposition between 'us' (the people) and 'them' (those at the top of the social hierarchy), and the party elite hence appeared suspicious. Stalin himself was the butt of jokes and critical remarks but was also widely seen as a benefactor and defender of the people.

Davies's Russians under Stalin and Kershaw's Germans under Hitler appear remarkably similar. They primarily saw the respective regimes from the vantage point of their personal concerns and interests. These were largely material in character, and given the sacrifices imposed on them, both Russians and Germans were mostly disgruntled if not outright negative. Moreover, their worldview was largely dominated by Orthodox, Catholic or Protestant Christianity, which made them resent and at times even oppose the various Stalinist and Nazi anti-clerical campaigns. Both had their share of preconceived stereotypes: against 'them' (the elite) in the Russian case, against 'Marxists' in the German, to some extent against the Jews in both countries. Only to the degree that their propaganda and action overlapped with these stereotypes were the two regimes able to appeal to the respective populace. This widespread discontent also explains why, as a way of compensation, the leaders Stalin and (more so) Hitler were successfully presented as exceptional individuals and enjoyed a significant popularity.

Is this parallel picture of dissatisfaction and passive compliance under Stalin and Hitler correct? Or is it rather due to the pitfalls of the two historians' approach, particularly their reliance on, and reading of, surveillance reports? Some critical reviewers certainly suggested as much. One of them pointed out that 'the kind of sources he [Kershaw] uses regularly turn up evidence of what might be construed as quite normal grumblings, and that, furthermore, given the Nazis' paranoid concern for information, these dissatisfactions [. . .] were magnified in the sources'.[12] Echoing this criticism, another historian provocatively asked Kershaw and others: 'Where did all the Nazis go?'.[13] He argued that the Nazi agencies writing and compiling the surveillance reports tended to focus on every instance of dissent (which was, after all, what they were there for) and thus to blow it out of proportion. The ever-complaining, self-centred and passive people emerging from these sources were at best one side of popular opinion in the 'Third Reich'. The other was a significant amount of active and ideologically committed support. This side was difficult to get at, but by analysing propaganda down to an everyday level as well as activities in Nazi organisations or denunciations of neighbours, one historian arrived at the conclusion that Germans were essentially 'backing Hitler'.[14]

In a parallel vein, some reviewers of Sarah Davies's book on Stalinist Russia argued that the author, while deserving credit for her pioneering work, had made sweeping generalisations based on anecdotal sources, fashioning an oppositional shadow culture out of harmless complaints and jokes.[15] Others went further and criticised Davies for downplaying the fact that the informants not only reported critical but also affirmative attitudes. According to them, the frequent grumblings should be interpreted not as the 'tip of the iceberg' of broader dissent but as the flip side of a widespread consent to at least some of the official values. Moreover, they pointed out that it was misleading to treat the surveillance reports as a mirror of popular opinion. Instead, they suggested 'that the mood summaries express the play of bureaucratic interests, the mentality of recorders, the bustle of toadies, and, most conspicuously, the deepest fears, even paranoia, of the authorities'.[16]

These criticisms demonstrate that it is not only possible to arrive at different empirical conclusions on the basis of the very same surveillance reports but also to hold contrary views as to the usefulness of this kind of source for getting at popular opinion. In a brilliant article, Peter Holquist came up with a new perspective on the reports which the Bolshevik regime produced. He suggested reading them not for what they reveal about popular attitudes but as part and parcel of the modern state's effort to transform the latter.[17] Focusing on the Don province in southern Russia and transgressing the boundary both between tsarist and Soviet Russia and between revolutionary Reds and counterrevolutionary Whites, Holquist highlighted the sea change of the First World War. Instead of simply keeping a close eye on potential troublemakers, thus securing order and obedience, the tsarist government already became actively interested in the hearts and minds of its subjects. It employed staff to read and summarise letters, eavesdrop on conversations and compile reports on the attitudes in different realms of society, not merely to prevent unrest but to have a basis for reshaping popular mood. The Soviet apparatus expanded this ongoing project rather than creating it. Moreover, the 'Whites', the counterrevolutionary forces in the post-1917 civil war, shared the Communists' interest in people's consciousness and set up their own surveillance system. Having thus dismantled the tendency to see the reports as typically Bolshevik, Holquist pointed to European similarities: after 1914, Germany, France and Britain alike sought to know and manage popular opinion by gathering systematic information about it. Total war brought about the emergence of what the author called 'national security states', and this was reflected in the genre of surveillance reports.[18]

Should we follow Holquist and abandon the idea that surveillance reports can tell us anything about 'popular opinion'? While we do not need to go that far we would be well advised to take his challenging argument seriously. An awareness of the shifting character of our source, depending on the respective political and institutional context, is a prerequisite for reading it in an informed way. For only if we know how, why and to what effect information on people's behaviour and attitudes was collected, written down, systematised, circulated and used can we hope to comprehend the specific foci of the reports. We can then interpret them on the one hand, as suggested by Holquist, as sources for a history of state surveillance, including its conceptual approaches, observation practices and textual devices. On the other hand, we can still draw careful conclusions about popular attitudes, provided that the reports are local or regional in scope rather than aggregated, and provided that their authors had an interest in knowing about the mood in their area and that their worldviews and stereotypes did not prevent them from doing so.

## Surveillance reports and the modern state – a brief history

What would a history of surveillance reports in modern times look like? A good early-modern starting point lies with the sources that the Paris police produced in the eighteenth century.[19] They offer detailed accounts of the communication that took place on the streets and markets of the French capital as well as the role of policemen therein. Rumours, jokes and minor confrontations emerge from the reports and provide us with fascinating glimpses into early modern social life. We can also learn which publications and songs circulated how and thus understand the dynamics of popular opinion – unfortunately, the police reports have only survived until 1781, not for the immediate pre-revolutionary period. Historians are thus reluctant to draw direct causal connections from popular opinion at mid-century to 1789 and after, even though some of them do argue that the monarchy had already lost a fair share of its legitimacy during the reign of Louis XV (1723–1774).

What is remarkable about the reports, compared to those discussed above, is the absence of systematic ambition. As suits a state with an absolutist self-understanding, popular discussions about things political were deemed illegitimate by the French authorities. Policemen and secret agents were partly there to observe it and thus prevent riots or revolts, which may have prompted them to blow critical remarks out of proportion. But they did not have as strong an ideological focus as the Nazi and Stalinist surveillance organisations, nor were the reports they wrote as standardised as their nineteenth-century counterparts. A higher authority summarising local findings in a more abstract way did not exist either. This absence of standardisation, the sheer wealth of unconnected stories, is precisely what makes these sources so colourful.

For the nineteenth century, there are hardly any instances of a similarly detailed glimpse into popular opinion through regular reports produced by the police or administration. Why is this so? States on the European continent modified their surveillance practices along two related lines. First, they frequently attempted to stifle subversive activities after the revolutionary shocks of 1789–1815 and, again, of 1848–1849. This prompted them to target surveillance specifically at oppositional groups representing the new ideological formations of the nineteenth century: the most important of these were the nationalist movements challenging monarchical authority and the socialist movements aiming at a radical transformation of class society. Complementing the censorship of newspapers, journals and other publications, police officers had to attend oppositional assemblies, while district administrators condensed the specific reports into more summary ones which also included general remarks on the mood of the populace. The standardised way in which these summary reports were drafted was part of a second trend: states became ever more interested in gathering and systematising information on society and in using this knowledge to exert control. Statistical tables, administrative forms and regular reports are reflections of this broader phenomenon.[20]

The standardised manner of gathering information on oppositional groups and of summarising the mood of the populace limits the usefulness of nineteenth-century surveillance reports. They may very well provide an accurate picture of, say, socialist activities in a certain region; after all, states had a vested interest in knowing about these. But the reports may, despite the careful work of their authors, just as well have missed the dynamic of grassroots politics. This depended on the grasp police officers and bureaucrats had on the respective subculture. Around the turn of the century, the observers themselves increasingly felt that routine methods no longer sufficed to pinpoint political unrest and social dynamics. In Russia, the newly founded 'Special Section' of the Police Department replaced the always somewhat dated yearly reports on the revolutionary movement by comprehensive and precise weekly or fortnightly bulletins. To the Tsar, it submitted juicier reports filled with colourful detail of underground activities, which he apparently enjoyed reading.[21] Despite these improvements, however, the security police could not cope with the growing popular unrest, much less prevent the revolution of 1905.[22]

Similarly, a police officer in the German city of Hamburg in the 1890s felt that the customary surveillance of assemblies no longer sufficed to grasp the shifts in urban society and control the rise of socialism therein.[23] He ordered several agents to visit working-class pubs in disguise and eavesdrop on the regulars' conversations. Not quite sure what their superiors wanted to read, the agents highlighted both discontent and its absence. The resulting detailed reports offer fascinating glimpses into the attitudes and interactions of working-class men which are otherwise hard to get at. But apparently, the vast majority of them were simply filed and stored under the heading 'useless reports'. There is no evidence of a concerted reaction by the police and the administration. The authorities of the late nineteenth century lacked the activist willingness to conquer people's hearts and minds that later was at the heart of 'national security states'.

The summaries of popular mood which regularly figure in the surveillance reports raise similar problems. Even if we grant the possibility that regional administrators had a good grasp of shifts in popular opinion, we still need to consider their own interests and agendas. The French prefects of the nineteenth century, for instance, had a clear stake in presenting the mood in their districts in a mostly positive vein. After all, it was their responsibility to keep it that way; to paint a negative picture meant that they could be reprimanded for not doing their job. It thus has a self-congratulatory ring and should be taken with a pinch of salt when one of them claimed in 1859: 'The spirit of the population is excellent, they are always extremely devoted to the government of the Emperor.'[24] In contrast, prefects had dramatised minor incidents and suggested an imminent revolution in 1851–1852. Through their reports, they had given propagandistic ammunition to the president of the Second Republic, Louis-Napoléon Bonaparte, for justifying his coup d'état to the anxious middle classes.[25] Yet another agenda brought the secret police in Venetia, one of the Italian provinces of the Habsburg Empire, to mention certain popular concerns in its reports. The officers communicated these problems to Vienna in the hope of prompting the Imperial government to react and thus prevent serious unrest.[26]

Even if we cannot detect any such agenda, it is not a given that the techniques used by policemen and administrators sufficed to provide them with a clear picture of popular moods and attitudes. The First World War with its contrast between the complex dynamics of society and the increased informational requirements of governments is a case in point. One perceptive French prefect explained to his minister in Paris:

> The prefect is in a bad position to know the state of public opinion. He does not have contact with the public. The persons whom he questions generally answer him in a sense which they think conforms to his wishes. He is thus at risk of

presenting as the spectrum of public opinion that which is but the outward projection of his own thinking.[27]

Right up to the first Russian Revolution in February 1917, some administrators in
the Don province still followed the nineteenth-century model and kept reporting
that 'the mood is satisfactory' and that in this respect 'no changes have occurred'.[28]
It is obvious that their conceptual approach no longer sufficed to grasp the rapidly
changing attitudes in a pre-revolutionary situation.

The example of German senior civil servants during and after the First World
War further highlights just how much the character and the results of surveillance,
a difficult activity to begin with, depended on the position of the administrative
elite in a highly conflictual field. Soon after August 1914, senior civil servants
found themselves cornered: they experienced a loss of actual power to the army
commands, which largely took over the government of the districts, while nevertheless being blamed for scarcity and injustice and thus facing increasing popular
resentment. Yet they attempted to shape attitudes and to define patriotic behaviour,
for instance by influencing who was awarded a decoration or by reducing the use of
contraceptive measures and foreign words. The results were rather disappointing,
since decorations were awarded by the army or through popular pressure, and senior civil servants were not able to put sufficient pressure on people. Things got
worse after 1918, when the administrative elite was faced with an unprecedented
degree of social unrest and popular mobilisation. Against this background, senior
civil servants resorted to medical metaphors such as 'depression' or 'nervousness'.
These quite obviously do not reflect a grasp of the popular mood from a position of
distant observation but rather show how the authors struggled to cope with a difficult situation. They are instead interesting for what they tell us about the way an
elite on the defensive reduced the complex dynamics of a society in crisis to a moral
illness of the German nation, while at the same time preserving some hope for an
ultimate regeneration.[29]

Thus the 'national security state' was at times more an ambition than a successful project. It also assumed a different outlook in different countries and underwent
significant transformations in the twentieth century. During the First World War,
Britain established a form of surveillance of soldiers and civilians based on military
intelligence that crossed the line between counter-espionage and political polic-
ing.[30] This system was continued and even expanded after 1918 in order to inform
the government about strike movements as well as, later, the activities of the British
Union of Fascists.[31] But during the Second World War, the new Ministry of
Information and its Home Intelligence Division no longer deemed it sufficient.
Military intelligence was therefore complemented by the reports of Regional
Information Officers in touch with voluntary societies, trade unions and business
leaders. In addition, the Ministry of Information consulted findings of the BBC's
listener research, surveys by 'Mass-Observation' (a group set up in 1937 by
left-wing intellectuals who wished to describe and criticise British society) and
opinion polls.[32] With this – at times uneasy – pluralism of reports, a system of
authoritarian surveillance moved towards a democratic polity in which 'the people'

were encouraged to voice their opinion which the government, facing public criticism and a future election, had to take it into account.

No such shift occurred in the Eastern Bloc. The idea of surveying public through opinion polls remained alien to the Communist system. Security services observed real or potential opponents and reported on popular opinion all the way to the revolutions in the autumn of 1989. The local Stasi officers in the German Democratic Republic, for instance, were well aware of the increasing dissatisfaction in the late 1980s.[33] But this information was watered down in the process of reaching the top of the secret service's hierarchy. Moreover, it was not fully communicated to the party leaders who were responsible for political strategy.

The Stasi leadership, limited by its ideological mindset and decades of practising surveillance, saw the 'people' as a passive crowd. Unable to comprehend the deeper causes of East Germans' dissatisfaction, it could only see 'hostile-negative forces' at work. It recommended cracking down on these, whilst defending the official viewpoint ever more vigorously. To the Stasi officers, this did not seem unrealistic, given that they perceived the 'progressive forces' as thinking that 'the development of social democracy and the growth of openness should not lead to the unrestricted expression of subjective opinions and judgements about people and processes'.[34] These hardliners still saw a chance for the Communist system to be saved but in the end, they felt let down by a party that succumbed to the unrest rather than fighting it.

## 'Liberalistic influences' in Nazi Germany – a secret report

After the discussion of reports on popular opinion in Nazi Germany and Stalinist Russia and the overview on the development of state surveillance, we have arrived at the following preliminary conclusion: these sources can tell us something about oppositional activities and popular attitudes, but only if read with attention to the agendas and stereotypes governing them and carefully contrasted with other sources. It is equally if not more interesting to view them against the background of the history of the modern state. An awareness of the shifting institutional contexts of surveillance reports as well as their textual qualities is key to such an interpretation. With these reflections in mind, we now return to Nazi Germany and look at one specific source extract. It is a small part of an over two hundred page-long survey of different oppositional activities and realms of society in 1938 by the SD, the security service which was part of the SS. The source extract is devoted to 'liberalism'.[35]

> The tense times of 1938 with its repeated crises have demonstrated that just by crushing liberalistic and pacifist organisations these circles of opponents are not eliminated. The significance of liberalism does not lie in its organisational forms, but in the inner attitude of the individuals carrying liberalistic ideas.
>
> In the intellectual circles of science and academia the liberalistic attitude predominates to this day and attempts to find among academic youth the necessary new recruits.

In the field of art liberalistic influences have become stronger. That the Provincial Museum of Breslau showed an exhibition on Chinese painting on the occasion of the German Gymnastics and Sports Festival must at the very least be regarded as a complete lack of instinct. Likewise, film and popular music [Schlagermusik] lapse more and more into the empty and exclusively erotic shallowness of the system period [the Nazi concept for the Weimar years].

With respect to community life, from which liberalism had been almost totally eliminated, one can even speak of a revival. Across the Reich, associations and informal organisations have flourished, which only represent societal concerns, constitute a counterweight to the party and its branches. [. . .]

The lack of a well-established National Socialist literature has led to authors of the system period re-emerging in the bookshops as well as to a preference for foreign books, some of which have a neutral, others a liberalistic-pacifist tendency.

To this day, formerly democratically-pacifistically inclined teachers are employed as educators and are a great danger to the ideological education of youth. For instance, a teacher in Hanover had to be disciplined, because as a participant in a sports camp he openly criticised such community training courses and labelled himself a liberal-minded [*freiheitlich gesinnten*] individualist.

Liberalistic influences are strongest in the economy. In cultural and community life National Socialism could exert a certain influence on staff policy. As a result, forces with an oppositional attitude drifted into business. Protection and corruption, which had dominated politics in the system period, are to this day not eliminated from business. Leadership positions in the chambers of industry and commerce as well as in industry are mostly held by people who distance themselves from any commitment to the *Volk* and the state. They tackle the tasks of the four-year plan grudgingly or use them to worsen the social situation of labourers and white-collar employees. Moreover, business circles are responsible for the bulk of the criticism which is directed against the politics of the state and deliberately spread.

This source extract shows how little such a summary of the mood in Nazi Germany had in common with any kind of early opinion poll. To treat reports by agencies of the 'Third Reich' as such would be problematic even for those produced at the local level, for while more in touch with attitudes on the ground, the authors tend to focus on instances of discontent. The SD summaries on the whole of Germany are moreover highly aggregated and have assumed the character of a memorandum for intragovernmental debate. In this particular extract, the evidence for 'liberalistic influences' is small to the point of caricature: at several points, the SD authors cite one single case to back up their view of a larger trend. It would therefore be quite obviously mistaken to take their assessment at face value and conclude that 'circles of opponents' were exerting their influence throughout German society. A reading of other sources results in a more balanced assessment highlighting the considerable degree of support for the 'Third Reich' by the late 1930s.[36]

Rather than telling us something about popular opinion, the source extract testifies to the ideological mindset and institutional agenda of the SD. These well-educated hardliners attempted to reshape the German public and create a homogenous *Volk*.[37] They measured everything they perceived against the yardstick of complete loyalty to Nazi principles. Consequently, they condemned any social activity outside the party and its branches as a 'counterweight'.[38] To them, an exhibition of Chinese painting on a 'German' occasion was evidence of a potentially dangerous lack of ideological conviction. And they had no patience for 'empty' and 'erotic' films and popular tunes, in contrast to the much more pragmatic Propaganda Minister Goebbels. While he and other Nazi leaders were content with compliance and outward signs of involvement, the SD expected true conviction from each and every 'Aryan' German. The authors of the report were outraged by the fact that one single teacher had dared define himself outside of the Nazi framework and, worse, as a 'free-thinking individualist'. While this man could be disciplined, business leaders' lack of ideological purity seemed a much bigger problem. After all, it was not possible to send all these people to concentration camps, due to their economic importance and social influence. The Nazi regime had to win them over, all the more since it required their participation for war mobilisation.

The concept 'liberalistic', as opposed to the more narrowly political 'liberal', served as a catch-all formula for any unpolitical or self-interested attitude. It identified such attitudes with the still all too prominent but ultimately outdated mindset of the 'system period' pre-1933. Thus, the report told a morality tale of old, stubborn and egotistic forces jeopardising the heroic project of reshaping Germany. Furthermore, the concept 'liberalistic' was closely related to the SD's radical anti-Semitism. One page later, the SD pointed out that many middle-class Germans had not concurred with Nazi ideology and voiced their reservations about the pogrom of 9 November 1938. It was important for the Nazi hardliners to dismiss both the widespread concern about the destruction of property and the ethically motivated dismay about the treatment of a minority. Hence the stern comment: 'Out of a liberalistic attitude many thought they had to stand up openly for Jewry.'[39] According to this view, the 'liberalistic' heirs of Weimar Germany were an intolerable barrier to the total elimination of Jews from society. At the same time, the term was used as a binary distinction serving to obscure the widespread popular rejection of the pogrom.[40] For a 'liberalistic' stance was by definition opposed to a 'German' one; whoever was not in favour of anti-Jewish policy was fundamentally wrong. In turn, the Jewish influence was time and again held responsible for potential or real opposition to the Nazi ideology.[41] Only if it was overcome could the identity of Germans and Nazis be complete.

This tied in with the SD's institutional agenda.[42] For years, the security service had strengthened its position amidst the different agencies that were dealing with the Jewish minority. It had pursued the line that Jews should be forced to leave the country through systematic isolation and pressure. After the pogrom of 9 November 1938, when street violence had caused economic damage as well as led to international protest and domestic criticism, the SD could offer the 'rational' line the Nazi leadership needed to reduce the Jewish presence in German society. The 'scientific' approach to ideological questions which the well-educated hardliners claimed for themselves had proven successful in terms of actual institutional influence. But this position always had to be justified and expanded. For this, it was, as usual in the 'Third Reich', necessary to frame it in the most radical terms. At the same time, the SD in particular had to assume a seemingly objective standpoint, which is very much reflected in the detached style of our source. The surveillance reports were attempts to produce such a 'reality effect' inside the framework of the Nazi state. To strengthen the security service's institutional position as well as to maintain its own drive to rid society of Jews and to purify Germans' attitudes the authors had to insist on the lasting significance of 'liberalistic influences'.

## Conclusion

The initial hope that popular opinion in Nazi Germany and Stalinist Russia could be discovered through a reading of surveillance reports has only partly been fulfilled. The historians who took this approach have fruitfully explored and contrasted a variety of reports by different institutions and from different perspectives. They have used reports compiled and written on a regional or local level to detail and correct the highly aggregated summaries on a whole country. Such a careful and critical reading has resulted in several important monographs. However, other historians have noted the persistent tendency of the reporting agencies to focus on, and thus overrate, instances of dissent. This was due to their security mission, their institutional agendas as well as their commitment to an ideal of total conformity. This still does not prevent us from drawing careful conclusions, on the basis of local and regional reports rather than of aggregated ones on a national level.[43] But it also suggests alternative readings.

Surveillance reports can be interesting for what they reveal about the observation of society by the modern state. While in the nineteenth century, the focus lay mostly on compliance and non-compliance, the First World War marks a shift towards a more activist understanding of surveillance. States now attempted to influence popular attitudes, to shape their citizens' hearts and minds. The reports were an integral part of this project, which the Nazi and Stalinist governments radicalised but did not invent. As the analysis of the extract from an SD report has demonstrated, historians should look at how the ideological mindset governed the perception of consent or dissent and resulted in certain concepts and binary distinctions. They should also include the dynamic context in which the respective agency pursued its institutional agenda by compiling reports. In this particular case, the ubiquity of 'liberalistic influences' reflected the SD's ambition to create a homogenous, morally and racially pure *Volk* while expanding its own position in the framework of the Nazi state.

Writing and compiling surveillance reports on oppositional activities and popular attitudes is a practice that is typical of authoritarian states. This is why after the Second World War it was continued in the Eastern Bloc but replaced by the commissioning of opinion polls in democratic Western Europe. However, this is not necessarily definitive. We are currently witnessing an increase in state surveillance on the European continent, in Great Britain and the United States. It is likely that reports will result from this surveillance – and that they will interest future historians.

## Notes

1 See A. Gleason, *Totalitarianism. The Inner History of the Cold War*, New York: Oxford University Press, 1995.
2 Classic statements of this shift include M. Broszat, *The Hitler State. The Foundation and Development of the Internal Structure of the Third Reich*, London: Longman, 1981; G.T. Rittersporn, *Stalinist Simplifications and Soviet Complications. Social Tensions and Political Conflicts in the USSR, 1933–1953*, Reading: Harwood, 1991.
3 See, for instance, J. Riordan (ed.), *Letters from the Dead. Last Letters from Soviet Men and Women Who Died Fighting the Nazis (1941–1945)*, Amsterdam: Fredonia, 2003.
4 L.D. Stokes. 'Otto Ohlendorf, the Sicherheitsdienst and public opinion in Nazi Germany', in G.L. Mosse (ed.), *Police Forces in History*, London: Sage Publications, 1975, pp. 231–261; Arthur L. Smith, Jr., 'Life in Wartime Germany: Colonel Ohlendorf's Opinion Service', *Public Opinion Quarterly* 36, 1972, 1–7.
5 M. Steinert, *Hitler's War and the Germans. Public Mood and Attitude during the Second World War*, Athens: Ohio University Press, 1977.
6 I. Kershaw, *Popular Opinion and Political Dissent in the Third Reich: Bavaria 1933–1945*, Oxford: Clarendon Press, 1983.
7 Ibid., p. 6.
8 Ibid., p. 10.
9 D. Bankier, *The Germans and the Final Solution. Public Opinion under Nazism*, Oxford: Blackwell, 1992 came up with similar findings but emphasised more strongly than Kershaw the underlying anti-Semitic consensus in German society.
10 I. Kershaw, *The 'Hitler Myth'. Image and Reality in the Third Reich*, Oxford: Oxford University Press, 1989.
11 S. Davies, *Popular Opinion in Stalin's Russia. Terror, Propaganda and Dissent, 1934–1941*, Cambridge: Cambridge University Press, 1997, p. 17. I should like to thank Malte Rolf for his briefing on the interpretation of Stalinism.
12 R. Gellately, 'Review of Ian Kershaw, *Popular Opinion and Political Dissent in the Third Reich: Bavaria 1933–1945*', *JMH* 57, 1985, 169–172, 171.
13 P. Fritzsche, 'Where Did All the Nazis Go? Reflections on Resistance and Collaboration', *Tel Aviver Jahrbuch für deutsche Geschichte* 23, 1994, 191–214. See also Fritzsche, *Germans into Nazis*, Cambridge, Mass.: Harvard University Press, 1998.
14 R. Gellately, *Backing Hitler. Consent and Coercion in Nazi Germany*, Oxford: Oxford University Press, 2001.
15 See the reviews by P. Kenez, *AHR* 103, 1998, 1658; M. Lenoe, *JMH* 71, 1999, 789–791; J.J. Rossman, *Russian Review* 58, 1999, 157–158.
16 S. Kotkin, 'Review of S. Davies, *Popular Opinion in Stalin's Russia. Terror, Propaganda and Dissent, 1934–1941*', *Europe-Asia Studies* 50, 1998, 739–742, 740; J. Hellbeck, 'Speaking Out: Languages of Affirmation and Dissent in Stalinist Russia', *Kritika: Explorations in Russian and Eurasian History* 1, 2000, 71–96, 76–79. For elaborations of the authors' viewpoints, see S. Kotkin, *Magnetic Mountain. Stalinism as a Civilization*, Berkeley: University of California Press, 1995; J. Hellbeck, *Revolution on My Mind. Writing a Diary under Stalin*, Cambridge, Mass: Harvard University Press, 2006.
17 P. Holquist, '"Information is the Alpha and Omega of Our Work": Bolshevik Surveillance in Its Pan-European Context', *JMH* 69, 1997, 415–450.
18 Ibid., 443–450.
19 For the following, see A. Farge, *Fragile Lives. Violence, Power and Solidarity in*

*Eighteenth-Century Paris*, Cambridge: Polity, 1993; A. Farge, *Subversive Words. Public Opinion in Eighteenth-Century France*, Cambridge: Cambridge University Press, 1994.

20  See H.E. Bödeker, 'On the Origins of the "Statistical Gaze": Modes of Perceptions, Forms of Knowledge and Ways of Writing in the Early Social Sciences', in P. Becker (ed.), *Little Tools of Knowledge: Historical Essays on Academic and Bureaucratic Practices*, Ann Arbor: Michigan University Press, 2001, pp. 169–195; L. Raphael, *Recht und Ordnung. Herrschaft durch Verwaltung im 19. Jahrhundert*, Frankfurt: Fischer, 2000, pp. 76–93.

21  J.W. Daly, *Autocracy under Siege. Security Police and Opposition in Russia 1866–1905*, DeKalb: Northern Illinois University Press, 1998, p.135, p.103.

22  Ibid., pp. 138–180.

23  See R.J. Evans (ed.), *Kneipengespräche im Kaiserreich. Stimmungsberichte der Hamburger Politischen Polizei 1892–1914*, Reinbek bei Hamburg: Rowohlt, 1989.

24  Quoted in B. Le Clère and V. Wright, *Les préfets du Second Empire*, Paris: Armand Colin, 1973, p. 58.

25  B. Chapman, *The Prefects and Provincial France*, London: Allen and Unwin, 1955, p. 37.

26  D. Laven, 'Law and Order in Habsburg Venetia, 1814–1835', *HJ* 39, 1996, 383–403, 400–401.

27  Léon Mirman, prefect of Meurthe-et-Moselle, to minister of the interior, 29 December 1917, quoted in J.-J. Becker, *1914: Comment les Français sont entrés dans la guerre. Contribution à l'étude de l'opinion publique printemps-été 1914*, Paris: Presses de la Fondation nationale des sciences politiques, 1977, p. 13. Similar to Kershaw, Becker is confident that despite this prefect's reservations, it is possible to get at public opinion by comparing surveillance reports of different types and from different regions. See also, in English, his *The Great War and the French People*, Leamington Spa: Berg, 1985.

28  Quoted in Holquist, '"Information is the Alpha and Omega of Our Work"', 428.

29  M. Föllmer, 'Senior Civil Servants and Nationalism in Germany, 1900–1933', forthcoming in P. Becker and R. von Krosigk (eds), *Figures of Authority. Contributions towards a Cultural History of Governance from the 17th to the 20th Centuries*, Berlin: Peter Lang, 2008; see also R. Bessel, *Germany after the First World War*, Oxford: Clarendon, 1993, pp. 238–253.

30  N. Hiley, 'Counter-Espionage and Security in Great Britain during the First World War', *EHR* 101, 1986, 635–670; D. Englander, 'Military Intelligence and the Defence of the Realm: The Surveillance of Soldiers and Civilians during the First World War', *Bulletin of the Society for the Study of Labour History* 52, 1987, 24–32.

31  K. Jeffery, 'The British Army and Internal Security 1919–1939', *HJ* 24, 1981, 377–397, 380; R. Thurlow, *The Secret State. British Internal Security in the Twentieth Century*, Oxford: Blackwell, 1994, pp. 107–113.

32  I. McLaine, *Ministry of Morale. Homefront Morale and the Ministry of Information in World War Two*, London: Allen & Unwin, 1979; P. Summerfield, 'Mass-Observation: Social Research or Social Movement', *Journal of Contemporary History* 20, 1985, 439–452, 444–449.

33  For the following, see D. Childs and R. Popplewell, *The Stasi. The East German Intelligence and Security Service*, Houndsmills: Macmillan Press, 1999, pp. 174–192.

34  Stasi report, 10 May 1989, quoted ibid., p. 184.

35  'Jahreslagebericht 1938', in H. Boberach (ed.), *Meldungen aus dem Reich 1938–1945. Die geheimen Lageberichte des Sicherheitsdienstes der SS*, vol. 2, Herrsching: Pawlak, 1984, pp. 7–214, pp. 71–72.

36  See, based on a critical interpretation of the reports by the Social Democratic exile organisation, B. Stöver, *Volksgemeinschaft im Dritten Reich. Die Konsensbereitschaft der Deutschen aus der Sicht sozialistischer Exilberichte*, Düsseldorf: Droste, 1993.

37 See P. Longerich, *"Davon haben wir nichts gewusst!". Die Deutschen und die Judenverfolgung 1933–1945*, Munich: Siedler, 2006, pp. 45–50.
38 For similar perceptions in Gestapo reports, see M. Föllmer, 'The Problem of National Solidarity in Interwar Germany', *German History* 23, 2005, 202–231, 224–226.
39 'Jahreslagebericht 1938', p. 73.
40 See the most recent assessment by Longerich, *"Davon haben wir nichts gewusst!"*, pp. 129–135.
41 A prime example is 'Bericht über den Stand der Arbeiten der Abtlg. II 112 in der Bekämpfung des Judentums', 28 August 1936, reprinted in M. Wildt (ed.), *Die Judenpolitik des SD 1935 bis 1938. Eine Dokumentation*, Munich: Oldenbourg, 1995, pp. 94–95. See also Föllmer, 'The Problem of National Solidarity', p. 228.
42 For the following, see the introduction to Wildt (ed.), *Die Judenpolitik des SD*. An excellent analysis of the broader context in which the SD operated is M. Geyer, 'The Nazi State Reconsidered', in R. Bessel (ed.), *Life in the Third Reich*, Oxford: Oxford University Press, 1987, pp. 57–67.
43 See especially Longerich, *"Davon haben wir nichts gewusst!"*.

## Select bibliography

Bödeker, H.E., 'On the Origins of the "Statistical Gaze": Modes of Perceptions, Forms of Knowledge and Ways of Writing in the Early Social Sciences', in P. Becker (ed.), *Little Tools of Knowledge: Historical Essays on Academic and Bureaucratic Practices*, Ann Arbor: Michigan University Press, 2001, pp. 169–195.

Childs, D. and Popplewell, R., *The Stasi. The East German Intelligence and Security Service*, Houndsmills: Macmillan Press, 1999.

Daly, J.W., *Autocracy under Siege. Security Police and Opposition in Russia 1866–1905*, DeKalb: Northern Illinois University Press, 1998.

Davies, S., *Popular Opinion in Stalin's Russia. Terror, Propaganda and Dissent, 1934–1941*, Cambridge: Cambridge University Press, 1997.

Englander, D., 'Military Intelligence and the Defence of the Realm: Tthe Surveillance of Soldiers and Civilians during the First World War', *Bulletin of the Society for the Study of Labour History* 52, 1987, 24–32.

Farge, A., *Subversive Words. Public Opinion in Eighteenth-Century France*, Cambridge: Cambridge University Press, 1994.

Fritzsche, P., 'Where Did All the Nazis Go? Reflections on Resistance and Collaboration', *Tel Aviver Jahrbuch für deutsche Geschichte* 23, 1994, 191–214.

Holquist, P., '"Information is the Alpha and Omega of Our Work": Bolshevik Surveillance in Its Pan-European Context', *JMH* 69, 1997, 415–450.

Kershaw, I, *Popular Opinion and Political Dissent in the Third Reich: Bavaria 1933–1945*, Oxford: Clarendon Press, 1983.

Schrecker, Ellen, *Many are the Crimes: McCarthyism in America*, Princeton: Princeton University Press, 1998.

Stokes, L.D., 'Otto Ohlendorf, the Sicherheitsdienst and Public Opinion in Nazi Germany', in G.L. Mosse (ed.), *Police Forces in History*, London: Sage Publications, 1975, pp. 231–261.

Theoharis, Athan G., *The FBI & American Democracy. A Brief Critical History*, Lawrence: Kansas University Press, 2004.

Thurlow, Richard C., *The Secret State. British Internal Security in the Twentieth Century*, Oxford: Blackwell, 1995.

# 5   Court Files

*Claudia Verhoeven*

## Law and history

The earliest peoples supposedly saw the source of the law as being with the gods: 'Anu and Bel called by name me, Hammurabi, the exalted prince, who feared God, to bring about the rule of righteousness' and 'When he had finished speaking with Moses on Mount Sinai, the Lord gave him the two tablets of the Testimony, stone tablets written with the finger of God.'[1] Historians, however, know that law emerged at a certain stage of civilization, say, some time in the beginning: countless college courses covering the *longue durée* of western history start with the Law Code of Hammurabi or the Ten Commandments. All that has happened in human history, it seems, happened on account of the law.

No sooner was there law, though, than there were law-breakers – sometimes quite literally:

> As he approached the camp, Moses saw the bull-calf and the dancing, and in a burst of anger he flung down the tablets and shattered them at the foot of the mountain . . . and about three thousand of the people died that day.[2]

Thus there is law and then there is something called higher law, which is invoked in the event of an emergency (for example, as in Exodus, idolatry and revelry) so that the law may be suspended (tablets that read 'Thou shalt not kill' are smashed, then three thousand people are killed) in order, ultimately, to be preserved (the political community is restored). From the point of view of the people, though, neither law nor higher law may look very lawful at all; consequently, there exists a long and venerable tradition of resorting to what the law calls 'lawlessness' (revolt, rebellion, or revolution). The point is: there is no one law; there are only laws, and they are not equal for all, nor are they intended to be.

But what does seem to be equal – across time – is that people refer their actions to law. Standards, norms, and rules exist in every society, and they can be observed, bent, or broken (however un-, pre-, or consciously). And this is why, for historians, the archives of the law hold such potential: they document how past peoples thought they should be *and* how they were, their ideals *and* their realities, theories *and* practice, rules *and* exceptions – which is to say that these archives present as near perfect a picture as possible of any given past.

This chapter addresses one aspect of these archives of the law: court files. It introduces their content and form, surveys how various historians have approached them, and draws out some of the problems involved in their interpretation. Then the chapter turns to a case study – the nineteenth-century trials of Russian revolutionary terrorists – and concludes with some thoughts on the law in modern history.

## Content and form

Like everything else, court files have a history, and this history began in the late middle ages. In older times, there was law, of course, but there were no real court files: Hammurabi's Code, for example, is a rich index of ancient Babylonian jurisdiction, but it includes no data-bank of cases. For court files, there are two basic requirements: one, that there is a 'court' that lords over crime and punishment, and two, that there are files, i.e. that there is a somewhat extensive written culture tracking the individual crimes. These requirements were first fulfilled by the Inquisition: in redirecting jurisprudence away from customs that were oral and open towards a culture of conducting criminal inquiries in camera, inquisitorial justice produced history's first proper – and, as is well-known, problematic – court files.[3] Thence developed our source, in accord with changes wrought by the switch from inquisitorial to adversarial justice, into its modern form.

Modern court files contain several sorts of sources. Usually, these include interrogation records; indictments; testimonies; speeches by the prosecution and for the defense; and then verdicts. Additionally, however, they may hold official memoranda and communiqués, legal briefs, procedural protocols, stenographic transcripts, supplications, and evidence, which in the modern period can mean criminal statistics and physiognomic 'facts', psychiatric profiles, telltale letters, smoking guns, bloody bullets, pharmaceutical samples, clothing, clots of hair, and so on and so on (or, when the materials no longer exist, references to these in the form of lists).

Some files, of course, are more complete, or more complex, or more diverse than others. For example, the investigation into the April 4, 1866, attempted assassination of Tsar Alexander II produced more than six thousand archival deposits. On the other hand, minor *lèse majesté* cases triggered by April 4 (say, the case of Timofei Krysa, a peasant, accused of having grumbled in a village tavern, 'Too bad they didn't kill him [the tsar]') may be entirely minimalist, at times consisting of no more than some summary sheets.[4] But historians must make do with what they have: 'The past is their tyrant,' as Marc Bloch wrote. 'It forbids them to know anything which it has not itself, consciously or otherwise, yielded to them.'[5] Governed by contingency (from accidental loss and damage to wilful destruction, judicial customs, and archival traditions), the content of court files is beyond the historian's control.

Nevertheless, skimpy as sometimes they may be, court files can be among the few primary sources that actually grant access to the world of popular culture, which is precisely why twentieth-century historians turned to them in the first place. So while it is true that the only time that Timofei Krysa appeared on the historical radar was when he was drunk enough to trip over the wires of the law and that, indeed, the archives may reveal nothing about what a fine figure he could have cut in sobriety, it is also simply the case that there he is, this Timofei – and it turns out he was not, as was long held about all Russian peasants, glad of the Tsar. At least since the 1960s, this has mattered to historians. But more on that below.

The multiplicity of content is surely one of the main challenges presented by court files, because, in turn, it implies a multiplicity of form. Each of the above-listed sources has its own logic, is constructed according to the rules of its own genre. Ideally, the historian learns these rules – mostly by reading widely, deeply, and slowly. Regarding this requirement, court files do not differ from whatever other source; it is just that they may present the historian with many more rules to learn. Moreover, these rules can be quite formal, so studying their application in concrete cases presupposes some familiarity with the procedures of the relevant legal system.

And yet, arguably, there is a qualitative difference, too. This has to do with the objectives and hazards involved in the creation of these sources. What is the purpose of a court case? Basically, to prove whether something alleged really happened, whether a certain subject committed a certain – illegal, mostly – act. Two important implications follow from this for the source base.

First, the sources are characterized by a high degree of intention, but it tends to be so that none of these intentions coincide; in fact, they often diametrically oppose one another. The testimony of someone falsely accused has a radically different aim from the speeches of the prosecution or the letters of the guilty supplicant. The result can induce a certain *Rashomon* effect: as in Akira Kurosawa's film, a case can be narrated from multiple, mutually exclusive points of view, leaving the historian with a dizzying sense of perspectivalism that seems to bar access to the truth.

Second, court files can be riddled by deliberate distortion. A great example of a blatant lie comes from testimonies of Ivan Khudiakov, who was trying to deny knowing Karakozov (Alexander II's failed 1866 tsaricide), whom in fact he knew well enough. Khudiakov, over the course of a single paragraph, names him, 'Kozyrev or Korozov, Korazov . . . Kozyrev or Karozov . . . some sick guy. That Korozy or Kozyrev (or Kozyrev, Koryzov, ~~Kozarev~~, ******, Korozovy).'[6] Most lies, however, are more difficult to detect, and thus present yet another obstacle to the truth. But the important point is that the very fact of deliberate distortion should serve as a reminder of what is probably the most essential fact about any trial: in whatever form, it is someone's life that is at stake. Khudiakov, for one, because he did know Karakozov, ended up in Siberia, where within a few years he got lost in his mind and then died.

In sum, it is true that court files are but a source like all others and, as such, require a hermeneutic approach like all others. And yet there is a sense in which court files push to the surface certain questions that are perhaps more grave. It is rare to read these sources and *not* wonder: What is a trial? What is proof? Law? Justice? Truth, then? And who decides all this?

## Historiography

It was not for history's most famous trials that the use of court files came to be rethought: not, say, for Socrates, or Christ, or even Louis XVI. Nor was it done, really, for anything modern: not for the Dreyfus Affair (1890s and 1900s), the 'Moscow Trials' (1936–38), or the Nuremberg Trials (1945–46). Rather, it was historians of medieval and early modern Europe who pioneered the new approach, and they did so largely for the sake of the historically marginal: workers, women, witches, etc.

All this began in the 1960s, when the practitioners of what would come to be known as *microstoria* (micro-history) and *Alltagsgeschichte* (the history of everyday life) pushed off from the shores of the anonymous and algebraic structures of the then dominant *Annales* school and social science history. They brought with them some of the central assumptions of the *annalistes* and their acquaintances – they were equally unconcerned, for example, with the high politics of kings and kin, and equally concerned, instead, with popular culture – but sought to move back to the centre of investigation individual subjects' experience of historical events. For example, in *The Night Battles* (1966) – one of the earliest works of micro-history and, significantly, one to make extensive use of court files – Carlo Ginzburg explicitly set off his emphasis on 'a rich variety of individual attitudes and behaviour' against an approach that would stress 'such general and vague terms as "collective mentality", or "collective psychology"', which were mainstays of *Annales* history.[7]

Where, though, to obtain evidence of the 'individual attitudes and behavior' of subjects who went unrecorded in the chronicles? This is where the law comes in: for centuries, the law caught in its nets and then preserved in its archives the likes of Timofei Krysa. 'Why then choose letters of remission?' asks Natalie Zemon Davis, eminent micro-historian and the author of *The Return of Martin Guerre* (1983) and *Fiction in the Archives* (1987). 'Because they are one of the best sources of relatively uninterrupted narrative from the lips of the lower orders.'[8] The law, for historians, is the largest accidental archive of whatever traditional historiography neglected to record.

What was innovative about the way these historians used court files? Certainly they were not the first to realize that the archives of the law existed. It had long been held, however, that these archives – and especially its court files – were the product of elite culture and could reveal nothing about those under investigation. The Inquisition, for one, was seen as an ignominious institution that imposed its views on anyone unfortunate enough to come into contact with it, and its sources were thus utterly worthless for the study of popular culture. A difference in degree, not kind, characterized what was assumed about other courts of law and the documents they produced.

To clarify this issue, take, for example, interrogation records. Depending (on the judicial tradition, literacy of the suspect, etc.), these are either transcriptions of oral interviews or depositions written out by the suspects themselves. In the first case, unless the transcriptions are verbatim, the original voices may largely be lost. For transcription is translation: the spoken idiom is converted into a written language whose form may have little to do with the suspect's style, which in turn is the suspect's truth (or at least the truth of the suspect's culture). Even in the second case, though, the depositions may not be *sui generis*. Often, they followed lengthy interviews or were overdetermined by set questionnaires, and the interrogators' questions imposed distinct narrative restraints on the testimonials. Thus, like the transcriptions, written depositions, too, can only be read through the grid of investigative procedure and the socio-cultural filters of those conducting the investigation. But is there any getting beyond these grids and filters? Most practitioners of micro-history believe there is, but they had to return to court files armed with a cache of new reading strategies and a new set of questions in order to prove it.

The new reading strategies and questions may be best introduced through their infamous absence in one of the best-known works to use court files, Emmanuel Le Roy Ladurie's *Montaillou: Promised Land of Error* (1978). Upon publication, *Montaillou* was exceptionally well-received by scholars and the reading public alike. Its immense popularity in France provided an impetus for the work's rapid translation into a condensed, English version, which was enthusiastically reviewed by Charles Wood in the *American Historical Review*. Wood lauded *Montaillou* as a work that had done 'more to enrich our understanding of life in the Middle Ages than any book since Marc Bloch's *La société féodale* (1939)'.[9] Wood particularly commended the work's innovative use of inquisitorial records, from which Le Roy Ladurie had reconstructed a total history of life in the early fourteenth-century mountain village of Montaillou. Initially causing *Montaillou* to be heralded as an instant classic of *Annales* history, it has been Le Roy Ladurie's approach to the source that has since had to sustain the most vigorous critiques. For what occurs on the pages of *Montaillou*, critics contend, may be characterized as a *writing over* or an *erasing of* the historical source, its referents, and its production – rather troubling for historians concerned with liberating the authentic voices of the past.

Hence the question of Le Roy Ladurie's approach to his source, or the question of method, on which the author remains largely silent – problematic since his source is in fact highly complex. Le Roy Ladurie's source, the so-called Fournier Register, came into existence when Bishop Jacques Fournier determined to root out a last revival of the Cathar heresy in southern France; it consists of 114 inquisitorial dialogues between Fournier, his accused, and witnesses. Spurred on by Fournier's insatiable appetite for details, the villagers' testimonials are littered with the descriptions of their daily lives, customs, and cosmologies that form the bedrock of Le Roy Ladurie's history.

The lacking explication of method raises a host of problems all in one way or another concerned with the multiplicity of filters that separate the modern reader from the villagers. Can the ecclesiastic linguistic conventions of the scribes accurately capture the mentalities of the villagers? How do the translations impede our access to authentic village voices? To what extent were villagers' descriptions determined by the guidance of questions? In his brief biographical sketch of the zealous Bishop, Le Roy Ladurie relates that, 'the whole Pamiers Inquisition Register bears the brand of [Fournier's] constant intervention'.[10] It is noteworthy then that after the reader is told that Fournier's intervention is constant, the Bishop largely disappears from the pages of *Montaillou*. The exclusion of his questions is particularly problematic since it complicates the reader's ability to assess not only the process of production of the villagers' description of daily life but ultimately also the conclusions drawn by the historian.

*Montaillou* has thus been criticized as a methodologically informed work that refuses to spell out its methods; that celebrates the richness of its source while obscuring it from the reader's view; and that illuminates the practices of long lost historical actors while it erases the dialogical context in which they spoke and lived. To avoid such paradoxical pitfalls, the historians whose innovative work with court files is discussed below explicate their method and deconstruct the production of the sources by highlighting their (1) dialogical nature; (2) narrative emplotment; and (3) cultural presuppositions. As stated above, these approaches were pioneered by early modernists (which is why works by Ginzburg and Zemon Davis have been included in the discussion), but for some twenty years now, historians have also been using them to analyse court files made in modernity.

## Examples: dialogics, emplotment, and the collective cultural unconscious

To move beyond elite 'representations' and 'perceptions' of popular culture, historians developed a reading strategy directed at uncovering the dialogical nature of their sources. Sometimes influenced by the work of literary scholars like Mikhail Bakhtin (particularly *The Dialogic Imagination*, written in the 1930s, but not published in English until the early 1980s), these historians hold that all texts, even the most seemingly monological, are in fact multivocal, and therefore multi-perspectival: other voices always sneak in, and it is the task of the historian to locate those voices, which, in turn, evidence alternate realities.[11] This strategy has been very gainfully employed by scholars engaged in exhuming from the archives of the law worlds long thought to be all, and permanently, dead.

Foremost among advocates of the dialogical approach is Carlo Ginzburg. Over the years, Ginzburg's method has become increasingly explicit, but his concern has always been, since his earliest work, with what he calls a 'gap' or 'discrepancy': evidence in the text of an irreducible difference between conflicting voices and realities.[12] For Ginzburg, a text is never 'only evidence of itself', or of the author's intentions: 'a conflicting cultural reality may leak out even from such heavily con-trolled texts as inquisitorial trials.'[13] Thus, for example, in *The Night Battles*, which excavates and traces the disappearance of the *benandanti* fertility cult in the Friuli between 1570 and 1640, Ginzburg collects, from the mismatch between the inquisitors' questions and the suspects' answers, traces of an autonomous peasant mentality, 'which was later deformed, and then expunged by the superimposition of the schema of the educated classes'.[14]

A fine example in this tradition but applied to the modern period is Regina Schulte's *The Village in Court* (1989). By unpacking criminal cases of arson, infanti-cide, and poaching, Schulte excavates the world of late nineteenth-century Bavarian peasants from underneath the projections of contemporaries and scholars alike.[15]

Now for studies centred on court files' emplotment. Decidedly post-linguistic turn, Zemon Davis's *Fiction in the Archives* knows that, 'shaping choices of language, detail, and order are needed' to achieve the requisite 'reality effect' (Barthes), but further suggests that people in the past knew this, too.[16] Analysing the storytelling skills of sixteenth-century people where they needed them most – in the highly literary petitions for the king's pardon from capital crimes – Zemon Davis uncovers the range of narrative patterns and plots that constituted the norms of a pardonable exception to the rule of law.

As legal tender, letters of remission had a standard form determined by the cultural elite ('*Francois, etc. Be it known to all present and to come. We have received the humble supplication of A,*' etc.), yet Zemon Davis insists that the true voices of the supplicants are preserved – and preserved precisely in the letters' fictive elements.[17] The supplicants are most like themselves when they are spinning stories, for there were characteristic peasant, artisan, and gentleman tales: 'When the learned Etienne Dolet tells a story to get pardoned for the printing of heretical books, he sounds different from the plowman Thomas Manny [who stoned and stabbed his faithless wife to death].'[18] There are common plot points, too: feast days (signal that the crimes happen outside normal time), uninvited guests (signal that they happen on the edge of social norms), and sudden outbreaks of 'hot bile' (that they happen beyond normal emotions). These the letters share with other forms of contemporary literature, with crime pamphlets, for example, but also with Rabelais's *Gargantua and Pantagruel* and Shakespeare's *Romeo and Juliet*. The latter, for one, features uninvited guests (Romeo and Benvolio) at a feast (the Capulets' masked ball), 'hot bile' (Tybalt's choler, Romeo's fury), and then death. But as Shakespeare's context differs (from that of Rabelais, crime pamphlet writers and pardon tale tellers), these elements are ordered into a different narrative constellation: 'hot bile' may pardon Thomas Manny in France, but 'does not serve as a sufficient excuse for pardoning, neither for the prince of Verona nor, for that matter, for the English law'.[19] Thus, as with the tales characteristic of various estates, the limits of each genre are exposed by its difference from the next. As such it matters who is speaking, when, where, and under what circumstances: specific subjects are not subsumed by the general context.

Sarah Maza has likewise looked at the link between literature and legalese, and done so for the modern period. In *Private Lives and Public Affairs: The Causes Célèbres of Prerevolutionary France* (1993), she examines the publicity surrounding sensational courtroom cases in order to make a larger argument about the emergence of the public sphere in the eighteenth century. The making of the modern public happened, she shows, against the background of a causes célèbres craze: the development of the new politico-juridical consciousness was mediated by the consumption of published 'legal briefs' (*mémoires judiciaires*). Regularly devoured by the reading public, the trial briefs were popular, Maza argues, because of their fictionalized form – which the lawyers borrowed from popular literature. For example, the brief of the defence lawyer Jean Blondel, writes Maza in 'The Diamond Necklace Affair, 1785–1786', is 'a consummate piece of dramatic writing'.[20] Blondel's accounts are crammed with theatrical terms ('*scène, jouer, représenter, personnage*'), all in an effort to convince the court that the *affaire* was a play staged by the main culprit, Jeanne de La Motte (and thus not by Blondel's client, Nicole Le Guay).[21] More specifically, Blondel's template for the briefs was *opéra-comique*: 'The Diamond Necklace Affair offered a complicated plot, disguises and mistaken identities, purloined letters, elegant settings, and luscious female characters.'[22] And most specifically, it was Beaumarchais's *Marriage of Figaro* (1784). When readers consumed Blondel's briefs, therefore, they swallowed whole the gender bias of a literary tradition dating back to Rousseau's misogynistic *Letter to d'Alembert* (1758) – with devastating effects for the place of women in the public sphere in both pre- and post-revolutionary France.

Finally, historians might select an especially extraordinary trial, sift its paperwork for discursive tics, and thence re- and/or deconstruct the case's unspoken cultural context. Here, the idea is that the key concepts used to make sense of the unprecedented will reveal that culture's presuppositions about what constitutes ordinary and/or acceptable behavior. In these cases, that is, the exception proves the rule. The example chosen to represent this last approach focuses on *fin-de-siècle* France and uncovers the covert gender politics operating during the period.

Just before World War I, Henriette Caillaux went to trial for shooting Gaston Calmette, editor of *Le Figaro*; her point was to avenge the honour of her husband, former French prime minister, Joseph Caillaux, whose reputation *Le Figaro* had done everything to besmirch. But was this a political crime or a 'crime of passion', that most female of nineteenth-century crimes – and the surest guarantee of an acquittal? After generations of historians fought for one side or the other, Edward Berenson's *The Trial of Madame Caillaux* (1992) revisits the scandalous case: irreconcilable as the sides may appear, what really matters is their shared participation in a gendered discourse about crime and politics. To put her away, the lawyer for the Calmette family sought to show that the shooting could not have been a crime of passion, for Henriette was not a 'real woman'; to set her free, the Caillaux's attorney strove to prove that she was precisely that. Whether they agreed that Henriette was a real enough woman or not, the two lawyers – and all of France with them – knew what *une vraie femme* should be: whatever would allow French males to heal the wounds inflicted on their masculinity by the loss of the Franco-Prussian War, the Paris Commune, etc. Thus Berenson can write, 'What gives the Caillaux Affair its continued importance is the extent to which the documents it produced . . . give us access to spheres of the Belle Epoque culture and politics that might otherwise be difficult to discern', for example: the norms of femininity in an age of emerging feminism.[23]

As the early modern turned into the modern and inquisitorial transformed into adversarial justice, the open court with its lawyers, juries, and journalists replaced the closed chambers of the inquisitors as the principal production site of court files. Interrogations and letters of supplications loom large in works by Ginzburg and Zemon Davis, but legal briefs and trial transcripts form the backbone of books by such scholars as Maza and Berenson: while the first set of sources addresses kings and judges, the latter speaks to the people (as public or peers), a difference that clearly reflects the shift in the source of political legitimacy that took place over the last several centuries. Court files from either period can refract the politics of the past, but what was unseen before the age of popular sovereignty, and the dynamics of which only modern court files can illuminate, is the veritable explosion, in modernity, of properly political trials, including the conscious use of the courtroom as a political platform. If there is one place that paradigmatically crystallized this politics of the court room, then this place is Russia. Principally this is so because of the notorious show trials under Stalin, but, as the next section shows, these had their roots in the revolutionary tradition of the imperial period.

## A case study: the trials of the Russian revolutionary terrorists

One of the most visible strands of the Russian revolutionary tradition consists of the celebrated sequence of state crimes committee by the Decembrists (1825), *Petrashevtsy* (1849), *Karakozovtsy* (1866), *Nechaevtsy* (1871), and *Pervomartovtsy* (1881). These are the concept names that have long represented the successive stages of revolutionary history – which is another way of saying that they are but the most famous ones. Indeed, over the course of the late imperial period, thousands were dragged before the tsarist courts for political crimes. Therefore, the political trial is undoubtedly one of the central sites in Russian revolutionary history, and court files among the most important sources for getting at this history.

Some of the most complete sets of court files were first published by the revolutionaries themselves, who were very interested in distributing the documentary record of their own trials. Why? Because the courtroom was the one public space where they could give (more or less) free expression to their political views. That the court could function as such a 'free zone' had to do with the particular circumstances of Russia during the mid-century.

Of all the 'great reforms' implemented during this progressive period of Russian history, the 1864 Judicial Statutes are considered the most far-reaching and successful: they redressed many of the abuses of the old, inquisitorial system and, once they were in place, it took longer to chip away at them again than at, say, freedom of the press laws. The Statutes established all the elements of adversarial justice: an independent court; counsel; orality, controversiality, and publicity; trial by jury; and irremovable judges. The public was enormously enthusiastic about the new courts and extremely curious about their workings, and the press catered to this by providing publications like *Glasnyi Sud* (*The Open Court*) and *Sudebnyi Vestnik* (*The Judicial Herald*) and regularly covering sensational cases. Suffice it to say that in the 1860s and 1870s, all eyes were on the court. For revolutionaries, therefore, the court held great potential as a media outlet: the trial was a chance to spread revolutionary propaganda and use the judicial system as a weapon against the autocracy.

Officialdom, however, quickly caught on, and at the very latest understood the need to start back-pedaling in 1878, when a jury acquitted Vera Zasulich for shooting the governor of St Petersburg. Henceforth, the history of the revolutionary movement shows the extent to which the new legal system was still subject to administrative abuse and autocratic intervention. It became par for the course to try revolutionaries before closed-door military tribunals, snatch away their rights, and execute them out of public sight. Increasingly, newspaper covered political trials with a gloss. Hence the zeal of revolutionary publishing: politicals could sometimes still talk in court, but they could only be heard in public through samizdat.

With some significant exceptions, however, there exist few scholarly treatments of these sources, especially *qua* sources. Partly to plead for their increased use, what follows below takes a closer look at two sets of trial transcripts – those of the 1881 tsaricides and of the 1866 Karakozov case – and specifically at the examples they provide of the use of the court as disputed political space.

The final assassination attempt on the life of Tsar Alexander II took place in broad daylight on Sunday March 1, 1881, on the banks of the Ekaterininsky Canal, right around the corner from St Petersburg's celebrated thoroughfare, Nevsky Prospect. Returning in a closed carriage from an inspection of the Marine Corps, Alexander II was killed by the explosions of two bombs thrown by Nikolai Rysakov and Ignatei Grinevitsky (who later died from wounds received in the blast), both members of the revolutionary group Narodnaia Volia (The People's Will), a.k.a. *Russkaia Sotsial'no-Revoliutsionnaia Partiia* (Russian Social-Revolutionary Party).

Rysakov was arrested on the spot and his trial promptly scheduled for March 3 (note the swift justice!), but then postponed in light of subsequent arrests. Ultimately, the trial of the six *pervomartovtsy* – Andrei Zheliabov, Sofia Perovskaya, Nikolai Kibalchich, Nikolai Rysakov, Timothy Mikhailov, and Gesia Helfman – commenced on the morning of March 26 and was concluded March 28 (again: justice at a clip). The foremost charge against the six reads as follows:

> That they did enter into a secret society calling itself the 'Russian Social-Revolutionary Party', having as its aim to overthrow, by means of a violent upheaval, the existing state and social regime in the Empire, and that the criminal activity of that society led to a series of infringements on the life of His Imperial Majesty; murders and attempted murders of official functionaries; and armed resistance to the powers that be.[24]

On March 28, after two days of witness testimonies, public prosecutor Nikolai V. Murav'ev delivered his prosecution speech, which lasted for about five hours, and, when printed, runs a little over fifty pages. In the end, all six were found guilty, condemned to death, and (except for Helfman, who was pregnant) hanged on April 3.

Both the formalized legal procedures and Murav'ev's rhetorical talents gave the trial a degree of legitimacy it would otherwise have lacked. Having suspended the defendants' right to trial by jury, the government varnished the proceedings with a veneer of legality, not only because it feared reprisals from revolutionary elements, but also because the assassination had unleashed a real media-frenzy both in Russia and abroad. The world-wide attention contributed to the fact that, while a jury trial was out of the question, the plan to hold a quick trial before a closed military district court was abandoned in favor of a public trial before a Special Commission of the Senate.

There exists, however, another explanation for the public nature of the trial. It was, as stated, by this time a known fact that revolutionaries used their trials to promote their politics – and that their idealistic stance often found favor with the public. As such, the Commission was informed that, 'His Imperial Majesty would prefer to see the proceedings made as short as possible; it would be undesirable for the accused to be allowed to make long speeches'; throughout the trial, the strictest measures were upheld to hinder the defendants in using the courtroom as a political platform.[25] Then, instead, the government – represented by Murav'ev – took the floor and promoted *its* politics. Upon deliverance, this exposition of autocratic ideology, including its perception of the revolutionary threat, was then distributed by all newspapers of significance.

Murav'ev's task was tricky. On the one hand, he had to prove that the accused, 'did enter into a secret society', and so on. This was hardly the taxing part, since, in Murav'ev's own words: 'they rush to proclaim that they are members of the party.'[26] However, on the other hand, Murav'ev had to show that, all appearances to the contrary, really, this party was not powerful at all.

In 1881, there were at least 50 active members of *Narodnaia Volia*, about half of whom were agents of the Executive Committee. The most visible of these became the six defendants who actively participated in the March 1 assassination, but there were many others who performed smaller tasks, such as organizing conspiratorial quarters and safe houses, printing the party's underground newspaper, and relaying information. The state, however, could only guess at the actual size of the opposition, and while multiple attempts on the life of the tsar had failed, each contributed to an increasing atmosphere of fear on the part of the authorities. On March 4, the adjutant to Grand Duke Konstantin Nikolaevich Romanov noted in his diary that, '[Petersburgers] have started to say that you won't be able to conquer the nihilists, and in fact the nihilists' rule would be better, so let [the government] grant a constitution.'[27] As Alexander III intended neither to grant a constitution, nor to admit that 'the nihilists would be better', it was imperative to demonstrate that the revolutionary threat could in fact be conquered. Public perception of the terrorists' omnipotence had to be countered.

Murav'ev's claim was simple: *Narodnaia Volia* was a small criminal gang and its Executive Committee a fiction whose agents no longer posed a threat, since all had been arrested. He urged the court to disregard the testimony of Zheliabov, Perovskaya, and Kibalchich, all of whom 'magnify the size [of the party] to fantastic proportions'.[28] It is true that the party, which obviously stood to gain from the impression that it was large and powerful, employed tactics to create an image of itself as effectively being able to penetrate and mobilize all strata of Russian society. More on where it learned these tactics below. But it is also true that the members of *Narodnaia Volia* themselves were partially ignorant of the scope of their support among the Russian people. By all accounts, they were genuinely disappointed and disillusioned when the assassination failed to trigger a mass uprising. The Executive Committee *did* exist, but it had far fewer members than was suspected by the public.

Murav'ev, however, reduced the existence of the Committee to cunning. 'I will simply venture to doubt the existence of the Executive Committee,' he exclaimed.[29] He held that leading members of *Narodnaia Volia*, under the direction of arch-bandit Zheliabov, deliberately created the fiction of the Executive Committee, 'that invisible, mysterious formation, which holds in its hands the strings of the conspiracy, moves people like marionettes, and sends them to their deaths', in order to deceive and intimidate recruits and to frighten the Russian people.[30] Zheliabov's claim to have worked 'under the close control of the Executive Committee', Murav'ev stressed, was a fiction: rather, the myth of the Executive Committee was carefully fabricated by Zheliabov himself to further a cause that served his own relentless ambition and vanity. For example, the process of recruitment to the Executive Committee, according to Murav'ev, occurred as follows: Zheliabov discovered someone 'suitable for participation in the crime', who was then sent to the Executive Committee for approval, and then returned to Zheliabov for training purposes. In other words, as the Executive Committee is a fiction, all procedures are controlled by Zheliabov. Murav'ev thus sought to replace the myth of the revolutionary community with the reality of Zheliabov's scheme to develop around his own person a hierarchically organized, obedient, criminal gang.

In effect, Murav'ev's argument hinged on revealing revolutionary truth as false rhetoric. Hence the red thread of discursive deconstruction that runs through his speech, the repeated efforts to ironically distance himself from the language of the accused:

> The so-called terrorist section of the working group or, using the defendants' technical expression, characteristic enough, 'the fighting working squad' . . . Zheliabov was ordered to occupy himself with the organization of that venture [tsaricide], as the accused love to express themselves in their special, specific language.[31]

All this was meant to rob revolutionary rhetoric of its reality effect. And what would be left, he hoped, after all the terms had been separated, was a very different truth behind the grand conspiracy all Russia thought it knew:

> The well-known union of the defendants . . . which it pleases them to honour with the resplendent name party, which the law calmly calls a criminal, secret society, and which reasonable, honest, but indignant Russian people call an underground band, a gang of political killers.[32]

Thus the revolutionaries were separated from the people, whom they claimed to represent, in the very place where they communed with them: the courts.

Interestingly enough, fifteen years earlier, when the terrorist threat first emerged, officialdom's politico-juridical strategy had been precisely the opposite. Following Karakozov's 1866 attempted assassination of Alexander II, official efforts were directed towards making 'conspiracy' seem as imminent and grand as possible (in order, of course, to secure the state a free hand in sweeping away the political opposition). One of the ways this was accomplished was, again, through language. The files of the Karakozov case clearly show that the words of the accused were always interpreted in such a way that they would fit the official image of the conspiracy. Just one example:

> President of the Court Gagarin: About which society did you tell Ishutin [Karakozov's cousin]?
>
> Khudiakov: I didn't tell him about any society.
>
> Gagarin: Ishutin positively testified: 'My connections with Khudiakov were such as with someone from the Petersburg socialist party, etc.'
>
> Khudiakov: Aside from telling him that I was acquainted with Nozhin, I said nothing about any party.
>
> Gagarin: Yes, now it's easy to point to Nozhin, now that he's dead.
>
> Khudiakov: He was my close friend, yes, and I knew him well, but we had no society of any sort.
>
> Gagarin: Here it talks of your belonging to a socialist party.
>
> Khudiakov: Yes, well, I did belong to a socialist party.
>
> Member of the Court Pinsky: A socialist party constitutes a society.
>
> Khudiakov: Ah, no. There's a big difference. A meeting of people, organized in a certain order, that's what constitutes a society. But a party is just a meeting of people thinking along a certain line.
>
> Pinsky: So finally a party is a meeting of people who meet to discuss various questions, various measures.
>
> Khudiakov: Ah, no, if there will be meetings, it'll already be an organization. We had nothing of the sort.
>
> Member of the Court Oldenburgsky: Who's 'we'?
>
> Khudiakov: Nozhin, Nikolsky, and I.
>
> Pinsky: Every party has a goal, without [a goal] it's not a party.
>
> Khudiakov: We did not have any sort of party; we were just people who saw eye to eye.[33]

During the investigation and the trial, all these terms – society, organization, party, meeting, etc. – were seen as synonymous and stigmatized as conspiratorial. Afterwards, they were even so declared by law. In early 1867, the law revisited article 318 of the Criminal Code, which named as a state crime membership of 'secret societies of whatever denomination' having as their aim to undermine government, law, and order: 'secret societies of whatever denomination' was reworded 'whatever unlawful societies', and these then defined these as 'all gatherings, meetings, groups, associations, circles, collectives, etc., under whatever name they might be existing'.[34]

Fifteen years later, revolutionaries had internalized the official policy of aggrandizing the conspiratorial threat and begun to use it to their own advantage. Thus, Murav'ev's speech at the trial of the 1881 tsaricides must be read not only as a conscious, strategic dismantling of revolutionary propaganda, but also as an unacknowledged emergency measure to seal shut a Pandora's Box of the autocracy's own making.

## Conclusion: law and modernity

Only rather recently did historians of the modern period join their medievalist and early modernist colleagues and turn towards a conscious, concentrated use of court files. As late as 1992, Berenson, in his preface to *The Trial of Madame Caillaux*, could write that the micro-historical methods associated with the use of trial records had not yet been applied to modern cases. Arguably, though, the questions asked of court files by medievalists and early modernists have a lot less urgency in modernity, when the source base for accessing popular culture expanded enormously. Madame Caillaux's trial crystallizes the implicit gender politics of *fin-de-siècle* France, yes, but possibly these politics could have been uncovered through different sources just as well. If this is true – if it is true that modernity 'frees' our source from its status as a means and makes it available, instead, as an end – then the time is right to definitively invert the relationship between history and law. Instead of looking at history through the law, we may now move towards looking at the law through history, which ultimately means moving towards illuminating what has long been mysterious to modernists, namely the very nature of law in modernity. Briefly, by way of concluding, a few words on this.

In many major European languages, the origins of terms for 'law' are literally grounded: they derive from roots meaning 'to place'. The idea is that 'something laid down' developed into law. The English term *law*, for example, derives from the Indo-European *loghom*, the root of which is *legh-*, 'to lie or lay'. Likewise, the German *das Gesetz* (n. 'the law') can be traced to *setzen* (vb. 'to put, place, set'). Law thus means something that was placed, something fixed, and something firm.[35]

This traditional understanding of the law, however, is entirely inadequate for coming to terms with one of the most difficult political problems of the modern period, namely the nature of the law in what used to be called 'totalitarian' states. This is so because under 'totalitarianism', the law loses its fixity and goes airborne; the old law exists in a state of suspension, and meanwhile the laws of history and nature – Marxist or Darwinian – go on the move. There was thus something *essentially* paradoxical about law in Nazi Germany and Stalinist Soviet Russia: these states were not lawful (because they either suspended or ignored all positive laws), but neither were they lawless (because they invoked higher law).[36] Therefore, for example, when Nikolai Bukharin stood accused of conspiracy during the Stalinist show trials, he could in all seriousness appear to be 'innocent in a juridical sense', but 'guilty in a party sense' – and then legally be killed.[37] It has, however, been suggested that this paradox is not peculiar to 'totalitarianism'. This is certainly intimated, for example, by the recent coinage of a logico-juridical *fictio* like 'enemy combatant', which places the person to whom the status applies in a permanent state of exception to the normal rule of law; for the enemy-combatant, the law is lifted indefinitely. Law on the move, this is the implication, may be characteristic for states other than those classified under the 'totalitarian' heading; it may be characteristic for modern states by definition. Consequently, Giorgio Agamben has recently begun to trace the history of the 'state of exception' through the democratic-revolutionary tradition of the last two hundred years.[38]

The implications for the historical analysis of law in modernity have yet to be drawn out. Undoubtedly, however, in this endeavour, court files – and above all those of modernity's many political trials – will be of the essence, and it may well turn out that they, especially, hold one of the keys to unlocking the political logic of the modern age.

## Notes

1   *The Code of Hammurabi*, trans. L.W. King (1910); Exodus 31:18, *The Oxford Study Bible. Revised English Bible with the Apocrypha*, (ed.) M.J. Suggs, K.D. Sakenfeld, J.R. Mueller, New York: Oxford University Press, 1992, p. 94.
2   Exodus 32:19–28, ibid., p. 95.
3   See G. Schwerhoff, *Aktenkundig und gerichtsnotorisch. Einführung in die Historische Kriminalitätsforschung*, Tübingen: Ed. Diskord, 1999, pp. 24–27.
4   Gosudarstvennyi Arkhiv Rossiskoi Federatsii (State Archive of the Russian Federation, hereafter GARF), 1 eks. 1866, fond (collection, hereafter f.) 109, opis' (inventory, hereafter op.) 222, delo (file, hereafter d.) 5, list (page or sheet, hereafter l.) 76.
5   M. Bloch, *The Historian's Craft. Reflections on the Nature and Uses of History and the Techniques and Methods of Those Who Write It*, trans. P. Putnam, New York: Vintage Books, 1953, p. 57.
6   Written testimony Ivan Khudiakov, April 13, 1866. GARF, f. 272, op. 1, d. 11, l. 154.
7   C. Ginzburg, *The Night Battles: Witchcraft and Agrarian Cults in the Sixteenth and Seventeenth Century*, Baltimore: Johns Hopkins University Press, 1983, p. xvii.
8   N. Zemon Davis, *Fiction in the Archives: Pardon Tales and Their Tellers in Sixteenth-Century France*, Stanford: Stanford University Press, 1987, p. 5.
9   C. Wood, 'Montaillou, village occitan de 1294 à 1324', *AHR* 81 (1976), 1090.
10  E. Le Roy Ladurie, *Montaillou: The Promised Land of Error*, trans. B. Bray, New York: Vintage Books, 1978, p. xiii.
11  M.M. Bakhtin, *The Dialogic Imagination: Four Essays*, (ed.) M. Holquist, Austin: University of Texas Press, 1981.
12  See for example Ginzburg's *The Night Battles*, p. xviii; C. Ginzburg, *The Cheese and the Worms: The Cosmos of a Sixteenth-Century Miller*, trans. J. and A. Tedeschi, Baltimore: Johns Hopkins UP, 1980, p. 33; C. Ginzburg, *Clues, Myths and the Historical Method*, trans. J. and A. Tedeschi, Baltimore: Johns Hopkins University Press, 1992, pp. 11 and 160.
13  Ginzburg, *Clues*, p. 161.
14  Ginzburg, *The Night Battles*, p. xviii.
15  R. Schulte, *The Village in Court. Arson, Infanticide, and Poaching in the Court Records of Upper Bavaria, 1848–1910*, Cambridge: Cambridge University Press, 1994.
16  Zemon Davis, *Fiction*, p. 3.
17  Zemon Davis, *Fiction*, p. 16.
18  Zemon Davis, *Fiction*, p. 23.
19  Zemon Davis, *Fiction*, p. 74.
20  S. Maza, *Private Lives and Public Affairs: The Causes Célèbres of Prerevolutionary France*, Berkeley: University of California Press, 1993, p. 198.
21  Maza, *Private Lives*, p. 202.
22  Maza, *Private Lives*, p. 204.
23  E. Berenson, *The Trial of Madame Caillaux*, Berkeley: University of California Press, 1992, p. 7.
24  *Delo 1-go marta 1881 g. Protsess Rysakova, Mikhailova, Gelfman, Kibalchicha, Perovskoi i Zheliabova. Pravitel'stvennyi otchet'*, Odessa, 1906, p. 43.
25  D. Footman, *Red Prelude: A Life of A.I. Zhelyabov*, London: Barrie and Rockliff, 1968, p. 33.

26  *Delo*, p. 151.
27  Cited in P.A. Zaionchkovsky, *The Russian Autocracy in Crisis, 1878–1882*, trans. G.M. Hamburg, Gulf Breeze, Fla.: Academic International Press, 1979, p. 192.
28  *Delo*, p. 154.
29  *Delo*, 159.
30  *Delo*, 159.
31  *Delo*, 157 and 159.
32  *Delo*, 138.
33  *Pokushenie Karakozova. Stenograficheskii otchet po delu D. Karakozova, I. Khudiakova, N. Ishutina i dr.* Ed. M. M. Klevenskii i K. G. Kotel'nikov. Seriia Politicheskie protsessy 60–80 gg. Ed V. V. Maksakov i V. I. Nevskii (Moscow, 1928), Vol. I, pp. 40–41.
34  *Svod zakonov ugolovnykh. Ulozhenie o nakazaniiakh ugolovnykh i ispravitel'nykh 1857–1866,* Moscow, 1867, pp. 113–114; *Polnoe sobranie zakonov Rossiskoi Imperii. Sobranie Vtoroe.* Vol. 42. Otdelenie I. 1867, Saint Petersburg, 1871, p. 330.
35  For further discussion, see E. Benveniste, *Indo-European Language and Society*, Coral Gables: University of Miami Press, 1973, pp. 379–384; *Chambers Dictionary of Etymology*, ed. Robert K. Barnhart, New York: Chambers, 1988, p. 582.
36  For further discussion, see H. Arendt, *Origins of Totalitarianism*, New York: Schocken Books, 2004, pp. 593–603. Originally published in 1966.
37  J.A. Getty and O.V. Naumov, *The Road to Terror. Stalin and the Self-Destruction of the Bolsheviks, 1932–1939*, translations by B. Sher, New Haven: Yale University Press, 1999, p. 323.
38  See G. Agamben, *State of Exception*, trans. K. Attell, Chicago: University of Chicago Press, 2005.

## Select bibliography

Agamben, G., *State of Exception*, trans. K. Attell, Chicago: University of Chicago Press, 2005.

Berenson, E., *The Trial of Madame Caillaux*, Berkeley: University of California Press, 1992.

Bloch, M., *The Historian's Craft. Reflections on the Nature and Uses of History and the Techniques and Methods of Those Who Write It*, trans. P. Putnam, New York: Vintage Books, 1953.

Ginzburg, C., *The Night Battles: Witchcraft and Agrarian Cults in the Sixteenth and Seventeenth Century*, trans. J. and A. Tedeschi, Baltimore: Johns Hopkins University Press, 1983.

Ginzburg, C., *Clues, Myth, and the Historical Method*, trans. J. and A. Tedeschi, Baltimore: Johns Hopkins University Press, 1989.

Ginzburg, C., *The Judge and the Historian. Marginal Notes on a Late-Twentieth-Century Miscarriage of Justice*, trans. A. Shugaar, New York: Verso, 1999.

Le Roy Ladurie, E., *Montaillou: The Promised Land of Error*, trans. B. Bray, New York: Vintage Books, 1978.

Maza, S., *Private Lives and Public Affairs: The Causes Célèbres of Prerevolutionary France,* Berkeley: University of California Press, 1993.

Zaionchkovsky, P.A., *The Russian Autocracy in Crisis, 1878–1882*, trans. G.M. Hamburg, Gulf Breeze: Academic International Press, 1979.

Zemon Davis, N., *Fiction in the Archives: Pardon Tales and Their Tellers in Sixteenth-Century France*, Stanford: Stanford University Press, 1987.

# 6  Opinion polls

*Anja Kruke*

Polls appear to be an almost natural part of our daily lives; they present public sentiments on almost everything, regardless of topic. The media report on them regularly; at least once a month changes in party preferences are published. But why is polling taken as a source in this volume? Polls, after all, consist of figures, so how can they be read like a text? In this contribution I will try to show that polls are more than statistics and that they can be analysed in varying perspectives and from different points of view, just like any other text.

According to the *Encyclopaedia Britannica*, '[p]ublic opinion polling can provide a fairly exact analysis of the distribution of opinions on almost any issue within a given population' and 'is a valuable tool for estimating the state of public opinion on almost any subject'.[1] This confident claim rests on the assumption that it is possible to construct a sample in which opinions are represented in the same proportions as in the population at large. This representation of society and its opinion in straightforward, quantified data has become so wide-spread that other concepts of public opinion have virtually disappeared.[2] This chapter will endeavour to give a differentiated picture of opinion polls, taking political polling as an example (rather than marketing surveys, general societal surveys or scientific empirical social research).

## Opinion polling in the twentieth century: the rise of cheap knowledge

Polling is a quantitative survey method which is used in many different contexts. It helped to establish empirical social research as a leading science in society in the middle of the last century and was closely connected with various uses in science, economy, politics and media.[3] The method originated in the 1920s in the field of consumer and marketing research and was tested by George Gallup and others at the US presidential election in 1936 with a forecast of the result. Until then, the magazine *Literary Digest* had run the popular 'straw poll', which asked readers to express their opinions on a postcard. This method, which tended to involve the handling of several million responses, had often predicted the election outcome correctly, but it went badly wrong in 1936 – in contrast to the pollsters' forecasts which were based on a carefully selected sample of only a few thousand voter preferences.

Owing to his success and his aggressive advertising, Gallup's name became a virtual synonym for public opinion polling. He soon started franchise institutes which exported his method to countries like Britain, where Henry Durant became active for Gallup in 1937 with the British Institute of Public Opinion (BIPO).[4] The rise of polling and its breakthrough in the public coincided with a discussion in the USA about the relation between mass media, public opinion and democracy that had started in the 1920s. It was inspired mainly by young researchers from the field of psychology and mass media.[5] In 1937 they founded the first journal devoted to problems of opinion polling, the *Public Opinion Quarterly* which is still the most important periodical in the field.[6] During the Second World War, the different strands of public opinion research were bound together (from the USA and Great Britain) and formed a kind of 'research front' which contributed to the acceptance of polls as a reliable scientific method to gain a picture of public opinion – which meant at least that public opinion came to be defined as a quantifiable entity.[7]

Public opinion polling continued to be a genuinely inter- and transnational phenomenon after 1945. The USA especially was striving for a wide distribution and use of polling, because it was regarded as 'democratic science': everybody could be asked and every opinion had its rights. This made public opinion transparent for everybody and it was believed that this transparency would prevent the rise of demagogues and dictators. Opinion polling was ascribed its status as a 'democratic science' when the Western Allies brought it to Germany in 1945 in order to find out what the German people thought and to support democratisation.[8] The post-Nazi German parties and authorities were quick to adopt polling as a method of observing society. Within only fifteen years after the foundation of the Federal Republic in 1949 it became institutionalised as part of the political process.[9]

Opinion polling was soon established in a large number of countries because it promised to be quick, cheap and reliable. It was expected to deliver reliable data on fields where popular opinion was insufficiently known to parties, governments, or the media. In comparison to other methods like statistics, polls would be much quicker and much cheaper because of the small data base. The basic idea of a poll is representativeness as understood in statistical and probability theory: a sample of ca. 2000 persons or less, selected randomly, speaks for a whole nation.[10] Pollsters would be able to discover the public's opinion on virtually any topic that might interest their clients. A clear procedure for polling has been developed. As a first step, clients formulate the questions to which they seek an answer, and the polling institute designs a possible questionnaire on that basis, formulating questions about the most important political issues for the voters, combined with questions relating to the strengths and weaknesses they would ascribe to a party. After some pre-testing of possible questions, the final questionnaire is devised in consultation with the client. Only after that process is the actual poll carried out. First results are delivered to the client shortly after that, followed by a thorough report by the pollster on the whole poll. The interpretation of a poll is often given in an oral report, as it saves the clients' time and leaves room for questions and for recommendations from the pollsters on how to make use of the data. Sometimes, these recommendations are given with some selected data in form of a memorandum (as with the source extract below).

In addition to quantitative polls, pollsters also carry out qualitative surveys. Often they use discussions in focus groups to gain insights into people's attitudes and lines of argumentation with respect to some specific subject or to prepare the ground for a questionnaire. A rather unusual kind of opinion observation was practised by Mass Observation in the late 1930s and 1940s. This group, set up by three English left-wing intellectuals, employed a panel of regular respondents who wrote narrative reports and diaries on set topics instead of answering questionnaires.[11] These methods of interviewing people should not be mistaken for surveillance reports which are secretly written by police or other state institutions for controlling purposes.[12]

All in all, clients hope to obtain information which gives them an advantage over competitors. Political parties, for example, want to know how they can influence voters and want to use the data to organise an effective election campaign, while the media are interested in knowing who voters would like to see as their next prime minister so their newspaper or news channel can be the first with newsworthy information. Historians can usually best reconstruct these processes from the perspective of the client, because parties, governments and the media possess archives. The interests that lead to the commissioning of a poll can usually be discovered by exploring these records, though it is harder to gain access to the archives of pollsters. However, in some cases data-as-processed-by the pollsters is collected by scientific institutes, stored in data banks and thus accessible for secondary analyses.[13]

The main types of documents coming under the heading of a poll are thus, (1) the correspondence between the client and the institute which contains information concerning the production process, (2) the reports and memoranda on the findings of a survey. The latter contain interpretations of the data as well as minutes of a party or a cabinet meeting and handouts distributed at such a meeting show how the survey was presented and discussed. The evidence of the archives suggests that the use of opinion polls by political parties was chiefly prompted by crises. Andrew Taylor shows that the first poll commissioned by the British Conservative Party, after their defeat in 1945, was a survey on the impact of their 'Industrial Charter' on the public.[14] But it also becomes clear that the party first had to learn how to use polls. The Conservatives' insecurity over the effects of mass affluence forced them to integrate polling as an integral part of their policymaking during the 1950s as they sought expert advice on how to address voters.[15] The material gives an idea of the conditions under which the poll in question originated and the uses to which the results were put. Archival sources enable us to reconstruct the concept of an entire election campaign, as has been done, for example, with the presidential campaign of John F. Kennedy in 1961.[16] Further materials, like notes for press conferences or speeches or material prepared for the media allow a detailed analysis of the applications of polls within the political context.

The main access to polls is often their coverage in the media. The media tend to present the polls as unbiased, 'scientific' news, often accompanied by some information on the circumstances under which the poll was taken. The results are usually compared with earlier polls in order to show a 'trend'. The reporting generally follows the rules of 'news value theory', i.e. particularly newsworthy features are stressed, such as discrepancies with former results, special emphasis on a particular person or issue etc. In using such particulars the media hopes to make the report appear different from its predecessors and thus to excite the readers' attention. Monthly or even weekly reports on political preferences have some of the attraction of a horse race, especially when a close finish is predicted. The data generally appear in three different contexts: as information, as instrument or on a meta-level that thematizes the poll as an instrument in politics.[17] In this way, the media's use of polls is somewhat contradictory; in the news part, polls are taken as news and in the features pages they are often dealt with critically, for example with discussion of the timing of the poll in relation to the campaign. In general, the headline-grabbing nature of journalism means that press reports often capture the attention of political actors, and even set the political agenda.[18] Sometimes, the media even deliberately seeks to influence politics, as was the case when the *News Chronicle* announced that public opinion (as measured out by BIPO) was against Neville Chamberlain's Appeasement policy.[19] The presentations of poll trends, giving the ground line of what is politically current and important, adopt an orienting function for the audience as well as for the political actors. By solely relying on data, polls constitute a new reality of their own.[20]

It has always been a financially attractive option for pollsters to publish polls on their own and to use them for publicity purposes. This is particularly true of election forecasts, as could be seen with the American presidential election in 1936. Depending on their contract with the client, pollsters are allowed to publish the poll or parts of it – or sometimes nothing: in some cases the extent to which polls are made public is left to the clients' discretion. The first poll commissioned by the West German government in 1950 showed a continuing high degree of anti-semitism in Germany and as a result remained classified. The government agreed to have a selection of its monthly questions published, without, however, revealing the fact that it was only a selection.[21] Polls are obviously regarded as an important means to influence public opinion, and even to swing elections. This turns them into highly important pieces of information for different actors within the political field (parties, media, the public itself). Indeed, the secrecy which has often surrounded polls has made them even more attractive, especially for the media who are keen to use information from secretly conducted polls as news in their reporting.

## How historians can use polls

Only in the past decade have historians become fully aware of the potential represented by polls both as historical sources and as an object of historical research in their own right. During that period attitudes towards them have become more cautious, and analysis of them more complex. Some historians treat them as mere facts of history while others have developed new approaches which focus on issues of political representation. All aspects of the political are touched: the different fields of political intervention (policy dimension), the exercise of power and decision-making (politics dimension), and the wider structure of the body politic (polity dimension). In all three dimensions, various perspectives and approaches to the reading of polls can be found.

Firstly, polling data can be taken simply as evidence for historical analysis. This is a popular way to deal with this source particularly in political history.[22] Data collections allow comparisons of different questionnaires or longitudinal studies that follow the opinion on a specific topic over time. For example, historians have studied the shifts in popular opinion regarding the reunification of Germany between 1949 and 1990.[23] Focusing on the data is a legitimate but sometimes quite restricted approach because the data themselves do not say anything about the context in which a particular poll was made, who ordered it, and for what purpose.

A second way to read polls also takes them at face value, but turns away from their use as illustrative or evidential purpose in some wider narration of political history. Instead, polls are consciously taken as sources. In this way, the historical analysis of polls can elucidate long-term trends and focuses on aspects such as changes in the wording of questionnaires on a particular topic. These changes are taken to indicate discursive developments and shifts in a political culture, for example what can be said and asked. It often happens that a question is phrased in many different ways, sometimes even by the same institute.[24] An analysis of these changes may reveal something about the context in which the poll was made, the purpose of the contractor, and even how the perception of a (political) subject evolved.[25] For the analysis of the latter aspect, one has to assume that the form of the questions represents the contemporary perceptions of a topic, because they have to meet the mindset of the interviewees in order to obtain adequate answers. For instance, when the German government polled popular opinion on Jews the words 'solution to the Jewish problem' were used without inverted commas. Such a formulation revealed that the ideological mindset of National Socialism was still intact, because the institute expected the interviewees to share the perception of a 'Jewish problem'.[26] The use of anti-semitic semantics in such questions on anti-semitism was replaced by different interpretational frames with other, more positive connotations of the 'Jews' in the following decades. A long-term analysis of these shifts can elucidate changes both in opinion and in the horizons of political comprehension.[27]

A third type of analysis is concerned with the details of political decision-making: was it informed by polls, and did the political actors follow the experts' advice? In this line of inquiry, polls are regarded as strategic elements within politics. For the USA, presidential polling in particular has become a relevant field of inquiry. One example is how Franklin D. Roosevelt used polling to navigate through the Second World War without losing the approval of the people. Public opinion – as represented by the polls – guided his decisions about domestic politics and orientated the way he used arguments and public relations in order to keep up the morale of the population.[28]

Let us now turn to the polity dimension. The question of how polls influence the constitutional and wider institutional bases of politics remains necessarily open-ended and is bound up with normative issues. A crucial debate has arisen regarding the consequences of polling for the democratic process. One side argues that polls have been used as a means of manipulation which tries to influence public debate in an instrumental fashion, enabling the government to pursue a hidden agenda. This view is taken by Lawrence R. Jacobs and Robert Y. Shapiro, who cite the presidency of Richard Nixon as an example of such a manipulative use of the polls.[29] On the other side, the rise of 'private' polling by presidents is regarded as an improvement. Robert Eisinger for instance takes polls as neutral elements which have been used increasingly by presidents to gain more political autonomy. Here, polls are seen as a necessary instrument to exert power appropriately. Eisinger demonstrates how polls were applied as a means to gain power and hence made the political system more responsive to public opinion and thus the popular will.[30] Another version of this interpretation is founded on the idea of a 'silent majority' that can be mobilised by clever strategic political communication. This idea has been formulated by the conservative German pollster Elisabeth Noelle-Neumann in the 1970s in her theory of a 'spiral of silence', a concept that is still the object of controversy and intense scrutiny.[31] The underlying idea of a 'silent majority' can be traced back to Richard Nixon's belief that, contrary to the poll data and the reports of the mass media, which were in his opinion heavily biased towards a left-liberal agenda, middle America was largely in favour of US intervention in Vietnam. Consequently, Nixon ignored the polls and relied on alternative measures of public opinion.[32]

The problem of the transparency of polls touches on the very foundations of any democratic system: when political actors can gain superior quantitative knowledge about public opinion, the relation between them and the voters, who have to make their choice on a political mass market, changes profoundly. Thus, polls affect the structure of the body politic in a democracy. In the controversy that has surrounded this aspect of polling in the USA and other Western democracies since the 1950s, the polls have been seen not only as a means for political actors to improve their knowledge of the population but also as an instrument for the manipulation of voters. This ambivalence has been scrutinised by Susan Herbst who shows how the growing transparency was used by different political actors in the USA, and also caused shifts in the imagination of how politics work.[33]

This understanding of polls as a means to engage in politics can in fact be extended to all participants in the political process. Publicly accessible polls benefit not only the political actors but also the electorate for they help voters to find their way through the contradicting 'offers' on the political mass market. Between elections, the 'sovereign will' of a people is measured by polls. Seen from this perspective, polls can be analysed as a political ritual, where only a few thousand people take part instead of the whole nation. The political scientist Lisbeth Lipari argues that the outcome of a poll, often visualised in pie charts, represents and unites the whole nation and thus transforms sovereignty by asking the people about their preferences between the elections. Since the people can be sure that the charts are perceived by the political actors, this pseudo-democratic ritual provides a new form of symbolic participation and thereby secures a responsive democratic leadership.[34]

A different approach to study the polity-dimension of polling is to analyse it as a means societies can use to describe and observe themselves.[35] Historian Sarah Igo has focused on this dimension in her recent study with the telling title 'the Averaged American', which suggests that polling as a method, irrespective of the actual quantitative data, contributed to the self-observation and self-description of US-society. The constant stream of polling data on various aspects of daily life deeply changed the ideas Americans held about themselves and affected the popular perception of what was deemed to be usual, typical or normal. Igo explains this process of 'normalisation' as a consequence of the ongoing statistical categorisation of various spheres of social life between the 1930s and 1950s. In particular, she takes the Kinsey reports as an important demonstration of how the conceptualisation of the private was reconfigured.[36] The biologist Alfred Kinsey, actually an expert in the study of gall wasps, had started to collect several thousand in-depth interviews with Americans, based on a quota selection rather than on a random sample. The first of his two volumes, *Sexual Behavior in the Human Male*, was published in 1948 and caused widespread outrage in the media. Many Americans were deeply disturbed and agitated by the new categorisation and quantification of sexuality offered in this study, because 'Kinsey was shifting the terms of what could be asked'.[37] Soon, however, they became accustomed to thinking about sex in quantitative terms. When the second study, *Sexual Behavior in the Human Female*, was published in 1953, the criticism was not as intense as it had been after the first volume. Sexual 'normality' was accordingly redefined through Kinsey's studies and a new stage in the 'second-order-observation' of society had been reached.[38] (Second-order observation suggests Americans compared their own sexual behaviour with the published figures about the lives of anonymous others and used them as a mirror to observe themselves.) People were now able to place their own experiences on a scale of normality or typicality represented by Kinsey's results, even in the most intimate aspects of their lives. Finally they started regarding themselves in statistical categories of the typical, the average, and the normal, thereby creating a 'new community'.[39]

These studies, with their focus on the wider framework of politics and society (for which we employed the term 'polity'), use polls to uncover the implicit normative rules of American society. Polls thus become an internal guide that sets normative rules which previously were set by other institutions. These examples show polls to be more than mere data: they allow a more complex reading as a text, contrary to what the data suggest at first glance.

## How polls can be used as a source – an example

In this section we take a closer look at a 1972 poll report. The poll report was provided by the institute Infratest Sozialforschung, a leading pollster in the Federal Republic and it was delivered to the West German government at the end of September 1972.[40] The government had commissioned the poll in preparation for the Bundestag election on 19 November 1972. That election had become necessary because the ruling coalition of Social Democrats (SPD) and Free Democrats (FDP) under Willy Brandt had failed to obtain a vote of confidence. Earlier in the year, a motion of no confidence, introduced by the opposition parties Christian

Democratic Union (CDU) and Christian Social Union (CSU) had failed to obtain the necessary absolute majority in the Bundestag [the Federal parliament].

Infratest, 28/9/1979

1  In 1969 the SPD obtained 42.7% [of the total vote], the FDP 5.8%, and SPD/FDP jointly 48.5%; the CDU/CSU obtained 46.1%.

2  Given the decline of the [extreme right] NPD [National Democratic Party] and other splinter parties [which had failed to pass the 5% hurdle at the previous general election], the coalition will need about 49% of the vote for a majority of seats in the Bundestag, against the 47.5% which sufficed in 1969. To secure a victory . . . 49.5% should be aimed at.

3  Since the turn of the year 1970/71 polls on potential voting patterns of the interviewees on a Federal election 'next Sunday' have shown:

   – *the CDU/CSU in the lead* before the governing coalition in the months. . . ;
   – *the governing coalition in the lead* in the months . . ..

   The biggest coalition lead was directly after the CDU/CSU's failure to obtain a vote of no-confidence . . .

4  A quick poll taken from 14 to 20 September 1972 shows again the CDU/CSU in the lead: . . .
   Extrapolating from declared preferences to the electorate as a whole, the voting potential at the time of the poll was: SPD 41% and FDP 6% = 47%; CDU/CSU 51%; other parties 2%.

5  The poll was taken a few days after the terrorist attack in the Olympic Village and the subsequent failure to free the hostages. It cannot be ruled out that these events caused the ruling parties an at least temporary loss of sympathy.
   On the other hand it is currently not clear whether the debate about the vote of confidence on 22 September brought a wave of sympathy for the government such as that observable after the failed motion of no confidence. This could be verified only by a further quick poll (to be carried out from 5 to 13 October, results [available] on 17 October). . . .

6  *16% of all voters declared that they were not yet entirely sure about their party choice for the Federal election, and said they would make up their minds only during the election campaign. . . .*
   This uncertainty was expressed particularly by voters in: big cities (metropoles); younger voters up to 25 years of age; women . . .

7  The priority is to fight against the apparent tendencies towards resignation and self-pity among the members and the followers of SPD and FDP. It appears that the belief in a victory of the coalition also in the upcoming Federal election has declined over the last few months. . . .

8  From August to September there has been hardly any change in the preference for the chancellor among the voters. Willy Brandt (44%) is still well ahead of [opposition leader and CDU chairman] Rainer Barzel (32%), while 23% of the voters are still undecided.

But since domestic issues are dominating the debate at the moment (see below), the chancellor's popularity is not making sufficient impact. Under no circumstances, however, should this lead to a change in the concept of the 'chancellor election campaign'.

Willy Brandt enjoys particular esteem in the three groups with the largest number of uncommitted voters . . ..

9   56% of the respondents stated that political problems like

- price stability
- securing social progress (health care, old age insurance etc.)
- internal security (protection against crime)
- external security (policies of peace and reconciliation [with Poland and the USSR])
- job security

would influence their voting decision.

From the 16% of all voters who stated earlier that their final decision for a party would be taken only during the election campaign, 71% will make their decision according to the parties' actions with regard to these issues. Among the '*two most important problems*' which will 'influence their electoral decision for a party' are:

|  | All voters | SPD | FDP | CDU/CSU |
|---|---|---|---|---|
| price stability | 33% | 27% | 35% | 38% |
| securing social progress | 23% | 29% | 15% | 18% |
| guaranteeing the external security of the FRG | 21% | 27% | 31% | 16% |
| guaranteeing internal security (protection against crime) | 18% | 12% | 17% | 24% |
| job security | 16% | 17% | 15% | 15% |

Potential SPD voters state their decision to vote for a certain party at the next Federal elections will be influenced by the aforementioned political 'issues' [English in the original!], they name the combination of 'securing social progress and external security of the Federal Republic' most frequently. . . .

10  During the next weeks, the following points should receive particular attention:

a   A decisive part of the election campaign has to be the political, publicly visible work of government members.

b   Under no circumstances must the CDU/CSU be allowed to dictate the topics and style of the election campaign . . . .

c   As a first priority issues of *foreign and intra-German [i.e. relations with the GDR] politics* will have to be updated (chancellor election campaign).

d  The government's *performance record* has to be highlighted more
strongly in order to improve the mood which has been affected by the
events of the last few days. The impression that the government is on the
defensive and has little to show in terms of positive achievements has to
be countered. Points to be stressed are the chancellor's declaration of
22 September and the preamble of the election manifesto.

In addition, a statement on economic and financial policies by Helmut
Schmidt [then chancellor of the exchequer and minister for economics]
seems indispensable to us. Such a statement is to be repeated on many
occasions. . . .

Perhaps the notion of stability in its 'CDU-specification' should be
countered with the concept of *productivity*. (This would have to be
explicated further.)

e  A clear link should be formed between the concept 'quality of life' and
'stability' understood in a more differentiated manner.

f  The impression that the governing coalition lacks competent people is
to be countered by giving more prominence to actual and potential
members of government . . . who stood rather in the background during
the last weeks. Perhaps there should be a debate on the composition of
the cabinet after 19 November [the election day]. . . .

The starting point for an analysis could be the 'politics' dimension. The report
begins with the results of the previous Bundestag election in 1969 and the percentage of votes that was then required for a working parliamentary majority. That percentage was comparatively low because a relatively large number of votes were
'wasted' on splinter parties which obtained less than 5% of the vote and thus
obtained no seats. According to the decline of these parties in the polls from 1969
to 1972, a coalition wanting to stay in power had to aim at a correspondingly higher
target. In accordance with the coalition's intention to stay in power the report points
out these changes and draws corresponding conclusions for the planning of the
election campaign. The descriptive analysis of the polls can thus be understood in
the 'politics' dimension as a prescriptive guideline. The recommendations in point
10 especially confirm this assumption.

The text is reduced to bare essentials and does not give a detailed analysis of the
situation which suggests that it was used as a handout for a meeting in which the
report would be presented in detail. Instead of alternatives the text presents only
one possible course of action. Infratest gives the recommendations on the basis of
highly selective data and short statements. The latter were selected to support the
line of argument because Infratest wants to hang on to the concept of the 'chancellor campaign'. The institute advised taking some specific measures to win undecided voters and to counter the negative impressions evoked by some data. The
warning against changing the basic concept suggests that this possibility was being
debated within the SPD. The report thus suggests alternative ways of interpreting
the data as the results in fact signalled insufficient support for the SPD and
could have pointed to the advisability of a new direction in the campaign. This is

particularly apparent in points 3 and 4 in which the changes in party preferences since 1969 are described and the latest trends (in which the opposition is leading with an absolute majority) are explained. In point 8 the chancellor's popularity, which rested on his foreign policy, is put forward as an argument for a certain kind of election campaign. The supporting argument aims at the result that the people who were in favour of Brandt were at the same time the undecided voters. The following point 9 contains arguments against a 'chancellor campaign' and in favour of a 'domestic issues campaign'. The institute's figures show that the majority of potential SPD voters wanted domestic as well as external security (Brandt's topic), which amounts to recommending a combination of both issues in the election campaign.[41]

The SPD and government followed the interpretation and recommendations of Infratest which had already conceptualised the earlier campaign in 1969 and had advised the party since then.[42] The 1972 election campaign was heavily centred on Brandt, who even lent his name to the main campaign slogan 'Vote Willy'. Also, the new term 'quality of life' (point 10e) became part of the standard repertoire of the SPD's political objectives.[43]

A second reading of this source concerns the implicit assumptions about the factors which determine public opinion, i.e. how voters make up their minds and hence may be influenced in their decisions. What is the mindset that structures the line of argument given in the extract? How are causal relations constructed in the report? Essentially, the report contains three major ideas about how public opinion was structured and could thus be influenced: the event, the mood and the performance as presented in the media.

First, public opinion as described in the extract displays a striking volatility; it is prone to abrupt changes under the impact of events. The slump in government support as registered by the quick poll (point 5) is attributed, though somewhat cautiously, to the Munich Olympic massacre without even considering an alternative explanation. The massacre, which ended the kidnapping of Israeli athletes by Palestinian terrorists on 5/6 September 1972, was a shock not only to the German public but also to the wider world, especially as the Olympics, the biggest international event to be hosted by the new Germany since the Second World War, had been conceived as 'cheerful games' that were to present West Germany as a friendly and peaceful nation.[44] The monocausal explanation of the latest slump in government support is immediately followed by a prediction which is again presented without possible alternatives. The lively media debate about the failed vote of confidence for Willy Brandt on 22 September that led to the dissolution of the Bundestag, may lead to a swing back in the government's favour. A decisive influence is attributed to the 'mood' of the public; measures are accordingly proposed to influence that mood in the desired direction (10d). Special attention is paid to the mood of the party's own followers, who are perceived as indulging in self-pity (point 7); this statement is contextualised with the bad expectations in the polls of the last months (points 3 and 4).[45]

Pollsters as well as politicians believe in some sort of 'laws' of decision-making. The so-called 'bandwagon effect' is thought to be especially important: Voters tend to be influenced by their perception of the voting intentions of other people and so to mobilise voters in general as well as supporters parties must give them the impression that they are going to be the winners.

The idea that public opinion is influenced by events and the mood created by them rests on the assumption that voting decisions of individuals are fluid as well. Points 6 to 9 show how the mechanisms of opinion-formation are perceived and how Infratest hoped to influence them. These ideas rest on the construction of one specific group of voters. The focus of political attention is directed at the volatile part of the electorate, the 'floating voter'. First used by the British Conservatives in the 1930s after the collapse of the Liberal Party, the term was adopted in the 1940s by psephologists and pollsters who were looking for a word to describe voters who shift their vote from time to time.[46] According to this view, the floating voters are perceived as tipping the scales between the solid blocks of firm party followers.[47]

The group of the 'undecided' is assumed to be best swayed by 'people' and 'issues'; the appeal to some 16 per cent of the electorate will thus determine the character of the election campaign more strongly than the long-term ideals of the committed supporters who were still in an overwhelming majority. As a consequence, the presentation of topical issues and of the political personnel as carriers of issues is put at the centre of the proposed campaign strategy. Such a strategy, it is believed, will affect the election result in favour of the government. The recommendations of point 10 all refer to certain aspects of performances in this regard. They allow conclusions about a conceptualisation of the political process that was probably shared by Infratest and its client, the SPD-led government. In the source extract, Infratest combines social aspects like the different groups of floating voters with psychological elements that refer to the perception of politics. The extract considers not a change of policies but of the way policies and personnel are to be presented to the electorate. Actions d) to f) are proposed in this form of reasoning, each concerned with questions of issues and personnel, like the 'quality of life'.

Since they take mechanisms of public opinion into consideration and give recommendations, polls do not only inform the political discourse by the data they obtain and interpret, they also influence its very structure. A third way of reading this source would thus focus on the discourse of politics. Polling has had a growing influence on the semantics of political presentation and hence on the way politics is discussed. Infratest makes suggestions in this direction, proposing to set 'productivity' against the CDU slogan of 'stability' in order to emphasize economic growth, thus connoting stability with stagnation. The background of the terms refers to the reforms that the coalition had introduced since 1969. Generally, the term 'quality of life' was symptomatic for this change in the political discourse. The concept did not only play its part in the election campaign, but also became a keyword for the social-liberal coalition between 1972 and 1974 and was almost a synonym for the aspirations for 'more democracy' and an overall better, more humane society. The use of this concept can be paralleled with the alleged 'value change' towards post-materialistic norms like 'self-realisation' in an affluent society which were discussed at the time.[48]

The more dynamic political semantics of the late 1960s and early 1970s caused a more flexible appeal to the voters, as shown in points 6, 8, 9 and 10 of the extract. It appeared that the only way to remain a serious competitor in politics would be to take the dimension of political language and political semantics into account and to address voters accordingly. After the devastating defeat in the 1972 Federal elections, the CDU/CSU contemplated strategies to regain the initiative in this embattled field of political semantics. The party's newly elected secretary general, Kurt Biedenkopf, thus developed the strategy of 'occupying the concepts' (*Begriffe besetzen*) in order to disseminate the aims of the party more successfully, and to regain an even playing field in the definition of key political concepts.[49]

## Conclusion

As we have seen in this chapter, polls do not only represent public opinion as a 'mirror' of society, but have also reformulated key structures of the political in its three dimensions, politics, policy, and polity. Returning to the introductory question, polls can be read as texts not only because the actual material includes survey reports and memoranda besides the actual figures but also because the media report and comment on the figures. The figures are not significant by themselves, they gain meaning only through the way they are presented and embedded into the political language of post-1945 politics. They are open to a textual reading with regard to their different dimensions. With their quantitative, allegedly 'hard' data, polls create 'reality effects' that provide us with a new perspective on the political process and suggest various conclusions for political action. The conclusions have to look compelling to achieve what the political actors want. As hard facts that create a 'soft' reality on their own, polls have become an indispensable part of the political process. This process has also been observed in economics, where market research faces problems in the collection as well as the interpretation of data which resemble those of political polling.[50]

A semantic reading shows the ways in which underlying beliefs about public opinion structure the people's perceptions of the political process and influence the way political actors think about politics and act or communicate politically. Finally, polls intervene in the political discourse by determining what can be deemed 'political' and how it can be expressed. This can also be observed occurring amongst the audience (the voters) too. People often adopt the categories which pollsters develop and start thinking with them as well, a phenomenon that Ian Hacking has labelled the 'classification loop'. As a consequence, the surveys observe a reality that was created by the data in the first place, and thus reconfirm themselves to a large degree. This process sets a loop of observation and classification in motion. In this chapter we have seen how this worked with regard to the public-private sphere of sexuality where people were first shocked by Kinsey's statistical classifications of sexuality but then took over the very categories of 'normality' his reports had suggested. The same could be said about the political realm when people learn to perceive themselves in categories of loyal followers and 'floating voters'. In several respects, therefore, polls can be interpreted as an important factor in explaining the political transformations of the second half of the twentieth century.

## Notes

1  *Encyclopaedia Britannica*, 15th ed., vol. 26, London 2003, pp. 314–316, p. 314.
2  A. Gollin, 'Polling and the Media', *Public Opinion Quarterly* 51, 1987, 86–94; S. Herbst, 'On the Disappearance of Groups: 19th- and Early 20th-Century Conceptions of Public Opinion', in T.L. Glasser and C.T. Salmon (eds), *Public Opinion and the Communication of Consent*, New York: Guilford Press, 1995, pp. 89–104.
3  For the history polls as part of survey research see M. Blumer, K. Bales, and K. Kish Sklar (eds), *The Social Survey in Historical Perspective 1880–1940*, Cambridge: Cambridge University Press, 1991; M. Bulmer (ed.), *Essays on the History of British Sociological Research*, Cambridge: Cambridge University Press, 1985.
4  See A. King (ed.), *British Political Opinion 1937–2000. The Gallup Polls*, compiled by R. J. Wybrow, London: Politico's, 2001; R. Worcester, *British Public Opinion. A Guide to the History and Methodology of Political Opinion Polling*, Oxford: Blackwell, 1991. For other countries see R.M. Worcester (ed.), *Political Opinion Polling. An International Review*, London: Macmillan, 1983; N. Moon, *Opinion Polls: History, Theory and Practice*, Manchester and New York: Manchester University Press, 1999; D.J. Robinson, *The Measure of Democracy: Polling, Market Research, and Public Life, 1930–1945*, Toronto and Buffalo: University of Toronto Press, 1999; L. Blondiaux, *La fabrique de l'opinion: Une histoire sociale des sondages*, Paris: Editions du Seuil, 1998.
5  See T. Osborne and N. Rose, 'Do the Social Sciences create Phenomena? The Example of Public Opinion Research', *British Journal of Sociology* 50, 1999, 367–396; W. Lippmann, *The Phantom Public*, New York: Harcourt, Brace, 1925; J. Dewey, *The Public and its Problems*, London: George Allen & Unwin, 1927. This discussion has continued until today. See Glasser and Salmon, *Public Opinion*; V. Price, *Public Opinion*, Newbury Park and London: Sage, 1992; S. Spichal, *Public Opinion: Developments and Controversies in the Twentieth Century*, Lanham: Rowman & Littlefield, 1999; J. Habermas, *The Structural Transformation of the Public Sphere: An Inquiry into a Category of Bourgeois Society*, Cambridge, Mass.: MIT Press, 1989; H. Mah, 'Phantasies of the Public Sphere: Rethinking the Habermas of Historians', *Journal of Modern History* 72, 2000, 153–182.
6  See URL of the journal, available at <http://www.oxfordjournals.org/poq/about.html> (accessed 30 April 2007).
7  Osborne and Rose, 'Social Sciences'; F. Keller, *Archäologie der Meinungsforschung. Mathematik und die Erzählbarkeit des Politischen*, Konstanz: UVK, 2001.
8  A.J. Merritt and R.L. Merritt, *Public Opinion in Occupied Germany. The OMGUS-Surveys 1945–1949*, Urbana, Chicago and London: University of Illinois Press, 1970, A.J. Merritt and R.L. Merritt, *Public Opinion in Semisovereign Germany. The HICOG Surveys 1949–1955*, Urbana, Chicago and London: University of Illinois Press, 1980.
9  A. Kruke, *Demoskopie in der Bundesrepublik. Meinungsforschung, Politik und Medien 1949–1990*, Düsseldorf: Droste, 2007.
10  You will find further technical information in many textbooks on empirical social research and statistics, e.g. R. Czaja and J. Blair, *Designing Surveys: A Guide to Decisions and Procedures*, Thousand Oaks, Calif.: Pine Forge Press, 1996; B.I. Newman (ed.), *Handbook of Political Marketing*, Thousand Oaks, Calif.: Sage, 1999.
11  A. Calder, 'Mass-Observation 1937–1949', in: Bulmer (ed.), *Essays*, pp. 121–136.
12  On surveillance reports, see the chapter by Moritz Föllmer in this volume.
13  See for example Inter-University Consortium for Political and Social Research at the University of Michigan at Ann Arbor, URL: <http://www.icpsr.umich.edu> (accessed 30 April 2007).

14  A. Taylor, 'Speaking to Democracy: The Conservative Party and Mass Opinion from the 1920s to the 1950s', in S. Ball and I. Holliday (eds), *Mass Conservatism: The Conservatives and the Public Since the 1880s*, London and Portland: Frank Cass, 2002, pp. 78–99, pp. 85–88.

15  A. Taylor, '"The Record of the 1950s is irrelevant"': The Conservative Party, Electoral Strategy and Opinion Research, 1945–64', *Contemporary British History* 17, 2003, 81–110, 87–95.

16  L.R. Jacobs and R.Y. Shapiro, 'Issues, Candidate Image, and Priming. The Use of Private Polls in Kennedy's 1960 Presidential Campaign', *American Political Science Review* 88, 1994, 527–540.

17  J. Raupp, *Politische Meinungsforschung. Die Verwendung von Umfragen in der politischen Kommunikation*, Constance: UVK, 2007.

18  See for an early analysis of the structural effect polls in the media have on American politics H.A. Mendelsohn and I. Crespi, *Polls, Television, and The New Politics*, Scranton, Penn.: Chandler, 1970.

19  L. Beers, 'Whose Opinion? Changing Attitudes towards Opinion Polling in British Politics, 1937–1964', *Twentieth Century British History* 17, 2006, 177–205, 187. Here, the criticism of polling is emphasised.

20  This is empirically scrutinised by S. Herbst, *Reading Public Opinion. How Political Actors View the Democratic Process*, Chicago and London: University of Chicago Press, 1998; N. Luhmann, *The Reality of the Mass Media*, Cambridge: Polity, 2000.

21  Kruke, *Demoskopie*, pp. 438–449.

22  As an example, see L. Black, *The Political Culture of the Left in Affluent Britain: 1951–64. Old Labour, New Britain?*, Basingstoke: Palgrave Macmillan, 2003.

23  See M. Glaab, *Deutschlandpolitik in der öffentlichen Meinung. Einstellungen und Regierungspolitik in der Bundesrepublik Deutschland 1949–1990*, Opladen: Leske und Budrich, 1999.

24  See M. Kohli, 'Die Entstehung einer europäischen Identität: Konflikte und Potentiale', in H. Kaelble, M. Kirsch, and A. Schmidt-Gernig (eds), *Transnationale Öffentlichkeiten und Identitäten im 20. Jahrhundert*, Frankfurt am Main: Campus, 2002, pp. 111–158; W. Bergmann, 'Survey-Fragen als Indikatoren für den Wandel in der Wahrnehmung politischer Probleme: Antisemitismus in der Bundesrepublik Deutschland 1949–1998', *Jahrbuch für Antisemitismusforschung* 12, 2003, 231–258.

25  Kruke, 'Western Integration'.

26  Bergmann, 'Survey-Fragen', p. 239.

27  Ibid., pp. 253f.

28  S. Casey, *Cautious Crusade. Franklin D. Roosevelt, American Public Opinion and the War against Nazi Germany*, Oxford: Oxford University Press, 2001. For the early use of polls by Roosevelt see M.G. Holli, *The Wizard of Washington. Emil Hurja, Franklin Roosevelt, and the Birth of Public Opinion Polling*, New York: Palgrave, 2002.

29  L.R. Jacobs and R.Y. Shapiro, 'Presidential Manipulation of Polls and Public Opinion: The Nixon Administration and the Pollsters', *Political Science Quarterly* 110, 1995, 519–538; L.R. Jacobs and R.Y. Shapiro, *Politicians Don't Pander: Political Manipulation and the Loss of Democratic Responsiveness*, Chicago: University of Chicago Press, 2000.

30  R.M. Eisinger, *The Evolution of Presidential Polling*, New York: CUP, 2003. Responsiveness is a term that arose at the same time when polls became a pivotal part of politics in the public. See for different studies V.O. Key, *The Responsible Electorate*, Cambridge, Mass.: Harvard UP, 1966; Jacobs and Shapiro, *Politicians Don't Pander*; B.I. Page, 'Democratic Responsiveness? Untangling the Links between Public Opinion and Policy', *Political Science and Politics* 27, 1994, 25–29.

31  E. Noelle-Neumann, *The Spiral of Silence: Public Opinion – Our Social Skin*, Chicago: University of Chicago Press, 1984; for the discussion see Spichal, *Public Opinion*.

32  See B. Rottinghaus, 'Following the "Mail Hawks". Alternative Measures of Public

Opinion on Vietnam in the Johnson White House', *Public Opinion Quarterly* 71, 2007, 367–391.

33  S. Herbst, *Numbered Voices: How Opinion Polling Has Shaped American Politics*, Chicago: University of Chicago Press, 1993.

34  L. Lipari, 'Polling as a Ritual', *Journal of Communication* 49, 1999, 83–102.

35  S. Igo, *The Averaged American. Surveys, Citizens and the Making of a Mass Public*, Cambridge, Mass.: Harvard University Press, 2006.

36  Igo, *The Averaged American*, pp. 234–280.

37  Ibid., p. 243.

38  For a more detailed definition of the idea of an orientation by second-order-observation and the constitution and role of the public see R. Stichweh, 'The constitution of a world public', *Development* 46, 2003, 26–29; Luhmann, *The Reality of the Mass Media*.

39  This is the general hypothesis of Igo, *The Averaged American*, see esp. p. 280.

40  Archive of Social Democracy (AsD), Bonn, Depositum Albrecht Müller, 1/AMAD000222.

41  For further reading on *détente* see A. Hofmann, *The Emergence of Détente in Europe. Brandt, Kennedy and the Formation of Ostpolitik*, London: Routledge, 2007.

42  Infratest Sozialforschung conducted the politically sensitive polls; other institutes were also under contract, but had to deliver more general polls that were distributed quite widely.

43  For detailed information on this campaign see A. Müller, *Willy wählen. Siege kann man machen*, Annweiler: Plöger, 1997.

44  U.A. Balbier, '"Der Welt das moderne Deutschland vorstellen": Die Eröffnungsfeier der Spiele der XX. Olympiade in München 1972', in J. Paulmann (ed.), *Auswärtige Repräsentationen. Deutsche Kulturdiplomatie nach 1945*, Cologne, Weimar and Vienna: Böhlau, 2005, pp. 105–120.

45  This is not explained further, but that is not necessary, because the aspect of mobilisation of one's own followers belonged to a longer lasting discourse on the different aspects of voter mobilisation under different circumstances in the SPD. Another pollster, Infas, that worked for the SPD and the government had postulated that it was most important to win its 'own reserve' completely, i.e. to mobilise the people who constantly vote for the SPD. See in detail Kruke, *Demoskopie*, pp. 283ff.

46  See Laura Beers, *Conceptualizing the Liberals in the 1930s*, manuscript (2007).

47  This is the founding idea of psephology. As a classical introduction see P.F. Lazarsfeld, B. Berelson and H. Gaudet, *The People's Choice. How the Voter Makes Up His Mind in a Presidential Campaign*, New York: Duell, Sloan and Pearce, 1944.

48  Originally, it refers to the concept of a 'value change', which had been brought forward in the influential study by R. Inglehart, *The Silent Revolution. Changing Values and Political Styles among Western Publics*, Princeton: Princeton University Press, 1977.

49  G. Pridham, *Christian Democracy in Western Germany. The CDU/CSU in Government and Opposition, 1945–1976*, London: Croom Helm, 1977, pp. 209–214.

50  For the example of the use of the Kinsey Reports by market research see Igo, *The Averaged American*, p. 241f.; for general aspects see A. Kruke, '"Atomwaffe im Propagandakampf"? Markt- und Meinungsforschung in Politik und Wirtschaft in der frühen Bundesrepublik', in H. Berghoff (ed.), *Marketinggeschichte. Die Genese einer modernen Sozialtechnik*, Frankfurt/Main: Campus, 2007, pp. 346–371.

## Select bibliography

Allport, F.H. 'Towards a Science of Public Opinion', *Public Opinion Quarterly* 1, 1937, 7–23.

Bulmer, M., Bales, K. and Sklar, K. (eds), *The Social Survey in Historical Perspective, 1880–1940*, Cambridge: Cambridge University Press, 1992.

Casey, S., *Cautious Crusade. Franklin D. Roosevelt, American Public Opinion and the War against Nazi Germany*, Oxford: Oxford University Press, 2001.

Converse, J.M., *Survey Research in the United States. Roots and Emergence 1890–1960*, Berkeley: University of California Press, 1987.

Eisinger, R.M., *The Evolution of Presidential Polling*, New York: Cambridge University Press, 2003.

Geer, J.G., *From Tea Leaves to Opinion Polls: A Theory of Democratic Leadership*, New York: Cambridge University Press, 1996.

Herbst, S., *Numbered Voices: How Opinion Polling Has Shaped American Politics*, Chicago: University of Chicago Press, 1993.

Igo, S., *The Averaged American. Surveys, Citizens and the Making of a Mass Public*, Cambridge, Mass.: Harvard University Press, 2006.

Kruke, A., *Demoskopie in der Bundesrepublik. Meinungsforschung, Politik und Medien 1949–1990*, Düsseldorf: Droste, 2007.

Kruke, A., 'Western Integration vs. Reunification? Analyzing the Polls of the 1950s', *German Politics and Society* 25, 2007, 43–67.

Mendelsohn, H.A. and Crespi, I., *Polls, Television, and The New Politics*, Scranton, Penn.: Chandler, 1970.

Noelle-Neumann, E., *The Spiral of Silence: Public Opinion – Our Social Skin*, Chicago: University of Chicago Press, 1984.

Robinson, D.J., *The Measure of Democracy: Polling, Market Research, and Public Life, 1930–1945*, Toronto/Buffalo: University of Toronto Press, 1999.

Worcester, R., *British Public Opinion. A Guide to the History and Methodology of Political Opinion Polling*, Oxford: Blackwell, 1991.

Worcester, R. (ed.), *Political Opinion Polling. An International Review*, London: Macmillan, 1983.

# 7   Memoranda

*Kristina Spohr Readman*

Memoranda are written communications that give directions and transmit information within bureaucratic structures.[1] For the purpose of this chapter, the bureaucratic apparatus of interest is the state, and here the distinctive feature of memoranda is political analysis and stocktaking, and then policy recommendation. With reference to the nation-states of the nineteenth and twentieth centuries, memoranda can be political position papers, opinion pieces, longer 'think pieces', or short briefing notes on topics varying from foreign policy to issues of state finances to social matters. Any of these types of memoranda can be both solicited and unsolicited documents, mostly produced and consumed within the governmental machinery – by which is meant the civil servants, personal political advisors, and ultimately the decision-makers; although certainly in the early modern period many of the unsolicited memoranda were written by (more or less expert) people from outside the government. Significantly, memoranda can also take the form of short notes of discussions or minutes.

As the nature of memoranda has varied and evolved over time, so too has the historian's approach to the genre developed – not least since Leopold von Ranke. Post-Rankean political and diplomatic historians have tended to see memoranda as an important document type amongst other key state papers (especially dispatches, telegrams, and emails, as well as minutes of meetings or telephone conversations, and reports), even if over the past decades their practice has evolved to encompass other types of primary sources as well. A particularly close link thus exists between a specific sub-discipline of history and the source type in question. Before turning to the post-Rankean practices of professional historians and their uses of memoranda, a brief comment on the origins of this source – its production, use and preservation since the early modern period – is necessary.

## The professionalisation of state bureaucracies and the rise of political history

As a genre, political memoranda appeared with the development of the state as a bureaucratic structure and state-state interaction: diplomacy. Inter-state relations could take many forms – those of competition, conflict, cooperation, partnership or neutrality – and hence, diplomacy was a crucial aspect of state activity from the start.[2] It was in the fifteenth century that modern diplomacy began among the major powers in northern Italy and Spain as the then most developed state structures in Europe.[3] By the sixteenth century, the Spanish monarchy's bureaucracy was the most advanced in Europe in terms of the organisation and structure of the political administration as well as in its internal and international communication and record keeping. Philip II of Spain was particularly receptive to and keen to read both solicited and unsolicited memoranda, or *memoriales* as the Spanish called them, as his frequent annotations reveal; his policy-making thus generated a considerable paperwork trail. Not only was the writing and the reading of important memoranda embedded in the routines of Spanish government bureaucracy, but moreover, the first modern depository of government documents – established in 1540 by Philip II's predecessor Charles V of Spain – became in 1578 the first 'national' archive, the Royal Archive at Simancas. Philip II was an avid collector of documents. He called for documents to be sent to his archive for preservation, and sent chroniclers to Rome to make copies of Italian documents. The English bureaucracy was as yet far less developed, and the French one far more casual.

While present-day historians certainly benefit from the increasingly organised state apparatuses of collecting and preserving governmental documents from the sixteenth-century onward, already some chroniclers or contemporary historians such as Italians Francesco Guicciardini (1483–1540) and Paolo Giovio (1486–1552) relied heavily on the existence and privileged access to these early state papers including memoranda. The former indeed became the 'father of Modern History' through his methodical research based on primary sources that included state papers. A century later, William Camden and Sir Francis Bacon followed the Italian authors in method and conception.[4] Among the methodological precursors of the scholarly historical works of the nineteenth century were the German Johann Christoph Gatterer (1729–1799) and Scot William Robertson (1721–1793). For Gatterer research, evidence and presentation were deeply intertwined, and he highlighted the necessity of distinguishing between important and unimportant events. Gatterer was keen to see histories that incorporated analysis founded on meticulous research and use of source materials rather than majestic chronological narratives.[5] Robertson, likewise emphasised exhaustive original scholarship, and was well acquainted with original documents: his *History of the Reign of the Emperor Charles V* (1769), had an extensive scholarly apparatus, including an appendix of proofs and illustrations. Edward Gibbon (1737–1794) – more famous and certainly scrupulous in his search for evidence – had, like many other important Enlightenment historians, a tendency to rely on existing works of synthesis. Meanwhile writers such as Voltaire, Hume and Smith pointed toward new areas of history, the social, economic and cultural.[6] Nevertheless, the expanding system of territorial states meant historians' increased focus on diplomacy and the predicament of war, as they sought to explain the principles underlying the conduct of international relations – albeit always in keeping with the didactic and moralising nature of eighteenth-century historical thought.[7]

The professionalisation of history as an academic discipline brought with it the exploration of the production, nature, use of and access to the most important categories of state papers kept in archives. Had previously access been granted to land documents and titles, as well as treaties, now – in the post-Napoleonic era – political state papers (including memoranda) were made available. This, together with the growth of critical philology, helped inspire the reinvention of history as a profession with the German historian Leopold von Ranke (1795–1886) playing the central role. While many of his methodological principles were not new, his skill in self-promotion and his visibility as a teacher of historical textual criticism in his University of Berlin seminar from 1830 onward determined the subsequent swift professionalisation of the discipline of history in Germany and throughout the West.[8] Ranke's approach to history, with his emphasis on 'objectivity' was indisputably 'more rigorous' than that of his predecessors.[9] But it was also narrower in its primary emphasis on diplomatic relations.

Ranke gave scientific history a firm orientation towards past politics and relations between states. German historicism had been closely associated with the school of Hegelian political thought, which according to John Tosh, 'endowed the concept of the state with a moral and spiritual force beyond material interests of its subjects making the state the main agent of historical change'. Nationalism and the rise of the nation-state from the eighteenth century onward inspired a great deal of historical writing; scholars focused upon competition between great powers and the struggles of submerged nationalities for political self-determination. These histories inevitably reflected nationalist and even determinist perspectives upon the development of their authors' chosen nations. They were part of nation-building projects: as a *Bildungsgut* within a rapidly expanding higher education system, they were intended to serve state and nation. In this context, the new access to the increasingly professionally run royal or state archives and the newly set-up Royal Commissions that published printed collections of government documents obviously fostered the Rankean emphasis on the critical study of primary sources as well as the predominance of diplomatic history with its distinctive methods and approaches, even if the most recent state papers remained classified.[10]

The emergence of highly specialised constitutional, political, diplomatic and military national and international history monographs; chronologically framed master narratives with massive bibliographical apparatuses; and the high proportion of articles of similar content in the first professional journals (including *Historische Zeitschrift* (1859), *Revue Historique* (1886), *The English Historical Review* (1886)) all reflected the parallel and interrelated developments of the professionalisation of history and the emerging primacy of diplomatic history in the context of the growing importance of the nation-state and a competitive great power environment.

## Historians' uses of memoranda and the evolution of diplomatic history

The evolution of government apparatuses and communication technology at a time of highly volatile international relations allowed the nineteenth and early twentieth centuries to become a high point for the production of the classic 'think pieces'.

Decision-makers looked for ever more detailed political analyses and policy recommendations, and in the increasingly hierarchical state bureaucracies some civil servants saw an opportunity to raise their own profile through document production and dissemination. Whilst the study of diplomatic correspondence (dispatches and telegrams) has predominated, memoranda have proven useful to diplomatic historians seeking to explain internal decision-making processes and the motives and rationale behind certain policies. Importantly, some memoranda have caused major historiographical debates, if not fierce controversies. Among twentieth-century memoranda of historical significance are the 'Crowe Memorandum' of 1907 (a study of the Anglo-German relations of the time), Imperial Germany's 'Septemberprogramm' of 1914 (on the Reich's war aims), Hitler's 'Four-Year Plan' of 1936 (a memorandum on the Nazi economic programme to prepare for war), the 'Hossbach Memorandum' of 1937 (a summary of a meeting where Hitler laid out his war plans), Sir Orme Sargent's memorandum 'Stocktaking after VE-Day' of 1945 (on Britain's postwar position), and Kennan's so-called 'Long Telegram' of 1946 (an analysis of Soviet policies).

Regarding the creation and dissemination of documents generally, media-theorist Friedrich Kittler has identified a growing estrangement of the author from his or her written word over the past two centuries.[11] He has argued that in the nineteenth century the writer acted as creator and linguistic controller whilst producing a handwritten work, whereas by the twentieth century the 'human author' became more distanced by the use of the typewriter, and today, of computers. Certainly, for much of their early history, memoranda were handwritten and underwent the stages of being drafted and redrafted, with passages 'overwritten' (corrected or amended), added to and deleted, before eventually a final clean version would be produced and passed to the selected few addressees, who might further annotate the document or write comments on the margins. This was a lengthy process, and one that provided historians an excellent opportunity to trace the train of thought of the author and others who commented on the memorandum when studying the drafts. The typewriter revolutionised the production of documents in terms of speed. The author of a memorandum would now type drafts or have them typed – often multiple copies or later carbon copies – which were disseminated and on which corrections, suggestions and comments would be noted by hand. Often a further fresh copy would be typed out, for circulation among the policy-makers (who might write minutes or longer comments on the paper). Unsurprisingly, with the bureaucratic machinery involved in producing and consuming documents ever growing by 1900, the constant flow of documents was much greater than a century earlier.

This coincided with the professional turn of historians, who now aimed at systematically piecing together the historical facts of high politics based on these written sources. Yet this methodology found also its 'abusers', as governments stimulated the writing of official national histories by declassifying pre-selected state documents early in order to promote their perspectives of events. For example, the volumes of documents regarding the origins of the First World War that were published in the interwar years by most great powers, and the Western governments' documents relating to the end of the Cold War era published in the 1990s, fulfil precisely such a purpose.[12]

As the discipline of history has grown more diverse during the twentieth century, so have diplomatic historians' methods become more wide-ranging. Political historians generally have begun seeking to bridge the traditional gap between high and low politics, between domestic and foreign policy, by exploring the interconnectedness of these different layers and by using new methodological approaches from the social sciences to cultural studies.[13] Historians of international affairs have moved away from using archival state papers as their predominant source, and their approaches to reading and interpreting these papers have evolved as well. The latest methodological trend affecting diplomatic history (and history more generally) has been the 'linguistic turn' – the focus on studying 'texts' and 'language'. This approach has included the 'history of concepts'[14] (Koselleck) and the study of emotion and tropes in texts (Costigliola). More sweepingly diplomatic historians have been challenged by 'culturalism', pushing them towards exploring the effects, for instance, of ideology and culture, gender, race, the 'other' as well as memory as areas of cultural attitudes on their sub-discipline.[15]

But did the linguistic or cultural turn then create a crisis for international history? Assuming nation-states continue to be recognised as the main organisational structures in the world, traditional questions about states, power and policy will persist. The questions relating to the reasoning and actions of individuals – why certain decisions were taken by governments, what alternatives there were, why they were rejected, and what led to certain events or developments – cannot be omitted. Thus, memoranda and other state papers remain a crucial source to political historians.[16] This is not to say that archival documents should not be used in conjunction with other sources, and also undergo textual scrutiny where useful.[17] To quote T.G. Otte: 'if the utterances of Foreign Office clerks ought not to be neglected by the historian, they need . . . to be set against a wider network of relationships of systemic, cultural, financial and economic nature.' But significantly, as David Reynolds has highlighted, some of the culturalist approaches – the issue of 'cultural' explanatory primacy aside – are not as novel as they may seem. Zara Steiner and later D.C. Watt had focused on bureaucratic culture and policy-makers respectively, while Christopher Thorne and Reynolds have paid attention to cultural and racial dimensions.[18] More recently Creswell and Trachtenberg, as well as myself, have analysed the interplay between political rhetoric and actual policy.[19] And certainly early modernist international historians, such as Ragnhild Hatton as early as the 1950s, have found it important to engage with language, political culture and *mentalités*.[20]

In practice this means that, although it is interesting to recover 'what was said' and to explore 'how the texts need to be understood' as the new culturalists do, the *explanatory primacy* of language theory and cultural factors promoted by some extremist culturalists must be rejected. International historians remain keen to find preserved drafts and final versions of memoranda, with their main aim to uncover the thought processes of individuals within the government apparatus, to glean information about the circle of recipients (and those omitted), and thus to understand the intricacies of policy-making. They are interested in more than the text *per se*. Memoranda are read against the historical background of the specific contingent situations, such as when they were written, and when and how they were used at the time. International historians continue being interested in exploring the context in which the document was created in order to gather what is 'meant' by what is 'written'; which influences affected the document's author; what aims they pursued, and whether these were achieved; and what the wider political impact was. In other words, they continue to concentrate on establishing human agency and causalities.

A brief excursus on the culturalist approach as applied by Frank Costigliola clarifies the above. Costigliola has argued that, since historical situations and events – such as his case studies on the origins of the Cold War – are complex and diffuse, and not all their causes are attributable to single agents or conscious intentions, the scope of diplomatic history needs to be widened. He suggests doing so by exploring the connections between the personal and private lives of foreign policymakers, and the importance of emotions (such as personal desire, anger, contempt and prejudice) tied to cultural perceptions and the domestic political agenda. Not least in relation to documents produced in the Cold War, cultural and ideological presuppositions influenced how political issues were perceived. In Costigliola's words: 'Documents speak with many voices. In evaluating those voices, we need to pay attention to all aspects of foreign relations: the circumstantial, personal, emotional, and cultural, as well as the general, official, rational and political.'[21]

While emphasising the necessity of a thorough study of both text of and metaphors in a document – something that many diplomatic historians would do when for instance analysing Communist documents laced with the ideological 'jargon' – Costigliola has gone further. Particularly interested in the gender aspect of diplomatic language, he has identified tropes of masculinity in a number of American papers, especially in those dealing with American relations with the USSR,[22] which he sees as emanating from a male-dominated political and military realm.

Costigliola's article on the 'Long Telegram' of 1946 by George Kennan (minister-counsellor for the US embassy in Moscow) is a particularly good case in point. The Long Telegram – effectively an analysis seen by many as the root of the policy of 'containment' that defined America's position toward the Soviet Union for much of the following two decades – has played an important role in traditional Cold War historiography. It has been used to emphasise Kennan's and the US government's detailed knowledge and solid evaluation of Soviet foreign policy in the early Cold War context.[23] Costigliola looks at the telegram for new facets and interpretations by analysing its language and metaphors. To this end, for nearly twenty pages, he contextualises the telegram against the background of Kennan's earlier personal views of the USSR and the Russian people which had been generally positive, and argues that:

> Kennan's strong emotions, his ambition to be persuasive, and the sensuality that he and his friends had experienced in the Soviet Union – all made gendered language a particularly important rhetorical strategy. As Soviet American

relations deteriorated in 1944-46, Kennan's emotive rhetoric helped delegitimate the wartime policy of striving to cooperate with the Soviets. Bitter at Soviet restrictions on access to the Russian people and to officials, Kennan disparaged and discouraged the ties that others might develop with the Soviet leaders. He depicted those Americans seeking postwar cooperation as prone to 'gushing assumption of chumminess'. The phrase called up an image of gullible United States officials, almost inevitably men, emasculating themselves and their nation with uncontrolled flows of homosocial feelings.[24]

To prove his points about Kennan's gendered language helping to construct an 'attention-grabbing morality tale', Costigliola then spends the last seven pages of his article analysing the actual telegram's text in detail, showing Kennan's rhetorical devices to portray US–Soviet estrangement. He notes Kennan's use of a discourse of pathological psychology (the US as the 'doctor' versus the USSR as a rapist), metaphors full of hypermasculinity ('courage', 'vigor', 'firmness'), the absence of references to Russian people ('propaganda machine', 'Russian rulers', 'Russian nationalism', 'political force'), and the use of a passive voice to dramatise. The closest to an overall conclusion regarding the historical importance of the telegram is Costigliola's statement that Kennan 'in [it], . . . channelled his complex feelings about the Soviet government, the Russian people, American society, and his own career into an emotional sermon that helped shape the meaning of the Cold War'.[25] Costigliola's main point seems to be a methodological one, when he postulates that, to understand text and context, one needs to understand that texts can also have shaped contexts by the use of allusive language which in turn conditions how we interpret the text.[26] But crucially he abstains from engaging in depth with what exactly can be gleaned from his findings regarding the telegram's impact on Cold War developments – a typical problem, as alluded to above, when the study of the text takes total precedence over establishing agency and causality.

## An Example: The Crowe Memorandum of 1907

The historical importance of the now iconic memorandum by Sir Eyre Crowe 'On the present state of British relations with France and Germany' of 1 January 1907 is undisputable. Since its publication in 1928 in *British Documents on the Origins of the War, 1989–1914*, it has triggered a major historiographical debate on the nature of London's foreign policy-making.[27] More specifically attention has focused on the F.O.'s (if not Crowe's) views on Germany and Foreign Secretary Edward Grey's policies in relation to the German Reich, France and Russia. Denounced by some (Hermann Lutz, Keith Wilson, Niall Ferguson) as blatantly anti-German and deliberately misleading in its embellishment of Germany's aims and objectives, others (D.W. Sweet, B.J.C. McKercher, Zara Steiner, Paul Kennedy, T.G. Otte) have praised the memorandum as a classic exposition of British statecraft, balance of power considerations as well as an accurate judgement of German *Weltpolitik* and the consequential problematic Anglo-German relations at the time.

Crucially, contemporaries did not consider this memorandum epoch-making.[28] Nevertheless, Foreign Secretary Grey considered the memorandum important enough to show it to Prime Minister Henry Campbell-Bannerman, and to circulate it among a small circle of politicians. Grey's own comments however were low key; he simply minuted that the document was 'most valuable' as a 'guide to foreign policy' and that it contained 'information and reflections, which should be carefully studied'. Steiner, as well as Wilson, has suggested that others such as Fairfax Cartwright, minister resident in Munich, Sir Louis Mallet, Grey's private secretary, Lord Fitzmaurice, Grey's parliamentary private secretary, and Sir Frank Lascelles, the ambassador to Berlin also saw it. But given the document's extraordinary length (at twenty-four pages in *British Documents*), it seems most likely that few actually read it in great detail. Debate only ensued among a handful of officials, as the Crowe-Sanderson correspondence reveals. While according to Wilson, Fitzmaurice and Lascelles expressed their keenness to combat what they perceived as an 'anti-German current in the F.O.',[29] the exposé which Lord Sanderson, former permanent under-secretary (1894–1906), prepared in response to Crowe's memorandum differed, as Steiner has explained, more in tone than substance.[30]

Before moving to interpreting the Crowe memo, some brief remarks on the document's genesis and its author. Independent of the issue of whether the King commissioned the memorandum or not, it is important to take notice of the increased freedom of initiative enjoyed by F.O. bureaucrats since the reforms of 1906.[31] The introduction of a new registry system, now performed by the second division of staff, had not only been intended to increase efficiency, but also to free the diplomatic establishment from their clerical functions. Instead, F.O. officials could devote their time to their advisory functions, expressing their ideas in minutes and memos that would go further up the F.O. hierarchy, even as far as Grey. While it was up to the foreign minister to accept or reject suggestions, it is crucial that that additional information and advice was now available on a daily routine basis.[32] Obviously, the men who served under Grey varied in importance and ability, and their influence in foreign policy-making differed accordingly. But 'no civil servant, no matter how highly placed, would have pursued an independent policy in direct opposition to Grey's wishes.'[33] The advice of officials, however strongly urged, was thus only one element in the foreign secretary's deliberations. Grey was his own master.[34] Still, Crowe's memorandum (as many of his other papers too) was read and found approval by the foreign secretary, who as mentioned above, considered it significant enough to be circulated to politicians and officials.

Too easily overlooked and yet of crucial importance to historical interpretation, is the issue of the background of the memo's author. Born and raised in Germany, bilingual, and related through both his mother and wife to members of the German establishment, with whom he cultivated close contact, Sir Eyre's knowledge of Germany and his specific interest in military and naval issues certainly gave his minutes and memos an unusual authority for a senior clerk. He had carved out a special niche for himself by becoming the leading expert in German affairs after his appointment as senior clerk in the Western Department at the beginning of 1906. Yet as much as his background and his cultural and political perceptions gave him authority and the clout of a rational and realistic analysis, the ways in which his emotions coloured the text must also not be overlooked.

By 1906–1907 – in particular after the crisis over Morocco in 1905, but also given the longer-term economic shifts and rising maritime rivalry – Britain's map of the world, and of Europe especially, was undergoing dramatic change.[35] There was within the F.O. a growing suspicion of Germany's aspirations and intentions in view of her increasing political and economic and especially military might. A consensus was emerging around the proposition that the threat posed by Germany had to take top priority in foreign policy considerations. Other commitments could be attended to only after this primary danger had been adequately addressed.

It is thus unsurprising that Crowe's advice merited Grey's and other British key policy-makers' special attention, and also came to be of great interest to historians from the 1920s onwards.[36] Even if coloured by Crowe's deep admiration for Germany's cultural inheritance and the 'enormous talents and capabilities with which she [Germany] contributed to many parts of European life', the 1907 memorandum reflected his fears regarding the Reich's foreign policy direction which he saw founded in its recent history as much as in its present activity.[37] Seen together with the F.O.'s rising general concerns over Germany's future behaviour, the memorandum surely consolidated F.O. thinking.

Yet what exactly did this famous memorandum say, and what can be extrapolated from it? How have historians read this document in view of the wider debate on the origins of the First World War and specifically regarding the interpretation of Grey's subsequent foreign policy direction and choices?

> ... Germany waited for the opportune moment for taking action, with the view of breaking up, if possible, the Anglo-French entente.
>
> ... England, more than any other non-insular Power, has a direct and positive interest in the maintenance of the independence of nations, and therefore must be the natural enemy of any country threatening the independence of others, and the natural protector of the weaker communities. ...
>
> History shows that the danger threatening the independence of ... [a] nation has generally arisen ... out of the momentary predominance of a neighbouring State at once militarily powerful, economically efficient, and ambitious to extend its frontiers or spread its influence. ... The only check on the abuse of political predominance derived from such a position has always consisted in the opposition of an equally formidable rival, or of a combination of several countries forming leagues of defence. The equilibrium established by such a grouping of forces is technically known as the balance of power, and it has become almost an historical truism to identify England's secular policy with the maintenance of this balance by throwing her weight ... in this scale ..., but ever on the side opposed to the political dictatorship of the strongest single State or group at a given time.
>
> If this view of British policy is correct, ... [England's] opposition ... assumes almost the form of a law of nature. ...

By applying this general law to a particular case, the attempt might be made to ascertain whether, at a given time, some powerful and ambitious State is or is not in a position of natural and necessary enmity towards England; and the present position of Germany might, perhaps, be so tested. Any such investigation must take the shape of an inquiry as to whether Germany is . . . aiming at a political hegemony with the object of promoting purely German schemes of expansion, and establishing a German primacy in the world of international politics at the cost and to the detriment of other nations.

With 'blood and iron' Prussia has forged her position in the councils of the Great Powers of Europe.

Germany had won her place as . . . the foremost Power on the European continent. But over and beyond the European Great Powers there seemed to stand the 'World Powers'. It was at once clear the Germany must become a 'World Power'. The evolution of this idea and its translation into practical politics followed with singular consistency the line of thought that had inspired the Prussian Kings in the efforts to make Prussia great.

It cannot for a moment be questioned that the mere existence and healthy activity of a powerful Germany is an undoubted blessing to the world. Germany represents in a pre-eminent degree those highest qualities and virtues of good citizenship . . . which constitute the glory and triumph in modern civilization. The world would be unmeasurably the poorer if everything that is specifically associated with German character, German ideas, and German methods were to cease having power and influence. . . .

So long then, as Germany competes for an intellectual and moral leadership of the world in reliance on her own national advantages and energies England can but admire, applaud and join in the race. If . . . Germany believes that greater relative preponderance of material power, wider extent of territory, inviolable frontiers, and supremacy at sea are the necessary and preliminary possessions without which any aspirations to such leadership must end in failure, then England must expect that Germany will surely seek to diminish the power of any rivals, to enhance her own by extending her dominion, to hinder the co-operation of other States, and ultimately to break up and supplant the British Empire. . . .

There is no pretence to completeness in the forgoing survey of Anglo-German relations. . . .The immediate object of the present inquiry was to ascertain whether there is any real and natural ground for opposition between England and Germany. It has been shown that such opposition has . . . existed in an ample measure for a long period, but that it has been caused by an entirely one-sided aggressiveness, and that on the part of England the most conciliatory disposition has been coupled with never-failing readiness to purchase the resumption of friendly relations by concession after concession.

It might be deduced that the antagonism is too deeply rooted in the relative position of the two countries to allow of its being bridged over by the kind of temporary expedients to which England has so long and so patiently resorted. On this view of the case it would have to be assumed that Germany is deliberately following a policy which is essentially opposed to vital British interests, and that an armed conflict cannot in the long run be averted, except by England either sacrificing those interests, with the result that she would lose her position as an independent Great Power, or making herself too strong to give Germany the chance of succeeding in a war. This is the opinion of those who see in the whole trend of Germany's policy conclusive evidence that she is consciously aiming at the establishment of a German hegemony, at first in Europe, and eventually in the world.

If, merely by way of analogy and illustration, a comparison . . . be permitted, the action of Germany towards this country since 1890 might be likened not inappropriately to that of a professional blackmailer, whose extortions are wrung from his victims by the threat of some vague and dreadful consequences in case of a refusal . . . The blackmailer's trade is generally ruined by the first resolute stand made against his exactions and the determination rather to face all risks of a possibly disagreeable situation than to continue in the path of endless concessions. But, failing such determination, it is more than probable that the relations between the two parties will grow steadily worse. . . .[38]

If we consider Crowe's memorandum as an attempt to produce a 'brief' and expert analysis of Anglo-German and Anglo-French relations based on facts, but which unavoidably does reflect some personal bias (and emotions) – then its long historical sections on the tradition of Prussian militarism and its most recent foreign political restlessness must be read in the following way: while Crowe accepted that German intentions were yet unclear, for him these historical developments foreshadowed the future. Even if Germany did not embark on an aggressive path, her ascent to a position of dominance would nonetheless 'constitute as formidable a menace to the rest of the world as would be presented by any deliberate conquest of a similar position by "malice aforethought"'. Crowe, as the extract shows, was undoubtedly worried about Germany's geopolitical ambitions, and his advice, as formulated at the very end of the document, was thus that British consent to a potential Anglo-German Agreement (which the Germans sought) had to depend on the circumstances of the moment. Berlin had to be treated with courtesy, but also with firmness and on a *quid pro quo* basis.[39]

As T.G. Otte, following Steiner's earlier reading of Crowe and her broader comments on a traditional, rather exclusive and isolated F.O. that saw the world in static terms, has emphasised, 'balance of power thinking' lay at the core of Crowe's thought and his memorandum.[40] Otte further inferred that in Crowe's view for Britain the continental equilibrium meant a 'positive power balance, as opposed to an overdrawn one'. If Britain could remain the 'linchpin of European politics', she would be better placed to protect her interests.[41] By studying the extract's language, we can see that Crowe's thinking transcended simple European power politics. Though only implicitly, Crowe described Britain as a 'World Power', not just as a 'European Great Power', and Germany's aspirations were believed to be the desire to forcibly enter into this elusive club of world powers and thus to challenge the existing equilibrium. With this language emphasising the high power-political stakes, Crowe clearly sought to influence the F.O. Whether the preservation of the balance of power was as consistent a principle in British foreign policy as Crowe assumed is debatable.

Steiner has argued that Crowe saw the problem of German-British relations also in moral terms, in that Britain, the naval and commercial might, had not and was not expected to abuse her strength, whereas an ascending Germany, as a military power, would very likely behave as offensively in the future as she had in the past.[42] From this she concluded that, despite Crowe's 'highly developed historical perspective', his memorandum was based on a static conception of world power. By contrast, Sanderson, in his response to Crowe, held that with careful diplomacy space could be found for the 'nervous giant' within the existing great power system. Yet according to Steiner the room for manoeuvre by 1907 already seemed to have become too restricted. [43]

As Crowe and other F.O. officials saw it at the time, the Franco-British *entente* had, contrary to its inception and in response to the threat posed by the Germans as reflected in the naval race and the Morocco crisis, turned into a relationship that was marked by an 'element of common resistance to outside dictation an aggression, a unity of special interests tending to develop into active co-operation against a third Power'.[44] It was in this *Realpolitik* and defensive vein that Britain, France and Russia were to form an informal coalition, the Triple Entente.

But was the German threat real or imagined? Behind the rationally presented argument, the references to Prussian military might and the German threat was there not outright Germanophobia? Can Crowe's memorandum and subsequent F.O. actions be taken at face value? Or was the German threat a fabrication, a rational calculation in the text used to justify the pursuit of ever closer Anglo-French and then Anglo-Russian ententes?

Interestingly, whereas Steiner and others have pointed to the danger, if not plain mistake, of believing that, based on this memorandum 'Crowe [and F.O. policy] was [plainly] anti-German',[45] Niall Ferguson in his *Pity of War* boldly categorises Crowe as among the 'Germanophobes'.[46] Ferguson devotes an entire subsection of his chapter 'Britain's War Illusions' to the memorandum, arguing that Crowe's 'alarmist claims of a German Napoleonic design' were in fact at odds with much of the intelligence gathered in Germany and only fuelled Grey's zeal for entente with France. He goes on to explain that, since Germany in reality was suffering acute fiscal weakness and thus was not at all as powerful as suggested, the whole idea of a direct German threat to Britain was exaggerated, if not fabricated, in order for Grey, the F.O. and the General Staff to be able to 'justify the military commitment to France'. Ferguson's main point is that the policy of 'appeasement of France and Russia' was a policy of the past, which Grey – fuelled by memoranda by the likes of Crowe in the F.O. – was bent on maintaining. Yet rather than representing a real threat, the grandiose plans for European domination were deliberately imputed to the Germans by elements of the Foreign Office and Grey.[47]

In this interpretation, Ferguson actually follows Keith Wilson's attack on Steiner's view of F.O. thinking about the 'German riddle'. Wilson wrote: 'However much, as time went by, the Foreign Office found it necessary to exaggerate and invent Napoleonic tendencies in the policy of the German empire . . . there was no German riddle.'[48] He blamed the F.O. and the Foreign Secretary for '*deliberately* [mistaking] the aims and objectives of Germany, and [crediting] her with intentions they did not believe her to possess'.[49] Moreover, Wilson, in direct contrast to Otte's recent findings but in some ways also in contradiction to Ferguson, held that 'there was no balance of power on the European continent, that the military power of Germany and Austria far outweighed that of all other Powers and that the main characteristic of German policy was . . . *its restraint'*.[50] Instead of looking to France and Russia, Britain – in Ferguson's and Wilson's views – should have sought engagement with what certainly in naval terms was a weaker Germany. Both strongly believed that Anglo-German rivalry was more or less fabricated, and that the ententes with France and Russia were pursued for other reasons than German blackmail, namely the preservation of Empire. Yet while Ferguson's analysis of the Crowe memorandum forms part of his book's overarching explanation of the outbreak of the First World War, Wilson uses the memorandum as an example to prove his point that the invention of German power was an indispensable part of the projection of Britain and indeed of building good relations with Russia – a primary end in itself. Both thus have ulterior motives as to how they use the memorandum, namely as part of a mosaic of explanations for a specific theory to prove the primacy of domestic politics in foreign policy-making. And it is this which makes their interpretations somewhat problematic.

At the risk of simplifying the complex, multilayered historiographical debate over Crowe's memorandum and British foreign policy in the run-up to the outbreak of the First World War more generally, the Steiner/Otte versus Wilson/Ferguson debate reveals how historians have read the same document in very different ways, and effectively for different purposes. Steiner and Otte have sought to study the document very closely, yet without going as far as Costigliola's approach of the study of the 'text' and 'metaphors' with view to teasing out 'emotions' and 'gender' versus 'supposedly' realistic calculations of national interest. They have analysed it with a focus on both its author's background, ideas and political influence within the F.O. and on the wider context of British foreign policy-making and thinking, before interpreting it in relation to the general contemporary international context. Certainly, in the references to Britain as a moral and even pacific great power in contrast to Germany with its 'erratic, domineering and often . . . aggressive spirit', its history of Prussia having 'forged her position with "blood and iron"'', Crowe's views of Germany as anti-British are obvious in his words and metaphors. Consequently, his rhetorical device of a disclaimer that German political actors may not have been as calculating and power-hungry as his early analysis may have laid out serves probably the purpose of further emphasising to his audience the serious threat posed by the Reich. Indeed, contrary to Ferguson's reading, the memorandum actually alludes to a need to end any appeasement policies with Germany.

Wilson and Ferguson, by seeking to bolster their theories, leave out a discussion of Crowe's personal motivations and some of the facts he states about the Anglo-French Entente. What seems to work in favour of Steiner's and Otte's interpretations is that Crowe's judgement was certainly rather realistic and also well-informed. Paul Kennedy similarly wrote on a developing Anglo-German antagonism between 1860 and 1914 (and certainly in the 1900s).[51] Crowe's interpretation was then not based solely on myths fabricated (as Wilson and Ferguson have tried to argue) by F.O. bureaucrats and the foreign secretary, but on serious thinking and calculations that the latter genuinely seemed to believe in when making their foreign policy judgements. To be sure, Crowe's use, for instance, of the metaphor of the 'professional [German] blackmailer' may have altered the F.O. mood in 1907. But as much as being a persuasive rhetorical tool, these words were also a reflection of longer-term political realities of an intensifying *real* German challenge to Britain's position, not just those of his perception.

As a coda to the above case-study, it ought to be pointed out that an even broader historiographical debate surrounding a not dissimilar premise grew out of a German memorandum, namely the question of Germany's guilt in the origins of the First World War, or rather the question whether primacy should be given to international relations or domestic politics in explaining the origins of the First World War. In the 1960s Fritz Fischer formulated a new theory based on Bethmann-Hollweg's 'Septemberprogramm' of 1914 (among other new archival sources), which called for annexations and economic mastery over central Europe. He postulated that Germany had a war plan (implying, by looking backwards to the 'War council' document, that they must have planned and wanted the war since 1912) and that the German power elite's machinations in 1914 brought about the war to stave off democracy and to attain continental hegemony. On top of this hypothesis, Fischer promoted a novel approach to the traditional high-politics historiography by studying the links between the domestic fears of the German power elite and the Reich's expansionist aims. Demanding a reinterpretation of the war's origins, he provoked what became known as the Fischer controversy in the 1960s.[52]

## Conclusions and prospects

Evidently, despite an overwhelming predominance of the study of diplomatic correspondence, topics related to foreign policy and policy-making in the late nineteenth and early twentieth century have also focused many a diplomatic historian's mind on analysing memoranda – key 'think pieces' in the classic sense – among other state papers, on which to build a particular argument. Yet with the onset of jet-setting, telephone diplomacy and the computer age from the 1980s onward, the speed both of politics and of document production has significantly increased. The nature of memoranda and other state papers has changed notably, as early declassified material from the end of the Cold War period reveals. Long 'think pieces' appear to have given way to shorter memoranda. The number of briefing notes by close advisors of the highest political actors has increased, and the sheer mass of minutes of conversations has rocketed.

The historian dealing with affairs after 1945, and especially from the 1960s or 1970s onward, thus has to look at the wider mosaic of the numerous types of government papers and other primary sources. The closer a historian comes to exploring events in the present, the less likelihood of finding a single key 'think piece' to establish a major causal nexus between document and political decision. These developments suggest the demotion of the civil servant from an auxiliary of high politics to a far more subaltern standing. The memorandum was of great significance in the policy-making machinery and processes from the late nineteenth to the second half of the twentieth century. But of late, direct communication between leaders, one-to-one meetings and telephone conversations, and most recently emails have heightened the importance of direct agency by individuals of the highest political position. In other words, technology has re-established the importance in politics, and in the practice of political history, of 'great men', and increasingly women, and of personal interaction at the highest levels. Independent of recent methodological trends in the historical profession and disputes over methodological primacy, emotion and psychology, gender, cultural perceptions, ideology and the reasoning of the individual against the background of national and international experiences will inevitably play an increased role in future historical enquiry.

The impact of the electronic revolution on the production and dissemination of memoranda, and on changes in the methods of preservation of electronic documents that affect the historian's practice, raises further issues.[53] The questions for the future are: will the historian find (printed out) drafts of longer or shorter 'think pieces' with comments and amendments in twenty, thirty, fifty or a hundred years' time? Will evidence of the addressees survive? Will email responses themselves survive? Will any action that might result be traceable? Or will digital sources simply vanish? The slow decline or disappearance of state papers as a source may result, unless archivists systematically print out and file electronic documents.[54]

From my own experience in studying unified Germany's Ostpolitik in the 1990s on the basis of pre-released documents, still classified material, newspapers, official sources, and interviews, political historians may wish to reconsider their overly historicist approach and their reliance on archives.[55] They may contemplate returning to the pursuit of the *most* contemporary history – which means that historians will have to combine written and oral testimony, just as they have already begun to use a variety of sources and approaches in the 'new' international history. Throughout the modern period as a whole, state papers (including memoranda) were, and remain, the crucial primary source for the historian of international affairs. Yet tracing, analysing and explaining the very recent past – events in the digital age – imposes peculiar and novel challenges to the historian, as government websites prove ephemeral, and political actors themselves 'make history' in a literal sense by choosing whether to save, or print and/or archive – or secure erasure of – electronic documents. Burning documents was scarcely unusual practice in the early modern period, but in the late nineteenth and early twentieth centuries, the naïve expectation developed that civil servants would discharge an implicit or explicit moral obligation to preserve all papers they produced. The result was shock at the widespread practice of deleting electronic files that emerged after Helmut Kohl's departure from the chancellorship in 1998. This chancellor – a historian by training – sought more insistently than many of his predecessors to shape the image and memory of his policies.[56]

The advent of freedom of information legislation in most Western liberal democracies and the leakage with ever-increasing frequency of emails and documents to the media has almost certainly made government officials far more guarded (consciously or subconsciously) than their predecessors in putting matters in writing at all, since papers that in the past remained indefinitely and reliably secret may now be released, or may escape prematurely into the public domain through other channels.[57]

Thus as the historian's approaches have diversified and evolved over time both thematically and methodologically, the nature and significance of memoranda, and the conditions of their preservation have likewise changed – in a process of reciprocal interaction whose end is not in sight.

## Notes

1 Memorandum – from Latin: something to be remembered; a note to assist the memory; a brief note of some transaction [law]; a summary of the state of a question [diplomacy]. *Chambers 20th Century Dictionary*, Edinburgh: Chambers, 1987.
2 T.G. Otte, 'Diplomacy and Decision Making', in Patrick Finney (ed.), *International History*, Basingstoke: Palgrave Macmillan, 2005, pp. 38–39.
3 V. Depkat, 'The Invention of State and Diplomacy: The Political Testament of Frederick III', in J. Gienow-Hecht and F. Schumacher (eds), *Culture and International History*, Oxford: Berghahn Books, 2003, pp. 233–242. K. Hamilton and R. Langhorne, *The Practice of Diplomacy*, London: Routledge, 1995, chapter 2.
4 A. Marwick, *The New Nature of History*, Basingstoke: Palgrave, 2001, p. 57.
5 G. Mollin, 'Internationale Beziehungen als Gegenstand der deutschen Neuzeit-Historiographie seit dem 18. Jahrhundert: Eine Traditionskritik in Grundzügen und Beispielen', in W. Loth and J. Osterhammel (eds), *Internationale Geschichte*, Munich: Oldenbourg, 2000, pp. 3–30.
6 Marwick, *Nature*, pp. 58–61. Cf. J. Black and K. Schweizer, 'The Value of Diplomatic History: A Case Study in the Historical Thought of Herbert Butterfield', *D&S* 17, 2006, 617–631, 619.
7 Black/Schweizer, 'The Value', p. 620.
8 G.G. Iggers and J.M. Powell (eds), *Leopold von Ranke and the Shaping of the Historical Discipline*, Syracuse: Syracuse University Press, 1990, p. 111.
9 J. Rüsen, 'Rhetoric and Aesthetics of History: Leopold von Ranke', *H&T* 29, 1990, 190–204.
10 J. Tosh, *The Pursuit of History*, Harlow: Longman, 2000, p. 73; Loth and Osterhammel, *Internationale*, p. 46; Black and Schweizer, 'The Value', p. 620. The Prussian crown founded its Geheimes Staatsarchiv Preussischer Kulturbesitz, which still exists today, in 1803. The Spanish Royal Archive at Simancas was opened to historians in 1844, while Britain's Public Record Office (PRO) for instance was founded in 1838.
11 F.A. Kittler, *Discourse Networks 1800/1900*, Stanford: Stanford University Press, 1990.
12 J. Lepsius *et al.* (eds), *Die Grosse Politik der europäischen Kabinette 1870–1914*, Berlin: Deutsche Verlagsgesellschaft für Politik und Geschichte, 1922–27. G.P. Gooch and H. Temperley (eds), *British Documents on the Origins of War 1898–1914*, London: HMSO, 1926–1938. K. Spohr, 'German Unification: Between Official History, Academic Scholarship, and Political Memoirs', *HJ* 43, 2000, 869–888.
13 J. Lawrence, 'Political History', in S. Berger, H. Feldner, K. Passmore (eds), *Writing History*, London: Arnold, 2003, pp. 183–202, p. 199. On different influences (e.g. culture, gender, intelligence, international relations theory) on international history, see Finney (ed.), *International History*; M.J. Hogan and T.G. Paterson, *Explaining the History of American Foreign Relations*, Cambridge: Cambridge University Press, 2004.

14 R. Koselleck (ed.), *Historische Semantik und Begriffsgeschichte*, Stuttgart: Klett-Cotta, 1979.

15 D. Reynolds, 'International History, the Cultural Turn and the Diplomatic Twitch', *CSH* 3, 2006, 75–91. For responses of A. Best and P. Finney to Reynolds and the latter's rejoinder, see *CSH* 3, 2006, 472–495.

16 Gienow-Hecht and Schumacher, *Culture,* fail to have a chapter on memoranda, although they discuss many other source types.

17 Otte, 'Diplomacy', p. 51. Cf. M.J. Hogan, 'SHAFR Presidential Address: The "Next Big Thing" – The Future of Diplomatic History in a Global Age', *D&S* 28, 2004, 1–21.

18 Reynolds, 'International History', fn. 53; D. Reynolds, *Rich Relations*, New York: Random House, 1995.

19 M. Creswell and M. Trachtenberg, 'France and the German Question, 1945–1955', *JCWS* 5, 2003, 5–28; K. Spohr Readman, 'Between Political Rhetoric and Realpolitik Calculations: Western Diplomacy and the Baltic Independence Struggle in the Cold War Endgame', *CWH* 6, 2006, 1–42.

20 'Introduction', in R. Oresko, G.C. Gibbs, H.M. Scott (eds), *Royal and Republican Sovereignty in Early Modern Europe,* Cambridge: Cambridge University Press, 1997.

21 F. Costigliola, '"I had come as a Friend": Emotion, Culture, and Ambiguity in the Formation of the Cold War', *CWH* 1, 2000, 103–128, 123.

22 F. Costigliola, '"Like Animals or Worse": Narratives of Culture and Emotion by U.S. British POWs and Airmen behind Soviet Lines, 1944–1945', *Diplomatic History* 28, 2004, 749–80, 754.

23 J.L. Gaddis, *We Now Know,* Oxford: Oxford University Press, 1997; V. Zubok and C. Pleshakov, *Inside the Kremlin's Cold War,* Cambridge, Mass.: Harvard University Press, 1996; K. Jensen (ed.), *Origins of the Cold War,* Washington: United States Institute of Peace, 1991.

24 F. Costigliola, '"Unceasing Pressure for Penetration": Gender, Pathology, and Emotion in George Kennan's Formation of the Cold War', *JAH* 83, 1997, 1309–1339, 1328.

25 Ibid., 1331.

26 Ibid., 1338.

27 Gooch and Temperley, *British Documents, vol. 3,* pp. 397–420.

28 Z. Steiner, *The Foreign Office and Foreign Policy 1898–1914,* Cambridge: Cambridge University Press, 1969, p. 112.

29 K.M. Wilson, 'Sir Eyre Crowe on the Origin of the Crowe Memorandum of 1 January 1907', *HRes* 56, 1983, 238–41.

30 Steiner, *The Foreign Office,* pp. 68–9, 114.

31 Wilson, 'Sir Eyre Crowe', 240–1.

32 Steiner, 'The Foreign Office under Sir Edward Grey, 1905–1914', in F.H. Hinsley (ed.), *British Foreign Policy under Sir Edward Grey,* Cambridge: Cambridge University Press, 1977, pp. 22–69, p. 23.

33 Steiner, *The Foreign Office,* p. 25.

34 Ibid., p. 69.

35 P. Kennedy, *The Rise of the Anglo-German Antagonism 1860–1914,* London: George Allen & Unwin, 1982, pp. 464–70.

36 Steiner, 'The Foreign Office', pp. 35–6; Steiner, *The Foreign Office,* p. 112.

37 Steiner, *The Foreign Office,* p. 112.

38 Gooch and Temperley, *British Documents, vol. 3,* pp. 397–420, pp. 400–416.

39 Steiner, *The Foreign Office,* p. 114.

40 Ibid., p. 210.

41 T. G. Otte, '"Almost a Law of Nature"? Sir Edward Grey, the Foreign Office, and the Balance of Power in Europe, 1905–1912', *D&S* 14, 2003, 77–118, 107.

42 Steiner, *The Foreign Office,* p. 115.

43 Ibid., p. 115.

44 Gooch and Temperley, *British Documents, vol 3,* p. 402.

45   Steiner, *The Foreign Office*, p. 114.
46   Niall Ferguson, *The Pity of War*, London: Penguin, 1998, p. 74.
47   Ibid., p. 75.
48   K.M. Wilson, *Empire and Continent*, London: Mansell Publishing, 1987, p. 53.
49   Idem, *The Policy of Entente*, Cambridge: Cambridge University Press, 1985, p. 106.
50   Ibid., p. 104.
51   Kennedy, *The Rise of the Anglo-German Antagonism.*
52   F. Fischer, *Germany's Aims in the First World War*, London: Chatto & Windus, 1967;
     F. Fischer, *War of Illusions: German Policies from 1911 to 1914*, London: Chatto &
     Windus, 1975; N Ferguson, 'Germany and the Origins of the First World War: New
     Perspectives', *HJ* 35, 1992, 725–52; A. Mombauer, *The Origins of the First World War:
     Controversies and Consensus*, London: Longman, 2002.
53   For discussions on digitalisation and digital history, see http://chnm.gmu.edu.
54   M. Moss, 'The Hutton Enquiry, the President of Nigeria and What the Butler Hoped to
     See', *EHR* 120, 2005, 577–92.
55   K. Spohr Readman, *Germany and the Baltic Problem after the Cold War*, London:
     Routledge, 2004.
56   Ibid., see postscript. Cf. Moss, 'Hutton', pp. 578–82.
57   See fn. 54.

## Select bibliography

Costigliola, F., ' "Unceasing Pressure for Penetration": Gender, Pathology, and Emotion in
    George Kennan's Formation of the Cold War', *JAH* 83, 1997, 1309–1339.
Finney, P. (ed.), *Palgrave Advances in International History*, Basingstoke: Palgrave
    Macmillan, 2005.
Gienow-Hecht, J. and Schumacher, F. (eds), *Culture and International History*, Oxford:
    Berghahn Books, 2003.
Hamilton, K. and Langhorne, R., *The Practice of Diplomacy: Its Evolution, Theory and
    Administration*, London: Routledge, 1995.
Hogan, M.J. and Paterson, T.G., *Explaining the History of American Foreign Relations*,
    Cambridge: Cambridge University Press, 2004.
Iggers, G.G. and Powell, J.M. (eds), *Leopold von Ranke and the Shaping of the Historical
    Discipline*, Syracuse: Syracuse University Press, 1990.
Loth, W. and Osterhammel, J. (eds), *Internationale Geschichte: Themen – Ergebnisse –
    Aussichten*, Munich: Oldenbourg, 2000.
Reynolds, D., 'International History, the Cultural Turn and the Diplomatic Twitch', *CSH* 3,
    2006, 75–91.

# 8  Diaries

*Christa Hämmerle*

*Translation by Andrew Evans*

Tuesday, August 1, 1944
Dearest Kitty,
. . . As I've told you many times, I'm split in two. One side contains my exuberant cheerfulness, my flippancy, my joy in life and, above all, my ability to appreciate the lighter side of things. By that I mean not finding anything wrong with flirtations, a kiss, an embrace, an off-color joke. This side of me is usually lying in wait to ambush the other one, which is much purer, deeper and finer. No one knows Anne's better side, and that's why most people can't stand me . . . Actually, I'm what a romantic movie is to a profound thinker – a mere diversion, a comic interlude, something that is soon forgotten: not bad, but not particularly good either.[1]

So wrote, in self-reflection, the then 15-year-old Anne Frank in her final diary entry on 1 August 1944. Only three days later, on 4 August, the SS and the Dutch Security Police stormed the so-called Achterhuis (Secret Annex), the Amsterdam hiding place of the Frank family, who had fled Germany several years earlier. Anne, her parents, her sister Margot and the four other Jewish people hiding in the building were arrested and subsequently deported. Except for Otto Frank, all died in Nazi concentration camps, and nothing survived of Anne apart from her diary, which has appeared in different editions since 1947 and was later made into a film. Today, it is still rightly considered to be a highly personal written legacy of one of the young, female Jewish victims of the Holocaust.

Anne Frank had begun in summer 1942 to confide in her Kitty, the name with which she personified her diary, on an almost daily basis. Oscillating between hope and despair, she noted news on the war and described her fears during the bombardment of Amsterdam, arguments with her mother, and the tensions between the families living in close proximity to one another. In addition, Anne wrote effusively about being in love for the first time, her wildly changing moods and an imaginary future as a successful author, which ultimately motivated her to rework earlier entries. In doing so, she was following the appeal of Gerrit Bolkestein, the member of the exiled Dutch government in London, who, in a foreign radio broadcast on 28 March 1944, called on people to compose authentic testimonies of the suffering of the populace under German occupation.[2] Personal writing, then, or in Anne Frank's own words, 'a collection . . . of diaries and letters dealing with the war', was meant to bear witness to a collective fate.[3]

Thus, Anne Frank's diary is both a particularly moving and unique historical source which draws upon its author's own tragic story, and equally a self-testimony which breaks through this singularity in many respects. This is true not only in view of its documentary character or the fact that these diaries have become a symbol for the expulsion and murder of millions of Jews in the Holocaust. The way in which Anne Frank tried (as in the passage quoted at the beginning) to depict and put into words the self that she perceived as contradictory, and even the simple fact that she was writing a diary at that time from the age of 13, has relevance for many girls then and since.[4] Similar diaries of young people have even been left behind from the Soviet Union under Stalin; one of them, by Nina Lugovskaia from Moscow, has been directly compared by commentators to the diary of Anne Frank.[5]

Although that may be a rather glib comparison, it cannot be overlooked that through her writing Anne Frank was participating in a youth diary culture that arose in the nineteenth century and reached a peak in the early twentieth century, perhaps especially among girls.[6] It was only thanks to this that Gerrit Bolkestein's radio call fell on fertile ground in the case of Anne Frank, and that at the same time diary-writing also flourished on the other side of the German *Volksgemeinschaft*. In recent years it has become apparent that there are not only far more diaries or diary-like writings by persecuted (Jewish) people than had long been assumed,[7] but also that many gentile German children and young people composed various forms of war diaries.[8]

What connects, then, the diary of Anne Frank with the culture of diary-writing that was so widespread at the time? In what respect can her example be generalised, and where is it situated in the context of established genre definitions and in respect to concepts and debates in the history and theory of the diary? Should girls' diaries be defined as a possible sub-genre when constructing canons? And when does this sub-genre begin?

## Defining the genre

With its inclination for self-exploration, the passage from Anne Frank's diary cited at the beginning leads us into the heart of the discussion. For example, self-exploration is a central issue explored in Ralf Wuthenow's much-quoted overview of the diary genre. He underscores the 'immediacy' of the diary genre which arises because a diary is 'composed almost in the midst of impressions and experiences, so to speak', and does hence not permit 'any summarising with the benefit of hind-sight or later understanding'. Yet of the many possible dimensions of a diary's con-tent, Wuthenow emphasises above all the fact that this is a form shaped by the 'reflective self which tries to envision, objectify and recall itself, and maybe also project itself'. He ranks as comparatively less important the frequent description of crude everyday reality, the reporting of impressions and experiences of books and landscapes, the formulation of religious or erotic thoughts, the confessional character of many diaries, and their tendency to approximate a collection of philosophical, literary or scientific plans, designs, outlines and commentaries.[9] His relatively open definition of the diary notwithstanding, Wuthenow locates the main feature of the genre in its self-centredness and self-reflexivity. In this he follows the criteria closely tied to literary history which for a long time represented *the* definitive parameters for the appraisal of autobiographic writing in the modern era.

Furthermore, Wuthenow continued a tradition which primarily focused on the diaries of male writers. It is no accident that in his sample women like Katherine Mansfield or Virginia Woolf make up a minority of around ten per cent of the authors examined, although these women did at least find a place in the history of the genre here, something which earlier could by no means be taken for granted.[10] Archetypal diaries were initially only canonised if they were written by male authors, as was the case with the conceptualisation of the autobiography – ideal examples of which were considered from the nineteenth century on to be *Les Confessions* (The Confessions, 1782) by Jean-Jacques Rousseau and *Aus meinem Leben. Dichtung und Wahrheit* (From my Life: Poetry and Truth, 1811–1813) by Johann Wolfgang von Goethe.[11] Only male self-exploration in diary form was attributed with the status of 'literature in its raw form' and ascribed aesthetic and artistic character.[12] This was true even when such texts did not conform to the ideal of a coherent and autonomous male self, as was the case with some of the best-known examples of the 'Journal intime' in the nineteenth century.[13] The prevailing view in the hegemonical literary industry was Gottfried Keller's maxim, formulated in 1838, that 'a man without a diary (whether on paper or in his head)' is like a 'woman without a mirror'. With this, Keller addressed the bourgeois gender dichotomy and equally the convention that a writer should keep a diary, for the writer's 'intellectual independence' could, he thought, 'only be preserved through continual reflection and strict self-observation', which was 'best achieved through a diary'.[14]

The watchword 'strict self-observation' also stands here for the primary function ascribed to the modern diary. In explaining its emergence, established definitions of the genre take as their starting-point a 'process of development of self-awareness' which took place in Europe from the eighteenth century onwards.[15] It is above all in this way that these definitions distinguish the journals of the pre-modern period, which on the whole describe exterior events and behaviour, from the diaries of the modern age.[16] Earlier self-description in diary form, as it was practised, for instance, by both men and women in the puritan New England of the seventeenth century or in the pietist religious circles of the eighteenth century on the European continent, document only early forms of modern self-reflexivity which were still strongly bound to religiously motivated self-observation and self-examination. This lineage includes Johann Caspar Lavater's *Geheime[s] Tagebuch. Von einem Beobachter seiner Selbst* (Secret Journal of a Self-Observer) which was initially published anonymously in 1771 and, in the German-speaking world, quickly became the literary prototype for a lively diary culture of the 'awakened', a classic example of a new subjective form of religiousness in the transition from 'self-portrayal motivated by pietism to one based on psychological motives'.[17]

It is above all the nineteenth century that is regarded as the golden age of the – then largely secular – private diary. 'By far the largest number of diarists wrote in the 19th century', writes the author of a study of female diaries in England from 1600 to 1939.[18] British female manuscript diaries of the nineteenth century have even been gathered in a separate bibliography, testimony to the large variety of this writing in the United Kingdom.[19] With regard to France in the nineteenth century, Alain Corbin has asserted that the bourgeois public virtually elevated the diary to a synonym for the 'mystique of the individual' that was especially pronounced in its circles. The market offered a variety of diaries, some rather luxurious, bound in real or imitation leather, adorned with golden lettering and lockable with a finely crafted miniature key. These were readily bought and sold, given as gifts and filled with writing to imitate the literary success of the 'Journal intime'[20]. The trend was also orientated around women, particularly as the polarisation of gender roles in the bourgeois era led to the fixation of women and girls in the private, non-public sphere. Women's ostensibly natural characteristics were located in the domains of reproduction, and associated with emotionality and the prosaic concerns of everyday life, while more publicly relevant qualities such as rationality and objectivity were ascribed to the male sex. The gendered private–public dichotomy characteristic of modernity gradually unfolded in the decades around 1800.[21]

This led effectively to a paradox with regard to diary-writing: although (almost exclusively) male authors continued to define the canon, the immense popularisation of diary-writing hinted at here caused parallel diary cultures to develop, practised by women and girls. This happened to such an extent that at the end of the twentieth century (female) scholars, inspired by feminism, were to ask, among other things, if the diary might not represent a genuinely female genre.[22] At the same time, they had to deal critically with the consequences of the social barriers to which female diary writers had been subjected. These writers could not come anywhere near the ideal of an autonomous or freely acting self, or an 'I', but rather focused much more on other writing traditions, their everyday life and a collective, usually family-centred 'We'.[23] Firmly wedged in the private sphere, they often cast themselves in correspondingly contradictory ways. As a result, this form of writing, especially the diaries of young girls, has repeatedly been judged negatively. It was devalued, for instance, by Jean-Paul Sartre, whose protagonist Antoine Roquentin in his 1938 novel *La Nausée* notes that in future he will refrain from charting his impressions 'day-to-day in a pretty notebook like the little girls'.[24] Bolshevik propaganda proceeded in similar fashion in its largely unsuccessful attempt to encourage workers on the Moscow metro to write 'production diaries'. These were to be 'unlike a bourgeois diary' which was considered 'a socially useless record filled with ineffectual talk' and as 'a girl's high school activity: a girl who sits down and writes all sorts of nonsense'.[25]

Philippe Lejeune's study of girls' diaries in France is, by contrast, completely free of such judgments, which have sometimes also permeated literary-historical portrayals of private diaries.[26] He takes a wholly non-discriminatory perspective that is indispensable for a historical analysis of such texts. Lejeune was able to identify more than 100 diaries written between 1783 and 1914 by girls or young women up until their marriage, but only a few written by boys. Almost all originated from the middle and upper strata of the bourgeoisie or from noble circles. The largest group of these diaries, whose production increased notably from around 1830, comprises those published, usually posthumously, in the course of the nineteenth century primarily for purposes of commemoration and instruction.[27] It was their pronounced religious content that made these diaries such suitable reading, and they were often reworked and corrected for a published edition, especially in the second stage of the history of girls' diaries from around 1850 to 1880 which Lejeune terms the 'moral order' phase. At this time it was common for middle-class girls to be urged to write diaries and for the mothers or teachers to monitor them for educational purposes. In this way, the time before their hoped-for marriage was used to educate girls in feminine conduct, in morality, devotion and godliness, and also in handwriting and style – often making these 'waiting-for notebooks' heavily censored texts.[28]

It was only in a third phase, from around 1880, as such religious and moral influences gradually retreated, that French girls could formulate their diaries in a more open and self-determined way. An example of this is the diary of Marie Bashkirtseff (1858–1884) who died at a young age and whose text found many imitators. Bashkirtseff's diary stands for a process of secularisation and democratisation of this popular sub-genre.[29] Such a tendency was driven not least by schools and was obviously conscious in the minds of educators, as the comments the Catholic abbé Laplace made in 1885 reveal. He welcomed the keeping of a diary in principle as 'an excellent thing' which had 'its place in the life of a pious girl'. At the same time he qualified this, warning that 'the hateful and cunning self, which creeps in under the appearance of the greatest humility, must be expelled from it at any cost'.[30]

Self-centredness and self-confidence, then, were not everyone's right, even at the end of the nineteenth century, and nor would they become a right later. The example should also demonstrate that diary-writing was able to retain a considerable religious function in the modern age. Until long into the twentieth century it remained the case that diaries were written, among other things, to reflect on and put religiousness into words, or even to enter into dialogue with God.

However, such tendencies only become apparent when we look at the whole spectrum of diary-writing in a particular period and when we recognise that the boundaries between the various different genres of self-writing were continually porous. Primarily introspective or self-reflective diaries should be placed alongside more calculative and chronicle-like housekeeping books, almanacs (*Anschreibebücher*, widely used in peasant households), notebooks chronicling births in the family and other books on family life, which often have their origins in much older traditions of popular writing. The effusive diaries of adolescents should be contrasted with the more documentary style of war and travel journals and 'eye-witness accounts', which can in turn be literary in form.[31] In practice, all the possibilities of diary-writing mentioned here tend to overlap and merge into one another, and the boundaries between diaries and other self-testimonies such as the letter-diary can be said to be open. According to the context in which a diary is composed, it can serve as the vehicle for many different self-depictions and self-projections which are motivated by the relevant cultures (both religious and non-religious) of self-thematisation and self-control. Writing a diary could thus serve spiritual purposes and the task of adapting to everyday life and expected social roles, and equally that of self-exploration in an individualising society. In some situations, therefore, diary-writing led the writer back into practising self-education and self-discipline. Irrespective of this, the twentieth century saw ever-increasing activity in the field of politically motivated diary-writing – some more, some less successful.[32]

The modern diary then, like any other source, is located in the tense relationship between the society and the individual, which can sometimes be complex to unravel. It is not simply private or intimate, as overly narrow genre definitions suggest. The diary should not be conceived of as exclusively private, even when it contains for example only the everyday writings of a young girl on her family, her school, her prayers and her dreams. Rather, this writing had, like any diary-writing, significance for gender politics, and ultimately social implications, and could ultimately, as mentioned before, also be published as an expression of such.[33] Felicity Nussbaum thus defines the diary as fundamentally 'poised between past and future, self and other, public and private, universal and particular'.[34] Here she agrees with other current appraisals of the genre which see the emphasis on the private as completely 'inadequate' and call for this 'phantom in our heads' to be dispensed with once and for all.[35]

This suggestion is to be welcomed, as are further ideas with respect to the established suppositions that diaries are 'formless' and 'monological'. According to Arno Dusini, the former is refuted by the diary's structure on the level of the speech act, while the latter, he points out, is untenable since there are many diaries written directly to someone else or, as in the case of Anne Frank, addressed explicitly to another person.[36] We should also be critical of the definition that diaries per se reproduce 'immediacy' and 'exactness' and distil the day's events rather than taking an ordering, retrospective narrative approach. For in many diaries, memories are thematised, or, as again was the case with Anne Frank, are subsequently reworked.[37] The diary should therefore be conceived rather as a text which is structured using the periodic passing of units of time and the highly selective narrative figure of a 'day' in particular. It is, thus, a genre that is 'rhymed on a day'.[38]

Finally, the aforementioned focus on the history of girls' diaries, which Lejeune, not by coincidence, published in a book called *Le Moi des Demoiselles* (The Self of the Damsels), should make clear one further indispensable theoretical premise for the analysis of historical diaries. For this programmatic title expresses the fact that the young diary writers of the nineteenth century also sought to articulate their selves, in whatever way they formulated this, and that such self-reference increased after 1880. This was the case in spite of the gender norms which their writing was meant to reflect, and leads to the question of subjectivity that forms the basis of the diary as a self-centred genre. If we wish to do justice to the historical diversity and heterogeneous nature of many diary cultures, we must not use an essentialist concept of the subject. Nor can we subordinate the subject to a linear process of development toward a growing, non-historicised 'self-awareness' in the modern age, not least because this would lead us to neglect a large proportion of the female self-positioning practised by women and girls in their diaries.

The idea that all forms of subjectivity, and thereby all concepts of the self, are genuine historical phenomena was first put forward by theorists such as Jacques Lacan, Louis Althusser and Michel Foucault. Especially pertinent was Foucault's theory that the 'care of the self' associated with the enlightenment was established with an 'entire activity of writing and speaking' and thus became a 'true social practice'.[39] Even the modern diary which came into being at this time, based upon a self constructed in this way, is therefore ultimately the result of corresponding social discourses.

The further development of such an approach has come especially from feminist theorists in connection with postmodernist positions. In view of the fact that it was feminism that made the diary prominent, as Harriett Blodgett described it in 1988, this seems perfectly logical and has motivated numerous research works on the self-positioning expressed in the most diverse examples of female self-testimonies and often marked by ambiguity and ambivalence.[40] With this work, the classical concept of a universal subject, which in reality was always based on the male subject, has been decentred in a lasting way.[41] It has become all the more clear that western ideals of a coherent and stable human self were always 'constructs rather than eternal truths'. This in turn, and in association with postmodernist approaches, has led ultimately to a concept of the subject which sees subjectivity as being generated through language and consequently assumes that the text contains multiple selves: 'Individuals construct themselves as subjects through language, but the individual . . . can only adopt positions within the language available at a given moment.'[42]

In the wake of the linguistic turn, the radical practice of attaching such importance to the power of discourse alone has been much questioned and adapted, especially in the controversial discussion about the concept of experience. This notwithstanding, there is currently general agreement in the cultural and historical sciences on the necessity of (de)constructionist approaches for analysing diaries, the definition of which has also been fundamentally modified in recent times. This redefinition of what constitutes a diary has also resulted from the unexpected abundance of modern auto/biographical writing that has been (re)discovered since the 1980s and the 'hybridity and diversity' of these texts.[43] Rather than getting caught up in seeking to classify them into sub-genres and categories it has been suggested that instead we should ask what function keeping a diary has for the respective writer.[44] This is a promising approach since it leads us away from the unfruitful genre debate and toward the question of the social uses of different forms of text, for instance in times of war or personal crisis, or in the tensions between resistance to and compliance with social norms.[45]

## Historiography and diaries

The question of the usefulness of diaries as a source for historical studies has not yet been fully clarified with these remarks, though. We have established that private diaries cannot simply be taken as authentic personal accounts of individuality and subjectivity, experiences and meaningful communications of actors in the past. Historians have repeatedly made this mistake, following rarely challenged basic assumptions of historicism which, with its focus on the individual as an autonomous personality, favoured those sources which 'are grouped around the achievements and development of the individual personality: diaries, letters, memoirs, autobiographies'.[46] In this way, the purpose of the 'limitless diversity of autobiographical writing' was thought to be its use in evaluating the 'development of the consciousness of personality in occidental society'.[47]

The hermeneutic tradition within the arts and humanities had a great interest in autobiography which manifested itself in numerous editions of such sources since the nineteenth century to which historians have long referred. In this process, canonisation took place in the sense that certain dairies, which often existed only in printed selections, were repeatedly drawn upon in order to investigate historical figures and their interpretations of the world. In principle, this changed only with the reorientation of the historical sciences after the Second World War and above all after the establishment of the social history paradigm from the 1960s on, when self-testimonies fell into disrepute. Many came to regard them as unreliable sources and they were used much less often – particularly in German historiography where structural and socio-historical approaches were an especially dominant orientation of the discipline. In the USA and in Great Britain, in contrast, William Matthews published his comprehensive annotated bibliographies of diaries in 1945 and 1950.[48] He had the explicit aim of making this 'splendid raw material for social historians and historical linguists' more easily accessible so that they would make 'fuller use of them'. Diaries were, as Matthews believed even then, good sources 'for studies of popular ideas, fashions, taste, manners'.[49]

It may be thanks to the specific orientation primarily of English social history that the aforementioned mistrust of diaries was much less pronounced here than elsewhere. In any case, important historical contributions using such sources were to be found here even in the 1970s, such as Lawrence Stone's much quoted study of the 'privatisation' of the family and the beginning of love-matches in the late seventeenth century.[50] A further example is Leonore Davidoff's impressive analysis of the diaries of Hannah Cullwick (1833–1902), a Victorian maidservant.[51] From such examples a continuous line can be drawn into the 1990s and Peter Gay's influential book *The Naked Heart*, which forms part of the new histories of culture and sexuality. Inspired by psychoanalysis, Gay's text reads intimate diaries of the nineteenth century as part of the bourgeois discourse on the self, on love and on sexuality.[52]

In the German-speaking world, it was the history of everyday life of the 1980s that gradually led the historical sciences to renew their interest in subjective testimonies. These were supposed to enable direct access to individual and collective life experiences, interpretations and value-judgements, and as a result ideas of 'authenticity' and 'vividness' were key. This was true at first with respect to the lower classes, although, understandably, they handed down to us far fewer written self-testimonies than did the bourgeoisie. These existed, for instance, in the form of farmers' almanacs (*Anschreibebücher*) which, alongside details of sowing, ploughing and weather conditions, only rarely included short personal reflections.[53] Social historians working on the history of the middle classes were more fortunate. For example, the Viennese social historian Michael Mitterauer, who also widely researched on life-histories 'from below', analysed unpublished diaries from the bourgeois-commercial milieu in Vienna in the context of his research on religion in everyday life. In his analysis, he emphasised above all the prayerful nature of the diary entries of Johann Leb (born in 1840) and their direct appeals to God and other holy figures. Mitterauer was interested in the information these diaries give about the practice of prayer at that time and the shift toward a shorter and more individual practice of prayer in the family, more strongly related to particular events.[54]

More recently, the scope of such isolated examples has been extended by studies in women's and gender history, and by work on the war experiences in the two World Wars. Diaries are, however, still not a particularly favoured source in mainstream historical studies. In historical analysis, they are usually reduced to the dimension of content, of 'what is meant', or used to 'illustrate ready-made hypotheses'.[55] This is a practice which treats passages in isolation and was in principle already practised by Lawrence Stone.

By contrast, a recently published study by Jochen Hellbeck on *Writing a Diary under Stalin* demonstrates in exemplary fashion the new historical insights into a particular epoch that are possible when we put its diary-writing cultures at the centre of our analysis. Contrary to what has long been assumed, many private diaries were composed even in the totalitarian Bolshevik system – by young people, by men and women, by members of the proletariat and by members of the intelligentsia. Hellbeck researched this 'popular genre of the period' after the opening of the Soviet archives in 1991 and analysed it using both systematic perspectives and model examples. He reveals, for instance, that specific forms of diary-writing were propagated in the Soviet Union after 1917 and that, contrary to persistent assumptions, the development of 'personality' or the 'appeal to the self' lay at the heart of Communist ideology.[56] Most diary writers therefore oriented their self-sketches on revolutionary narratives or on the Communist concepts of the 'New Man' and 'New Woman', even though the contemporary language of self built largely on traditions of writing within the Russian intelligentsia. Many of them believed they were living in an exceptional historical period which 'required work and struggle' – and this applied equally to their private diaries which they sometimes kept for periods of up to 30 years.[57] On the basis of a meticulous analysis of these diaries, often together with other self-testimonies by the same individuals, Hellbeck can throw light on the dynamic interaction of ideology and individual agency, something which has long eluded researchers of totalitarian systems.[58]

## On the vulnerability of diaries – and an example

'... il n'est pas de texte plus vulnérable que le journal "intime" [... there is no more vulnerable text than the journal "intime"]'.[59] With this formulation, Béatrice Didier was not only referring to the fact that private diaries were frequently destroyed, but also had in mind editorial practices of the genre. These are, as Dusini also believes, 'a story of censorship, concealment and retraction, correction and rewriting'.[60] This was done by family members or friends when they published diaries of a loved one or relative posthumously, as well as by other editors who often only made a selection from the original diary entries. Examples of this are Leonard Woolf's edition of Virginia Woolf's diaries or the case of Henri-Frédéric Amiel, whose extensive diary-writings have only been published for the first time in their entirety from 1976 onwards. To these could be added countless other cases, beginning with Samuel Pepys's journals from the seventeenth century (of which there are so many different editions that they sometimes give different accounts of the very same day), right through to the diaries of Sylvia Plath, whose mother even added her own commentary.[61] In this respect too, Anne Frank's diary, which today exists in three versions, is no exception.

All this means that when interpreting edited diaries historically, we have always to ask about their complex relation to the original. If possible, we should use the original in order to analyse the edited version as a 'life rewritten'.[62] We must ask how things stand with the opposition between edited version and original, also with regard to the format, the handwriting or typeface, the writing implements and paper. What is irretrievably lost when diary entries are recompiled in printed form? What is left out, changed or given new meaning? Here we do not only have to consider that the original script can provide information as to the emotions of the writer – for instance where the writing suddenly becomes large and expansive. We must also think of everything that is placed or drawn inside the diary. Original diaries are particularly fascinating in this material sense: instead of words they repeatedly use dried flowers, photographs, theatre ticket stubs, bills, pencil sketches or simply exclamation marks as modes of expression. At the other end of this scale of diversity are war diaries which were sometimes even written in trenches, hurriedly in pencil, on loose slips of paper or in small notebooks and calendars.

Whether in edited form or in the original, all diaries are obviously to be treated as texts which, by means of various methods of text and discourse analysis, can and must be interpreted. This is because diary writers do not, as has been made clear, simply write in a personal language about themselves, and do not only describe their private daily experiences and activities. Rather, they also use 'borrowed languages' from the wide field of literature and other media, from the institutions of the Church, school education, political systems and so on, and they appeal to terminology, metaphors and other rhetorical devices which must be precisely reconstructed.[63] Only in this way can we work out the different traditions of discourse and the fragments and strands of discourse on self-thematisation and self-reference – all of which often clash and contradict one another in real examples of diaries – and make them relevant for a historical perspective on the many forms of modern diary-writing. When we carry out the essential task of putting diaries in the context of their medium, of history and of their authors' biographies, we can ascertain why diary writers choose particular – not always coherent – textual strategies to carry the narration in particular personal, social, political or historical situations.

This also applies to the strategies of silence, insinuation and periphrasis chosen by the author. Here, we touch on an aspect which in my view constitutes the particular 'vulnerability' of a private diary. In order to demonstrate this, an example of a woman's diary will be used here.[64] It displays, in a particularly drastic way, the impact of violence on private writing under the Nazi regime, and with this the genre's strong dependency on context. To decode this adequately, it is important to use intertextual analysis alongside the study of a particular text. This can often be achieved by interpreting a diary in relation to other available editions of the same work, or to further (auto)biographical texts and documents on and by the same person, written before, after or at the same time as the diary. Such comparisons make the process of interpretation more time-consuming but also guard against serious misjudgements which can arise when only a small number of sources are used.

The 'diary narrative' presented in the following would, however, only be of limited use if we did not have a larger palette of texts at our disposal to aid our understanding. The diary is by Therese Lindenberg (née Trestl) who was born illegitimately in the foundling hospital in Vienna in 1892 as the only child of a Catholic farmer's daughter and a Jewish father. She never wrote this herself, however, in any of her unpublished works which are archived in the Sammlung Frauennachlässe (Collection of Women's Personal Papers) at the Institute of History at Vienna University.[65] We know it only because two students from a research seminar, inspired by reading left-behind fragments of a novel on the fate of a foundling, examined the relevant records at the foundling hospital and found her name. Therese Lindenberg did not even disclose this secret shame to her descendants, and instead took it with her to the grave when she died at a great age in Vienna in 1980. An awareness of this history is useful to today's readers when interpreting her diaries.

Throughout her life, Lindenberg, who was a trained singer, wrote an abundance of different texts, not least because she would have liked to have become an author. Her writings include diaries and travel itineraries, letters and autobiographical manuscripts and also numerous (unpublished and to some extent autobiographical) novels, stories and poems. Beginning with her adolescent diary in 1909, she continually depicted and devised herself and the people she lived with in new ways and wrote about her life which was closely bound to the crisis-laden history of the twentieth century – even during National Socialism when she and her family were exposed to life-threatening persecution. The original diaries still exist from this time when Therese, who had been legitimised ex post by her Catholic stepfather, upheld her 'mixed marriage' (a term coined by the Nazi state) with the Jew Ignaz Lindenberg and in so doing rescued him from the regime. Another version of these diaries, entitled 'The Apocalyptic Years', which she compiled and rewrote herself in her old age in 1975, also remains in existence. This as yet unpublished manuscript, composed for her children and grandchildren, is much shorter in length than the original diaries: 39 pages of typescript compared to four full paperback volumes from the years 1937-1946 which are complemented by a sort of letter-diary and by entries on the war in a later diary. All in all, the manuscripts of Lindenberg's writings from the time comprise more than 200 pages of typescript.

However, the later compilation and reworking of the original diaries decodes much more information on what Therese Lindenberg and her husband had to endure in the years from the Anschluss of Austria by Nazi Germany in 1938 to the liberation of Vienna by the Allies in April 1945. For Lindenberg not only cut sections but also added and rewrote some entries entirely so that, in connection with a few other entries she wrote long after the war, we discover only with this diary-version what she had concealed in the original out of fear and worry. This is true, for example, with respect to the flight of her daughter to Manila in spring 1938 when it became clear that the Nuremberg race laws also classed her as 'Jew', or with respect to the repeated forced changes of address when Therese and Ignaz Lindenberg had to leave their high-quality rented apartment for a series of 'Jewish houses' [Judenhäuser]. From there, they had to watch the deportations; Ignaz Lindenberg himself was continually threatened; many friends and relatives were deported – even those from 'mixed marriages' whose 'Aryan' partners lived apart or had separated under pressure from the Nazi Party.

Despite all this, large parts of the original diaries consist of countless, almost romantic-looking descriptions of nature and the weather, as well as reports on the author's many excursions to other districts of the city and the areas around Vienna. She hardly mentions that these were primarily undertaken to support herself and her husband, since Therese Lindenberg carried out work in various locations in return for money. She was also extremely religious during these years; prayer and appeals to God, the examination of her own conscience and even spiritualism are all basic themes of these diaries, as well as the intense longing for her daughter, who had married and settled with her children in exile in the remote Manila. Apart from these topics, allusions predominate: the situation described above is addressed and lent an air of fear and danger, but is not explained at length. The scant references to it are dotted throughout the text in the form of concise pieces of Nazi jargon, which obviously had a protective function, for example '*Polentransporte*' (transports to Poland), '*Polenaktion*' (the action against Poles, deportation) and '*Parteimann*' (party man) and others. This tactic is seen in the diaries only when the danger was particularly great, as is shown by the following examples:

23rd January [1940]
And so life races wildly on. ... It's bitterly freezing here. Minus 14–16° almost every day. A bit milder today. –5° In Hetzendorf yesterday, surrounded by snow.

29th January [1940]
I read the pages earlier. Restful evenings in the child's room. Gone, gone forever. Letters today from the Waitzenkorn sisters. Depression. Being dependent on favours and support from other people. That's hard. . . . I want to be patient, I said at communion today. And always: protect my child . . . I'm dreading the days to come. Snow, so much snow. And war. And hardship, hardship. What could you say about it! All trapped in my heart. Skiing with Edith on Sunday 25th. On the Hamean. Then home via the Dreimarkstein. What a feeling!

6. II. [1940]

Colossal snowfall the day before yesterday and yesterday. In Hetzendorf today. Maxingpark. I greeted the snowy scene in tears. Little fir trees, coated in snow. Then home via Schönbrunn. The violet veil of the setting sun. The sun huge, golden [above the Gloriette]. My husband better. The action against Poles. No trams yesterday.

15/II./

Still no news from the child. 10 weeks tomorrow. Party man the day before yesterday. Deep depression in the evening, sadness . . . Lord I'm timid. I'm despairing. I know you're protecting us – yet still the tears run. Oh Lord, take care of my husband.

On the 19th February [1941]

Deepest despair. Maybe separation from my husband.

Saturday 22/II [1941]

11 weeks tomorrow since Lisl last wrote. The transports to Poland. At Edith's on Tuesday 18th. Coming from the Rudolfinum I heard blackbirds whistling in the garden. How it made my heart ache.

9th March [1941]

Every day I think: will the card come today? A sword of Damocles. Wedding celebration yesterday at Hilda's. My soul was far away. With the children. Letter from Hans – my joy!

Sunday, 15th February [1942]

I always think of the child, full of deep, deep longing. 'I'm really missing mother and father.' About this passage of a letter I reflect. Shovelling snow. Transports.

19th February [1942]

Still cold. Minus 3–4°. Walls of snow. Masses of snow on the 16th and 17th. Husband's suffering. Can't go out. Looks terrible. My heart aches when I look at him. The woman on the wagon the day before yesterday. Her fine face. She'd come from shovelling snow. The ebony furniture today. The portrait of the beautiful radiant woman. Where might she be? 11 weeks yesterday and no letter from the child.[66]

In the later compilations of the contemporary diaries, precisely such entries were taken up and revised, while the themes of nature and religion were played down. As the comparison shows, it was less important to Lindenberg to stick to the precise dates of the events described than to give more precise information on the things that her understandable fear had initially prevented her from picking out as a central theme. After all, she knew that her diaries could be confiscated at any time and could have posed a danger for those around her. This explains why she initially wrote only rarely and laconically of the 'husband' and, much more often, of the 'child' or 'Lisl', her daughter – features that are retained in the later version of the diaries. Other areas have been supplemented in a highly targeted way, as some matching excerpts from 'The Apocalyptic Years' will demonstrate:

> 10th [February 1940]
> And so life races wildly on . . . We hear about the deportation of the Jews. Mr Waitzenkorn, my student, comes for a 'farewell visit'. I have to go away, he tells us, the polite old guy.
> . . . 'Where to?' 'To Poland'. He thinks it's right that the Jews have to move closer to each other now, away from the tyrant . . . Oh, he'll reach them there too . . . Poland partly belongs to him now, doesn't it? . . . Very cold. Minus 14–16°. Somehow I've got hold of some coal. The room is warm. We live on the 3rd floor. And the husband has to fetch the coal from the cellar . . . He's so patient . . . I can only love and protect him.

> 15th February [1941]
> Husband still ill – since 16th January. Coughing, fever, no doctor . . . The party man came, to convince me to divorce . . . Deepest despair . . . And yet I feel protected . . . The experience with the ring.

> Sunday 22nd February [1941]
> 11 weeks tomorrow since Lisl's last letter.
> The tranports to Poland. There're eight of us in the Sandwirtgasse. One after the other has to leave. Litzmannstadt, 'resettlement' it says. Poland . . .

> 9th March [1941]
> Every day I think: will the card come today about deportation? A sword of Damocles.

> 15th February [1942]
> I'm always thinking of my loved ones, always full of deep, deep longing. Lisl writes: 'I'm really missing mother and father' . . . The transports. How the thought of them lies heavy in my heart . . . And my whole body hurts when I look at my husband. He looks so terrible. 14 weeks yesterday since the last letter from Manila came . . . The snow shovellers. Only Jews . . . A beautiful, elegant woman stood on the collection wagon . . . Her fine face! What a radiant woman she must have been . . . On the furniture wagon where all the 'Jewish furniture' was loaded I once saw a portrait of such a woman . . . Ebony furniture stood there . . . and then a wagon with the finest linen! 2 Marks a bundle – which people were snatching at – about 6 cushions, sheets – shirts – a bundle certainly worth more than 100–150 Marks . . .[67]

'The Apocalyptic Years' thus contributes considerably to our understanding of the diaries Therese Lindenberg composed during the Holocaust. But beyond this, the manuscript is also a new diary in which the years of fear and anxiety have been reworked. In so doing, Lindenberg retains many original passages and above all the elliptic, often telegram-like style with which she tells her story in the original diaries. This doubtlessly lessens the degree of difference between the two versions. However, there are significant differences in the self-references, the language of self. The original war diaries appeal primarily to religious and bourgeois-romantic discourses, while in 'The Apocalyptic Years', the central concern is documentation and commemoration for her descendants and the general public she imagines reading her reworked diary of the years of the Holocaust. It is for this reason that the elderly Lindenberg reawakens her memories of the past – not least in order that she might bequeath a written testimony of her courage during the Holocaust.

## Conclusion

All this again demonstrates aspects of the diary genre which have been examined in this chapter. While the diary is virtually dedicated to the day on which it is written, the past, the present and the future all mesh and overlap with each other in complex fashion within its pages, opening the genre to questions of how meaning is created and the world interpreted in different historical contexts. Furthermore, the boundaries between the diary and other autobiographical texts are fluid so that narrow definitions of the genre do not help us if we want to understand why and to what purpose people wrote diaries and which textual strategies they employed accordingly.

This chapter also showed that historical and theoretical dimensions of the modern diary cannot be fully understood without taking a gender perspective. For through the association of the genre with the modern bourgeois self, which in the hegemonic discourse denoted the male self, and through the genre's orientation on the private sphere, the domain assigned to the female sex, the diary is a strongly gendered medium and must be explored as such in any analysis. As has been shown here, we can only do justice to such a gendered genre by using concepts of subjectivity which integrate the ambivalence and fluidity contained in the self-sketches drawn by diaries.

## Notes

1 A. Frank, *The Diary of a Young Girl. The Definitive Edition,* ed. O.H. Frank and M. Pressler, trans. S. Masotty, New York: Bantam, 1997, pp. 330–331.
2 Ibid, foreword, p. vii.
3 Ibid, entry for Wednesday, March 29, 1944, p. 241.
4 For the USA see for example: M. Culley, *A Day at a Time. Diary Literature of American Women from 1764 to 1985,* New York: Feminist Press, 1985; for Great Britain, H. Blodgett, *Centuries of Female Days. Englishwomen's Private Diaries,* New Brunswick, N.J.: Rutgers University Press, 1988; C. Huff, *British Women's Diaries. A Descriptive Bibliography of Selected Nineteenth-Century Women's Manuscript Diaries,* New York: AMS Press, 1985; for France, P. Lejeune, 'The "Journal de Jeune Fille" in Nineteenth-Century France', in S.L. Bunkers and C.A. Huff (eds), *Inscribing the Daily. Critical Essays on Women's Diaries,* Amherst: University of Massachusetts Press, 1996, pp. 107–122; for Germany and Austria, M. Soff, *Jugend im Tagebuch. Analysen zur Ich-Entwicklung in Jugendtagebüchern verschiedener Generationen,* Weinheim and Munich: Juventa, 1989, and especially the diaries collected, published and commented by the founder of youth psychology, Charlotte Bühler, such as: C. Bühler, *Zwei Mädchentagebücher,* Jena: Fischer 1927.
5 See the comparison by L. Ulitzkaja in the foreword of the German edition: N. Lugowskaja, *'Ich will leben.' Ein russisches Tagebuch 1932–1937,* Munich: Hanser

Verlag, 2005. The English edition is N. Lugovskaya, *The Diary of a Soviet Schoolgirl (1932–1937),* Moscow: Glas, 2003.

6  See C. Hämmerle 'Ein Ort für Geheimnisse? Jugendtagebücher im 19. und 20. Jahrhundert', in P. Eigner, C. Hämmerle and G. Müller (eds), *Briefe – Tagebücher – Autobiographien. Studien und Quellen für den Unterricht,* Innsbruck and Vienna: StudienVerlag, 2006, pp. 28–45.

7  See, as a very important and often discussed example: *The Diaries of Victor Klemperer 1933– 1945,* London: Phoenix, 2000.

8  N. Stargardt, *Witnesses of War. Children's Lives under the Nazis,* London: J. Cape, 2005, has used a huge range of such diaries from both sides.

9  R.-R. Wuthenow, *Europäische Tagebücher. Eigenart–Formen–Entwicklung,* Darmstadt: Wissenschaftliche Buchgesellschaft, 1990, pp. ix–x, 1–13.

10  Anne Frank's diary is not included.

11  F.A. Nussbaum, 'Toward Conceptualizing Diary', in T.L. Broughton (ed.), *Autobiography. Critical Concepts in Literary and Cultural Studies,* vol. IV, London and New York: Routledge, 2007, p. 4.

12  Wuthenow, *Tagebücher,* p. ix.

13  One example is Stendhal (Henri Beyle), whose 'Journal 1801–1823' was published posthumously, another is Henri-Frédéric Amiel, extracts from whose monumental 'Journal intime' were also edited shortly after his death. See Wuthenow, *Tagebücher,* pp. 70–85.

14  Quoted in M. Brink, *Ich schreibe, also werde ich. Nichtkeitserfahrung und Selbstschöpfung in den Tagebüchern von Marie Bashkirtseff, Marie Lenéru und Catherine Pozzi,* Königstein: Ulrike Helmer Verlag, 1999, p. 40.

15  Wuthenow, *Tagebücher,* p. 7.

16  In the secondary literature a more documentary or protocolary character is often attributed to the 'journal', whereas a 'diary' is seen as a more personal form of writing. Other authors stress that both terms are interchangeable, or make inverse definitions. Cf. Blodgett, *Centuries,* p. 262, note 12; R. Cottam, 'Diaries and Journals: General Survey', in M. Jolly (ed.), *Encyclopedia of Life Writing. Autobiographical and Biographical Forms,* vol. 1, London and Chicago: Fitzroy Dearborn, 2001, p. 268; Nussbaum, *Conceptualizing,* p. 5.

17  A.M. Melichor, '*Liebesprobleme . . . waren schon immer ein Anlaß für mich, Tagebuch zu führen' Liebe, Ehe und Partnerschaft in Frauentagebüchern,* Königstein: Helmer Verlag, 1998, p. 20.

18  Blodgett, *Centuries,* p. 10.

19  Huff, *Women's Diaries.*

20  See A. Corbin, 'Das Geheimnis des Individuums', in M. Perrot (ed.), *Geschichte des Privaten Lebens. 4. Band: Von der Revolution zum Großen Krieg,* Frankfurt am Main: S. Fischer, 1992, pp. 466–468. For Britain in the nineteenth century see Huff, *Women's Diaries,* pp. xiv–xvi, who states that the market here offered special 'Ladies' Diaries' as printed formats for diary writing. The term 'Journale intime' denotes hence the literary diaries of the nineteenth century and is also a specific French term for private diaries in general. See P. Lejeune and C. Bogaert. *Le journale intime. Histoire et anthologie,* Paris: Les éditions Textuel, 2006, p. 23.

21  See for example D.O. Helly and S.M. Reverby (eds), *Gendered Domains. Rethinking Public and Private in Women's History,* Ithaca: Cornell University Press, 1992; L. Davidoff, *Worlds Between. Historical Perspectives on Gender and Class,* Cambridge: Polity Press, 1995.

22  See for example Blodgett, *Centuries,* p. 5; Cottam, 'Diaries', p. 269.

23  Huff, *Women's Diaries,* xviif.

24  Quoted in Brink, *Ich schreibe,* p. 96.

25  Quoted in J. Hellbeck, *Revolution on My Mind. Writing a Diary under Stalin,* Cambridge, Mass.: Harvard University Press, 2006, p. 44.

26 See for example P. Boerner, *Tagebuch*, Stuttgart: Metzler, 1969, p. 52.

27 Lejeune, *Journal*, p. 108.

28 Lejeune, *Moi*, p. 160f. This was also a common practice in nineteenth-century Britain; see Huff, *Women's Diaries*, pp. xxv–xxvi.

29 Lejeune, *Journal*, p. 120.

30 Quoted in Brink, *Ich schreibe*, p. 44. See also, for diary-writing of school girls at this time: R. Rogers, 'Schools, Discipline and Community: Diary-writing and Schoolgirl Culture in Late Nineteenth-century France', *Women's History Review* 4, 1995, 525–554.

31 See W. Hardtwig, 'Der Literat als Chronist. Tagebücher aus dem Krieg 1939–1945', in Hardtwig and E. Schütz (eds), *Geschichte für Leser. Populäre Geschichtsschreibung in Deutschland im 20. Jahrhundert*, Stuttgart: Franz Steiner, 2005, p. 149.

32 For the Soviet Union under Stalin see Hellbeck, *Revolution*, as well as: V. Garros, N. Korenevskaya, T. Lahusen (eds), *Intimacy and Terror. Soviet Diaries of the 1930s*, New York: The New York Press, 1995; for diaries in Nazi Germany Hardtwig, 'Literat', and S. zur Nieden, *Alltag im Ausnahmezustand. Frauentagebücher im zerstörten Deutschland 1943–1945*, Berlin: Orlanda Frauenverlag, 1992.

33 Nussbaum, *Coneptualizing*, p. 5. See also Huff, *Women's Diaries*.

34 Nussbaum, *Conceptualizing*, p. 9.

35 A. Dusini, *Tagebuch. Möglichkeiten einer Gattung*, Munich: Wilhelm Fink, 2002, pp. 70–71.

36 Dusini, *Tagebuch*, p. 68; see also Huff, *Women's Diaries*, pp. xviii–xix.

37 Dusini, *Tagebuch*, p. 73.

38 Ibid., pp. 83–108; on dates as a basis for diary-writing see also Lejeune and Bogaert, *Journal intime*, p. 23.

39 M. Foucault, *The Care of the Self. The History of Sexuality*, Vol. 3, London: Penguin, 1990, p. 51.

40 Blodgett, *Centuries*, p. 3; Cottam, 'Diaries', p. 269. See for example the collection of some of these theoretical texts in S. Smith and J. Watson (eds), *Women, Autobiography, Theory. A Reader*, Madison: University of Wisconsin Press, 1998; D. Riley, *The Words of Selves. Identification, Solidarity, Irony*, Stanford: Stanford University Press, 2000.

41 Cottam, 'Diaries', p. 269.

42 Nussbaum, *Conceptualizing*, p. 6.

43 Cottam, 'Diaries', p. 268.

44 Brink, *Ich schreibe*, p. 46.

45 See for example C. Hämmerle, '"Il libricino da chiudere a chiave." Diari popolari femminili dell'Otto-Novecento', in A. Iuso (ed.), *Scritture di donne. Uno sguardo europeo*, Arezzo: Protagon Editori Toscani, 1999, pp. 33–51.

46 H. Oncken, 'Aus der neueren Memoirenliteratur' (1905), quoted in D. Günther, '"And now for something completely different." Prolegomena zur Autobiographie als Quelle der Geschichtswissenschaft', *Historische Zeitschrift* 272, 2001, 26–27.

47 G. Misch, 'Geschichte der Autobiographie' (1962–1976), quoted in Dusini, *Tagebuch*, p. 65.

48 M. Matthews, *American Diaries. An Annotated Bibliography of American Diaries written prior to the Year 1861*, Berkeley: University of California Press, 1945; *British Diaries. An Annotated Bibliography of British Diaries Written between 1442 and 1942*, compiled by W. Matthews, Berkeley: University of California Press, 1950.

49 Matthews, *British Diaries*, pp. vii–viii.

50 L. Stone, *The Family, Sex and Marriage in England 1500–1800*, London: Weidenfeld and Nicolson, 1977, list of diaries pp. 763–765.

51 L. Davidoff, 'Class and Gender in Victorian England: Diaries of Arthur J. Munby and Hannah Cullwick', *Feminist Studies* 5, 1979, 104–141. These diaries were edited a few years later: L. Stanley (ed.), *The Diaries of Hannah Cullwick, Victorian Maidservant*, New Brunswick. N.J.: Rutgers University Press, 1984.

52  P. Gay, *The Naked Heart*, New York: W.W. Norton, 1995.
53  See for example J. Peters, H. Harnisch and L. Enders, *Märkische Bauerntagebücher des 18. und 19. Jahrhunderts. Selbstzeugnisse von Milchviehbauern aus Neuholland*, Cologne, Weimar and Vienna: Böhlau, 1989.
54  M. Mitterauer, ' "Nur diskret ein Kreuzzeichen." Zu Formen des individuellen und gemeinschaftlichen Gebets in der Familie', in A. Heller, T. Weber and O. Wiebel-Fanderl (eds), *Religion und Alltag*, Cologne: Böhlau, 1990, pp. 154–204.
55  Günther, *And now*, p. 45.
56  Hellbeck, *Writing*, pp. 4, 13.
57  Ibid., pp. 54–55.
58  Ibid., p. 12.
59  B. Didier, *Le Journale intime*, Paris: PUF, 1976, p. 21.
60  Dusini, *Tagebuch*, p. 49.
61  Ibid., pp. 43–47.
62  Ibid., p. 51.
63  See the introduction to this volume, and S. Titscher, M. Meyer, R. Wodak, and E. Vetter, *Methods of Text and Discourse Analysis*, London: Sage, 2001; R. Wodak and M. Meyer (eds), *Methods of Critical Discourse Analysis*, London: Sage, 2003.
64  C. Hämmerle, L. Gerhalter, in collaboration with I. Brommer and C. Karner, *Die Tagebücher der Therese Lindenberg (1938–1946)*, Cologne, Weimar and Vienna: Böhlau, 2008 (in press).
65  See <http:///www.univie.ac.at/geschichte/sfn> (accessed 26 August 2007).
66  Extracts from C. Hämmerle, L. Gerhalter, *Tagebücher* (in press).
67  Ibid.

## Select bibliography

Amigoni, D. (ed.), *Life Writing and Victorian Culture*, Aldershot: Ashgate, 2006.

Blauvelt, M.T., *The Work of the Heart: Young Women and Emotion 1780–1830*, Charlottesville: University of Virginia Press, 2007

Blodgett, H., *Centuries of Female Days. Englishwomen's Private Diaries*, New Brunswick, N.J.: Rutgers University Press, 1988.

Broughton, T.L., (ed.), *Autobiography. Critical Concepts in Literary and Cultural Studies*, 4 volumes, London and New York: Routledge, 2007 (especially chapters in vol. IV).

Bunkers, S.L. and Huff, C.A. (eds), *Inscribing the Daily. Critical Essays on Women's Diaries*, Amherst: University of Massachusetts Press, 1996.

Culley, M., *A Day at a Time. Diary Literature of American Women from 1764 to 1985*, New York: Feminist Press, 1985.

Dusini, A., *Tagebuch. Möglichkeiten einer Gattung*, Munich: Fink 2005.

Hellbeck, J., *Revolution on My Mind. Writing a Diary under Stalin*, Cambridge, Mass.: Harvard University Press, 2006.

Langford, R. and West, R. (eds), *Marginal Voices, Marginal Forms: Diaries in European Literature and History,* Amsterdam: Rodopi, 1999.

Lejeune, P. and Bogaert, C.. *Le journale intime. Histoire et anthologie*. Paris: Textuel, 2006.

Mallon, T., *A Book of One's Own. People and Their Diaries*, Saint Paul, Minn.: Hungry Mind Press, 1995.

Sinor, J., *The Extraordinary Work of Ordinary Writing: Annie Ray's Diary*, Iowa City: University of Iowa Press 2002.

Wink, A.L., *She Left Nothing in Particular. The Autobiographical Legacy of Nineteenth Century Women's Diaries*, Knoxville: University of Tennessee Press, 2001.

# 9  Novels

*Julia Reid*

Since the 1980s, the 'linguistic turn' in history and the advent of New Historicism in literary criticism have led to an apparent synergy between history and literary studies, a convergence captured in Louis Montrose's formulation, 'the historicity of texts and the textuality of history'.[1] What are the implications of this interest in the dynamic interplay of text and historical moment for the status of one literary genre – the novel – as a source? To address this, I shall focus on the nineteenth-century novel, as its engagement with realism renders it particularly crucial to the debate. The chapter will introduce the main features of the genre before outlining how historians have used the nineteenth-century novel as a source and considering the questions raised by its deployment as historical evidence. Finally, it will analyse a passage from a late-Victorian romance, H. Rider Haggard's *She* (1887), to explore some of these issues.

## The novel as a genre

Two features are central to the novel genre and to its relationship to its historical context: its association with realism and its connection with emergent class structures and reading practices. Critics have often regarded the nineteenth-century novel reductively, portraying it as naïvely realist in its narrative perspective and tainted by its bourgeois credentials. However, the genre was undoubtedly much more complex than this suggests: it was self-conscious in its negotiation of debates about realism and objectivity, and – far from being the ideological preserve of the middle classes – was traversed by competing class discourses.

For critics, the nineteenth-century novel's realist aesthetic indicates its adherence to a crude belief in scientific objectivity. The historians Hayden White and Dominick LaCapra, for example, have condemned modern historiography by associating it with the nineteenth-century novel's mode of representation, a mode which allegedly sought to 'render a literal copy of a presumably static reality'.[2] Yet the nineteenth-century novel, even in its realist heyday, was not unquestioningly empiricist. Ironically, the genre's origins and development articulate many of the epistemological debates which have exercised recent historians: debates about the blurred boundaries between realism and fictionality, objectivity and subjectivity, empiricism and theory, and fact and fiction.

As the genre rose to prominence in the eighteenth century, writers sought to distinguish the novel from romance, citing its realism, its objectivity, and its fidelity to empirical fact. As Euphrasia in Clara Reeve's critical dialogue *The Progress of Romance through Times, Centuries and Manners* (1785) explains:

> The Romance is an heroic fable, which treats of fabulous persons and things. – The Novel is a picture of real life and manners, and of the times in which it is written. The Romance in lofty and elevated language, describes what never happened nor is likely to happen. – The Novel gives a familiar relation of such things, as pass every day before our eyes, such as may happen to our friend, or to ourselves.[3]

By the mid-nineteenth century, indeed, realism had become central to the European novel. In France, the novelists Honoré de Balzac and Gustave Flaubert engaged in debates about realism. In Britain, George Eliot looked to the scientist as the model for the realist novelist's practice. As she wrote in *The Mill on the Floss* (1860):

> In natural science . . . there is nothing petty to the mind that has a large vision of relations, and to which every single object suggests a vast sum of conditions. It is surely the same with the observation of human life.[4]

This scientism culminated in the *fin-de-siècle* naturalist novel, in which Emile Zola and others drew on physiological medicine and positivist philosophy to investigate human activity as a product of inheritance, environment, and historical circumstance.[5]

For later critics, nineteenth-century novelists' appeals to science were deceptive, fostering an illusion of objectivity, and presenting the world of the novel as a direct, unmediated external reality rather than an artistic creation. In the French critic Roland Barthes's phrase, realism cultivated the '*referential illusion*'.[6] Such an illusion has been seen as either unsophisticated or ideologically suspect. Ioan Williams asserts for example that 'the mid-Victorian novel rested on a massive confidence as to what the nature of Reality actually was', and J.P. Stern describes realism as 'epistemologically naïve'.[7] Other critics relate the parallels between realism's narrative omniscience and science's rhetoric of objectivity to writers' quest for professional power. For Lawrence Rothfield, Flaubert's use of medical models of the 'clinical gaze' in *Madame Bovary* (1857) forms part of this attempt to assert epistemological authority.[8]

Yet despite realist novelists' frequent recourse to science, they arguably used scientific analogies more critically, to question the possibility of transparency. Eliot's novel, *Middlemarch* (1871–2), highlights the *limits* of human vision: 'Even with a microscope directed on a water-drop we find ourselves making interpretations which turn out to be rather coarse'.[9] This emphasis on 'making interpretations', on subjectivity and fallibility, informs even her more classically realist novel, *Adam Bede* (1859), where the narrator explains that:

I aspire to give no more than a faithful account of men and things as they have mirrored themselves in my mind. The mirror is doubtless defective; the outlines will sometimes be disturbed.[10]

Here, Eliot unsettles the idea of mimesis, undermining the popular image of holding a mirror up to nature. This doubt about narrative objectivity intensified as the Victorian period ended, shaping modernism's problematization of omniscient narration and its tendency to locate narrative in its characters' subjective consciousness, and, eventually, postmodernism's deliberate emphasis on its own fictionality.[11]

The novel's relationship to developing class formations and reading practices is equally important for historians exploring the genre's engagement with its historical context. The novel was not simply an uncomplicatedly middle-class genre (a significant point for historians concerned with the 'representative' nature of their source). Ian Watt argued seminally that the rise of the novel reflected the triumph of a dominant bourgeois experience.[12] However, critics have recently challenged this assertion, showing that the novel was the site of competing discourses, and enjoyed a broader social base and appeal.[13] Indeed, by the late-Victorian period, subgenres proliferated, as the Gothic novel, domestic romance, sensation novel, detective novel, science fiction, and imperial adventure vied with realism for readers' attention. Nor is it helpful to think in terms of a binary opposition between 'high' and 'popular' fiction. Certainly, many novels – such as the so-called 'penny dreadfuls' – were written specifically for working-class men.[14] Nonetheless, as Roger Chartier observes, there is no clear division between 'popular' and 'high' culture; he draws attention, rather, to the 'fluid circulation and shared practices that cross social boundaries'.[15] Thus Charles Dickens's *Pickwick Papers* (1836–7) emerged partly from comic traditions within popular culture, and re-entered this world when it was illustrated – and plagiarized – by the popular press.[16] From mid-century, publishers brought out cheap reprints of contemporary literature, and a burgeoning mass literacy, fuelled by the 1870 and 1880 Education Acts, further blurred the division between high and popular culture.

Reading practices were similarly rooted in the rapidly developing mass market for literature, with many Victorian novels first appearing, in serialized form, in magazines or periodicals. As Linda Hughes and Michael Lund have shown, encountering a novel in serial instalments produced a very different experience from reading it in volume form.[17] As well as encouraging a distinctive rhythm of reading, serial fiction was more obviously engaged with the 'real' world of non-fictional discourses, in the shape of the adjacent articles. The instalments of sensation novels, for example, were frequently engaged with the surrounding articles in intertextual debates on topical issues such as insanity, class, and crime.[18]

In its reading practices, then, as in its relationship to emergent class structures and its negotiation of realism, the nineteenth-century novel appears a peculiarly open-ended literary form, characterized by fluid and shifting boundaries between high and low culture, text and context, and fiction and fact.

## The novel as historical source

The realist novel, with its appeals to objective, scientific truth, has been a tempting source for historians. Novelists have frequently been imagined as preserving historical evidence which would otherwise have been obliterated. Thus Thomas Hardy aimed to provide, in his Wessex novels, 'a fairly true record of a vanishing life'.[19] Zola too researched the Anzin coal strikes in what James Smith Allen describes as 'a methodical manner closely resembling that of an historian'; his novel *Germinal* (1885) has outlasted many of his sources.[20] Friedrich Engels testified to the historical researcher's debt to the realist novelist, claiming that he learned more about French society from Balzac than from 'all the professional historians, economists and statisticians of the period put together'.[21]

Since the end of the nineteenth century, though, historians have been more sceptical about the novel as a source. LaCapra suggests that their attraction to an empirical and scientific model of history has relegated novels to the status of 'questionable literary evidence'.[22] Writing in 1948, William Aydelotte exemplified this attitude, warning that 'the attempt to tell the social history of a period by quotations from its novels is a kind of dilettantism which the historian would do well to avoid'.[23] He asserted that a work of art illuminates only the writer's 'background and interests . . . [and] his artistic purpose' and not 'the spirit of the age'.[24] From the 1930s, even this biographical approach to literature was called into question, as New Criticism in the United States and practical criticism in Britain promoted a decontextualized, formalist approach to literature. The work of art, according to these schools, was free-standing, and criticism should not concern itself with the writer's intention any more than with the historical context.[25]

From the 1950s, however, literary studies have been revitalized by successive post-formalist approaches – most notably reception theory, structuralism, deconstruction, and New Historicism.[26] These approaches have fed into history's linguistic turn and led to a rejuvenation in historical approaches to the novel. Reception theory, associated with Wolfgang Iser, Barthes, Stanley Fish, and others, looks at the production of meaning as an active negotiation between readers and text, and provides insights into how historians might think about readers' responses to fiction. For Barthes, meaning is produced in the process of reading, and this entails a shift of critical attention from the writer to the reader: the 'death of the Author' is required by the 'birth of the reader'.[27] The structuralist movement took issue with a representative view of language, asserting that language constitutes rather than records the world. While some structuralists were ahistorical in approach, others stressed the social nature of language, and examined the struggle by different discourses to fix meaning. Moving into the late 1960s, post-structuralism or deconstruction, which has been understood as a response to the failure of radicalism in 1968, viewed language as less stable than the structuralists had imagined. For Jacques Derrida, language and discourse is engaged in an infinite, open-ended play of signification; no text has determinate meaning; and there is nothing outside discourse. Post-structuralism was soon critiqued as an ostensibly apolitical, but essentially reactionary, formalism. However, the 'return to history' in the 1980s saw post-structuralist approaches used by more politicized schools, such as New

Historicism in the United States. New Historicism scrutinizes the interaction of texts with diverse social and political contexts, including those of sexuality, gender, ethnicity, and colonialism and postcolonialism. It is indebted to Michel Foucault's postmodern history, absorbing his interest in the relations between discourse and power but also his resistance to notions of historical truth and causation.

These theoretical approaches have been immensely fruitful for historians' thinking about textuality and history, and offer particular insights for their interpretation of novels. Nonetheless, many commentators have felt uneasy about this, viewing the linguistic turn, broadly conceived, as anti-realist. For those committed to the traditional historical task of establishing causation, the new cultural history evades this central responsibility. Peter Mandler asserts that emphasizing textual indeterminacy undermines the possibility of making objective claims about causation; charging that cultural history now lacks 'methodological rigour', he calls for a 're-infusion of discipline'.[28] Others, though, have mounted a robust defence of the new cultural history and New Historicism, one which is particularly pertinent to historians' use of novels. Carla Hesse welcomes the 'discursive turn', and applauds New Historicism's insistence on the dynamic interactions of text and context.[29] She insists that, while the notion of causality should not be jettisoned, 'to understand how meanings arise and how they operate . . . we need to investigate both how the text works as a system of signification, and also how it is produced, used and interpreted'.[30] Indeed, uniting historians' assimilation of these disparate theoretical approaches is the idea that one should consider texts not simply as illustrative documents but as part of wider discursive systems, and as linguistic negotiations of their historical contexts.

Despite this burgeoning interest in language and discourse among historians, theoretically sophisticated approaches to the novel are by no means the norm. Many historians have continued to use novels in an illustrative or documentary way, as apparently unmediated sources of factual information. Jerome Blum, for example, views novels by Hardy, Balzac, Anton Chekhov, and others as valuable social history sources, claiming that the 'realists'' intimate first-hand knowledge of the rural world and their artistic genius enabled them to provide us with an awareness of the realities of peasant life that the accounts of scholars cannot hope to achieve'.[31] Here, there is no understanding of language as constructing rather than representing reality. The force of 'artistic genius', rather than creating a fictional world, merely gives the writer more direct, unmediated access to the 'realities of peasant life'. Textbooks are perhaps the most prone to use novels in an illustrative way. Asserting that the 'cult of progress was very generally accepted by the mid-Victorians', Asa Briggs adduces as evidence, in the following order, Mr Gradgrind, the philosopher Herbert Spencer, and Charles Darwin.[32] Yet surely Dickens's Gradgrind, and his comic success with readers, provides, if anything, a measure of public *hostility* towards his self-confident belief in material progress and his mantra of 'Fact, fact, fact'?[33] At the other end of the spectrum are the historians who recognize the complexities of questions about genre in source analysis, but are reluctant to confront them. Michelle Perrot, who discusses her schooling in a tradition of historical sociology and quantification which was 'wary of a history that was "literary"', treats Zola's novels rather suspiciously in her work on French strikes: 'Did people die of hunger as in *Germinal*? . . . The historian always has some qualms about entering into the meaning of works of art'.[34]

Nonetheless, cultural historians, historians of science, and New Historicists are producing excellent work which draws on novels as a source in illuminating, challenging, and critical ways. I shall now consider some of the questions central to historians' use of novels by examining three areas in which this work is proceeding apace – representations of the city, the relations of Victorian literature and science, and imperial romance. At the heart of historians' work in these three fields are questions about generic difference, the relationship between readers, authors, and texts, the relation of fiction to ideology, and the construction of meaning.

### The city

One exciting recent strand of urban history seeks to tease out the ways in which the city has been imagined and experienced. As Peter Fritzsche has shown of Berlin, textuality and the modern city enjoy an intimate, mutually constitutive relationship.[35] In British history, Judith Walkowitz's *City of Dreadful Delight* (1992) and Seth Koven's *Slumming: Sexual and Social Politics in Victorian London* (2004) are particularly important attempts, informed by post-structuralism, to examine how the metropolis has been represented and understood in fictional and non-fictional discourses.[36] Koven eschews a model of transparent representation, seeing the novels he explores as 'attempts by their authors to organize self-consciously what they saw, thought, and read about the world of slum philanthropy'; he examines 'the discursive resources [the novelists] mobilized as writers of fiction' to 'make sense of this world'.[37] Koven's work usefully destabilizes the relationship between fact and fiction, tracing how the documentary exposés of conditions in 'Outcast London' were influenced by Dickens and the French novelist Eugène Sue, and how, in turn, realist novels paraphrased reports of evangelical agencies.[38] Readers' responses, of course, are central to the production and circulation of meaning within discourses of the city. While Koven examines middle-class reformers' testimony to the inspirational effect of the novels they read, individual working-class responses are harder to excavate.[39] Jonathan Rose's research on working-class readers develops this point. Asking rhetorically 'What did the Artful Dodger think of *Oliver Twist*?', Rose notes the divergent, often surprising, and sometimes subversive lessons which readers extracted from Dickens's work.[40] Urban historians working in this vein thus use the novel innovatively to explore how representations of city life breach the borders between fact and fiction, and between textual meaning and readers' response.

### Science

Scholars working on the relations of science and the novel have been particularly alert to the importance of genre in the construction of knowledge, meaning, authority, and subjectivities. An increasingly relativist and externalist approach to the history of science, fostered by Thomas Kuhn's *The Structure of Scientific Revolutions* (1962), has recognized science as a product of culture rather than a transcription of nature. This has generated substantial critical literature on the relations between science and the novel in the Victorian period. At the heart of this work are questions about the dynamics of influence between the two discourses. There is, as Gillian Beer has demonstrated, no 'one-way traffic' from science to fiction, but a complex pattern of mutually influential relations.[41]

However, while critics have emphasized patterns of assimilation and absorption as ideas travel between discourses, Helen Small critiques as too simple a 'one culture idea', contesting the assumption that 'the evidence of nineteenth-century medical and fictional texts [on insanity] is bound to be complementary'.[42] In fact, ideas originating in one discourse are resisted and challenged as often as they are assimilated in another field. Divergent generic conventions and discursive imperatives remain important, then, and New Historicism and new cultural history, valuable though they are in unsettling the categories of 'literary' and 'non-literary' texts, should not blind us to these differences. Indeed, Mary Poovey challenges the equation between literary and scientific realism made by critics including Rothfield.[43] She argues that 1840s social realist novelists radically rewrite and individualize the 'anatomical realist' narratives of political economy and social analysis.[44] The work of these interdisciplinary scholars productively uses the novel's negotiation of science to examine how ideas, values, and meanings travel between discourses and are thereby affirmed, contested, and modified.

### *Imperial romance*

The late-Victorian imperial romance has proved another fertile field for historicist interpretations of fiction. In some ways the historicization of romance novels has been too easy, as their influence on the formation of imperial attitudes and subjectivities has been unquestioningly assumed. J.S. Bratton, for example, argues that children's fiction presented 'an idealised England as the motive and reward of the Empire-builder', but does not discuss readers' responses to this apparent textual psychology.[45] Martin Green, who pioneered the idea that adventure tales formed 'the energizing myth of English imperialism', also offers a curiously monolithic model of readers' engagement with imperial texts ('Clearly the reader feels ...').[46] But this model of fiction fuelling imperialism fails to engage with questions about the debatable relation of culture to ideology. As Mandler asks in a different context, 'What cultural work does art do?'[47] Might not these tales of exciting adventure have provided escapist fantasy, and reconciled readers to their mundane home life, rather than inspiring them to enter the service of the Empire? These questions return us to the field of reader-response criticism. Moreover, to what extent did cultural forms create or merely respond to popular imperialism? John MacKenzie makes this point in a series of terse questions: 'Reflection or instrument? Supply- or demand-led?'[48]

The imperial romance has also been historicized by considering how imperial, masculine identities are constructed against a non-European or female 'other'. For the postcolonial critic Edward Said, the romance was integral to the discursive production of the 'Orient' as 'other', while feminist critics including Elaine Showalter have examined its foundation in misogynistic energies.[49] This mining of novels for binary oppositions can, unfortunately, lead to reductive readings. For example, John Tosh argues that empire was represented in popular culture as:

> the complete antithesis of feminine domesticity. This message came over loud and clear in the work of [Robert Louis] Stevenson and [H.] Rider Haggard ... Their heroes hunted, plundered or conquered, shored up by the silent bonds of men's friendship; and they were unencumbered by the presence of females.[50]

As a caricature of Stevenson's work this is particularly misleading. For instance, his novella 'The Beach of Falesá' (1892) amounts to a critique of imperialist masculinities: it is the tale of a Briton who comes to value his Polynesian wife over his fellow white settlers.[51] Stevenson was unusually equivocal about imperialism, but historians and critics have become increasingly alert to the tensions inherent within imperialist discourse more broadly. As Catherine Hall explains, Said's emphasis on 'certainties about the divisions between "us" and "them" has been undermined as the focus has turned to the ambivalence of colonial discourse'.[52] Stephen Arata's analysis of the male romance, indeed, argues that rather than being 'unambiguously celebratory of late-Victorian masculinist ideals', it is marked by profound anxieties about masculinity.[53] But where, finally, does this attention to ambivalence leave traditional historical questions about agency, causation, and power? In other words, how does textual uncertainty relate to the realities of imperial aggression and power? Anne McClintock offers a salutary reminder that, 'If colonial texts reveal fissures and contradictions, the colonials themselves all too often succeeded in settling matters of indecision with a violent excess of militarized masculinity'.[54]

In recent work on representations of the city, the relations between Victorian science and the novel, and the imperial romance, then, historians have deployed a new, more dynamic model of the construction of meaning and identities, one indebted to post-formalist theoretical approaches. They have examined the fluid, sometimes collaborative, sometimes resistant processes by which ideas move between reader, text, and author, between fictional and non-fictional discourses, and between text and context. In the final part of this chapter, I shall analyse a passage from Rider Haggard's *She* in order to consider how these issues might inform the historical source analysis of a novel.

### Extract and analytical interpretation: H. Rider Haggard, *She* (1887)

> [T]he handsomest of the young women ... deliberately advanced to [Leo], and, in a way that would have been winning had it not been so determined, quietly put her arm round his neck, bent forward, and kissed him on the lips.

I gave a gasp expecting to see Leo instantly speared; and Job ejaculated, 'The hussy – well, I never!' . . .

When we came to understand the customs of this extraordinary people the mystery was explained. It then appeared that, in direct opposition to the habits of almost every other savage race in the world, women among the Amahagger are not only upon terms of perfect equality with the men, but are not held to them by any binding ties. Descent is traced only through the line of the mother, and while individuals are as proud of a long and superior female ancestry as we are of our families in Europe, they never pay attention to, or even acknowl-edge, any man as their father, even when their male parentage is perfectly well known . . . When a woman took a fancy to a man she signified her preference by advancing and embracing him publicly, in the same way that this handsome and exceedingly prompt young lady, who was called Ustane, had embraced Leo. If he kissed her back it was a token that he accepted her, and the arrange-ment continued till one of them wearied of it. I am bound, however, to say that the change of husbands was not nearly so frequent as might have been expected . . . It is very curious to observe how the customs of mankind on this matter vary in different countries, making morality an affair of latitude, and what is right and proper in one place wrong and improper in another. It must, however, be understood that, as all civilised nations appear to accept it as an axiom that ceremony is the touchstone of morality, there is, even according to our own canons, nothing immoral about this Amahagger custom, seeing that the interchange of the embrace answers to our ceremony of marriage, which, as we know, justifies most things.[55]

How might we approach this extract as a historical source? Clearly the narrator Holly's account of Amahagger practices tells us nothing about the realities of nine-teenth-century African societies, despite suggestions, denied by Haggard, that the Amahagger were based on the Transvaal Lovedu.[56] It reveals much, though, about late-Victorian culture, illustrating the complex ways in which fiction negotiated contemporary historical contexts and non-fictional – especially scientific – discourses.

The rhetoric of the 1880s 'romance revival' may suggest that the form is disen-gaged from history: the romancers emphasized fictionality and repudiated realism. A brief plot synopsis will establish the novel's fantastic premises. *She* relates the adventures of three Englishmen who set out to the 'darkest heart' of Africa. Leo, the ward of the Cambridge scholar Holly, discovers that he is descended from an ancient Egyptian, Kallikrates, who was murdered by an African Queen, Ayesha. Leo and Holly set off with their trusty servant, Job, on a mission to kill the two-thousand-year old Ayesha. In the apparently primitive heartland of East Africa, they find her cave-dwelling Amahagger, who form a matriarchal society (as we see above). Central to the adventures which follow is the struggle between Ayesha and Ustane for Leo's heart. Ayesha prevails, but she is finally and dramatically destroyed by the fire which first endowed her with mysterious longevity.

Yet despite this emphasis on the marvellous, the late-Victorian romance was dynamically related to its historical context and intimately interwoven with non-fictional discourses. *She* is structured by this tension between 'adventure' and 'facts' (Holly insists that his narrative is 'the most wonderful history, as distinguished from romance').[57] The narrative tension between romance and history, fact and fiction, informs the extract above: exotic mystery is countered by a dry, ethnographic narrative voice. Indeed, Haggard's fiction – and late-Victorian romance more generally – was deeply engaged with contemporary anthropology. The novelist and scientific popularizer Grant Allen hailed Haggard's fiction, along with that of Stevenson, as a new genre, the 'romance of anthropology'.[58] Haggard, whose interest in anthropology stemmed from his work in colonial South Africa, dedicated *She* to the folklorist Andrew Lang. The extract exemplifies the novel's attention to custom and belief. Contrasting Amahagger courtship practices with the 'habits of almost every other savage race in the world', Holly not only exhibits his own anthropological knowledge, but assumes equal knowledge on the part of his readers.

More specifically, the extract reveals the articulation, across scientific and fictional discourses, of the late-Victorian debate about matriarchy.[59] From the 1860s, anthropologists queried the assumption that patriarchy was universal, suggesting instead that matriarchy was the original form of social organization. The heated debate which ensued was clearly marked by anxieties about the emergent feminist movement. (Darwin's theory that female sexual selection among animals precedes male sexual selection among humans was marked by similar concerns, and also informs the extract.[60]) Anthropologists including John F. McLennan and John Lubbock offered a triumphant narrative of progress from primitive and promiscuous matriarchy to civilized, monogamous patriarchy. More radical thinkers, however, urged a return to matriarchal values. The fraught debate soon crossed disciplinary borders between anthropology and fiction, as a cluster of novels envisaged the resurgence of matriarchy.

While critics have usually read *She* as a fiercely misogynistic fantasy, a straightforwardly dystopian vision of matriarchy, the extract demonstrates a more equivocal negotiation of the debate.[61] At least three voices are in dialogue in the passage, communicating a mingled sympathy and revulsion at the idea of female rule and sexual empowerment. Holly's understanding undercuts not only Job's censure but also – implicitly – that of the anthropologists. Thus while Job judges Ustane by comically inappropriate Victorian values, calling her a 'hussy', Holly's detached, ethnographic tone signals a more liberal cultural tolerance. His appreciation of plural cultures (he deems morality 'an affair of latitude') also subverts anthropology's hierarchical narrative of progress from primitive matriarchy to civilized patriarchy. He directly confounds two of the anthropologists' commonest slurs on matriarchy. First, he refutes the idea that matriliny was due to promiscuity and to the consequent ignorance of fatherhood.[62] Holly points out, on the contrary, that matriliny is maintained even when paternity is 'perfectly well known'. Secondly, he denies that sexual freedom leads to licence, noting that 'the arrangement continued till one of them wearied of it. I am bound, however, to say that the change of husbands was not nearly so frequent as might have been expected'. This is also an oblique comment on the British debate about divorce, a debate that entered fiction most famously in Hardy's *Jude the Obscure* (1895). Holly unsettles the cultural hierarchies assumed by Job and by the anthropologists, recognizing that there is 'nothing immoral about this Amahagger custom', and also commenting wryly on British customs ('our ceremony of marriage', he judges, 'justifies most things'). His observations articulate some of the tensions within late-Victorian culture, as a unilinear and ethnocentric evolutionism was challenged by an incipient cultural relativism.[63] The scene thus shows that fiction does not simply *reflect* scientific ideas, but is able to engage dynamically and critically with scientists' theories. Here, Haggard's novel, alternately enticed and threatened by 'primitive' matriarchy, questions the anthropologists' confidence that the future lies with patriarchy.

Equally important in analysing the novel's cultural meaning are readers' responses to Haggard's matriarchal fantasy. While reconstructing reader reception is often a speculative business, the limited evidence provided by the novel's serialization and by the critical response to its volume publication does suggest that readers were prompted to make connections between the literary text and its historical context. The novel was serialized in the generously illustrated *Graphic* magazine between October 1886 and January 1887, and published in volume form in 1887.[64] The serialized text differs in places from the volume edition (though only slightly in the case of the extract), but more striking is the extra dimension supplied by the *Graphic* itself. As Andrew Stauffer claims, the novel's 'serial incarnation' points to the British middle classes' 'increasingly global imagination'.[65] The magazine's interest in events all over the globe, and especially across the British Empire, resonates with Haggard's preoccupations in *She*. Readers of the serial version, therefore, would probably have been alert to connections between the text and historical context which were subsequently effaced. The number in which the extract appears includes articles which engage intertextually with Haggard's concern about relations between indigenous peoples and colonizers. A short piece on 'The Congo Railway' hopes that the railway will teach 'the African . . . that the outer world is not entirely composed of Arab slave-dealers, or even of enterprising explorers very much armed with repeating rifles'.[66] The writer notes that '[a]t present, that must be the impression of the tribes in the interior', and looks forward to Africans' recognition that 'white men' are not bent solely upon 'the destruction of human life'.[67] The advertisements in this number stress the imperial reach of British commerce, offering beds 'specially adapted for mosquito curtains, used in India, Australia, and the colonies', gems 'FROM THE ENDS OF THE EARTH', and, 'for big game shooting', 'CAPE GUNS' and 'COLONIAL GUNS'.[68] These themes reverberate with the extract, but even more with the accompanying illustration, which depicts a later incident: a cannibal feast. The engraving shows Holly shooting 'the diabolical woman who had been caressing Mohamed [a minor character]' to prepare him for being killed and eaten.[69] The illustration deepens the extract's ambivalence about 'primitive' matriarchy and about the travellers' responses to it. The Amahagger are depicted as clearly degenerate, but their degeneracy is mirrored in Holly's simian looks. Moreover, Holly's use of his revolver interestingly recalls the magazine's description of 'enterprising explorers very much armed with repeating rifles' and the advertisement for guns. Questions about the European travellers' behaviour are intensified, then, by viewing the extract in its original publication context.

*She* was published in volume form by Longmans, Green in January 1887, and sold for six shillings.[70] It proved immensely popular. Charles Longman, Haggard's publisher, wrote that '*She* keeps on selling capitally. We have printed 25,000 already and have ordered another 5,000 and I do not think we shall have many left when the printers deliver them . . . last week we sold over 1,000 copies!'[71] Haggard's fantasy of female power clearly chimed with his readers: his uncertainty whether 'any reader of the book is but half as much in love with *She* as I confess to being' was indirectly answered by reviewers' testimony that Ayesha 'haunts the imagination' and that '[w]e come to love [her] ourselves'.[72] Yet even while they stressed this apparently emotional response, reviewers were alert to the questions about sexual politics and colonialism which underlay the narrative. The *Blackwood's* reviewer was quick to align Haggard's ancient matriarch with the modern British woman: 'Notwithstanding this respectable period of duration, [Ayesha] is still as full of all the arts of coquetry as if she were a young lady of the nineteenth century.'[73] The *Spectator* reviewer, meanwhile, seems to have valued the novel more as a factual piece of colonial travel-writing than as fantastic adventure fiction: he celebrated Haggard's 'minute acquaintance with the scenery and physiognomy of savage African life' and lamented that this was overlaid by 'marvellous' and 'sensational' elements.[74]

Reviewers' opinions are clearly far from representative of readers' responses more generally (several reviewers, indeed, took care to distinguish their responses from those obtaining among 'the masses' or in 'the sphere of the "largest circulation"').[75] Nonetheless, the evidence provided by reviewers and by the novel's serial publication suggests that readers were impelled to, and did, make connections between text and social and political contexts. As we saw too in analysing the extract itself, Haggard's novel, far from being an ahistorical fantasy, intervened in contemporary debates about female rule, and can tell us much about late-Victorian ambivalence regarding sexual politics and evolutionary hierarchies.

## Conclusion

The analysis of the extract from *She* as a historical source draws on many of the theoretical perspectives discussed in the earlier part of the chapter. At the core of my reading of Haggard's matriarchal fantasy is a New Historicist interest in the construction of meaning across fictional and non-fictional discourses, and in the interaction of texts with historical contexts such as colonialism, sexual politics, and science. The interpretation draws, additionally, on a postcolonialist understanding of how imperialist discourse not only 'others' its colonial (and female) subjects, but also harbours underlying ambivalences. My emphasis on the material context of the extract's publication is indebted to reader reception theory and the history of reading, as well as to new work on periodicals and serial fiction. My interpretation thus draws on a number of critical approaches which are often theoretically divergent, but which unite to offer fruitful opportunities for analysing novels as a historical source. Together, these approaches illuminate the porous and shifting nature of the boundaries between novelistic and scientific discourses, serial fiction and periodical articles, and literary text and historical context.

## Notes

1 L. Montrose, 'Professing the Renaissance: The Poetics and Politics of Culture' (1989), rpr. in Julie Rivkin and Michael Ryan (eds) *Literary Theory: An Anthology*, Oxford: Blackwell, 1998, p. 781. See also T. Spargo, 'Introduction: Past, Present and Future Pasts', in Spargo (ed.) *Reading the Past: Literature and History*, Basingstoke: Palgrave, 2000, pp. 1–11.

2 H. White, *Tropics of Discourse: Essays in Cultural Criticism*, Baltimore: Johns Hopkins University Press, 1978, pp. 43, 50. Similar points are made in D. LaCapra, *History and Criticism*, Ithaca: Cornell University Press, 1985, p. 122. See also L.S. Kramer, 'Literature, Criticism, and Historical Imagination: The Literary Challenge of Hayden White and Dominick LaCapra', in L. Hunt (ed.) *The New Cultural History*, Berkeley: University of California Press, 1989, pp. 97–128, p. 117.

3 C. Reeve, *The Progress of Romance through Times, Centuries and Manners: . . . In a Course of Evening Conversation*, 2 vols, Dublin: Price, Exshaw, et al., 1785, vol. 1, p. 111.

4 G. Eliot, *The Mill on the Floss* (1860), Oxford: Oxford University Press, 1996, p. 273.

5 L. Rothfield, *Vital Signs: Medical Realism in Nineteenth-Century Fiction*, Princeton: Princeton University Press, 1992, pp. 123–129; A. Rothwell, 'Introduction', in E. Zola, *Thérèse Raquin*, Oxford: Oxford University Press, 1992, pp. vii–xxxv.

6 R. Barthes, 'The Reality Effect' (1967), rpr. in D. Walder (ed.) *The Realist Novel*, London: Routledge and Open University, 1995, pp. 258–261, p. 260.

7 I. Williams, *The Realist Novel in England: A Study in Development*, London: Macmillan, 1974, p. x; J.P. Stern, *On Realism*, London, 1973, p. 54. For defences of the realist novel which emphasize its self-conscious awareness of its own fictionality, see C. Prendergast, *The Order of Mimesis*, Cambridge: Cambridge University Press, 1986, p. 15, and G. Levine, *The Realistic Imagination: English Fiction from Frankenstein to Lady Chatterley*, Chicago: University of Chicago Press, 1981, pp. 15–22.

8 Rothfield, *Vital Signs*, pp. 37–40, 85, 71–78.

9 G. Eliot, *Middlemarch: A Study of Provincial Life* (1871–2), Oxford: Oxford University Press, 1997, p. 55.

10 G. Eliot, *Adam Bede* (1859), Oxford: Oxford University Press, 1996, p. 175.

11 D. Lodge, *Consciousness and the Novel: Connected Essays*, Cambridge, Mass.: Harvard University Press, 2002, pp. 49–50, 81.

12 I. Watt, *The Rise of the Novel: Studies in Defoe, Richardson and Fielding* (1957), Harmondsworth: Penguin, 1963.

13 M. McKeon, 'Generic Transformation and Social Change: Rethinking the Rise of the Novel', *Cultural Critique* 1, 1985, 159–181; J.A. Bull, *The Framework of Fiction: Socio-Cultural Approaches to the Novel*, Basingstoke: Macmillan, 1988.

14 L. James, *Fiction for the Working Man 1830–1850: A Study of the Literature Produced for the Working Classes in Early Victorian Urban England* (1963), Harmondsworth: Penguin, 1973.

15 R. Chartier, 'Texts, Printings, Readings', in Hunt, *New Cultural History*, pp. 154–175, p. 169.

16 James, *Fiction*, pp. 54, 51–82.

17 L.K. Hughes and M. Lund, *The Victorian Serial*, Charlottesville: University Press of Virginia, 1991.

18 See D. Wynne, *The Sensation Novel and the Victorian Family Magazine*, Basingstoke: Palgrave, 2001.

19  T. Hardy, 'General Preface to the Wessex Edition of 1912', in *Far from the Madding Crowd*, London: Penguin, 1978, p. 469.

20  J.S. Allen, 'History and the Novel: *Mentalité* in Modern Popular Fiction', *History and Theory* 22, 1983, 233–252, 234. For the ways in which Zola distorted his sources, see R. Magraw, *A History of the French Working Class*, 2 vols, vol. 1: *The Age of Artisan Revolution, 1815–1871*, Oxford: Blackwell, 1992, pp. 238–239.

21  Cited in J. Blum, 'Fiction and the European Peasantry: The Realist Novel as a Historical Source', *Proceedings of the American Philosophical Society* 126, 1982, 122–139, 126.

22  LaCapra, *History*, p. 117.

23  W.O. Aydelotte, 'The England of Marx and Mill as Reflected in Fiction', *Journal of Economic History* 8, 1948, 'Supplement: The Tasks of Economic History', 42–58, 43.

24  Aydelotte, 'England', 43, 53.

25  See W.K. Wimsatt and M.C. Beardsley, 'The Intentional Fallacy', in Wimsatt, *The Verbal Icon: Studies in the Meaning of Poetry*, Lexington: University of Kentucky Press, 1954, pp. 3–18.

26  For an account of these developments, see T. Eagleton, *Literary Theory: An Introduction* (1983), 2nd edn, Oxford: Blackwell, 1996.

27  R. Barthes, 'The Death of the Author' (1968), rpr. in D. Lodge, (ed.) *Modern Criticism and Theory: A Reader*, London: Longman, 1988, pp. 167–172, p. 172.

28  P. Mandler, 'The Problem with Cultural History', *CSH* 1, 2004, 94–117, (here 116 and 95).

29  C. Hesse, 'The New Empiricism', *CSH* 1, 2004, 201–207, 206–7.

30  Hesse, 'Empiricism', 206.

31  Blum, 'Fiction', 139.

32  A. Briggs, *The Age of Improvement 1783 to 1867* (1959), 2nd edn, Harlow, Essex: Longman, 2000, p. 341.

33  C. Dickens, *Hard Times* (1854), London: Penguin, 1994, p. 6.

34  M. Perrot, *Workers on Strike: France 1871–1890*, trans. C. Turner, Leamington Spa: Berg, 1987, pp. 2, 141–142.

35  P. Fritzsche, *Reading Berlin 1900*, Cambridge, Mass.: Harvard University Press, 1996.

36  J. Walkowitz, *City of Dreadful Delight: Narratives of Sexual Danger in Late-Victorian London*, London: Virago, 1992; S. Koven, *Slumming: Sexual and Social Politics in Victorian London*, Princeton: Princeton University Press, 2004.

37  Koven, *Slumming*, p. 204.

38  Koven, *Slumming*, pp. 35, 38, 95.

39  Koven, *Slumming*, pp. 205, 350n.

40  J. Rose, 'How Historians Study Reader Response: Or, What Did Jo Think of *Bleak House*?', in J.O. Jordan and R.L. Patten (eds) *Literature in the Marketplace: Nineteenth-Century British Publishing and Reading Practices*, Cambridge: Cambridge University Press, 1995, pp. 195–212.

41  G. Beer, *Open Fields: Science in Cultural Encounter*, Oxford: Oxford University Press, 1996, p. 173.

42  H. Small, *Love's Madness: Medicine, the Novel, and Female Insanity 1800–1865*, Oxford: Oxford University Press, 1996, pp. 35–36.

43  M. Poovey, *Making a Social Body: British Cultural Formation 1830–1864*, Chicago: University of Chicago Press, 1995, p. 204.

44  Poovey, *Making a Social Body*, pp. 74, 133. For an opposing reading, which suggests that a shared 'humanitarian narrative' unites 'the realist novel, the autopsy, the clinical report, and the social inquiry', see T. Laqueur, 'Bodies, Details, and the Humanitarian Narrative', in Hunt, *New Cultural History*, pp. 176–204, pp. 177–179.

45  J.S. Bratton, 'Of England, Home and Duty: The Image of England in Victorian and Edwardian Juvenile Fiction', in J.M. MacKenzie (ed.) *Imperialism and Popular Culture*, Manchester: Manchester University Press, 1986, pp. 73–93, p. 78.

46 M. Green, *Dreams of Adventure, Deeds of Empire*, London: Routledge and Kegan Paul, 1980, pp. 3, 33.

47 Mandler, 'Problem', 107.

48 J.M. MacKenzie, 'Introduction', in MacKenzie, *Imperialism*, p. 13.

49 E. Showalter, *Sexual Anarchy: Gender and Culture at the Fin de Siècle*, London: Bloomsbury, 1991, pp. 80–82; E. Said, *Culture and Imperialism*, New York: Random House, 1993, pp. 149, 160.

50 J. Tosh, *Manliness and Masculinities in Nineteenth-Century Britain: Essays on Gender, Family and Empire*, Harlow: Pearson Longman, 2005, p. 206.

51 See J. Reid, *Robert Louis Stevenson, Science, and the Fin de Siècle*, Basingstoke: Palgrave Macmillan, 2006, pp. 151–157. R. Jolly examines the tale's generic shift away from imperial adventure and towards the realistic and 'feminine realm of domestic fiction': 'Stevenson's "Sterling Domestic Fiction": "The Beach of Falesá"', *Review of English Studies* 50, 1999, 463–482, 463.

52 C. Hall, 'Introduction: Thinking the Postcolonial, Thinking the Empire', in Hall (ed.) *Cultures of Empire: A Reader. Colonizers in Britain and the Empire in the Nineteenth and Twentieth Centuries*, Manchester: Manchester University Press, 2000, pp. 1–33, p. 15. On the ambivalence of colonial discourse, see H.K. Bhabha, 'Signs Taken for Wonders: Questions of Ambivalence and Authority Under a Tree Outside Delhi, May 1817' (1985), rpr. in B. Ashcroft, G. Griffiths, and H. Tiffin (eds) *The Post-Colonial Studies Reader* (1998), 2nd edn, London: Routledge, 2006, pp. 38–43.

53 S. Arata, *Fictions of Loss in the Victorian Fin de Siècle*, Cambridge: Cambridge University Press, 1996, p. 89.

54 A. McClintock, *Imperial Leather: Race, Gender and Sexuality in the Colonial Contest*, London: Routledge, 1995, p. 16.

55 H. Rider Haggard, *She* (1887), ed. D. Karlin, London: Penguin, 1991, pp. 81–82.

56 M. Cohen, *Rider Haggard: His Life and Works*, London: Hutchinson, 1960, p. 109.

57 Haggard, *She*, pp. 1, 6, 4.

58 Unsourced quotation, cited in R.L. Green, *Andrew Lang: A Critical Biography with a Short-Title Bibliography of the Works of Andrew Lang*, Leicester: Edmund Ward, 1946, p. 115.

59 For details, see A.T. Allen, 'Feminism, Social Science, and the Meanings of Modernity: The Debate on the Origin of the Family in Europe and the United States, 1860–1914', *American Historical Review* 104, 1999, 1085–1113.

60 R. Jann, 'Darwin and the Anthropologists: Sexual Selection and Its Discontents', *Victorian Studies* 37, 1994, 287–306.

61 S.M. Gilbert and S. Gubar, *No Man's Land: The Place of the Woman Writer in the Twentieth Century*, 3 vols, vol. 2: *Sexchanges*, New Haven: Yale University Press, 1989, pp. 6–7, 20, 34–36; N. Auerbach, *Woman and the Demon: The Life of a Victorian Myth*, Cambridge, Mass.: Harvard University Press, 1982, pp. 36–38, 42–43; P. Murphy, 'The Gendering of History in *She*', *Studies in English Literature, 1500–1900* 39, 1999, 747–772.

62 On this belief, espoused by McLennan and L.H. Morgan, see A.P. and H.D. Lyons, *Irregular Connections: A History of Anthropology and Sexuality*, Lincoln: University of Nebraska Press, 2004, pp. 76, 78.

63 Historians continue to debate just when this epistemic shift happened – and if indeed it ever did. See J. Buzard, *Disorienting Fiction: The Autoethnographic Work of Nineteenth-Century British Novels*, Princeton: Princeton University Press, 2005, pp. 5–11.

64 For the *Graphic*, a popular, sixpenny rival to the *Illustrated London News*, see J.S. North (ed.) *The Waterloo Directory of English Newspapers and Periodicals 1800–1900*, series 2, 20 vols, Waterloo, Ont.: North Waterloo Academic Press, 2003, vol. 5, pp. 430–433.

65 A.M. Stauffer, 'Introduction', in H. Rider Haggard, *She: A History of Adventure*, ed. A.M. Stauffer, Peterborough, Ont.: Broadview, 2006, p. 18.

66  'The Congo Railway', in the *Graphic: An Illustrated Weekly Newspaper* 34, no. 882, 23 October 1886, 426.

67  'Congo Railway', *Graphic* 34, no. 882, 426.

68  *Graphic* 34, no. 882, 440, 447, 448.

69  Engraving by E.K. Johnson, *Graphic* 34, no. 882, 441.

70  P.B. Ellis, *H. Rider Haggard: A Voice from the Infinite*, London: Routledge and Kegan Paul, 1978, p. 111.

71  Cited in Ellis, *Haggard*, p. 118.

72  H. Rider Haggard to the editor of the *Spectator*, 22 January 1887, rpr. in Haggard, *She*, (ed.) Stauffer, p. 288; review, *Public Opinion*, 14 January 1887, rpr. in Haggard, *She*, (ed.) Stauffer, p. 283; review, the *Queen: The Lady's Newspaper*, 15 January 1887, rpr. in Haggard, *She*, (ed.) Stauffer, p. 284.

73  Review, *Blackwood's Edinburgh Magazine*, February 1887, rpr. in Haggard, *She*, (ed.) Stauffer, p. 289.

74  Review, *Spectator*, 15 January 1887, rpr. in Haggard, *She*, (ed.) Stauffer, p. 286.

75  Review, *Blackwood's*, rpr. in Haggard, *She*, (ed.) Stauffer, p. 289; review, *Pall Mall Gazette*, 4 January 1887, rpr. in Haggard, *She*, (ed.) Stauffer, p. 282.

## Select bibliography

Allen, J.S., 'History and the Novel: *Mentalité* in Modern Popular Fiction', *History and Theory* 22, 1983, 233–252.

Eagleton, T., *Literary Theory: An Introduction* (1983), 2nd edn., Oxford: Blackwell, 1996.

Hunt, L. (ed.), *The New Cultural History*, Berkeley: University of California Press, 1989.

Jordan, J.O. and Patten, R.L. (eds), *Literature in the Marketplace: Nineteenth-Century British Publishing and Reading Practices*, Cambridge: Cambridge University Press, 1995.

LaCapra, D., *History and Criticism*, Ithaca: Cornell University Press, 1985.

McClintock, A., *Imperial Leather: Race, Gender and Sexuality in the Colonial Contest*, London: Routledge, 1995.

Poovey, M., *Making a Social Body: British Cultural Formation 1830–1864*, Chicago: University of Chicago Press, 1995.

Spargo, T. (ed.), *Reading the Past: Literature and History*, Basingstoke: Palgrave, 2000.

# 10  Autobiography

*David Carlson*

To begin a discussion of potential approaches historians might take in reading autobiography, we must first acknowledge that autobiography (perhaps more than any
other non-fiction genre) has been a form notoriously resistant to precise definition.[1]
Indeed, surveying the critical history, one finds scholars struggling almost as
mightily to determine the boundaries between autobiography and other forms of
writing as to determine what type of knowledge can be gleaned from reading autobiographical texts themselves. The term 'autobiography', we should note, is of relatively modern origin. Probably first used in English by the poet Robert Southey in
1809, it only appeared in wide circulation during the 1830s.[2] Even then, however,
the precise meaning of the word was a source of debate. The history of texts that
might be labelled autobiographical has been traced back (by Georg Misch and
Avram Fleischman) as far as ancient Egypt or Nineveh.[3] However, many other critics (such as James Olney) view Augustine's *Confessions* as the best origin point for
the history of the genre.[4] And still other commentators (Georges Gusdorf, Karl
Weintraub) have argued that truly 'autobiographical' writing (which, they contend,
takes as its object the individualistic self of post-Enlightenment Europe) dates only
from the eighteenth century, with the works of writers such as Jean-Jacques
Rousseau and Benjamin Franklin.[5] What these divergent claims illustrate, of
course, is the truly varied nature of autobiographical discourse. Even if most critics
would agree that autobiography is a kind of narrative that aspires truthfully to relate
the story of an individual life, and where the writer of that story takes his or her own
distinct experience of selfhood as the central subject, the historical contingency of
those very categories ('narrative', 'self', 'individual', 'life', and 'truth') has made
autobiography a focal point for scholarly debate. Particularly in the wake of the
many varieties of postmodern theory addressed in the introductory chapters of this
volume, autobiography has become a problematic, but increasingly rich, type of
source material for historical study.

## Autobiography as narrative

The best way to rehearse the complex interpretive potential of autobiography as a
genre may be to highlight a series of key moments in the development of autobiography scholarship during the last several decades. One of the most interesting

things that such a survey reveals is a gradual departure from normative and formalist definitions of the genre (definitions focused on pinning down the typical content
features and structures of autobiographical texts) in favour of what we might call
'performative' or 'functional' models (critical modes focused on considering the
effects that autobiographies generate as acts of language, a move that requires
locating specific autobiographical texts as rhetorical acts rooted in particular discursive contexts). In many ways, what lies at the heart of the postmodern turn in
autobiography criticism is this shift away from asking 'what is an autobiography?'
or 'what does an autobiography tell us, objectively, about the life of its author?'
toward considering 'what constitutes the shifting parameters of autobiographical
expression?' or 'how do autobiographies contribute to the formation of subjectivity?' Tracing the history of this turn in autobiography studies will expose a number
of corollary questions relevant to literary and historical scholarship that can illuminate autobiographical texts.

Prior to the 1960s, autobiography was generally regarded both by historians and
literary critics simply as a source of factual, biographical information. In literary
circles, such information typically was used to provide insight into an author's
intentions in writing his or her works, thus supplementing the process of textual
analysis. Of course, during the 1940s and 1950s, the so-called 'New Criticism'
dominated Anglo-American literary criticism; as that school of thought tended to
de-emphasize the value of authorial intention in the process of textual interpretation, autobiographical discourse was effectively marginalized in literary studies.
Historians of this era were almost equally disinterested in autobiographical texts,
albeit for different reasons. As Jeremy D. Popkin reminds us, the efforts of historians during the nineteenth century to define their field as objective and scientific
helped to build a 'wall' between history and autobiography, one that persisted well
into the twentieth century.[6] Indeed, as Popkin rightly points out, the personal narratives of prominent writers such as Rousseau (in *The Confessions* of 1781) and
Goethe (in *Poetry and Truth* of 1812–31) had created a clear association between
autobiography and imaginative writing, a linkage that caused nineteenth-century
historians increasingly to distrust the form as a reliable data source.[7]

When considered by modern, specialized academics trained to rigorously challenge the objectivity of documentary sources, autobiography could not help but
appear suspect. This tendency, interestingly, represented a clear departure from
earlier methodological assumptions (dating back to Herodotus) that chroniclers
directly involved in events represented the best sources of historical memory. In the
wake of nineteenth-century positivism, however, autobiographical texts came to be
used by historians primarily as secondary sources: less desirable than quantitative
or normative materials, but still holding some potential to offer up useful supple-
mental information if subjected to sufficiently rigorous critical inquiry. The
most significant exceptions to this general rule would be, first, the use autobiography as a data source for scholars writing biographies of famous individuals and,
second, social historians' use of autobiographical texts to thicken their description
of social dynamics and to add vividness to their own narratives.[8] Nevertheless, as
Popkin suggests, the fundamental separation between history and autobiography

remained a 'structural feature' of the professional training of historians well into the twentieth century.

The 1960s mark a watershed period in the study of autobiography, the point at which the perceived scholarly limitations of autobiography for both literary criticism and historical inquiry began to break down. Initially, at least, this change was driven primarily by innovations in the field of literary studies. During this period, we can discern a transition from critical approaches that William Spengmann describes as 'historical' (reading autobiography as 'self-biography') to those that he calls 'fictional' (reading autobiography as an imaginative act of self-definition).[9] The appearance of Roy Pascal's *Design and Truth in Autobiography* in 1960 marks the beginning of this transition.[10] Pascal's motivating insight was that autobiography offers its readers insight into the 'consciousness' of an author (the way that his or her memory reshapes past experience), rather than simply into the objective 'truth' of that author's life. Though not always factually true (in an objective sense), an autobiography tells us a great deal about both the personality of an author and the process by which that individual makes sense of his or her own experience by converting it into narrative form. If the 'fictionalization' of autobiography initially renders such texts a questionable data source (in the older, positivistic sense), it simultaneously opens up the possibility of studying autobiographical narratives as complex rhetorical and artistic performances. This does not remove autobiography as an object of historical interest. Rather, it expands the kinds of questions a historian or literary critic might ask of, and through, an autobiography.

If we follow Pascal in assuming that the subject-matter of autobiography is a person's 'experience' of a life (the retrospective selection and organization of events into a meaningful narrative pattern), we can analyse any autobiography with an eye toward understanding the social and cultural conditions that affect such pattern-making work. Focusing on autobiography *as narrative*, then, becomes a tool for indexing not just literary shifts, but also broader kinds of historical changes. For example, if we read with a more 'literary' sensibility a seventeenth-century work such as the Puritan minister Thomas Shepard's *Autobiography*, and then situate that work alongside Benjamin Franklin's eighteenth-century *Autobiography*, the differences in the *way* these two individuals narrate their lives may help sharpen our sense of other differences between two periods in the history of colonial British America.[11] Attention to Franklin's narrative approach to organizing his life experience reveals the fact that he takes the time to flesh out his portraits of the other 'characters' he encounters in his young life, often focusing on his contractual relationships with those individuals. In contrast, Shepard's treatment of interactions with others is quite thin, and generally focused on how his encounters with them serve as indices of divine providence. Franklin's narrative, in this respect, is much more novelistic than Shepard's work, which draws its narrative voice directly from the Ramist sermon-rhetoric of his time.

But what can these kinds of textual details tell us about the differences between the Anglo-American worlds of the mid 1600s and late 1700s? There are many possibilities. The contrasts uncovered by a narratological reading of these autobiographies might offer us additional insight into the gradual emergence of a market-oriented Atlantic world, with its emphasis on contractually defined public relationships. They might enable us to think more deeply about shifting notions of cultural authority and the ways such authority might be legitimised. They might even draw into sharper focus the increasing importance of 'sociability' during the emergence of what we today call 'civil society'. Granted, to cull this kind of historical information from autobiographies such as Shepard's and Franklin's requires considerable analytical effort, for neither text directly addresses these issues as part of their overt thematic content. Nevertheless, when we read attentively for their *narrative* components, the fact that Franklin's or Shepard's accounts of their experiences may fall short as sources of objective 'truth' does not undercut their value as historical sources. That Franklin's recollection of events may be (1) faulty, (2) selective, and (3) tailored to a particular audience for a particular purpose, does not alter the fact that readers can use his narrative as *one* piece of data to begin reconstructing a sense of the historical conditions within which self was experienced and articulated during the American Enlightenment. The primary caution that 'literary' readers of autobiography need to observe, then, is to avoid drawing overreaching conclusions from one such piece of data, however rich the autobiographical narrative in question may be.

## Post-structuralism and autobiography

Part of what the previous section has been implying is that, when approached as narrative, autobiography becomes a tremendously useful source of information for the study of the history of ideas, especially ideas about the 'self'. It should not be surprising, then, that many post-structuralist critics and theorists have treated autobiography as foundational in their larger projects to (1) historicize the very concept of selfhood (as in Michel Foucault's efforts to explore how changes in institutional power structures and systems of knowledge production impact the way we conceive of self over time), or (2) to deconstruct the very possibility of any coherent self (as in Paul de Man and Jacques Derrida's consideration of the notion that identity is little more than a textual effect, forever unstable and collapsing on itself). Most historians, it seems to me, are likely to find more value in Foucault's focus on 'discourse' than in Derrida's insistent problematization of the Western intellectual tradition. Nevertheless, because the deconstructive understanding of autobiography has raised important questions about the nature and function of autobiographical expression, we should rehearse its main points as part of the present discussion.[12]

Derrida's discussions of autobiography are littered throughout his voluminous writings, so it can be a challenge to cull a discrete Derridean theory of autobiographical discourse. Nevertheless, it is fair to say that Derrida's interest in autobiography resides not so much in the study of a historically specific genre, but rather in what we might call an autobiographical impulse, something that he sees permeating many forms of writing. According to Derrida, autobiography is the ultimately impossible attempt to make manifest a coherent 'self' in writing. Indeed, growing out of his larger deconstructive project, Derrida sees this idea of a stable, coherent, and textualized self to be a myth needing to be exploded. Said myth only persists, he suggests, due to our failure to recognize that 'self' is always fragmented. The mistaken idea of coherence derives from a refusal to recognize the centrality of what Derrida calls '*différance*' (the way in which language creates meaning through a constant interplay of unstable terms, binary categories, and fluid signifiers) in the discourse of human identity.[13] Derrida insists that the meanings of any of the words that we might use to define ourselves emerge only in the context of the system of language as a whole – a system which itself is subject to constant change. To use a crude example, we can observe that the term 'man' signifies only in relation to a range of other terms – 'woman', 'animal', 'child', 'savage', 'deity', and so on. To define oneself as a 'man', then, requires situating oneself in an enormous network of other signifiers that are, themselves, relationally defined. (This simplified example does not even begin to raise the related issues of historical change in this signifying network, or of complications raised by adding further modifiers to the noun 'man'.) Discerning and revealing such patterns of regression (with meaning always being in a process of emergence involving constant 'deferral' to the next term in the signifying network), stands at the heart of Derrida's deconstructive project. A deconstructive 'reading' of autobiography, then, seeks to expose the ways in which the discourse of self continually relies on terms that are, in turn, reliant upon others.

In practice, the place where the deconstruction of the autobiographical myth of coherent selfhood can most easily be seen is in both Derrida's and Paul de Man's treatment of the issue of the 'signature' of the autobiographical subject – his or her proper name, and the personal pronoun 'I' that stands in for the name. In Derrida's case, the move to deconstruct the signature of autobiography represents an attempt to counter the work of the most prominent French critic of autobiography, Philippe Lejeune. Lejeune's influential idea of an 'Autobiographical Pact' stresses the existence of a kind of genre-confirming 'contract' between autobiographical writer and reader (an agreement regarding both the nature of autobiography as a kind of writing and its truth claims).[14] This contract, or 'pact', is ratified by the assumed correspondence between the author's proper name on the title page and the first-person 'I' used in the narrative. What distinguishes autobiography from other kinds of prose narrative, in other words, is the textual assertion that author and narrator (and, by extension, the narrator and the self as 'character' in the text) are one, and the reader's acceptance of that assertion. For Derrida, of course, such a presumption is fundamentally false. In his most sustained work dealing with the autobiographical impulse, Derrida looks in detail at *Ecce Homo* by the German philosopher Friedrich Nietzsche (1844–1900).[15] Nietzsche, Derrida reminds us, begins his autobiographical work with the claim, 'so I tell my life to myself'. This phrase asserts a closed and autonomous subjectivity (a form of total 'self-possession', we might say).[16] Derrida, however, argues that Nietzsche's formulation quickly reveals its own impossibility. In addressing his text to himself (and transforming himself into his own reader), Nietzsche is, in effect, addressing himself as a 'you'. Attempting to render himself as both author and reader of his own life, in other words, Nietzsche enacts a split in self, at precisely the moment when he is attempting to assert maximum coherence and closure. 'I' becomes 'you', regardless of how Nietzsche tries to obscure this division through his own language. Furthermore, in attempting to fix himself within the medium of language, Nietzsche inevitably renders his own identity an effect of constantly expanding systems of signification, much larger than his own powers of rhetorical control. He has no way to guarantee that his 'signature' (and his textual representation of 'I') will be received by other 'addressees' in the way that he desires. He has no way of stabilizing the network of signifiers that make up his text. The more he tries to write himself into existence, the more 'split' he will be.

The approach of the other major deconstructive critic of autobiography, Paul De Man, draws additional attention to the paradox examined above. De Man explores the instability of the autobiographical 'signature' in his famous essay 'Autobiography as De-Facement', where he emphasizes the temporal gap that is papered over by the first-person pronoun.[17] Like Derrida, De Man sees 'autobiography' not as a genre, but as an impulse (which he calls a 'figure of reading') occurring to some degree in many kinds of texts. De Man is even more interested than Derrida, however, in the temporal split that autobiography seems to try to repress. Generally speaking, de Man argues that the autobiographical 'I' represents an attempt to disavow the historical inconsistency between the self as author of an autobiographical text (the 'I' present at the moment of writing) and self as subject of that text (the 'I' present in the moment of prior experience).[18] Autobiography, for De Man, can thus be characterized in terms of the literary figure of prosopoeia, or personification (an attempt to ascribe human consciousness to something inanimate or lacking those qualities). Autobiography is an attempt to give 'living' voice to something 'dead' (the self of the past). De Man's approach to reading autobiography, then, becomes an exercise in exposing a kind of tragic melancholy lurking beneath the surface of our attempts to translate experience into textual form.

Obviously, deconstructive approaches to autobiography raise serious questions regarding the historical value of autobiographical texts, if autobiography is to be conceived as essentially an act of self-deception. Such questions draw attention to a profound source of frustration and dissatisfaction regarding deconstruction on the part of thinkers from many disciplines – the fact that deconstructive critics often seem engaged in a far-reaching kind of nihilistic scepticism. The key to finding methodological value and relevance in deconstructive approaches to autobiography, however, may be to see that the line of inquiry followed by Derrida and de Man draws attention to *textual* features in autobiography that *should* be attended to, even if doing so does not require us to draw the same unsettling conclusions they do. Take, for example, the point deconstruction makes about the 'gaps' between author, narrator, and character (gaps which are often masked by the presence of the first-person pronoun). This is an important insight, one that informs the work of many recent readers of autobiographical narrative. Rather than focus on the incommensurability of the 'selves' marked by 'I', however, an alternative interpretive approach has been to engage in a more systematic attempt to contextualize these various selves. Building on an awareness of the ambiguities of the 'signature', in other words, postmodern autobiography studies recognize that an autobiography is likely to offer at least as much illumination of the period *during which* it is written (the period of the authorial 'I') as of the period *about which* it is written (the period of the narrative 'I').

In reading Benjamin Franklin's *Autobiography*, for example, a careful reader will probably want to distinguish between 'Benjamin Franklin', the author of Part I of that text (which was begun at Twyford, England in 1771), and the older 'Benjamin Franklin', who began Parts II and III in Passy, France in 1784 and 1788. Similarly, it is important to see Franklin's autobiographical representation of his younger self (the 'I' within the text) more as a reflection of his mature conscious-ness than an objectively accurate depiction of the actual state of his mind at age twenty. Perceiving such 'splits' in the autobiographical self, of course, need not lead us to reject the possibility of 'self', as Derrida and de Man would seem to have it. Instead, that perception may help us to appreciate what Elizabeth Bruss has char-acterized as the 'performative' aspect of the autobiographical act – the way that 'self' is actually called into being by autobiographical expression in a dialectic between memory and imagination.[19] Franklin's 'autobiographical act' in his text, then, is to create an identity that did not exist outside of its narrative expression – an identity compounded from his past and present selves and called into being at the historical moment of textual composition. It is that historical moment, then, that can be studied through close reading of the text. When viewed in this light, we can see that the deconstructive exposure of the complexity of the autobiographical 'signature' opens up an appreciation both of the rhetorical contexts that shape auto-biographical expression and the historical specificity of its 'performance' of self.

The second major post-structuralist influence on autobiography studies derives from of the work of Michel Foucault. As with Derrida, the relevant Foucauldian pronouncements on autobiography are spread throughout a wide range of pub-lished works. Probably the two most significant of these, however, are *The History of Sexuality*, volume 1 (1976) and the widely anthologized essay, 'What is an Author?' (1969).[20] Foucault's work, in general, explores the idea that human beings (particularly those living in the modern world) are 'subjects' of 'discourse'. Discourse, as Foucault uses the term, refers to a historically specific and institu-tionally diffused system of meaning-production, enacted through the medium of language. Human self-consciousness, in turn, is something that is made possible only through the decentralized 'power' of these various discourses. According to Foucault's theories, we know ourselves only insofar as we are socialized (made 'subject') into various institutional contexts (many of which may operating on us at any given time) that produce specific forms of self-awareness. The discourses of education, religion, law, economic systems, and so on, all have their own languages (conceptual terms and categories, implied narratives, etc.) and disciplinary struc-tures that lead individuals to think of themselves in terms of those terms, categories, and narratives.

Self-definition, then, is not a process whereby autonomous individuals freely choose and articulate an identity in a vacuum. Instead, it is process where institu-tionally specific discourses speak through us, transforming us into particular kinds of individuals. Thus, in 'What is an Author?' Foucault actually suggests that the term 'author-function' is a more accurate term to designate the form of subjectivity that is typically referred to as an 'author'. And in a manner with clear applicability to the study of autobiography, Foucault raises a series of new questions that should be asked of texts (questions that I will slightly rephrase for purposes of the present discussion). Rather than wondering what an autobiographer reveals of him or herself through language, Foucaults' work suggests that we instead ask (1) what are the discourses that lead to the emergence of a self? (2) what are the histories and modes of circulation of these discourses? and (3) what possible models of self-definition (and range of subject-positions) do those discourses allow?

Foucault's theories regarding the interaction of knowledge and discursive power (which is, by definition, widely diffused and difficult to challenge) have been both useful and controversial for students of autobiography. Feminist critics, in particular, have been drawn to Foucault's persuasive account of the way that sexual desire (and, indeed, the body itself) has been regulated by a variety of discourses (medical, legal, psychological, and religious). At the same time, however, many scholars have noted that, especially in their early formulations, Foucault's theories take on a profoundly deterministic tone, seeming to leave no room for individual agency in the face of overwhelming and pervasive discursive power. Autobiography critics, not surprisingly, have been resistant to seeing 'authors' as nothing more than functions of discourse and 'selves' as nothing more than over-determined social constructions. In the end, therefore, a type of middle position has emerged – one that combines attentiveness to the presence and influence of powerful models of self on autobiographical acts of self-definition with a belief in the possibility of individual agency and innovation within specific discursive contexts.

## The historical study of autobiography: a case study

A relatively recent book, Paul John Eakin's *How Our Lives Become Stories*, offers a useful synthesis of autobiographical theory that occupies the middle ground just mentioned.[21] Eakin's book represents both a summation of the ideas of one of America's foremost autobiography scholars and an attempt to connect the study of autobiographical writing to advances in both the social and natural sciences (especially neuropsychology). Eakin accepts the notion that the autobiographical 'I' is 'fictional' (that it is constructed in the act of self-narration) but questions the wisdom of deconstructing something ('self') that all human beings seem to experience, in some form or other. Instead, what Eakin takes from deconstructive (and feminist) approaches to autobiography is the need to challenge the 'myth of autonomy' and embrace instead the notion that all identity is, in some degree 'relational'. One of the challenges in studying autobiography from a historical perspective, Eakin suggests, is cultivating an awareness of the culturally available 'models of self' upon which an autobiographer draws in individualizing him or herself. In this respect, his work connects with Foucault's interest in discourse. Another challenge is to recognize that an autobiographical act of self-definition always takes place in implicit dialogue with others. Here Eakin draws insight from the work of feminist scholars who have emphasized the communal nature of self-definition in women's autobiography. (Eakin, however, questions whether this emphasis on relationality is, in fact, distinctly 'feminine'.)

In the end, pulling together a range of ideas about identity-formation derived from cognitive psychology, Eakin argues that readers need to attend to a multiplicity of 'selves' that are made visible in autobiographical writing. These would include the 'ecological self' (the self that emerges through interaction with the physical environment), the 'interpersonal self' (the self emerging through interaction with others), the 'extended self' (the self emerging through acts of memory and anticipation), the 'private self' (the reflective self emerging through reflection on experiences unavailable to others), and the 'conceptual self' (the self that emerges either explicitly or implicitly through interaction with of a wide range of discursive contexts). Reading autobiography, then, is an analytical act that seeks to understand how individuals integrate these various registers of self into an 'identity', a process that is both fluid and ongoing throughout human life. We are always 'self-narrating' in some form, Eakin suggests. What an autobiographer, in particular, does is to isolate the process of self-narration during a relatively discrete moment of his or her life and then render that process into a text that can be encountered by others. When we read an autobiography historically, then, what we are understanding is this *process* of self-narration by looking at its personal, biological, environmental, and cultural parameters.

Based on the critical survey I have been presenting, then, historical scholars seeking to read autobiography in light of the most recent theoretical approaches to the genre might well ask at least some of the following questions of the texts before them:[22]

–   What did it mean to be an author at the time when the autobiographical narrative was written? How does that idea of 'authorship' affect the content and form of the narrative?
–   Who was the audience of the autobiography when it was first written? How might that audience have affected the manner in which the author narrates his or her life?
–   What gaps can we discern between the authorial 'I', the narrating 'I', and the historical 'I' in the autobiography? What explains these differences?
–   What models of identity were available to the author when he or she was writing? What models are used in the autobiography? How might we explain the presence and influence of those models? How does that author use or reinterpret those models?
–   What narrative patterns are used to structure the autobiographical story? (Is the autobiography organized according to the generic pattern of a bildungsroman, a conversion narrative, a confession, a Plains Indian 'coup tale', etc.?)[23] Why and how would these patterns be available to the author of the autobiography?
–   To what extent does the autobiography foreground 'relational' selfhood? What kinds of relationships matter most for the author's act of self-definition? What interpretive methods does the narrator seem to employ to explore the significance of his or her own experiences?

All of these questions help draw readers of autobiography into a broad form of historical inquiry, helping us to understand not only the textual features and rhetorical complexity of an autobiographical work, but also the historical period from which the text itself emerged.

To illustrate one manner in which such an interpretation of autobiography might proceed, I will turn in conclusion to a brief consideration of a text that first appeared in print in the United States in 1798, the *Memoirs of Stephen Burroughs*.[24] Stephen Burroughs was a notorious and disreputable con-man and convicted felon whose adult life was characterized by numerous run-ins with the law, stints in prison, and changes of identity. The choice of an autobiography by such an individual, in this context, is intended to highlight, first of all, the point that the unsettled nature of the 'truth claims' in a particular autobiographical text need not invalidate that work as a source for historical study. Burroughs made his living as a liar, and his 'signature', in this respect, most assuredly does not mark a 'coherent' or consistent self; indeed, there are many versions of Stephen Burroughs appearing in the *Memoirs*. When approached with a 'literary' sensibility, however, the specific nature of Burroughs's autobiographical act reveals much more than the duplicity of its author. It begins to provide considerable insight into the nature and reach of the discourse of criminality in post-Revolutionary America.

A complete analysis of a four-hundred page work is impossible in this context. Looking closely at just a few passages from Burroughs's *Memoirs*, however, will suffice to illustrate a few of the insights a 'discursive' approach to his autobiography can provide. Consider the following passages, quoted from the introductory epistle and the first chapter of the *Memoirs*, as representative examples of Burroughs's approach to the autobiographical act of self-definition:

> My life, it is true, has been one continued course of tumult, revolution, and vexation; and such as it is, I will give it to you in detail . . . You say my character, to you, is an enigma; that I possess and uncommon share of sensibility, and at the same time maintain an equality of mind which is uncommon, particularly in the midst of those occurrences which are calculated to wound the feelings. I learned fortitude in the school of adversity.[25]
>
> . . .
>
> The state of mind is the only criterion of happiness of misery. The Cynic Diogenes was more happy than the Conqueror Alexander, and the Philosopher Socrates more happy than either. They all had, undoubtedly, passions and feelings alike, which, not properly regulated would have rendered them unhappy. Yet whenever reason stood at the helm, the vessel was brought into the haven of peace.[26]
>
> . . .
>
> I am the only son of a clergyman, living in Hannover, in the state of New Hampshire; and, were any to expect merit from their parentage, I might justly look for that merit. But I am so far a republican, that I consider a man's merit to rest entirely with himself, without any regard to blood or connection.[27]
>
> . . .

I should hardly mention the insipid anecdotes of my childish years, were it not for the purpose of showing how these small occurrences had a decided influence in giving a tone to the character which I sustain at this time, and in directing the operations of my after life. So much do the greatest events depend upon circumstances so minute, that they pass unobserved, and consequently, wrong causes are attributed to the effects which take place. Being passionately fond of information, I embraced all opportunities for reading, which my desultory life would admit, and unfortunately many novels fell in my way, of that kind, which had a direct tendency to blow the fire of my temper into a tenfold rage.[28]

. . .

I have endeavored to study the operations of the human heart, that I might be able to afford that instruction which would be salutary; and in this, I find one truth clearly established, viz. a child will endeavor to be, what you make him think his parents are . . . Give him an idea, that the inhabitants of the world esteem virtue, integrity, mildness, and modesty, and that the contrary are obnoxious to them, he will be most likely to pursue that course unremittingly.[29]

. . .

To censure the faults of youth beyond what they ought to bear, is generally attended with fatal consequences. It destroys the object of their pursuit, viz. approbation; they revolt at the injustice, which they sensibly feel; therefore, inflicting unjust punishment is generally attended with fatal consequences in the system of education. It destroys the principles of equity in the youthful breast, and it substitutes in their room, the despotic principles of tyranny . . . I have often seen instances where the ambition of youth has been destroyed, by censuring their faults with too much severity.[30]

The first things we might notice about these passages from the *Memoirs* are Burroughs's self-conscious treatment of himself as a 'man of feeling' and his use of sentimental conventions. Thus begins our exploration of 'models of identity' and 'narrative patterns', as described in the question set above, a move that grows out of our recognition of the gaps in the autobiographical 'signature'. Looking back on his early years from the perspective of an adult life where he has seen himself defined publicly as a notorious criminal, the older Burroughs (the narrating 'I') adopts an epistolary narrative form common to sentimental novels to describe the younger Burroughs (the historical 'I'). The audience for the autobiography is defined as the 'you' referenced in the first excerpt above, a genteel 'friend' of the authorial 'I' to whom the entire book is addressed as a letter. This conceit serves to position the general reader as a cultured person likely to be receptive to balanced appeals to reason and feeling. The next pointed interpretive question we might ask ourselves, then, is what historical insights can we draw from the fact that Burroughs (in the 1790s) would choose this narrative structure and rhetorical approach for his autobiographical apologia? One possible answer derives from the fact that eighteenth-century sentimental literature had a deep investment in the epistemological assumptions (derived from philosophers such as John Locke) that human emotional and intellectual life originates in sense experience, and that specific ideas of morality are not innate. A related focus of sentimental fiction, therefore, is the need for cultivation of the moral sense through education and experience. Finally, sentimental writing explores the workings of human sympathy, the imaginative ability to 'feel' along with others by placing ourselves in their situations. Sympathy, understood thus, was a central pillar of Anglo-American political theory of the time, offering a way both to explain the innate sociability of humankind (a key source of social cohesion) and to theorize the way that self-interest could modulate into benevolence. When all of these elements are foregrounded, we can begin to make sense of Burroughs's rhetorical choices in his autobiographical act. Sentimental discourse provides him with both a logical complement and effective counterpoint to the late eighteenth-century legal discourse and its powerful model of the criminal self; it gives narrative structure to his autobiographical act.

A full examination of the discourse of criminality would require consideration of a wide range of texts and penal institutions. In the present context, however, we must be content with a succinct introduction to a central legal *definition* of the criminal that informed Anglo-American legal institutions in the mid-to-late eighteenth century – one drawn from William Blackstone's widely read *Commentaries of the Laws of England*.[31] In Volume IV ('Of Public Wrongs'), Blackstone defines a crime simply as 'an act committed or omitted in violation of public law'.[32] Public law, in turn, derives from what he calls 'the original contract'. This point makes a criminal a person who violates what political thinkers of the time also referred to as the 'contract of government'. Unlike the 'social contract' where individuals come together to create a society, the 'original contract' was understood to mean the agreement whereby members of an already existing society form a government with the responsibility to protect the rights – to life, liberty, and property – of the individuals in that society. Blackstone adds to this definition later in Volume IV, in the section 'Of the Persons Capable of Committing Crimes'. For an act (and actor) to be 'criminal', he argues, there must be a union of rational will, intention, and action in violation of the law. One is only a criminal, he notes further, if (1) one is not coerced into criminal behaviour, (2) one is not merely unfortunate – trying to do good and inadvertently doing harm, (3) one is not in an extreme situation requiring action for self-preservation, and (4) one has a properly formed understanding (a term Blackstone uses in its Lockean sense to refer to the capacity to reflect on sense experience to build up a store of knowledge and judgement). From these comments, then, we can derive a general picture of the model of criminal identity disseminated by the legal discourse of Stephen Burroughs's time. To be called 'criminal' by the state is to be defined as an individual who rationally, knowingly, and without the spur of self-preservation, violates the original contract of government and thus abdicates the rights and protections afforded to the people in his society. The legal 'model' of criminal selfhood, in this sense, is that of a person who is unrestrained by the bonds of sociability and who subsequently chooses to become an enemy of the people, existing in something analogous to a state of war against other members of his country.

As we can begin to see from the preceding discussion, sentimentalism offers Burroughs a vehicle by which he might challenge the way he is defined by the state

– as a man of deficient feeling whose unrestrained self-interest thus leads him into a state of unjust war against his fellow men. Against the legal model of his 'criminal' self – one who rejects the power of sympathy and spurns the original contract of government for self-interested reasons – Burroughs presents himself as a kind of ideal subject of eighteenth-century Anglo-American moral philosophy, a man well attuned to the affective impulses of sociability and sympathy that pulls societies together in the original 'social contract'. Burroughs presents himself as a 'student of the human heart' and, thus, one who is potentially a good 'republican'. In this manner, he begins to recast his career as a criminal as the story of a man of feeling and champion of liberty who is victimized by a tyrannical government and legal system that undercuts his moral potential. Burroughs's rhetoric and the narrative pattern of his act of self-definition align him, in this way, with the Whig Sentimentalism that influenced many of the American founders. By recognizing this fact, even as we also recognize that Burroughs's autobiographical 'confession' is motivated strongly by self-interest (and thus not always entirely reliable as a source of 'objective' information), we can begin to use the *Memoirs* as a source of historical 'data'. Read with an eye towards its narrative characteristics, the *Memoirs* can begin to tell us something about the relationship between the discourses of crime and feeling in post-Revolutionary America.

Continuing our discursive reading of these opening passages, we might notice also that Burroughs presents his life (again following sentimental narrative conventions) very much as a tale of 'education' (in his case, a flawed education). The memoir begins (in chapter one) with what Burroughs calls a 'digression' on this subject, but this digression also draws closer attention to the dominant interpretive framework (sentimentalism) through which he organizes his memories into an account of 'experience'. Stressing the impressionable nature of children (drawing on Locke's idea of the young mind as *'tabula rasa'*, or blank slate), Burroughs comments on the early effects of his 'uncommon share of sensibility' (a term that refers to 'passion' in this context) and 'volatile temper of mind'. Doing so, he links his own personal experience to a larger point about the need for all human beings to harness feelings and sensations through the application of reason in order to develop their moral sense and love of law. And yet, passions must not simply be restrained in youth, he suggests. Instead, judgement must be cultivated, a process that relies heavily on the presence of moral exemplars (and effective social 'parents'). As Burroughs puts it, 'a child will endeavour to become what you make him think mankind in general are'. Punishment, in this regard, must be carefully applied to avoid crippling the moral sense. The mere hint of arbitrary punishment undercuts the very social bonds to be fortified.

The problem for Burroughs, according to his narrative, was that he came of age during a time of social upheaval (the American Revolution) where he was surrounded by failed exemplars, tyrannical abuses of power, and inconsistent applications of punishment and disciplinary violence ('tumult, revolution and vexation'). Time and again, as the *Memoirs* continues, Burroughs will recount tales of individuals in positions of power whose example impedes the development of his moral sense and his understanding of the proper relationship between punishment and action. Burroughs's account of his own repeated attempts to establish himself as a schoolmaster reads as a kind of ironic commentary on the failure of the 'parent-figures' in his world to nurture his understanding (a point that, once again, links Burroughs's outlaw behaviour with the revolutionary ideology of the American patriots). This decision to emphasize the failure of parental authority in his autobiographical act, of course, can be explained as another shrewd type of 'appeal' against the legal discourse defining him as a criminal self. This, in turn, can lead us to a range of larger, more complex historical questions, beginning with these: Was the language of sentiment used commonly at this time in the legal system? Does Burroughs's autobiographical 'defence' offer insight into the ways in which criminal courts actually were functioning? To what extent were the philosophical discourses of moral sentiments and penology interacting at this time? Is Burroughs unusual in linking them?

Admittedly, the kind of discursive analysis I am beginning to develop here can only be called provisional. The type of interpretive work involved in producing a self-contained reading of Burroughs's *Memoirs* represents only a piece of a larger historical study. Nevertheless, I hope that at this point it is possible to imagine how a 'literary' reading of autobiography could add to many different types of historical inquiry. Stephen Burroughs's autobiographical act can clearly contribute to a study of the relationship between political theory, moral philosophy and penology in the 1790s. It can offer us insight into the cultural reach of both the discourse of criminality and the sentimental language of feeling in the United States at the same time. It can also, obviously, contribute to a history of changing ideas of the criminal 'self'. In all of these cases, a 'discursive' approach to Burroughs's text offers a different kind of evidence in service of historical projects than a more traditional positivistic reading of the book. Granted, the *Memoirs* may still yield conventional historical information about jail conditions, approaches to prosecutions, and the functioning of courts during the 1790s, though Burroughs's bias in penning the narrative has the potential to undercut the value of such data. What Burroughs seems unlikely to be able to feign or falsify, however, is the nature of the legal discourse confronting him, something revealed by the complexity of his response to that discourse. The narrative choices he makes in writing his life story may therefore tell us even more about the actual workings of law at this time than tabulations of court records or prison statistics. There may, in fact, be no better way to get a sense of the *effects* that the legal language and institutions of this time had on the criminals they sought to define and circumscribe than to consider a performative act of self-definition by one of these very criminals. A 'literary' reading of criminal autobiography opens up a broader form of legal history.

## Conclusion

Throughout this chapter, I have been suggesting how, in the wake of the 'literary' turn in autobiography study, personal narratives have been recognized as complexly constructed narratives. The challenge for contemporary historians working with such material is to find ways to examine the relationship between these narratives and the historical contexts from which they emerge. This is not to say that autobiographies will no longer yield 'facts' (names, dates, places, confirmation of major events, etc.) in the manner that they always have; only the most extreme deconstructionist will waste time quibbling over the availability and utility of such information. When approached though the lens of literary theory, however, autobiographical texts can provide an even richer vein of potentially useful information. If we ask ourselves not just *what* an autobiography says, but *why* and *how* it says, we enable ourselves to develop alternative understandings of the interactions between creative human minds and the social institutions that surround them. Such a move does not undercut the storytelling power of the historian; it only expands his or her repertoire.

## Notes

1 We should distinguish here between autobiography and memoir. Memoir is typically understood to be a life narrative that locates its subject in a specific social environment, focusing attention on the lives and actions of others and on significant historical incidents of which the subject was a witness or participant. Autobiography is usually understood to be (comprehensively) focused on its author's personal experience.

2 The term 'autobiography' appeared in German encyclopaedias even earlier, in 1800.

3 G. Misch, *A History of Autobiography in Antiquity*, London: Routledge, 1907; A. Fleischman, *Figures of Autobiography: The Language of Self Writing in Victorian and Modern England*, Berkeley: University of California Press, 1983.

4 J. Olney, *Metaphors of Self: Meaning in Autobiography*, Princeton: Princeton University Press, 1972.

5 G. Gusdorf, 'Conditions and Limits of Autobiography' (1956), rpr. in J. Olney (ed.) *Autobiography: Essays Theoretical and Critical*, Princeton: Princeton University Press, 1980, pp. 28–48; K. Weintraub, *The Value of the Individual: Self and Circumstance in Autobiography*, Chicago: University of Chicago Press, 1978.

6 J. Popkin, *History, Historians, and Autobiography*, Chicago: University of Chicago Press, 2005.

7 J.J. Rousseau, *The Confessions of Jean-Jacques Rousseau*, Harmondsworth: Penguin, 1953; J. W. von Goethe, *The Auto-Biography of Goethe. Truth and Poetry: From My Own Life*, London: Bell and Daldy, 1872.

8 Relatively recent examples of these approaches would include E. Morgan, *Benjamin Franklin*, New Haven: Yale University Press, 2002, P. Gay, *The Naked Heart: The Bourgeois Experience, Victoria to Freud, Volume IV*, New York: W.W. Norton., 1995; M. Maynes, *Taking the Hard Road: Life Course in German Workers' Autobiographies in the Era of Industrialization*, Chapel Hill: University of North Carolina Press, 1995. Further examples of the kinds of autobiographical texts of interest to social historians can be found in A. Kelly, *The German Worker: Working Class Autobiographies from the Age of Industrialization*, Berkeley: University of California Press, 1987.

9 W. Spengmann, *The Forms of Autobiography: Episodes in the History of a Literary Genre*, New Haven: Yale University Press, 1980.

10 R. Pascal, *Design and Truth in Autobiography*, Cambridge: Harvard University Press, 1960.

11 J. Albro (ed.), *The Works of Thomas Shepard*, 3 vols, Boston: Doctrinal Tract and Book Society, 1853; B. Franklin, *The Autobiography of Benjamin Franklin*, New Haven: Yale University Press, 1964.

12 The term 'deconstruction' is notoriously difficult to pin down and Derrida himself has never provided a clear explanation of the word. See the glossary for definition.

13  The term 'signifier', taken from the linguistic theory of Ferdinand de Saussure, has become a staple of literary criticism in the wake of postmodernism. Again see the glossary for detailed explanation.

14  P. Lejeune, *On Autobiography*, Minneapolis: University of Minnesota Press, 1989.

15  J. Derrida, *The Ear of the Other: Otobiography, Transference, Translation: Texts and Discussions with Jacques Derrida*, Lincoln: University of Nebraska Press, 1988.

16  F. Nietzsche, *On the Genealogy of Morals and Ecce Homo*, New York: Random House, 1967, p. 221.

17  P. DeMan, 'Autobiography as De-Facement', *Modern Language Notes* 94 (1979), 919–930.

18  De Man ignores the fact that many autobiographers (Protestant writers of conversion narratives such as John Bunyan or Jonathan Edwards, American Indian writers of 'post-colonial' autobiographies such as Charles Eastman or N. Scott Momaday, and immigrant writers) foreground and meditate on historical changes in personal identity.

19  E. Bruss, *Autobiographical Acts: The Changing Situation of a Literary Genre*, Baltimore: Johns Hopkins University Press, 1976.

20  M. Foucault, *The History of Sexuality*, vol. 1, New York: Pantheon Books, 1978; M. Foucault. 'What is an Author?', *The Foucault Reader*, New York: Pantheon Books, 1984, pp. 101–120.

21  P.J. Eakin, *How Our Lives Become Stories: Making Selves*, Ithaca: Cornell University Press, 1999.

22  This list of questions is adapted from S. Smith and J. Watson, *Reading Autobiography: A Guide for Interpreting Life Narratives*, Minneapolis: University of Minnesota Press, 2001.

23  'Bildungsroman' refers to a novelistic form that focuses on the moral, intellectual, social, or psychological development of a young protagonist, typically beginning in childhood and ending at maturity. A 'coup tale' is a traditional form of oral narrative that involves recounting acts of bravery and exploits in war.

24  S. Burroughs, *Memoirs of Stephen Burroughs*, Boston: Northeastern University Press, 1924.

25  Ibid., p. 1.

26  Ibid., p. 2.

27  Ibid., p. 3.

28  Ibid., p. 4.

29  Ibid., p. 5.

30  Ibid., p. 6–7.

31  W. Blackstone, *Commentaries on the Laws of England*, 4 vols, Chicago: University of Chicago Press, 1979.

32  Ibid., p. 332.

## Select bibliography

Bruss, E., *Autobiographical Acts: The Changing Situation of a Literary Genre*, Baltimore: Johns Hopkins University Press, 1976.

De Man, P., 'Autobiography as De-Facement', *Modern Language Notes* 94 (1979), 919–930.

Derrida, J. *The Ear of the Other: Otobiography, Transference Translation: Texts and Discussions with Jacques Derrida*, trans. P. Kamuf and A. Ronell, ed. C. McDonald, Lincoln: University of Nebraska Press, 1988.

Eakin, P.J., *How Our Lives Become Stories: Making Selves*, Ithaca: Cornell University Press, 1999.

Gusdorf, G. 'Conditions and Limits of Autobiography' (1956), rpr. in J. Olney (ed.)

*Autobiography: Essays Theoretical and Critical*, Princeton: Princeton University Press, 1980, pp. 28–48.

Lejeune, P. *On Autobiography*, trans. Katherine Leary, (ed.) P.J. Eakin, Minneapolis: University of Minnesota Press, 1989.

Olney, J. *Metaphors of Self: The Meaning of Autobiography*, Princeton: Princeton University Press, 1972.

Pascal, R. *Design and Truth in Autobiography*, Cambridge, Mass.: Harvard University Press, 1960.

Smith, S. and Watson, J., *Reading Autobiography: A Guide for Interpreting Life Narratives*, Minneapolis: University of Minnesota Press, 2001.

Spengmann, W.C., *The Forms of Autobiography: Episodes in the History of a Literary Genre*, New Haven: Yale University Press, 1980.

# 11 Newspapers

*Stephen Vella*

Newspapers offer a wealth of information about the social, political, economic and cultural life of the past. They easily lend themselves to the work of comparative textual analysis, opening windows onto the intellectual culture that prevailed in a particular time, place or community. A critical reading of newspapers can lead to significant insight into how societies or cultures came to understand themselves and the world around them.

At their most superficial level, newspapers reveal those events of which contemporary readers were made aware. But newspapers do much more: they document the ways in which reporters and editors thought about their own society and the world around them, how they organized and presented information, filtered out or neglected other potential news reports, created influential categories of thought and established, enforced or eroded conventional social hierarchies and assumptions. Far from simply reflecting contemporary events or public wants in objective, mirror-like fashion, newspapers often shaped the news and views of their readers by employing a particular framework for understanding events and institutions. In the words of historian Roger Chartier, 'representations of the social world themselves are the constituents of social reality'.[1] In this sense, one can appreciate how newspapers have influenced society as much as they have reflected it.

In a similar vein, Anthony Smith has argued that 'journalism was the art of structuring reality, rather than recording it'. Though newspapers 'developed a mission (and a defense) of "objectivity" in the twentieth century', their claim to objectivity remains highly dubious. The journalist 'weaves the tapestry of reality which society accepts – or rejects – as being a true image of "things as they really are"'. A speech may be written as spoken, stock prices accurately recorded, battles described as they have been fought; yet even in these apparent instances of objective journalism, 'who directs the attention of the reporter from one arena to another?' Smith asks. 'What forces motivate the feature writer to weep for one cause and scoff at another?'[2]

More news takes place in a given day or week than can possibly appear within a newspaper. The raw material of news events must therefore pass through successive filters that narrow the range of stories published. Reporters and editors determine the news to which the public will have access, including the standard of what is 'newsworthy' in the first place. They also fix the premises of discourse and interpretation for their stories once they have been selected. Newspapers are not then neutral conduits of information, but rather gatekeepers and filterers of ideas. These decisions even come to affect readers' own expectations. As Smith writes, 'we approach the newspaper product having absorbed certain routines of comprehension, accepting the special codes of the newspaper genre' and so read it with a set of 'habitualised assumptions'.[3] The task of scholarship is to dismantle these routines and examine them with care.

While newspapers are not often transparent about themselves, their expressions in print can reveal much to a careful reader. Newspapers differ considerably from other cultural products such as letters, memoirs and novels, behind which creations usually sits a single author (even as we grant that the 'discourse' employed by an author is informed by a larger social context of thought). Behind a newspaper lies a vast, complex machinery of literary production and layered social networks, for which no single individual is wholly responsible, even at the level of a news article.

Concentrations of wealth and power in any society inevitably influence the spectrum of topics and opinions expressed in its newspapers. The dominant domestic groups that own and control the mainstream newspaper press naturally see their priorities and interests reflected in news coverage, though this is never perfectly accomplished, even in police states. Rather than simply report a reality 'out there', newspapers filter, frame and report news and analysis in a manner supportive of established power structures under whose authority they function, thus limiting the bounds of debate and discussion accordingly. This process is more complex and subtle in nominally democratic societies than in despotic regimes, but the fact of a constraint upon the public discourse of newspapers is all but universal, as is its denial by those who operate within such systems. These filters have come to work so naturally over the past two centuries, and the constraints have become so powerful, and are built into newspapers in such a fundamental way, that alternative modes of news production often prove difficult to imagine.

During the past two decades, advances in information technology have allowed for wider and deeper access to historical news print and the interdisciplinary field of media studies has achieved recognition within academic institutions. As a result, scholars have come to appreciate newspapers as both sources and subjects in their own right, rather than as mere funds of data into which to dip in order to buttress claims made about the past from traditional archival sources. Still, the availability of published circulation, subscription and pricing figures for most historical newspapers remains very limited and uneven. When extant, however, these statistics, along with advertisements, allow scholars exciting opportunities to piece together a picture of newspaper readership as well as the demographic of reader that publishers coveted. Published letters to the editor reveal the responses of certain readers to news coverage. Nevertheless, short of systematic polling and survey information or an extensive search for reactions in contemporary letters and diaries, scholars find it a great challenge to assess newspaper reception (that is, how contemporary readers absorbed, interpreted and judged the news reports set before them).

So what is a newspaper? It is at once a text, a record of historical events, a representation of society and a chronicle of contemporary opinions, aspirations and debates. A newspaper is also a business enterprise, a professional organization, a platform for advertisements and itself a commodity. Newspapers are simultaneously open and closed systems of communications: on the one hand, newspapers are and have been available to anyone with enough change to spare; yet as private enterprises or centralized state organs, newspapers shroud their inner workings in secrecy. Newspaper scholars can thus focus upon content (what the reader saw in print) and, where archival sources permit, institutional history (managerial and hiring practices, growth and competitive strategies, changes in ownership and political and business ties, for example).

What most distinguishes a newspaper from any other writing genre, however, is *timing*. By definition, newspapers generate writing on fresh developments and must publish with speed. Just what constitutes 'the new' in newspapers, however, is historically relative. Daily newspapers were rare in most of Europe and North America until the late nineteenth century. For the average reader, the most common sources of news were weekly papers, whose reports a twenty-first-century reader likely find too 'dated' to accept as 'news' at all. In the early nineteenth century, news from parts of the British Empire, like India, averaged between two and three months to reach London. By the time it was published as 'news' in the UK, the event was already history in India. The spread of telegraph cables in the 1850s thus revolutionized the meaning of news and heralded the creation of publications like the *Daily Telegraph* (1855). Newspapers without telegraph cables of their own could subscribe to press agencies – such as Havas (France), Reuters (UK) and Wolff (Germany) – for access to breaking news from across the globe. Because of the high cost of this new technology, however, telegraphic dispatches were initially extremely terse and colourless in writing style, a compromise made for timeliness.

In its study of reading strategies, this chapter emphasizes British newspapers at the consumption end (as a finished textual product) rather than at the production end (as a business organization or state/party organ). However, the socio-political, economic and ideological structures from which news stories arise remain crucially important background to a full understanding of newspaper texts. Even where this context is lacking, a savvy reading of news reports and editorials can allow scholars to discern the kind of institutional framework that generated them.

## Historiography: histories of newspapers and newspapers in history

In 1846, Charles Mitchell published the first book devoted to the study of newspapers in the United Kingdom. His annual *Newspaper Press Directory* summarized and compared the price, circulation, ownership, political character and local context of British newspapers while offering advice to readers, publishers, politicians and journalists. In a chapter on the 'philosophy of advertising', Mitchell advanced rules that took for granted the newspaper 'as an advertising medium' and cautioned advertisers 'to regard [the readership's] *quality* rather than its *quantity*. Some of the most widely-circulated journals in the empire are the worst possible to advertise in,' he warned. 'Their readers are not purchasers and any money spent in them is so much thrown away.' A newspaper that had won 'the confidence of the monied and respectable classes of society' would prove to be 'a better medium for advertising, with a circulation of 2000, than another with a circulation of 4000, that circulation being chiefly confined to inns, public-houses, and beer-shops.' Why was this so? So-called respectable families, who typically read at home, 'look to advertisements as a part of the contents of the paper in which they may be interested', whereas those in the public houses, who often heard the articles spoken aloud, 'read for the news and the politics, *not* for the advertisements'.[4] As the logic went, newspapers should not seek to raise their general circulation numbers in order to improve profits, but rather aim to concentrate circulation amongst affluent circles. In the twentieth century, this common strategic manoeuvre would come to be known as 'moving up-market'.[5]

Thus before the middle of the nineteenth century, one can already trace in Britain the development of a strikingly modern, sophisticated business attitude towards the class and social identities of readers. Mitchell's book also revealed divergent definitions of newspaper content by contemporaries: one which included advertising as an intrinsic component of newspaper reading and another which saw it as entirely separate from the broadsheet proper.

Yet newspapers were more than mere businesses; they were shapers of ideas, even of nations. In 1834 Thomas Carlyle recognised to his chagrin that:

> Journalists are now the true Kings and Clergy: henceforth Historians . . . must write not of Bourbon Dynasties, and Tudors and Hapsburgs; but of Stamped Broad-sheet Dynasties, and quite new successive Names, according as this or the other Able Editor, or Combination of Able Editors, gains the world's ear.[6]

Mitchell himself highlighted the central importance newspapers had already assumed in the life of the British nation as a social salve. Queen Victoria, he noted, unwittingly 'owes the stability of her throne, and the tranquillity of her reign, more to the press than to the rude contrivance of a standing army'.[7] A quarter-century later, another press historian concurred. 'Public feeling, not only politically and morally, but socially, is powerfully influenced in all countries by the tone of their public journals', wrote James Grant in his multi-volume *History of the Newspaper Press*. 'It is impossible it could be otherwise', he continued, 'for the community in every country must, however unconsciously, imbibe the spirit of the newspaper which they daily read.'[8] Few scholars today would disagree.

The decade of the 1850s saw the first burst of interest in newspapers by book publishers. Not least of these was the first major history of newspapers in the United Kingdom, Frederick Knight Hunt's *The Fourth Estate: Contributions Towards a History of Newspapers, and the Liberty of the Press*. As the title immediately indicated, Hunt shared Carlyle's estimation of the social power of newspapers and measured journalism as an index of the progress made in the struggle to secure English liberties.[9] Hunt was no disinterested outsider either: he worked for the *Daily News* as an editor from 1846 to his death in 1854.[10] Surprisingly, booklets on the history of the English-language newspaper press of British India anticipated these domestic histories.[11] In part, such public attention arose from long-lived concerns for the scarce civil liberties granted to British servants of the East India Company, as press advocates complained that Parliament failed to extend the same measure of domestic liberties to newspapers produced in the British Empire.[12] Controversy surrounded the reduced free-speech rights of 'free-born Englishman' in India until it was surpassed by the same demands made by Indian nationalists at the century's end.[13]

General histories of Victorian newspapers emerged before 1900 as journalists, editors, and other newspapermen sought to assess and assert their own profession's triumphs, critique competitors and engage in gossip as they surveyed the state of the contemporary press. Despite the many golden nuggets of information contained within them, these dry histories usually fail the standards of modern scholarship, indulging as they often did in unstructured ambles down memory lane, the settling of personal and political scores and the propagation of colourful inaccuracies.[14]

While their quality improved considerably over the late nineteenth and twentieth centuries, the great bulk of newspaper histories continued to adopt a classic Whig interpretative framework. This conventional wisdom portrayed the commercial press as engaged in a heroic battle against state censorship and government taxation in the cause of civil liberties, principally from the period of the French Revolution until the Second World War. This contest resulted in a slow but steady 'transition from official to popular control' of the press, according to the standard account. At the core of this Whig school of thought existed a presumed linkage between the 'progress' of the commercial press one the one hand and democracy, or the more general 'broadening of political liberty', on the other.[15]

Since the 1960s, this grand narrative has come under fire as cultural theorists, literary scholars and historians have identified more subtle forms of ideological and social control at work in the discursive realm of the text. In their role as exponents of bourgeois liberal values, newspapers came to function as key ideological agents in class, gender and race oppression even as they contained the potential for radical critiques of such systems of power. In escaping more direct forms of government censorship, the press did not come under popular democratic control. Instead, newspapers largely passed from state control into the hands of private power interests and thus failed to democratize themselves as they became enmeshed in the gears of capital.

In their reassessment of newspaper history in the United Kingdom, James Curran and Jean Seaton detailed the rise of a radical press in the early nineteenth century that reached a national working-class audience. Evading the duties imposed by the state, the 'unstamped' press flourished, as did some of its radical commercial brethren, most prominently the Chartist *Northern Star*. This alternative press proved instrumental in fostering an alternative value system for disenfranchised labourers and a shared framework for looking at the world. When coercive attempts by the state to squelch these publications failed in the early nineteenth century, they were abandoned by mid-century in favour of the liberal view that the free market itself would enforce a tendency towards 'respectable' newspapers. Curran and Seaton demonstrate that this strategy largely accomplished what direct state intervention failed to do. Following the repeal of government taxes on newspapers between 1853 and 1869, a new daily commercial press came into existence, while the radical press collapsed. Not one new local working-class daily was established through the rest of the nineteenth century.

In its efforts to reach larger audiences for advertisers, newspapers saw a vast rise in scale and a corresponding increase in capital costs from the mid-nineteenth century onward. The expansion of the free market was accompanied by an 'industrialization of the Victorian press'. As radical newspapers with low-income working class readers failed to attract sufficient advertising from the business community and were forced to raise prices above levels that workers could afford, 'advertisers thus acquired a de facto licensing authority since, without their support, newspapers ceased to be economically viable'.[16] Profitable commercial newspaper publishers with great financial reserves stepped in to cater to the new 'popular' taste with a focus on entertainment, sensation and scandal. 'The repression, the isolation, the containment and eventually the incorporation of an autonomous popular press had nothing inevitable about them', Raymond Williams wrote. '[T]hey began as conscious political acts and continued as an effective deployment of financial resources to keep poor men's reading matter in rich men's hands.'[17]

When he wrote his preface to *Animal Farm* in the early 1940s, journalist George Orwell took for granted that most daily newspapers are 'owned by wealthy men who have every motive to be dishonest on certain important topics'.[18] Yet of greater interest to Orwell was the prevalence of journalistic self-censorship, 'a general tacit agreement that "it wouldn't do" to mention' certain facts in print:

> At any given moment there is an orthodoxy, a body of ideas which it is assumed that all right-thinking people will accept without question. It is not exactly forbidden to say this, that or the other, but it is not done 'to say it',

just as a Victorian gentleman would not mention trousers in the presence of a lady. 'Anyone who challenges the prevailing orthodoxy finds himself silenced with surprising effectiveness', Orwell concluded. 'A genuinely unfashionable opinion is almost never given a fair hearing, either in the popular press or in the highbrow periodicals.'[19]

The most sustained efforts to subject periodicals to historical examination in the last half century have in a sense been elaborations upon Orwell's sketch, deploying theories of ideology, hegemony and discourse to locate the ways in which newspapers inculcated in their readers a culture of conformity with the economic or social status quo.[20] Historian Brian Harrison reasoned that 'in modern conditions social cohesion could no longer be taken for granted: it needed to be energetically worked for'.[21] In the late eighteenth century, the Gordon and Priestly riots, reinforced by the role of the 'crowd' in the French Revolution, convinced both conservatives and reformers of the need to forge new links between government and people. Williams argued in his study of England in the 1840s that scholars should view newspapers as part of a 'chain of significations and determinations, and its nature and function as a signifying practice and a reproducer of ideologies'.[22] Leslie Williams has also emphasized, in examining British press coverage of the Irish famine of the late

1840s, that 'Victorian publications were also disseminators of ideas, bulwarks of values, normative gatekeepers, and social barometers'.[23] Joanne Shattock and Michael Wolff have argued that it was during the Victorian period (1837–1901) specifically that 'the press, in all its manifestations, became . . . the context within which people lived and worked and thought, and from which they derived their . . . sense of the outside world'.[24]

In the last two decades, newspaper studies have drifted away from institutional brands of social critique and have instead come to focus upon the ways in which texts betray complex ambivalences towards power, nation, empire, race, class and identity. Rather than being seen as pure ideological monoliths, newspapers are recognized as a contested ground in wars of cultural meaning.[25] In part the close attention paid by newspaper scholars to textual patterns and devices in the construction of that meaning continues the work of the 'linguistic turn' in literary studies. At the same time, growing numbers of newspaper scholars have followed an 'imperial turn' in their work, recovering long-ignored networks that linked newspapers and the wider world of empire.[26] This growing movement in the literature has taken inspiration from Benedict Anderson's positioning of newspapers as co-creators of the 'imagined communities' (the modern nation-state and empire) to which nearly all modern peoples have formed sustaining allegiances, including nationalist movements for independence in European colonies.[27]

## Analytical toolkit

The questions that scholars bring to newspapers divide generally into three broad categories of investigation: institutional structure (the social context), format (the textual context) and content (the text). Each of these impinges upon how one reads a newspaper.

Readers interested in the institutional setting and structure of a newspaper ask questions about its internal organization and how it fits into the broader society and its systems of power. Newspapers are, above all things, human institutions: fallible, imperfect, with material or ideological interests of their own. Rarely do existing archives provide a detailed record of newspapers' internal hierarchies, decision-making processes or outside influences. To the extent that the structure is known, one can hypothesize what the news product will look like. One can then study the news product itself and decide whether it conforms to obvious assumptions about the nature of the newspaper in question. In conducting such an institutional analysis, readers may raise the following sorts of questions: Who controls the newspaper? Is it owned by the local community or the state, a family, private company or public investors? Is it affiliated with a political party, religious group, trade group, advocacy group or is it independent? Is it national, regional or local in its reach? How regularly is the newspaper published? Are its revenues derived primarily from street sales, subscriptions or advertising? Who are its advertisers and what kinds of products or services do they market to readers? For what socio-economic class are they appropriate? What is the ratio of news content to advertising in column inches?

Take, for example, the *Washington Post*. It is itself a corporation, owned by a larger media parent company that is traded on the public stock exchange. As a business, this national newspaper sells a product to a market. Publishers earn relatively little income from newspaper sales; its owners and shareholders would lose money if they relied solely on street purchases or subscriptions for revenue. Its product is therefore not its latest edition; that is but a vehicle for its real product: readers. In particular, its product is a readership of relatively privileged, educated professionals in decision-making positions within society. This product is sold to a market: advertisers (largely other businesses), who pay for the opportunity to attract those privileged readers to buying or investing in their products or services. The *Washington Post*, then, in a purely business sense, is a corporation that sells readers (consumers with buying power and social influence) to other corporations. What can one predict about this newspaper's content, given just that set of circumstances? What is the null hypothesis: assuming nothing further, what conjectures could one make? The obvious assumption is that the media content (what appears, what does not appear, the way the news is framed, etc.), will reflect the values, priorities and interests of the buyers, the sellers, the product and the professionals that serve them.[28] Unless the newspaper were dysfunctional, any other outcome would be surprising.

When evaluating the visual context of a given newspaper edition, its layout, graphics, images, font size and type style all matter. Design affects reception, and does so with intent. The visual sophistication of newspapers grew enormously over the course of the twentieth century as technological changes and the concentration of media ownership accelerated. In this connection, readers may ask what newspapers do to attract the eye to particular bits of the page, or to move it in a particular direction. Is the news article in question on the front page or buried deep inside the paper? Historians that rely upon newspaper clippings in their research can easily lose this context of spatial placement. Does it make use of photographs, sketches, charts and maps? How are advertisements placed in relation to news? How does the ad shape our perception of the news? Does it create a certain mood? Does the news influence the context for the ad? Does it seem 'natural' for advertisements to be published alongside news or do the juxtapositions create a sense of friction?

Finally, the reader arrives at the textual content of the article itself. When addressing the text, one may put to it the following questions: Is the author named? Where and when was the article written? What is the writer's tone, vocabulary, choice of metaphors or mode of address? What are the denotation and contemporary connotation of its key terms? Who is the implied reader? Does the content cater to a niche audience or to a local, regional or national audience? Is there an implicit 'us' and 'them' voiced? What are the report's sources? (Government officials, opposition party members, experts, eye-witnesses, dissenters, victims, anonymous sources, etc.) Can you articulate any assumptions behind the point of view expressed? Are they stated explicitly or implicitly? What knowledge is the author assuming that the audience shares? How does the author use these assumptions to make his or her point persuasive? To what emotions does it seem to appeal? Does it position itself against another point of view? What other relevant information does the author leave out? Are there ideological limits beyond which the article does not go? If so, what is its doctrinal framework? Finally, does the article in question conform to your expectations for the genre or does it defy or modify expected conventions? Why?

Newspapers often engage in elaborate and unfolding debates with one another, playing with one another's words and consciously turning meanings around in competing narratives. Therefore, in order to understand a newspaper article, it is often essential to use the comparative method: to read the text alongside parallel articles in other newspapers as well as in comparison with what preceded it in its own newspaper. In this vein, one may inquire: How does a story's length compare with that of other news stories? Do you note a sustained as opposed to a casual or fitful attention to the issue over time? If looking at other newspapers, do you detect evidence of inter-textuality (an awareness of and response to reports in other newspapers or journals)?

## Case study: The Times and Sind (1843)

The archival record of news reporting on the British Empire offers modern scholars particularly rich opportunities to delve into the crowded mental landscape of another time and to test the theories that have emerged from media and literary studies. For its case study, this chapter selects articles from *The Times* on Britain's conquest of Sind in 1843.

Founded in 1785, *The Times* established itself as the nation's pre-eminent newspaper in the nineteenth century. *The Times* was more than a city daily; read avidly by businessmen, politicians, intellectuals and the educated middle and upper classes throughout the British Isles and Continental Europe, it set the agenda for news reporting. Its vast resources allowed it to gather news from across the globe and maintain its status as the overwhelmingly dominant press voice. In 1841, *The Times* sold twice as many copies as its rivals, the *Morning Post, Morning Herald,* and *Morning Chronicle,* put together; by 1850 it sold four times as many. At this time, the paper's foreign news budget alone amounted to more than £10,000 a year and supported agents in locales as far away as Marseilles, Malta and Alexandria.[29] As they lacked sufficient journalistic manpower, many city and provincial newspapers published extracts from *The Times* to supply their own national or international news.

The relatively quiet conquest of Sind followed a militarily disastrous and domestically controversial campaign in Afghanistan (1839–1842), from which Britain's reputation in Asia was only with great difficulty restored. Its 'Opium War' with China (1838–1842) aroused a mixture of moral dissent and xenophobic sentiment at home. Both wars took longer to win than expected and yielded few obvious benefits. The independent kingdom of Sind, on the other hand, fell into British hands quickly and unexpectedly. With no convincing military justification for the unprovoked conquest, General Charles James Napier and Governor-General of India Lord Ellenborough defended the annexation of Sind as an opportunity to project British might to the world and to acquire new economic resources for imperial trade along the Indus River. The spoils (in looted gold bullion, treasure and jewels) amounted to more than £500,000, of which a handsome cut of £21,000 was deposited into the Bank of England.[30] Napier's famously terse victory telegraph to London, 'Peccavi' ('I have sinned/Sind'), captured the ambiguity of the moment better than he could have known. For close to a year, *The Times* reported periodically on the conquest of Sind and the 17 February 1843 Battle of Miani that achieved it. A selection of this news coverage follows:

[Editorial]
We yesterday announced to our readers a brilliant victory obtained by Sir C. Napier, at the head of 2,700 of our own troops, over 22,000 Beloochees – a satisfactory evidence that, in military power at least, the days of Plassey and Assaye are not gone by. Such as the difference then was between the rabble-army of a native prince and the noble and disciplined array of Sepoys trained and led by English officers – such it remains . . . we find Sir C. Napier's victory brilliant, and in itself satisfactory, as it is, little consolation for the fact which it betrays, that the north-west of India is still unsettled . . . It is disappointing to find that a fresh war has proved necessary at the very moment when we fancied ourselves grasping an honourable and permanent peace. To have plunged in it, if it be proved *unnecessary*, will be more than disappointing – it will be disgraceful.

(*The Times*, 6 April 1843)

[Editorial]
On the 17th [of February] a battle took place, which can only be compared to the celebrated one at Plassey, in which, after a severe struggle of three hours, the Ameers were totally routed and their troops dispersed. The loss of the British troops was considerable . . . The capture of this most important position is of immense value; the valuable and fertile districts along the Indus can now be restored to industry and the arts of peace, and millions, as of old, will soon live in happiness in those plains where those despots have during a century scattered misery and desolation. The official accounts are subjoined. It appears that the plan of an attack in order to exterminate all the British in Scinde was not confined to Hyderabad, it extended itself throughout the territories of the Ameers, but their utmost efforts have been baffled, and they are now prisoners.

(*The Times,* 7 April 1843)

[News article]
The Affairs of India.
Private Correspondence.
Deccan, March 28.
. . . In the proclamation, the Governor General has made the best of the subject, and Scinde now belongs to the British Government, except such part as his Lordship may bestow on his faithful ally and base traitor to his family, Meer Ali Morad, Ameer, &c. I dare not trust myself to comment upon Lord Ellenborough's notification now, and I leave it to abler pens than mine – he has

glossed over his own acts in the opening paragraph, left it to be inferred that the Ameers were in the wrong altogether, that his usurpation and total *bouleverse-ment* of affairs there were strictly justifiable and needful, and has made the most, as of course he would, of the attack on [diplomat Sir James] Outram [in Hyderabad]. We have a flourish of trumpets too about the blessings of our own rule in future, and though this may be the only part of our conduct which may hereafter become subject for praise we have to account for what has been done to a higher tribunal than sits on earth. Read the gallant Napier's despatch, and if it does not stir your blood, ay, that of every man in England who reads it, then you had needs warm it somehow. Eloquent, just, spirited, it is worthy of the gallant old veteran . . . It was, indeed, a hard fought and daringly-contested field on both sides, and I question if ever before in India there was so much hand to hand, sword to bayonet fighting as on this occasion, nor ever more dis-parity of odds – the victory, indeed, seems a miracle. May it be the last. It will be a wise and beneficent policy, now that the deed of blood is done, to pour a large body of troops into Scinde, so as completely to put it beyond the means of the Ameers and the haughty Beloochee chiefs to attempt to regain by force what has been lost. As to the former, they are our prisoners and at our mercy; the others may be thorns in the side of the Governor-General, if he remain. As a territorial acquisition the importance of Scinde cannot be denied: the com-mand of such a river and such a country, capable of becoming a second Bengal in wealth and productiveness, is beyond all question.

(*The Times*, 8 May 1843)

[Editorial]
We remain masters of Scinde . . . The opportune accident of a family dispute impaired the irregular strength of the Ameers. One of those usurpations so common in Oriental sovereignties furnished us with an excuse for interfering in the quarrel. We interfered only to divide; and from the divisions which we encouraged, we already begin to speculate on the aggrandizement of our Indian empire . . .

While we do not mean to justify these aggressions by the success which has attended them, nor to assert that, because the districts on the banks of the Indus may be cultivated to the highest point of fertility, the occupation of Scinde was, on that account, a measure to be advised or applauded; at the same time we do not hesitate to affirm, that, as things have turned out, it is the duty of the Indian Government to make the best use they can of this new acquisition. Whether their mode of acquiring it be defensible on the score of political morality or no, there can be no question that they may retain it both on safer and more hon-ourable terms than those whom they dispossessed. They could not by any pos-sibility be worse rulers of the country than the old Ameers. It is no great compliment to say that we expect they will be much better. The territory is represented as being of great capabilities. Let them improve these to the utmost. They will thus improve the physical, and with it the moral, condition of the people. When we are reproached with the treachery, the ambition, and the violence by which we have extended our Eastern empire, let us at least be able to answer, in our own defences, that in destroying dynasties we have not substituted one slavery for another, but that in every case we have made the people more happy, more wealthy, and more secure than they ever dreamed of being under their native princes. Let us point to more enduring and substantial reigns of our power than the Sepoy camp or the tax-collector; let us point to the change in manners, morality, and jurisprudence, which best attests the influence and the honesty of a paternal government.

*(The Times*, 24 October 1843)

[News article]
Indian Affairs.
(From Our Own Correspondent.)
Camp, Deccan, Oct. 24.
Scinde.
. . .

The country has become unhealthy because it was neglected by the oppressive Ameers, who seem to have considered that there were but two objects of government – that of screwing money out of the people, and that of creating hunting grounds for their own pastime. A scientific system of drainage will soon alter the face of the country and remove all cause of complaint on the score of unhealthiness . . .

However defective may have been our right to dispossess the Ameers, it is allowed by all, even by those who most violently impugn [Governor-General] Lord Ellenborough's policy, that we cannot relinquish the country without committing an act of unparalleled madness. To restore it to its former rulers and thus establish a new and independent, perhaps a hostile, power on the frontiers of India, would bring in question our capacity for governing the rest of the country. If the Indus is to be regarded as the natural limit of our empire, we cannot spare a foot of land within that boundary; and the sooner the anomalous independence of the various chiefs, whom our forbearance has spared, ceases, and the whole country is brought under the same scheme of administration, the better for the interests of the people, and the better also for the consolidation of our empire . . .

*(The Times*, 5 December 1843)

A number of basic contextual points arise from this reading. First is the plain fact of the anxiety-inducing delay between an event in India and the arrival of news reports in London (by about six weeks). While the recent introduction of steamships shortened the eight- to twelve-week journey of the 1820s, it must be observed that reading news reports from India was a bit like gazing into the stars: one never could be certain whether what one saw, no matter how brightly it shone, still existed in fact. Another point is the anonymity of the field reporter; readers are left in ignorance as to whether he is an independent agent or an employee of the East India Company, be it as officer, soldier, veteran or merchant, all of which hold important implications. (This is one indication that the journalistic profession was still in its infancy, and certainly so in colonial spaces. The personalized reporting of William Russell on the Crimean War in the 1850s would signal an important shift in journalistic authority here.) Finally, there is the distinction between the news article written in India and the editorial column composed in London, which synthesizes and interprets the former for the reader in sometimes unexpected ways.

Within the text itself, one notes the recurring deployment of several key words and ideas. The very first is 'we', creating an implied unity amongst the military, the East India Company, the newspaper, the nation, and the reader as well as a tone of celebration over the outcome of events. To promote the British 'side' in these events is not to suffer from subjective bias, but rather to practise objective and neutral journalism. In a sense, the anonymity of the reporter noticed above supports this ideological notion, casting the story beyond the subjective experience of any particular writer. The repeated discussion of the small number of British forces relative to their Baluchi opponents advertise the superior quality of each Company officer, soldier and sepoy (native Indian recruits, who comprised some 80 per cent of the Company army's rank-and-file). As with the reporter, both Baluchi and British soldiers go unnamed (in army lists of the killed and wounded only officers are delineated), revealing a striking adherence to social hierarchies. The army becomes a simple extension of the will of Sir Napier. The use of the term 'British soldier' also creates ambiguity, allowing readers to imagine the army as more European than it was in fact, while word of the 'miraculous' turn of this violent contest hints at the hand of Providence.

The reports assume common knowledge amongst readers of two historical British victories in South Asia. One was the 1757 Battle of Plassey (Palashi) between Nawab (governor) of Bengal Siraj ud-Daulah and General Robert Clive, establishing British rule in Bengal. Then in 1803 the Battle of Assaye gave Britain an important victory over the Maratha Empire of south-central India, its last serious rival for power on the subcontinent. By forging these links with an established noble past, news writers attenuated any hint of moral scandal surrounding the attack upon Sind.

At the same time, these articles betray anxiety about the fundamental illegitimacy of the attack upon Sind. They therefore raise multiple and repeated rationalizations for it: the amirs as 'Oriental' despots; false rumours of a plan to 'exterminate all the British' from Sind; the Indus River as a 'natural' limit to Britain's eastern empire; the promise of economic trade for Britain; the scientific, agricultural and economic improvements that Britain will bring to the regions' inhabitants; and the moral, cultural and political improvement of the people of Sind, left in the dark ages by their oppressive amirs. British imperial warfare and expansion, then, are presented as benign tools to bring about the real benefits of 'peace' and 'civilization' to unenlightened natives as imperial subjects. Newspaper coverage thus limited the many possible impressions of Sind to several options: a land of internal oppression, menacing threat, outright violence or peaceful progress under British tutelage. The possibility of British wrongdoing (beyond well-intentioned error) is simply not a category of thought here. To return 'a foot of land' would be an act of 'madness'. Even where British aggression is acknowledged, there is no contemplation of decrying the imperial enterprise itself. British expansion by definition means progress, modernity, liberty.

Victorian news accounts of imperial warfare clearly worked to galvanize loyal sentiment at home.[31] *The Times*, alongside other broadsheets, increasingly addressed its readers as politically engaged persons and as though Indian events naturally touched their lives, discursively positioning Britons as an imperially invested people. In the press, Britons were formidable frontiersmen and sober soldiering men bringing order and tranquility to a broad landscape peopled with diverse tribes, but emphatically unchanged by them.

## Conclusion

Despite the prodigious bounty that newspapers bring to the intellectual table, the promising evolution that newspaper scholarship has undergone, the growing accessibility of newspaper writing and their enormous contemporary relevance, newspapers have inspired relatively few historical monographs as a subject in themselves and fare even less well within general history writing. In 1990, Brian Maidment lamented the fact that 'there is almost no attention paid to Victorian periodicals in themselves, though many articles and essays depend on evidence drawn from periodicals to substantiate, illustrate, or reinforce arguments constructed out of other kinds of scholarly evidence.' Maidment found 'a startling absence of any well-developed corpus of work studying the generic issues specific to periodicals' such as editorial policy, print technique, readership definition, sales figures, distribution patterns, and finance, all of which 'underlie, or perhaps even construct, the statements of opinions, beliefs, or values which scholars read off from the diligently researched page or microfilm'. Maidment called upon scholars to move beyond the use of newspapers as mere illustrations and to adopt an authentically interdisciplinary approach worthy of the genre:

> If we regard periodicals not like fossil hunters, in search of specimens to fill a cabinet, but like theoretical geologists or theologians, as expositions of processes by which change occurs and is made legible, then I think a quite major shift in thinking will have occurred.[32]

Nearly two decades later, it is no longer true that 'a case still has to be made for the centrality of the study of newspapers as a scholarly project'.[33] The fruit of that recognition has yet to grow and multiply, but the prospects for researchers to break new ground in this genre and to shape its future are without limit.

## Notes

1 R. Chartier, 'Intellectual History or Sociocultural History? The French Trajectories', in Dominic Lacapra and S.L. Kaplan (eds), *Modern European Intellectual History: Reappraisals and New Perspectives*, Ithaca: Cornell University Press, 1982, p. 30.

2   A. Smith, 'The Long Road to Objectivity and Back Again: The Kinds of Truth We Get in Journalism', in G. Boyce, J. Curran and P. Wingate (eds), *Newspaper History from the Seventeenth Century to the Present Day*, London: Constable, 1978, pp. 168 and 170.

3   Smith, 'The Long Road to Objectivity', p. 152.

4   C. Mitchell, *Newspaper Press Directory: Containing Full Particulars Relative to Each Journal Published in The United Kingdom and the British Isles; Together with A Complete Guide to The Newspaper Press of Each County, Etc. Etc. Etc.*, London, 1846, p. 327.

5   For evidence of the advance of this logic in the contemporary commercial press, see R. Perez-Peña, 'Why Big Newspapers Applaud Some Declines in Circulation', in the *New York Times*, 1 October 2007.

6   T. Carlyle, *Sartor Resartus; The Life and Opinions of Herr Teufelsdröckh*, London, 1920, Book I, pp. 48–49.

7   Mitchell, *Newspaper Press Directory*, p. 22.

8   J. Grant, *History of the Newspaper Press*, vol. 2, London, 1871, p. 402.

9   The phrase 'fourth estate' arose early in the nineteenth century as a short-hand for journalists and newspaper editors. In early modern England and France, those who represented the nation and participated in the life of the body politic were divided by tradition into three orders or 'estates': the clergy, the nobility and the commons. In its power to monitor and limit state action through its influence upon public opinion, the press had in the nineteenth century become an unofficial 'fourth estate' of the realm, according to writers such as William Hazlitt and Thomas Carlyle.

10  A. Jones, *Powers of the Press: Newspapers, Power and the Public in Nineteenth-Century England*, Brookfield: Ashgate Publishing Company, 1996, p. 52. See also F. Knight Hunt, *The Fourth Estate: Contributions towards a History of Newspapers, and of the Liberty of the Press*, 2 vols, London, 1850; P.-A. Cucheval-Clarigny, *Histoire de la Presse en Angleterre at aux Etats-Unis*, Paris, 1857 [English transl. Andrews (London, 1870)]; and A. Andrews, *The History of British Journalism: From the Foundation of the Newspaper Press in England, to the Repeal of the Stamp Act in 1855, with Sketches of Press Celebrities*, 2 vols, London: Richard Bentley, 1859.

11  L. Stanhope, *Sketch of the History and Influence of the Press in British India* (1823) and S. Arnot, *A Sketch of the History of the Indian Press During the Last Ten Years, With A Disclosure of the True Causes of Its Present Degradation . . . With a Biographical Notice of the Indian Cobbett, Alias 'Peter the Hermit'* (1829).

12  *Report of the Second Anniversary Meeting of the Newspaper Press Benevolent Association, Held at the Freemason's Tavern*, 13 July 1839.

13  Jones, *Powers of the Press*, pp. 25–27. See also *Papers Relating to the Public Press in India* (House of Commons, 1858).

14  J.D. Vann and R.T. VanArsdel (eds), *Victorian Periodicals: A Guide to Research*, New York: The Modern Language Association of America, 1978, p. 87.

15  For a classic example of this interpretive framework, see S. Koss, *The Rise and Fall of the Political Press in Britain*, 3 vols, London: Hamish Hamilton, 1981.

16  J. Curran and J. Seaton, *Power Without Responsibility: The Press and Broadcasting in Britain*, 4th edn, London: Routledge, 1991, pp. 35 and 39.

17  R. Williams, 'The Press and Popular Culture: An Historical Perspective', in Boyce, Curran, Wingate (eds), *Newspaper History*, p. 50.

18  As if to prove Orwell's theory, the British Ministry of Information suppressed his preface; it sat unknown until its publication in the 1970s. See B. Crick, 'How the Essay Came to Be Written' in *The Times Literary Supplement*, 15 September 1972.

19  G. Orwell, *Animal Farm*, London: Penguin, 2000, Appendix I.

20  Marxist theorists such as Louis Althusser, Raymond Williams and Terry Eagleton have used ideology to refer to a coherent system of ideas that rely upon certain basic assumptions about the social world that ultimately advance a particular class interest. The principal theorist of hegemony was Antonio Gramsci, though his ideas were not well known

until the latter third of the twentieth century. Hegemony points to the capacity of dominant social groups to cause others to accept, adopt and internalize their values and norms without the brute use of force, though force may be available. Postmodern theorists like Michel Foucault, in shifting away from any search for singular truths, looked instead at how knowledge and experiences are produced and sustained through discourses, such as texts, beliefs, attitudes, policies and practices. Discourse analysis seeks to reveal the wider social processes of legitimation and power contained within texts and practices.

21  Shattock and Wolff, *The Victorian Periodical Press*, p. 262.

22  L. Brake, A. Jones and L. Madden (eds), *Investigating Victorian Journalism*, London: Macmillan Press, 1990, p. 10.

23  L. Williams, 'Bad Press: Thomas Campbell Foster and British Reportage on the Irish Famine, 1845–1849', in L. Brake, B. Bell and D. Finkelstein (eds), *Nineteenth-Century Media and the Construction of Identities*, London: Palgrave, 2000, p. 295.

24  J. Shattock and M. Wolff (eds), *The Victorian Periodical Press: Samplings and Soundings*, Leicester: Leicester University Press, 1982, p. xiii.

25  See J.F. Codell (ed.), *Imperial Co-Histories: National Identities and the British and Colonial Press*, Madison. N.J.: Fairleigh Dickinson University Press, 2003, and Brake, Bell and Finkelstein (eds), *Nineteenth-Century Media*.

26  Some of the most ground-breaking work in this field deals with the rich English-language newspaper history of South Asia. See D. Finkelstein and D.M. Peers (eds), *Negotiating India in the Nineteenth-Century Media*, London: Macmillan, 2000; M. Israel, *Communications and Power: Propaganda and the Press in the Indian Nationalist Struggle, 1920–1947*, Cambridge: Cambridge University Press, 1994; C. Kaul (ed.), *Media and the British Empire*, London: Palgrave Macmillan, 2006; C. Kaul, *Reporting the Raj: The British Press and India, c. 1880–1922*, Manchester: Manchester University Press, 2003; and S. Potter, *News and the British World: The Emergence of an Imperial Press System*, Oxford: Clarendon Press, 2003. For two important bibliographies of imperial newspaper collections, see E.M. Palmegiano, *The British Empire in the Victorian Press, 1832–1867. A Bibliography*, New York: Garland Publishing, 1987, and J.D. Vann and R.T. VanArsdel (eds), *Periodicals of Queen Victoria's Empire: An Exploration*, Toronto: University of Toronto Press, 1996.

27  B. Anderson, *Imagined Communities: Reflections on the Origin and Spread of Nationalism*, London: Verso, 1993. For an influential thesis on the role of newspapers and print media on the creation of bourgeois civil society, see J. Habermas, *The Structural Transformation of the Public Sphere*, Cambridge, Mass.: MIT Press, 1989.

28  For detailed case studies of the effect of corporate ownership upon US news reporting in the latter half of the twentieth century, see E. Herman and N. Chomsky, *Manufacturing Consent: The Political Economy of the Mass Media*, New York: Pantheon Books, 1988.

29  M. Walker, *Powers of the Press: The World's Great Newspapers*, London: Quartet Books, 1982, pp. 33–36.

30  *The Times*, 24 November 1845, citing *Allen's Indian Mail* (n.d.).

31  For a sampling of the eighteenth-century analogue, see P.J. Marshall, '"Cornwallis Triumphant": War in India and the British Public in the Late Eighteenth Century', in L. Freedman, P.M. Hayes and R. O'Neill (eds), *War, Strategy and International Politics: Essays in Honour of Sir Michael Howard*, Oxford: Oxford University Press, 1992, pp. 57–74 and P. Lawson, '"Arts and Empire Equally Extend": Tradition, Prejudice and Assumption in the Eighteenth-Century Press Coverage of Empire', in K. Schweizer and J. Black (eds), *Politics and the Press in Hanoverian Britain*, Lewiston, N.Y.: E. Mellon Press, 1989, pp. 119–146.

32  B.E. Maidment, 'Victorian Periodicals and Academic Social Discourse', in Brake, Jones and Madden (eds) *Investigating Victorian Journalism*, pp. 147–148.

33  Maidment, 'Victorian Periodicals', p. 153.

## Select bibliography

Boyce, G., Curran, J. and Wingate, P. (eds), *Newspaper History from the Seventeenth Century to the Present Day*, London: Constable, 1978.

Brake, L., Bell, B., and Finkelstein, D. (eds), *Nineteenth-Century Media and the Construction of Identities*, London: Palgrave, 2000.

Brake, L., Jones., A., and Madden, L. (eds), *Investigating Victorian Journalism*, London: The Macmillan Press, 1990.

Curran, J. and Seaton, J., *Power Without Responsibility: The Press, Broadcasting and New Media in Britain*, 6th edn, London: Routledge, 2003.

Finkelstein, D. and Peers, D.M. (eds), *Negotiating India in the Nineteenth-Century Media*, London: Macmillan, 2000.

Jones, A., *Powers of the Press: Newspapers, Power and the Public in Nineteenth-Century England*, Brookfield: Ashgate Publishing Company, 1996.

Kaul, C., *Reporting the Raj: The British Press and India, c. 1880–1922*, Manchester: Manchester University Press, 2003.

Koss, S., *The Rise and Fall of the Political Press in Britain*, volume 1, *The Nineteenth Century*, London: Hamish Hamilton, 1981.

Potter, S., *News and the British World: The Emergence of an Imperial Press System*. Oxford: Clarendon Press, 2003.

Shattock, J. and Wolff, M. (eds), *The Victorian Periodical Press: Samplings and Soundings*, Leicester: Leicester University Press, 1982.

Vann, J.D., and R.T. VanArsdel (eds), *Periodicals of Queen Victoria's Empire: An Exploration*. Toronto: University of Toronto Press, 1996.

**Online sources:**

*C19: The Nineteenth Century Index* <http://c19index.chadwyck.com> [This archive supersedes The Wellesley Index]

*The Times Digital Archive* <http://www.gale.com/Times/> [This archive supersedes Palmer's Index]

# 12  Speeches

*Paul Readman*

'The great men's speeches in this exciting time are the most interesting reading in the world. Nothing could be more absorbing than one's own sentence of death.'[1] Thus Lady Monkswell confided to her diary on 30 January 1878, at the height of the controversy over the British government's foreign policy in the near east. The political debate over this policy, which saw Britain and Russia come close to war, were largely fought out by means of public speeches such as those of the great Liberal leader William Gladstone, who delivered open-air orations to audiences of thousands on the unwisdom and immorality of the line taken by his Conservative antagonist Benjamin Disraeli, the earl of Beaconsfield, who was then Prime Minister. In Britain and elsewhere, this was the golden age of public speaking, that moment in history which extended from the mid nineteenth to the mid twentieth century, when the progressive democratisation of political cultures served to make the set-piece speech vital to the very stuff of a newly popularised politics. In these years before the advent of television, speeches were the primary means of political communication and persuasion, being routinely reported in detail by the newspaper press. Even as early as 1855, a single number of *The Times* could contain nearly 60,000 words of reportage on proceedings in parliament.[2] Yet speechmaking retained its importance with the twentieth-century arrival of new broadcast media. While radio and television may have meant the eventual demise of hours-long addresses in the style of Gladstone, privileging excerpts and soundbites over the full coverage of old, speeches remained of key historical significance. It may be, for example, that the length of excerpts from speeches shown on American news programmes during presidential elections had fallen to an average of just nine seconds by 1988, but while Harry Truman gave 58 speeches in his first year of office, Ronald Reagan gave 211, and in all, American presidents spoke nearly 10,000 times in public in the forty years after 1945.[3] These observations suffice to illustrate the central importance of speeches as sources across the whole chronological range of modern history, and particularly modern political history, which will form the focus of the present chapter.

Scholars interested in speech before the nineteenth century face difficulties finding the sources they need to carry out their research. As James Axtell, the distinguished historian of early modern North America has commented, '[o]ur best evidence about human history, people's words, have almost wholly vanished into thin air because they were spoken and not written down'.[4] Historians of the later modern period, however, are far less troubled by this problem, as the sources recording speech that are available to them are many and various. They range from the first-hand accounts of contemporary witnesses, often summary in form rather than verbatim, to more accurate reports in newspapers and official parliamentary records. They also include typescripts of speeches preserved in the private papers of those who delivered them, popular and scholarly collections of important speeches, and the texts of public utterances as printed in leaflets, pamphlets and other ephemeral publications. In addition, many twentieth-century speeches (or extracts from speeches) are preserved in radio, film and television archives, as well as on the internet.

## Historians' use of speeches as sources

Historians have always made use of speeches. Unsurprisingly, given the prestige and importance of oratory in classical civilisation, they were extensively deployed by Greek and Roman historians like Herodotus, Thucydides and Tacitus. Thucydides' account of the Peloponnesian War (431–404 BC) for example, contains three long speeches by Pericles, all of considerable and continuing scholarly importance.[5] Later on, nineteenth-century historians such as Thomas Carlyle and T.B. Macaulay also deployed the spoken word in their accounts, although like their classical predecessors, they often lacked the documentary evidence for the words that they put in the mouths of their historical subjects. To the extent that pre-Rankean history writing was seen as a fount of moral object-lessons as much as a rigorously exact account of 'how things actually were (wie es eigentlich gewesen)' – Carlyle, for one, saw it more as a branch of poetry or literature – this was a matter of little enough concern to most contemporaries. For them, speeches added much colour and drama to heroic narratives, such as the teleological chronicle of English national progress constructed by 'Whig' historians for a reading public interested to know the origins of Britain's greatness.

Notoriously, of course, Leopold von Ranke changed all this. Although its impact was not felt immediately and varied from place to place, Rankean methodology transformed the character of historical writing, especially within the academy. Its stress on painstaking research in the name of factual accuracy and concern with the details of statecraft fractured the expansive narrative approach of old, and sent scholars scurrying to the archive in pursuit of government documents and the minutiae of policy-making. Within political history, this led to a focus on what statesmen *did* – in terms of legislation, diplomatic initiatives and so on – at the expense of what they *said*, especially in public. This view of speechmaking as ancillary rather than central to the stuff of politics was further entrenched by the rise of Namierism from the late 1920s on. A historian of late eighteenth- and early nineteenth-century England, Lewis Namier gave rise to a whole school of historical thought that tended to downplay the role of ideology and belief in political motivation, instead emphasising personal and material factors, not least individual self-interest. Its effects are still being felt today. While it is true that recent historical writing does make use of speeches, in political history at least, some of it still conveys the sense that the spoken word provides evidence of secondary rather than primary importance, and that the record of the 'real' business of politics still lies buried in the archive, residing in organisational documents, private papers, diaries, memoranda and the like.

However, the view of speeches as window-dressing or 'mere rhetoric' ignores the philosophical insights of Ludwig Wittgenstein, J.L. Austin, John Searle and others, who argued that words do not simply have certain 'meanings' which can be understood in isolation, but are used in specific contexts to do specific things; words, in short, can be deeds, or 'speech-acts'.[6] As Wittgenstein put it, 'the *speaking* of language is part of an activity, or of a form of life.'[7] Yet according to this perspective, which Austin developed with considerable precision in his seminal *How to Do Things with Words*, the activities language perform are not limited to conveying information: the 'locutionary' act *of* saying something can be distinguished from the 'illocutionary' (what is done *in* saying it) and the 'perlocutionary' (what is done *by* saying it). The policeman who tells a skater 'the ice over there is very thin' is saying precisely that (locutionary), but may also be issuing a warning (illocutionary), and depending on the skater's response – fear, annoyance, whatever – may have succeeded in causing a (perlocutionary) effect. In this way, utterances can be seen to convey particular intentions and have particular impacts, depending on the context, form and mode of their delivery. Led by Quentin Skinner, historians of political ideas have recognised the significance of these linguistic-philosophical observations for the study of the past, applying them to analyses of the thought of Thomas Hobbes or Niccolo Machiavelli (to take two examples).[8] However, the focus of these scholars has necessarily been on the written rather than the spoken word. And while other – rather different – manifestations of the 'linguistic turn', such as those associated with the post-structuralist theories of Jacques Derrida and Michel Foucault, have not left the analysis of speeches completely untouched, it is nevertheless true that many modern historians who have been influenced by such approaches have also evinced more interest in written than in spoken texts.[9]

That said, however, there are signs of an increasing scholarly willingness to use speeches as sources for the elucidation of the pattern, character and meaning of contemporary discourses. One recent example would be Antoinette Burton's analysis of an address given by the Conservative Prime Minister Lord Salisbury at Edinburgh in 1888, during which he had commented that the failure of the Indian Liberal candidate Dadabhai Naoroji to be elected as MP for the London seat of Holborn at the 1886 general election proved that 'however great the progress of mankind has been. . . I doubt if we have yet to go to that point of view where a British constituency would elect a black man.' As Burton shows, the speech and the outcry it generated reveals much about contemporary views on race, not least the racism implicit in the Liberals' protestations that to describe Naoroji as 'black' was to suggest he was uncivilised. For them, Salisbury's statement was outrageous because it conflated 'black' Africa with 'brown' India, the backward with the less backward, and thus threatening to upset the established taxonomies of Victorian racial discourse.[10] A further example, more wide-ranging in scope, is provided by David Green's work on the language of American politics from presidents

McKinley to Reagan, specifically his use of presidential speeches to investigate changes in the meanings of political labels over time. Franklin Delano Roosevelt's interwar exploitation of the longstanding linguistic connection between 'liberal' and 'liberality', for example, re-orientated the label of 'liberalism' around New Deal-style state intervention to assist the less fortunate in society, so transforming popular expectations of government for more than a generation.[11]

It is worth pointing out that these new self-consciously 'linguistic' approaches bear some similarity to older traditions of scholarship, not least that of 'high political' history. It is true that historians of high politics have often placed considerable emphasis on behind-the-scenes tactical manoeuvring between politicians, an emphasis that requires the study of private correspondence and government papers, and it is equally true that, being concerned with 'the politicians who mattered', they have avoided discussion of popular, extra-parliamentary discourse, usually declaring scepticism as to its influence on the thinking of governing elites.[12] That said, however, it is also the case that few high political historians have disdained the study of ideology and its use in the public sphere. This fact has often gone unrecognised in some of the more recent, theoretically inflected work on political discourse, perhaps because of an ideological reluctance to acknowledge any methodological affinity with scholars like Maurice Cowling, whose own ideological inclinations – like many in the high political school – were very far removed from those of the Parisian Left Bank. In any case, as made clear in Cowling's own classic definition, high politics is 'primarily a matter of rhetoric and manoeuvre'; its study therefore requires that attention be paid both to private doings in smoke-filled rooms *and* public doings in parliament and on the platform.[13] Indeed, if anything, recent research in the high political tradition has paid more attention to the public than private activities of politicians. Two examples from the field of modern British history bear this out. Jonathan Parry's work on the parliamentary politics of nineteenth-century Liberalism is largely reliant on the speeches of statesmen;[14] while Philip Williamson's biographical study of Stanley Baldwin draws even more heavily on public utterance to present a sophisticated account of the Conservative premier's ideological outlook. As Williamson argues, in a democratic environment, 'the qualities that really distinguish and explain a politician's effectiveness' are most 'likely to be revealed in speeches – in public presentation and argument'.[15]

Historians have not only used speeches to examine the ideological outlook of statesmen and the character of contemporary political discourse, however. They have also been deployed in the investigation of political culture. Here, the focus has been on the form as much as the content of political speech. In the British context, Jon Lawrence's work on the role of speeches in the partisan struggle for control of local public space demonstrates the central importance of public utterance to constituency-level politics in the late nineteenth and early twentieth centuries.[16] Moreover, despite the claims of some accounts that film, radio and television spelled the death knell of the political speech, it persisted as a crucial element of political culture throughout the interwar period and beyond. While only one-fifth of Gladstone's public addresses were made outside of parliament, over one-half of the many thousands given by Churchill were delivered beyond the walls of

Westminster, and even at the general election of 1951, 30 per cent of voters claimed to have attended a platform meeting.[17] Recent quantitative work on twentieth-century American political culture also supports the view that speechmaking remained important despite the advent of mass media. Hart's study of presidential rhetoric between 1945 and 1985, for example, found that the location of speeches was still important. Speechmaking was concentrated in densely populated and politically marginal states; whom a president talked to and where he did it remained crucial, even if his words were broadcast nationally.[18]

Work such as that of Lawrence, Meisel and Hart points to two new directions which historians might usefully take in studying political speech. First, as Lawrence himself has suggested, scholars could address the lack of an integrated approach to the study of public utterance, one that connects the discourse of high and low politics; typically, the focus has either been on the national rhetoric of statesmen or that of the local constituency platform, rarely on both.[19] Second, historians of modern Britain and Europe have been remarkably reluctant to take cognisance of the methods and insights of social scientific approaches to the analysis of speech. This is not the case in North America, where the disciplines of rhetorical criticism and communication studies are well established, and have produced the historically literate work of Hart, Karlyn Kors Campbell, D.W. Houck and others.[20] Houck's prize-winning *Rhetoric as Currency*, to give one example, shows how both Hoover and Roosevelt believed increasing public confidence was vital to economic recovery in the era of the Great Depression, and both deployed sophisticated rhetorical strategies aimed at effecting this, such as Hoover's extensive use of metaphors of 'war' in 1931–2.[21] Indeed, Houck's analysis of metaphor is especially noteworthy. European historians have proved rather unwilling to devote much attention to the use of metaphor in public speech, despite the incontrovertible significance of images such as Churchill's 'iron curtain'. Yet, if social scientists like George Lakoff are right, humans' cognitive processes are largely structured around metaphor: '[i]n all aspects of life . . . we define our reality in terms of metaphors and then proceed to act on the basis of the metaphors'.[22] Hence, for example, the metaphorical conceptualisation of labour as a 'resource' in the utterances of modern politicians has had clear policy implications: those accepting of the metaphor have been inclined to agree that the cost of labour should be kept down, and that cheap labour is necessarily a positive good.[23] Such theoretical insights offer much to historians of modern Europe, but have remained largely unexploited.

## Issues of interpretation

Like all sources, speeches present historians with their own particular set of interpretive problems. These problems are most obvious for the classical, medieval and early modern periods, for which issues of authenticity are most fraught, but they are also of considerable and perhaps underappreciated moment for the period after 1800. Accounts can be partisan, partial, bowdlerised, edited (as often the case in radio or television broadcasts) or simply inaccurate, and the modern historian needs to be aware of this. For example, newspaper reports of speeches often give most coverage to speeches by politicians of the party to which the publication is aligned, while also presenting these utterances in a positive light. As the *Exchange Telegraph* (which supplied reports of speeches to British newspapers) testified to a 1947–8 Royal Commission, '[s]ubscribers to whom the opinion expressed [in a speech] are sympathetic and in line with their own convictions will require perhaps 800 words. Organs with a different frame of mind will require 200 words only.'[24]

Even what might be considered the gold standard of historical authenticity, the official report, has its pitfalls for the unwary researcher. *Hansard*, the record of British parliamentary debates, provides an excellent case in point. Although not published by parliament itself until 1909, *Hansard* functions as the standard source for nineteenth- and twentieth-century parliamentary history, and its reliability is rarely called into question. Yet, it is far from being an entirely accurate record. Before 1909 and the installation of a parliament-appointed staff of reporters, *Hansard* did not provide a verbatim account. Its text being largely compiled from newspaper coverage, only the speeches of front-benchers, ministers and ex-ministers were ever reported in full, with the speeches of everyone else being accorded third-person summaries. Moreover, poor grammar and infelicities of expression were routinely corrected, and proofs of speeches were sent to MPs for amendment, with many politicians making full use of the opportunity this offered for ex post facto alterations to what they had said in the chamber.[25]

Historians' relative lack of concern about the accuracy of British parliamentary records is troubling. As an important article by Olive Anderson has shown, *Hansard*'s heavy reliance on the reports of *The Times* newspaper throws doubt on the authenticity of its accounts of key debates, such as that over the 1857 Divorce Act. Omissions and amplifications in *The Times*'s reportage, often made in accordance with the paper's editorial line, were carried over into the record presented in the columns of *Hansard*. Thus, Anderson concludes, in order to obtain an accurate picture of what exactly went on in the mid nineteenth-century House of Commons, the historian needs to read *Hansard* in conjunction with newspaper reports, such as those contained in the pages of the *Daily News* (which, in contrast to those of *The Times*, were far more likely to leave bad grammar uncorrected and record MPs' reactions, such as cheering, laughter and interruptions).[26] Anderson's article was published in 1997; to date, few scholars have taken on board its lessons.[27]

Aside from issues of authenticity, a second set of problems faced by historians when using speeches as primary sources relates to questions of reception and agency. While it is straightforward enough to analyse the construction and content of public utterances, it is much more difficult to assess their contemporary impact. How were particular speeches regarded by their audiences, and what effect did they have on politics and society? In answering these questions, conventional written sources are in fact helpful enough: informed views on the significance and reception of speeches can readily be found in memoirs, diaries, newspaper commentaries, and so on. Even the bald text of reports can be revealing, as in this example, taken from the press coverage of an address by the Tory leader Arthur Balfour at the 1906 general election:

Now what is the point in debate? (Cries of 'Free Trade' and 'Protection'.) What is the point in debate between us? (Cries of 'Free Trade' and cheers.) I will come to free trade a little later . . . What is a Radical? (A voice – 'Joe Chamberlain'.) . . . I ask, what great changes are desired by the school of thinkers of whom Sir Edward Grey is the leader? (A voice – 'The abolition of Chinese labour'.). . . But there is another. (A voice – 'We do not want a shilling income tax'.) I quite agree. (A voice – 'Then why don't you take it off?' Cheers, and laughter.) I do not think you are listening very well, some of the gentlemen at the back. (A voice – 'Buck up, we'll soon be dead'.) . . . What is dumping? (A voice – 'Dumping them down', and laughter.) Well, what is dumping them down, as the gentleman prefers to say? (Interruption.) Gentlemen, are you not even going to listen to me on free trade?[28]

It hardly needs saying that this tells us much about the strength of popular pro-free trade feeling in early twentieth-century Manchester, while also providing a good illustration of the combative, confrontational rhetorical culture of the time. But such sources do not necessarily give the historian all the answers when it comes to the evaluation of contemporary reactions to any given speech or speeches. The same utterance can mean different things to different people: one witness's opinion of a speech and its impact can be wildly different from the judgement of the majority, which may remain unsaid. As J.G.A. Pocock has pointed out, '[p]olitical statements are such that they may convey more than one meaning and be of more than one order; they are made up of terms of many origins, bearing many possible implications'.[29] So a speaker can have conveyed something to his audience that he did not mean to convey. Moreover, he might have expressed himself differently in different contexts to make the same point: a politician in 1906 setting out his views on free trade to an audience of farmers might well have used a different rhetorical vocabulary to that he deployed in doing the same thing for an audience of bankers. These are obvious points, but it is important that historians be sensitive to them, especially those scholars who read the records of public utterances as discursive 'texts', because the language used in a speech will often vary depending on the circumstances of its delivery.

Occasionally, historians will encounter particular sources which seem especially well-suited for assessing the reception and impact of speeches. Containing numerous reports of the public reaction to Hitler's set-piece orations, the Security Service (SD) files of National Socialist Germany provide one such example. Ian Kershaw has demonstrated how these records can be used to chart the changes in popular attitudes to the Nazi regime over time.[30] But even when dealing with such richly detailed sources, which seem to offer a goldmine of information, the historian needs to tread carefully and remain alert to the context in which such records were produced, as insensitivity here can lead to questionable claims.[31] As Kershaw makes clear, the SD's 'opinion research' was carried out in the context of totalitarianism: in conducting their surveys, some officials were doubtless influenced by a desire to record a positive reaction, for fear of offering uncongenial news to their masters (after Hitler's speech on the twentieth anniversary of the 1923 Putsch, one

SD agent approached a Nazi Party member with: 'Well then, didn't the Führer speak well?'). Similarly, the ordinary German could be reluctant, when questioned, to give negative assessments of Hitler's oratorical efforts, out of understandable fear that this would be followed by reprisals.[32]

The use of speeches as sources thus presents the historian with a variety of methodological problems, and these problems are not always addressed adequately in the extant scholarship. Historians of rhetoric are especially apt to make quite sweeping claims as to the transformative impact of public utterance on politics and society. Yet in many cases, such arguments are more suggestive than compelling, and in some, they tend towards unsubstantiated assertion. K.J. Musolf's recent rhetorical history of Nancy Astor's 1919 election campaign is one example. Although strongly of the view that rhetoric was a powerful persuasive force in politics, Musolf provides little more than a descriptive account of Astor's platform utterances, and while her book does examine the various rhetorical strategies of her subject, it does not prove their impact.[33] Similarly, Andrew W. Robertson's comparative study of the language of democracy in nineteenth-century Britain and North America is also heavy on the recovery of discourse, but weak on explaining its significance. Wanting to argue that rhetoric functioned as a means of 'integrating a mass audience into meaningful political debate', Robertson leaves largely unexplained quite how it performed this function, and aside from distinguishing between two main types of rhetoric ('laudatory' and 'hortatory') simply presents the reader with a surface-level treatment of public political discourse in both countries.[34]

These two examples are illustrative of a wider methodological problem in modern history: in much recent writing, agency and causation have been eschewed in favour of the recovery and analysis of political cultures and discourses. One reason for this, of course, is the post-structuralist assault on older epistemological certainties. What Adrian Jones has called the 'hollow words-only history' of the linguistic turn dispensation has presented us with a profusion of discourses, but its sceptical epistemology ('there is nothing beneath the text') can sometimes inhibit proper evaluation of these discourses' significance.[35] To recognise this is not to reject discursive notions of 'the actual', as some have done.[36] Myths, images and other forms of representation prevalent in the past cannot be dismissed as 'unreal' just because they might have conflicted with contemporaries' day-to-day experiences; they were as much a part of reality as anything else. But it is to say that scholars need to recognise the limits of narrowly textual readings of public utterances, and make more of an effort to assess what in another context Peter Mandler has aptly termed the 'weight and throw' of discourse.[37] Speech-act theorists' insistence on the importance of the illocutionary and perlocutionary dimensions of speech is worth noting here, offering a 'linguistic' approach that is not disdainful of agency or reception. As writers like Austin have insisted, the extent to which an individual succeeds in doing things with words depends on their audience's understanding of and response to what is said.[38] In addition, scholars would perhaps also do well to heed the claim that 'structural context' and material 'reality' still constitute legitimate factors of consideration for the serious historian, despite the postmodernist onslaught. Both, according to Jon Lawrence, should be reintegrated into scholarly accounts of political history. And as Lawrence further points out, recognition that 'actions often speak louder than words' implies that scholars – even scholars of discourse – ought not to neglect the relationship between what politicians said and what they did, between rhetoric and legislation, platform oratory and policy-making.[39] Thus it is important to use speeches in conjunction with other sources. Accounts based solely on the record of public utterance can miss the interaction between historical actors' private and public personas, and tell us little about questions such as the processes through which state policy was made or how diplomatic initiatives were conducted.[40]

But for other questions, however, speeches remain crucial sources. For the political historian, archival records are only of limited utility for the investigation of ideology, thought and doctrine.[41] In politicians' papers, tactical considerations often loom very large – and so accounts that are over-reliant on private correspondence can give the impression that such considerations were the dominating motive force behind political action.[42] In fact, since the mid nineteenth century politics has largely been about what politicians said in public.[43] In the context of advancing democracy, oratorical ability was seen as the key index of political authority, the sine qua non of high office: at least until recently, no amount of administrative competence could compensate for lacklustre speechifying. Salisbury remarked in 1894:

> [W]hen party leaders have to select for a certain number of the offices of the Government, members of the House of Commons who have never held office before, one of the qualifications, which they consider with the greatest care, is that of being able to speak and act in a manner acceptable to the House of Commons; and if a man who has held office before has shown a marked incapacity in this respect, the party leaders will always be glad of any decorous method of excluding him from ministerial office.[44]

This explains why Churchill invested so much effort in preparing his speeches, and why – as he once remarked – a 45-minute address to parliament took him 18 hours to prepare.[45]

Speech was important because it was largely through speech that political leaders communicated their ideas and sought to persuade their publics of the merits of particular policies. Thus if we are interested in recovering the historical experience of politics, we must read the speeches that people at the time heard (and read). After all, the letters and papers so privileged by many historians had tiny contemporary audiences, even among the political elite, whose opinions (on Hitler's views about Jews, for example) were shaped at least as much by public utterance as they were by private correspondence. This implies that speech was central to the quotidian business of leadership and government. As Hart has shown, the speechmaking activities of American presidents since the Second World War have increasingly tended to be spread throughout the year, rather than concentrated at election times.[46]

It is also worth repeating that rhetoric is *never* 'mere rhetoric': as speech-act theory teaches us, words themselves have agency. Publicly enunciated party doctrine can act to constrain political behaviour by making clear what the rank-and-file can and cannot say or do.[47] Moreover, politicians are constrained by their own words. Public utterances can be committing in ways other than those which the speaker intended: '[t]o speak at all is to give some other power over us', as Pocock has observed.[48] One obvious example of this is the way in which voters can hold politicians to account for past promises at election time, but policy-making itself is also affected by public statements made. At the end of the Cold War, for example, the western powers' historical use of a language of national self-determination (used as a rhetorical weapon against the USSR since 1945) constrained the policy options of their governments. In particular, it compelled them to pursue a policy of support for Baltic independence, despite the fact that their *Realpolitik* priorities lay elsewhere.[49] Finally, as social scientists have shown, to speak in favour of something has a self-persuasive effect; it is cognitively quite difficult to feel one thing and say or do another quite different thing, at least over extended periods of time.[50] It may be, for example, that Lyndon Johnson's huge rhetorical campaign to sell the Vietnam War to the American people did more to convince *him* of the rightness of his policy, hence leading to greater presidential commitment to the war effort.[51]

## Benjamin Disraeli's Crystal Palace speech, 1872

Benjamin Disraeli's famous Crystal Palace speech of 24 June 1872 provides an excellent case study for the historical analysis of speeches. Delivered at a mass meeting of the Tory Party's popular organisation, the National Union of Conservative and Constitutional Associations, the speech was a long one, and it is only possible to print a short extract here:

> My Lord Duke and Gentlemen, – I am very sensible of the honour which you have done me in requesting that I should be your guest to-day . . . In the few observations that I shall presume to make on this occasion I will confine myself to some suggestions as to the present state of the Constitutional cause and the prospects which you, as a great Constitutional party, have before you . . . Gentlemen, the Tory party, unless it is a national party, is nothing. It is not a confederacy of nobles, it is not a democratic multitude; it is a party formed from all the numerous classes in the realm – classes alike and equal before the law, but whose different conditions and different aims give vigour and variety to our national life.
>
> Gentlemen, a body of public men distinguished by their capacity . . . seized the helm of affairs in a manner of which I do not for a moment question, but they introduced a new system into our political life. Influenced in a great degree by the philosophy and the politics of the Continent, they endeavoured to substitute cosmopolitan for national principles; and they baptized the new scheme of politics with the plausible name of 'Liberalism.'. . . But the tone and tendency of Liberalism . . . is to attack the institutions of the country under the

name of Reform, and to make war on the manners and customs of the people of this country under the pretext of Progress. During the forty years that have elapsed since the commencement of this new system . . . the real state of affairs has been this: the attempt of one party to establish in this country cosmopolitan ideas, and the efforts of another . . . to recur to and resume those national principles to which they attribute the greatness and glory of the country . . .

Now, I have always been of opinion that the Tory party has three great objects. The first is to maintain the institutions of the country . . . We associate with the Monarchy . . . the majesty of law, the administration of justice, the fountain of mercy and of honour. We know that in the Estates of the Realm and the privileges they enjoy, is the best security for public liberty and good government. We believe that a national profession of faith can only be maintained by an Established Church . . . Well, it is a curious circumstance that during all these same forty years of triumphant Liberalism, every one of these institutions has been attacked and assailed – I say, continuously attacked and assailed . . .

[T]he Act of Parliamentary Reform of 1867–8 . . . was founded on a confidence that the great body of the people of this country were 'Conservative'. When I say 'Conservative', . . . I mean that the people of England, and especially the working classes of England, are proud of belonging to a great country, and wish to maintain its greatness – that they are proud of belonging to an Imperial country, and are resolved to maintain, if they can, their empire – that they believe, on the whole, that the greatness and the empire of England are to be attributed to the ancient institutions of the land . . .

Gentlemen, there is another and second great object of the Tory party. If the first is to maintain the institutions of the country, the second is . . . to uphold the Empire of England. If you look to the history of this country since the advent of Liberalism – forty years ago – you will find that there has been no effort so continuous, so subtle, supported by so much energy, and carried on with so much ability and acumen, as the attempts of Liberalism to effect the disintegration of the Empire of England . . .

Gentlemen, another great object of the Tory party . . . is the elevation of the condition of the people . . .

I ventured to say a short time ago, speaking in one of the great cities of this country, that the health of the people was the most important question for a statesman . . . What is the opinion of the great Liberal party . . . on this subject? Why, the views which I expressed in the great capital of the county of Lancaster have been held up to derision by the Liberal Press. A leading member . . . among the new Liberal members – denounced them the other day as the 'policy of sewage'. . .

I have touched, gentlemen, on the three great objects of the Tory party . . . I have told you . . . with frankness what I believe the position of the Liberal party to be. Notwithstanding their proud position, I believe they are viewed by the country with mistrust and repugnance. But on all the three great objects which are sought by Toryism – the maintenance of our institutions, the preservation of our Empire, and the improvement of the condition of the people – I find a rising opinion in the country sympathising with our tenets, and prepared, I believe, if the opportunity offers, to uphold them until they prevail.[52]

Now, how should the historian go about interpreting a source such as this? First and foremost, context is vitally important. Many scholars have read the speech as an important statement of Conservative Party ideology, yet they have often done this without considering the circumstances in which the address was delivered. Unlike his great opponent Gladstone, Disraeli was no populist, and the Crystal Palace speech was one of the very few forays the Conservative leader made into mass politics during a long career.[53] In making this departure from his usual political style, Disraeli was deliberately sanctioning the growth of popular Conservatism, as represented by the National Union, while also simultaneously atoning for his refusal to address that organisation's inaugural meeting – also held at the Crystal Palace – in November 1867.[54] But there were further circumstantial factors at work, too. The early months of 1872 had seen mounting dissatisfaction in some sections of the Tory Party at what was seen as Disraeli's dilatory leadership in opposition to Gladstone's Liberal government, and his oratorical efforts at Crystal Palace – and also at Manchester earlier that year – should be seen as an attempt to re-impose his authority. This *context* helps explains why the *content* of the speech contained such hot attacks on Liberalism and its principles; Disraeli wanted to scotch any suggestions that he was prosecuting the Conservative ideological attack on Gladstonian reformism with insufficient vigour or clarity of purpose. Hence Liberalism was condemned not simply as an inferior political creed, but as unpatriotic, unconstitutional 'cosmopolitanism', the exponents of which sought 'to make war on the manner and customs of the people of this country under the pretext of Progress' and 'effect the disintegration of the Empire of England'. This was very strong, combative language indeed, and its use was triumphantly successful in cementing Disraeli's position at the head of his party: after 1872, no further challenges to his leadership emerged.

The reasons for Disraeli's success lay in what he said, and historians have devoted much attention to analysing the wider significance of the language he used. His remarks on empire have attracted the most comment. For some scholars, the claim that the second of the Tory Party's three 'great objects' was 'to uphold the Empire of England' did much to establish a close connection between the Conservative Party and imperial patriotism, while signifying a personal shift in opinion away from an earlier view of colonies as 'deadweights' towards support for expansionist imperialism. For others, however, this is an anachronistic perspective, one that accords Disraeli's speech a significance it never had at the time by linking it to later events – notably the partition of Africa – to which it was not in fact connected by any causal relationship.[55] There is much force in this objection, which recognises the importance of the context in which public utterances are made. However, perhaps influenced by a general view of Disraeli as an opportunist rather than ideological politician, a number of scholars have suggested that his statements on empire – indeed the whole speech itself – was little more than 'demagogic self-advertisement' bearing scant relation to practical policy: after all, when Disraeli came to power in 1874, he showed little interest in the details of colonial affairs.[56]

Such scepticism is not justified, however. It is true that Disraeli found the details of imperial (and other) policies uncongenial, but this is not to say he was uninterested in ideas, or that his speech did not reflect a genuinely held ideological position.[57] Again, context is crucial. Examination of the speech in the light of other sources for Disraeli's ideas is revealing, suggesting ideological consistency over time: Crystal Palace was neither a new departure in the Conservative leader's thinking, nor was it a purely tactical ploy. For example, letters published in *The Times* in 1836, in which Disraeli had accused the then Whig government of threatening the empire's integrity, show that the views he expressed on imperial issues in 1872 reflected a long-held position.[58] Similarly, it is also clear from other sources that the opinions Disraeli voiced at Crystal Palace on the Church, the monarchy and social welfare were in line with already-settled convictions.[59] While the stress on 'the elevation of the condition of the people' as the third 'great object of the Tory party' was certainly designed to appeal to working-class voters newly enfranchised by the Second Reform Act, Disraeli's public utterances earlier in the 1860s had already presented the Conservative Party as a 'national' party committed to the welfare of all. Moreover, the fact that Disraeli had privately consulted a noted factory reformer six days before his speech does suggest he had been thinking seriously about the issue.[60]

That Crystal Palace marked no sea-change in Disraelian Conservatism – or Conservatism generally – is further illustrated by contemporary assessments of the speech (showing once again the need to read the records of public utterance in conjunction with other sources). Witnesses saw nothing remarkable in what Disraeli had said. It was a 'good orthodox Conservative speech' in the judgement of *The Times*, while the Tory grandee Lord Derby recorded in his diary that Disraeli 'had nothing to tell his friends that was either new or important. His chief point was that the Liberals represent cosmopolitan, the Conservatives national ideas.'[61]

This is not to say, however, that the speech was of no ideological significance. Disraeli's utterances may have been consistent with established Conservative doctrine, but their delivery to a mass audience had an important effect on the character of the party's public appeal. It is clear that Disraeli intended to use the speech as a means of installing empire, church, crown and constitution, along with a moderate commitment to social reform, as key focal points of a patriotic *popular* Toryism. Throughout the address, this intention is made plain by his repeated claims that 'the great body of the people of this country' were 'Conservative', that they shared his own view that 'the greatness and empire of England are to be attributed to the ancient institutions of the land' and viewed the Liberal alternative with 'mistrust and repugnance'. As Paul Smith has argued, Disraeli's rhetorical involvement of ordinary working people in the Tory political project was a major innovation, and established the foundations of the Conservative Party's popular appeal for at least one hundred years.[62] It is a moot point, however, as to whether or not this meant that henceforth the Conservatives had an effective monopoly on the 'language of patriotism'.[63] While there is no doubt that popular Toryism became more patriotic after 1872, recent research would suggest that alternative vocabularies of patriotism continued to be used in the platform appeals of Liberals and socialists up to and throughout the twentieth century – one example was the left-wing pro-Boer 'Little Englandism' at the time of the South African War (1899–1902).[64] Despite Disraeli's best intentions, patriotism remained a contested concept, available to politicians from all parts of the ideological spectrum.

## Conclusion

The example of Disraeli's Crystal Palace address demonstrates how speeches can tell historians much about contemporary ideologies; for the study of discourse, political discourse especially, they are a vital source. Yet as it also shows, the scholarly use of speeches needs to be handled with care. In order to tell us anything meaningful about the representativeness or impact of any given idea – its 'weight and throw' – speeches need to be read alongside other sources. Only by examining the records of Disraeli's earlier views on the subject can we know that what he said about empire in 1872 was no new departure in his thinking, being consistent with long-held convictions. Similarly, only by consulting contemporary reports (like that of Lord Derby's) can we come to an informed assessment of the reception of any public utterance. Sensitivity to context, then, is crucial. Even if we are interested in understanding a statesman's public persona, or discussing the ideological significance of a particular political issue in public debate, it will not do to study speeches in isolation from other historical sources.

## Notes

1  E.C.F. Collier (ed.), *A Victorian Diarist: Extracts from the Journals of Mary, Lady Monkswell 1873–1895*, London: J. Murray, 1944, p. 30.

2  J.S. Meisel, *Public Speech and the Culture of Public Life in the Age of Gladstone*, New York: Columbia University Press, 2001, p. 78.

3  M. Atkinson, 'Mere Rhetoric?', in D. Brack and T. Little (eds), *Great Liberal Speeches*, London: Politico's, 2001, p. xxxiii; R.P. Hart, *The Sound of Leadership: Presidential Communication in the Modern Age*, Chicago: University of Chicago Press, 1987, pp. xix, 8–9.

4  J. Axtell, 'History as Imagination', *The Historian* 49, 1987, 451–462, 454.

5  Thucycides, *History of the Peloponnesian War*, Harmondsworth: Penguin, 1972, pp. 118–123, 143–151, 158–163.

6  L. Wittgenstein, *Philosophical Investigations*, 2nd edn, Oxford: Basil Blackwell, 1958; J.L. Austin, *How to Do Things with Words*, Oxford: Clarendon, 1962; J. Searle, *Speech Acts*, Cambridge: Cambridge University Press, 1969.

7  Wittgenstein, *Philosophical Investigations*, p. 11 (emphasis in original).

8  For Skinner's methodology, see his *Visions of Politics*, 3 vols, Cambridge: Cambridge University Press, 2002, I. For the 'policeman' example, see ibid., pp. 104–105, 133; cf. P.F. Strawson, *Logico-linguistic Papers*, London: Methuen, 1971, p. 153.

9  See, for example, P. Joyce, *The Rule of Freedom: Liberalism and the Modern City*, London: Verso, 2003.

10  A. Burton, 'Tongues Untied: Lord Salisbury's "Black Man" and the Boundaries of Imperial Democracy', *Comparative Studies in Society and History* 43, 2000, 632–661.

11 D.E. Green, *Shaping Political Consciousness: The Language of Politics in America from McKinley to Reagan*, Ithaca: Cornell University Press, 1987, pp. 119–163.

12 M. Cowling, *The Impact of Labour 1920–1924*, Cambridge: Cambridge University Press, 1971, p. 3.

13 Ibid., pp. 3–12.

14 J. Parry, *The Rise and Fall of Liberal Government in Victorian Britain*, New Haven, Conn.: Yale University Press, 1993, and *The Politics of Patriotism: English Liberalism, National Identity and Europe, 1830–1886*, Cambridge: Cambridge University Press, 2006.

15 P. Williamson, *Stanley Baldwin*, Cambridge: Cambridge University Press, 1999, p. 14.

16 J. Lawrence, *Speaking for the People: Party, Language and Popular Politics in England, 1867–1914*, Cambridge: Cambridge University Press, 1998.

17 J. Meisel, 'Words by the Numbers: A Quantitative Analysis and Comparison of the Oratorical Careers of William Ewart Gladstone and Winston Spencer Churchill', *HRes* 73, 2000, 262–295, 290; D.E. Butler, *The British General Election of 1951*, 2nd edn, Basingstoke: Macmillan, 1999, pp. 141–142.

18 Hart, *Sound*, pp. 177–189.

19 J. Lawrence, 'Political History', in S. Berger et al. (eds), *Writing History: Theory and Practice*, London: Routledge, 2003, pp. 183–202, pp. 196–198.

20 See, for example, Hart, *Sound*; D.W. Houck, *Rhetoric as Currency: Hoover, Roosevelt, and the Great Depression*, College Station: Texas A&M University Press, 2001; K.K. Campbell, 'Style and Content in the Rhetoric of Early Afro-American Feminists', *Quarterly Journal of Speech* 72, 1986, 434–445. For a useful overview of the field, see S.E. Lucas, 'The Renaissance of American Public Address: Text and Context in Rhetorical Criticism', *Quarterly Journal of Speech* 74, 1988, 241–260.

21 Houck, *Rhetoric as Currency*, pp. 54–93.

22 G. Lakoff and M. Johnson, *Metaphors We Live By*, Chicago: University of Chicago Press, 1980, p. 158.

23 Ibid., pp. 67, 156–158, 236.

24 H.C.G. Matthew, 'Rhetoric and Politics in Modern Britain, 1860–1950', in P.J. Waller (ed.), *Politics and Social Change in Modern Britain*, Brighton: Harvester, 1987, p. 55.

25 MPs could, if they wished, return a clean typescript, and there is even one recorded example of a politician deleting two-thirds of his speech: H.D. Jordan, 'The Reports of Parliamentary Debates, 1803–1908', *Economica* 11, 1931, 438–441.

26 O. Anderson, 'Hansard's Hazards: An Illustration from Recent Interpretations of Married Women's Property Law and the 1857 Divorce Act', *EHR* 112, 1997, 1202–1215.

27 One notable exception is B. Griffin, 'Male Legislators and Women's Rights in Britain, 1866–86', PhD Dissertation, Cambridge, 2004.

28 P. Clarke, *Lancashire and the New Liberalism*, Cambridge: Cambridge University Press, 1971, p. 140.

29 J.G.A. Pocock, *Politics, Language and Time*, London: Methuen, 1972, p. 23.

30 See also Moritz Föllmer's chapter in this volume.

31 For example, Stephen Kotkin has suggested that Sarah Davies's use of similar reports produced by party and secret police officials in the USSR under Stalin reflects an excessive readiness on her part to interpret any recorded expressions of public discontent as evidence of significant political dissent. See S. Davies, *Popular Opinion in Stalin's Russia*, Cambridge: Cambridge University Press, 1997 and cf. S. Kotkin's review of ibid. in *Europe-Asia Studies*, 50, 1998, 739–742.

32 I. Kershaw, *The 'Hitler Myth': Image and Reality in the Third Reich*, Oxford: Clarendon, 1987, p. 6, 88–90, 157–158, 180–185, 211–213. On the problems in using such reports, see also Kershaw, *Popular Opinion and Dissent in the Third Reich: Bavaria 1933–1945*, Oxford: Clarendon, 1983, pp. 6–10.

33  K.J. Musolf, *From Plymouth to Parliament: A Rhetorical History of Nancy Astor's 1919 Campaign*, Basingstoke: Macmillan, 1999.

34  A.W. Robertson, *The Language of Democracy: Political Rhetoric in the United States and Britain, 1790–1900*, Ithaca: Cornell University Press, 1995.

35  A. Jones, 'Word *and* Deed: Why a *Post*-poststructuralist History is Needed, and How It Might Look', *HJ* 43 (2000), 517–541, 528.

36  See, for example, L. Stone, 'History and Post-modernism', *P&P* 131, 1991, 217–218 and *P&P*, 135, 1992, 189–194.

37  P. Mandler, 'The Problem with Cultural History', *CSH* 1, 2004, 94–117.

38  Austin, *How To Do Things With Words*, especially pp. 98, 116.

39  Lawrence, 'Political History'.

40  On this, see M. Bentley, 'Party, Doctrine and Thought', in M. Bentley and J. Stevenson (eds), *High and Low Politics in Modern Britain*, Oxford: Clarendon, 1983, pp. 137, 141–142.

41  Ibid., p. 141.

42  See, for example, A.B. Cooke and J. Vincent, *The Governing Passion: Cabinet Government and Party Politics in Britain 1885–86*, Brighton: Harvester, 1974.

43  See Williamson, *Baldwin*, pp. 13–16 for extremely perceptive comments.

44  Salisbury to Sidney Low, cited in G.H.L. Le May, *The Victorian Constitution*, London: Duckworth, 1979, p. 154.

45  Meisel, 'Words by the Numbers', 262–295, 280.

46  Hart, *Sound*, pp. 11.

47  Bentley, 'Party', pp. 148–149.

48  Pocock, *Politics*, pp. 23–24.

49  K. Spohr Readman, 'Between Rhetoric and Realpolitik: Western Diplomacy and the Baltic Independence Struggle in the Cold War Endgame', *CWH* 6, 2006, 1–42.

50  See, for example, K.K. Reardon, *Persuasion: Theory and Context*, Beverly Hills: Sage, 1981, pp. 61–90. Reardon argues that: 'advocating a position discrepant with one's initial position on an issue could conceivably lead one to qualify that initial stance', p. 80.

51  Hart, *Sound*, pp. 90–93.

52  T.E. Kebbel, *Selected Speeches of the Late Right Honourable Earl of Beaconsfield*, 2 vols, London: Longmans, Green, 1882, II, pp. 523–535.

53  J.P. Parry, 'Disraeli and England', *HJ* 43, 2000, 699–728, P. Smith, *Disraeli*, Cambridge: Cambridge University Press, 1996, p. 156.

54  R. Shannon, *The Age of Disraeli, 1868–1881*, London: Longman, 1992, pp. 18–21, 142.

55  C.C. Eldridge, *England's Mission: The Imperial Idea in the Age of Gladstone and Disraeli 1868–1880*, London: Macmillan, 1973, p. 172.

56  R. Koebner and H.D. Schmidt, *Imperialism: The Story and Significance of a Political Word, 1840–1960*, Cambridge: Cambridge University Press, 1964, pp. 107ff.

57  Parry, 'Disraeli and England'.

58  A. Hawkins, *British Party Politics, 1852–1886*, Basingstoke: Macmillan, 1998, p. 183; T.A. Jenkins, *Disraeli and Victorian Conservatism*, Basingstoke: Macmillan, 1996, pp. 14, 73.

59  Hawkins, *British Party Politics*, pp. 182–183.

60  Smith, *Disraeli*, p. 162 and *Disraelian Conservatism and Social Reform*, London: Routledge, 1967, p. 160; Hawkins, *British Party Politics*, pp. 183–184.

61  Eldridge, *England's Mission*, p. 176; J. Vincent (ed.), *A Selection from the Diaries of Edward Henry Stanley, 15th Earl of Derby (1826–93) between September 1869 and March 1878*, London: Royal Historical Society, 1994, p. 110.

62  Smith, *Disraeli*, p. 165.

63  Matthew, 'Rhetoric and Politics', p. 49; Smith, *Disraeli*, p. 166; H. Cunningham, 'The Language of Patriotism, 1750–1914', *HWJ* 12, 1981, 8–33, 22.

64  P. Ward, *Red Flag and Union Jack: Englishness, Patriotism and the British Left, 1881–1924*, London: Royal Historical Society, 1998; P. Readman, 'The Liberal Party

and Patriotism in Early Twentieth Century Britain', *Twentieth Century British History* 12, 2001, 269–302.

## Select bibliography

Green, D.E., *Shaping Political Consciousness: The Language of Politics in America from McKinley to Reagan*, Ithaca: Cornell University Press, 1987.

Hart, R.P., *The Sound of Leadership: Presidential Communication in the Modern Age*, Chicago: University of Chicago Press, 1987.

Houck, D.W., *Rhetoric as Currency: Hoover, Roosevelt, and the Great Depression*, College Station: Texas A&M University Press, 2001.

Jones, A., 'Word *and* Deed: Why a *Post*-poststructuralist History is Needed, and How It Might Look', *HJ* 43, 2000, 517–541.

Jordan, H.D., 'The Reports of Parliamentary Debates, 1803–1908', *Economica* 11, 1931, 438–441.

Lawrence, J., *Speaking for the People: Party, Language and Popular Politics in England, 1867–1914*, Cambridge: Cambridge University Press, 1998.

Matthew, H.C.G., 'Rhetoric and Politics in Modern Britain, 1860–1950', in P.J. Waller (ed.), *Politics and Social Change in Modern Britain*, Brighton: Harvester, 1987.

Meisel, J.S., *Public Speech and the Culture of Public Life in the Age of Gladstone*, New York: Columbia University Press, 2001.

Steinmetz, W., '"A Code of its Own." Rhetoric and Logic of Parliamentary Debate in Modern Britain', *Finnish Yearbook of Political Thought* 6, 2002, 84–104.

# 13 Testimony

*Devin O. Pendas*

In Primo Levi's memoir, *Survival in Auschwitz*, there is a moment where the inmate Levi tries to break off an icicle to quench his tormenting thirst, only to have a guard knock it out of his hand. When Levi asks the guard why, the guard merely replies 'Hier ist kein warum (There is no why here)'.[1] As an inmate and a victim, Levi is singularly ill positioned to know much about the motivations or goals of his tormenters, the guards. It is not the case that there was no 'why' to Auschwitz, only that no guard would have, or would have been able to, explain it to a prisoner. To the victims, the why of Auschwitz remained the mysterious purview of their tormenters. This exchange between a victim of Auschwitz and one of its perpetrators reveals something quite fundamental about the value and limitations of testimony as a source of historical evidence.[2] As a historical source, testimony is extremely valuable for answering some kinds of questions but nearly useless for addressing others.

In particular, what this exchange highlights is the fact that testimony is bound by the personal experience of the witness. His or her position in relations of power (Levi as a victim of German perpetrators) limits not only the kinds of information he or she has access to but the perspectives available for interpreting and understanding that information. Moreover, because testimony is based on direct experience, it cannot offer much useful information about historical processes that extend beyond the scope of individual experience. The structural workings of a capitalist economy or the long-term trends in standards of living or processes environmental change, for example, elude testimony as a source. In other words, questions of macro-structure and long-term change are not well suited to using testimony as a source. On the other hand, testimony provides a unique insight into the meanings of historical experience, to the way that people understood and felt about their lives. If history is as much about people as it is about broad social processes, then testimony provides an invaluable source for historical analysis. Yet how exactly ought we as historians approach testimony as a historical source? How ought we interpret it and weigh it in relation to other kinds of sources? The answers to these questions hinge on how we understand evidence more generally and testimony more particularly.

## Forms of evidence: intentional and unintentional

How do we know what we claim to know about the past? This is, in many ways, one of the most basic questions one can ask of the historian. The short answer that almost any historian would give is that what we know about the past, we know because it is what the evidence tells us. This short answer, of course, simply begs the question. What is evidence? And what can it tell us? Whatever one thinks of the claim that history is simply another genre of writing, like poetry or novels, one must be clear that the crucial generic characteristic of history is that it is a form of writing that relies on evidence.[3] This is precisely what defines history as a genre, distinct from novels or poetry. So the question of what evidence is and what it says is virtually indistinct from the question of what history itself is.

The great French Jewish historian, Marc Bloch, executed by the Nazis in 1944, gave us perhaps the canonical account of historical evidence. Bloch proposed distinguishing two broad categories of historical evidence: intentional and unintentional.[4] Intentional evidence comprises, according to Bloch, those forms of evidence which are 'consciously intended to inform their readers'. These are generally narrative sources, i.e. they seek to tell a story and, in so doing, shape the way events will be perceived and interpreted by others. The classic examples of intentional evidence are memoirs, journalism and testimony. As narratives, intentional sources are self-consciously historical, deliberate attempts to create history. Unintentional evidence, on the other hand, informs the reader despite itself and, as such, is generally non-narrative in form. Government documents, private letters, statistical data, archeological findings are all examples of unintentional evidence. They are sources of information created for some purpose other than informing posterity.

Since the advent of modern, scientific history in the nineteenth century, historians have had a marked preference for unintentional evidence.[5] It is not hard to see why this should be so. With any form of intentional evidence, there is always the possibility that its author is seeking to deliberately mislead his or her reader. And even if the intentional source is not lying in the strict sense, by virtue of the simple fact that its author is deliberately trying to convey information to a reader, it is safe to assume that he or she has a definite and possibly self-interested perspective on the events in question. One is reminded here of Winston Churchill's famous quip that 'history will be kind to me, for I intend to write it'. Generally, historians have assumed – not always correctly – that unintentional sources will, in effect, be more honest. Whatever the distortions of unintentional evidence, Bloch argues, 'at least, [it] has not been especially designed to deceive posterity'.[6]

Yet this historian's preference for unintentional evidence is not as unproblematic as it may seem. That preference originates, as I have indicated, in the sense that such sources are significantly more honest. Because they were created for other purposes, they are thought to be more likely to reveal what was 'really going on' at some point in the past. However, it is imperative to remember that, although unintentional sources were perhaps not created in order to deliberately influence posterity, they were nevertheless *created*. As such, they too have an agenda. This can be, and often is, deliberate, as in, for instance, a government memo seeking to influence policy. But it can also be the product of unconscious forces.

All language has meaning only in the context of shared rules, not simply of grammar, but also of cultural understanding. This is why translation is always such a difficult task. Because language only acquires meaning in specific cultural contexts, it is crucial for the historian to enter into the logic of that cultural context in order to decode his or her evidence. Otherwise, the evidence would either simply be gibberish or, alternatively, the historian would be reading it in light merely of his or her present-day understanding, and thus would be committing the originary historical fallacy: anachronism.[7] Yet all cultural contexts are in part products of power relations and consequently, all meaning reflects the power structures in which it was created. This means that even unintentional sources reflect the power relations of their time period. If read naively, this can distort the historian's analysis of these sources by incorporating the power structures of the past directly into the historian's present day analysis without sufficient critical distance. Above all, it is crucial to read sources not only for what they say but for what they fail to say, because it is in their silences and omissions that their underlying power structures frequently reveal themselves most clearly.[8]

Take for example, the first general history of the Nazi genocide of the Jews written by Gerald Reitlinger in 1953. His title? *The Final Solution: The Attempt to Exterminate the Jews of Europe, 1939–1945.*[9] This is a remarkable book, especially for the time when it was written, and one cannot help but admire Reitlinger's achievement. Yet his very choice of title shows the core problem of unintentional sources. 'The Final Solution' is, of course, the Nazi term for their systematic extermination of European Jewry. It is short for 'the final solution to the Jewish question'. As such, the very phrase 'final solution' implies there is a Jewish question, that there really was a Jewish problem needing to be solved. But the idea that there is a Jewish problem in modern European history is an intrinsically anti-Semitic notion. There was no Jewish problem in Europe; there was only an anti-Semitic one. So to pick up this intrinsically anti-Semitic and Nazi concept and use it as the label for the historical genocide of the Jews is, however unwillingly and unwittingly, to view that event through the eyes of the perpetrators, to give credence to the notion that there was a problem that needed solving in the first place. Unintentional evidence, in this case, unintentionally skews historical perception, subtly, perhaps, but significantly.

There is also the problem of gaps and omissions in unintentional evidence, no less than in intentional evidence. In the context of genocidal violence, for instance, one of the goals of the perpetrators is to dehumanize and silence their victims, to in effect remove them from history. Not surprisingly, then, Jewish voices appear only sporadically and in highly distorted form in the German documentation of the Holocaust. The long-standing cliché that the Jews were passive victims in the face of Nazi violence, that they went to their death like sheep to the slaughter, that, in effect, they had no historical agency during their extermination, is an artifact of precisely this reliance on German sources. There was nothing the Nazis feared more than Jewish agency. Consequently, they sought to disguise, minimize and malign it at every opportunity.[10] Moreover, since most Jewish efforts during the Holocaust would have been directed at either evading or resisting Nazi initiatives, Jews obviously had every incentive to keep as much of this secret from the Germans as possible. Finally, there is the simple technical limitation that few unintentional Jewish sources for the history of the Holocaust survived the war and many of those that did are in languages other than German and hence inaccessible to a significant number of Holocaust historians, who speak no Hebrew, Yiddish, Polish, Hungarian, Russian or any of the myriad other languages of European Jewry. For all of these reasons, then, the Jewish dimension of the Holocaust has proven singularly inaccessible using unintentional German sources. As a consequence, much of the historiography of the Holocaust, as with other traumatic events, tends to focus on the perpetrators, rather than the victims. As Philip Gourevitch has said of the Rwandan genocide: 'The more the dead pile up, the more the killers become the focus, the dead are only of interest as evidence.'[11]

What is crucial to note here is that once one recognizes that unintentional sources can be as deceitful as intentional ones, the *prima facie* preference for the former is less compelling. Bloch himself noted that even those forms of unintentional evidence 'which seem the clearest and the most accommodating will speak only when they are properly questioned'.[12] In particular, he insisted, we must cross-examine our sources sceptically. For Bloch, a crucial part of that cross-examination was to deploy as many different forms of evidence as possible in a given context. Why then exclude intentional evidence from that variety? If we must read even unintentional evidence against the grain, for its silences and hidden logics, if we must cross-examine every piece of evidence before deeming it reliable, then why would intentional evidence be any less valuable than its unintentional counterpart? It seems, then, that the a priori case against intentional evidence becomes quite weak on closer examination and that, if approached properly, intentional evidence – like testimony – can be every bit as valuable to the historian as unintentional evidence.

## Testimony as a genre of intentional evidence

Of the forms of intentional evidence testimony forms a distinct subgenre. In his *Lectures on Logic and Metaphysics,* Sir William Hamilton offered one of the first systematic definitions of the term. 'Testimony,' he wrote, 'in the strictest sense of the term, therefore, is the communication of an experience, or, what amounts to the same thing, the report of an observed phænomenon, made to those whose own experience or observation has not reached so far.'[13] Taking this definition as a starting point, what are the defining characteristics of testimony? I would argue there are three. The first has to do with the status of the witness. Testimony is a report of firsthand experience or observation. As such, it is distinct from many other kinds of intentional evidence, such as past histories, newspaper reports, documentary films etc. Second, it differs from yet other kinds of firsthand intentional evidence, chiefly memoirs, in that testimony is principally an oral genre. Although testimony can certainly be written down and, indeed, that is the form in which it will most commonly be used by historians, the origins of testimony are verbal. As the nominal form of the verb – to testify – indicates, the roots of the concept of testimony are both religious and juridical. In Judaism, for instance, the divine injunction to remember carries with it, perforce, an injunction to tell as well.[14] Even more explicit is the mandatory courtroom oath to 'tell the truth, the whole truth, and nothing but the truth'. In both of these contexts, the injunction to tell the truth initially concerns an oral context. Thus, as a form of truth-telling, testimony is, in its structure, more about what people say, than what they write down. This basic orality of testimony has profound implications for how we evaluate it as a historical source, even though, again, most historians will in fact read testimony, rather than listen to it directly.

Finally, testimony differs from oral history, another kind of spoken intentional evidence, in that the interlocutor is not the historian directly. In oral history, the historian talks to the witness him or herself and, as such, is in a position to carefully craft the questions being asked, to follow up on points of uncertainty, to shift topics in pursuit of serendipitous points of interest.[15] When using testimony, the historian has none of these luxuries. The questions are asked by others and may or (more frequently) may not be precisely those which the historian wishes to address. Testimony has been gathered for a wide number of reasons but, at least in the twentieth century, two have been the most common. One frequent source of testimony has been court proceedings, where eye-witness testimony has a long, if troubled, history as a major source of evidence. Testimony in this context is guided by the legal proceedings at hand and is shaped by the evidentiary concerns of the court, e.g. the determination of criminal guilt or civil liability. Matters extrinsic to this concern, however interesting to the historian, rarely appear.[16] In this respect, legal testimony often remains strongly perpetrator-oriented, treating only tangentially the experience of the victims. Alongside material from legal trials, one might also include testimony gathered by so-called Truth and Reconciliation Commissions, such as the ones created in post-Apartheid South Africa.[17] Based on the premise that national regeneration requires the disclosure of past atrocities, truth commissions are generally more interested in the victims' experience than are trials, although they share with trials the fundamental feature that the questions posed may not be those of interest to the historian.[18]

If legal or quasi-legal proceedings thus form one principal venue for testimony in the twentieth century, memorial projects, broadly construed, form the other. Particularly in the aftermath of traumatic events, even when there is no prospect for political or legal redress, efforts are often undertaken to collect the testimony of survivors so as to record their experiences. These efforts can be quasi-official, as with the German government's documentation of the experience of expellees from Eastern Europe after the Second World War or the current Veterans History Project by the American Folklife Center of the Library of Congress.[19] Alternately, these can be entirely private, as with the Fortunoff Video Archive of Holocaust Testimony at Yale University or Steven Spielberg's Survivors of the Shoah project (now the USC Shoah Foundation Institute for Visual History and Education), both of which videotape testimony by Holocaust survivors.[20] Earlier examples of such testimony can be found for the Armenian Genocide.[21]

We can thus define testimony for our purposes as follows: it is a form of oral evidence of firsthand experience, gathered by others and accessed by the historian indirectly, usually through reading. It is a form of intentional evidence, in that it seeks to deliberately shape the response of its audience, but it is different from memoirs or oral history in that it is not necessarily aimed directly at posterity.

This then raises the larger question: what use is testimony as a historical source? To answer this question, one must focus on the oral structure of testimony. Even if written down or transcribed, it is usually spoken first; even if never spoken, it is modeled on speech and meant to be comprehended as such. This means that the operative approach to testimony is not reading, as is typical of historical sources. Rather, it is listening and hearing. What difference does this make? Because, in a manner of speaking, we listen to and hear testimony (even when we read it), our mode of understanding it is more immediate and more directly inter-subjective. Reading is a relationship to a text, not a person. Listening and hearing, though, bring us into a relationship with the speaker. This may only form half of a conversation, since testimony is a monologue by the witness, not a dialogue with the historian, but the implicit inter-subjectivity is still there.

At this point, it becomes important, however, to distinguish the precise mode of this relationship by distinguishing listening from hearing. According to the *Oxford English Dictionary*, to hear means 'to perceive or have the sensation of sound'.[22] To listen, on the other hand, means 'to hear attentively; to give ear to; to pay attention to (a person speaking or what is said)'.[23] The crucial difference, then, between listening and hearing is the degree of attentiveness involved and, by extension, the degree of inter-subjective recognition accorded the speaker. I can hear what someone is saying without acknowledging his or her humanity but I cannot listen to it without recognizing him or her as a fellow human being, even if I ultimately reject what is actually being said. This may seem to imply that hearing is inferior to listening, that it is callous and indifferent. This can be the case, but often hearing is not so much inferior to listening as it is a different mode for accessing a different kind of truth.

When thinking of evidence as a way of reconstructing the past, one ought to keep in mind that there are in fact different forms of historical truth that are being accessed thorough that evidence. This is by no means to say that there is no such thing as historical truth, much less its cognate opposite, that there is no such thing as historical falsehood. Both truth and falsehood most definitely exist but neither is homogeneous or unitary. There are multiple forms of truth and of falsehood, even with regard to any single instance or event. Different forms of evidence are useful for accessing different forms of truth. Similarly, different modes of interpreting the same evidence will likewise generate different forms of truth.

In the case of testimony, it makes a difference whether we listen to it or whether we hear it because each will produce a different register of truth. If we *hear* testimony, that is, if we take in its information without thereby establishing a strong, attentive inter-subjective bond with the speaker, the truth we are thereby accessing is what might be termed 'forensic truth'. This is truth at its most basic, the truth of facts, of either/or propositions, of location, of sequence and of timing. Something either happened at some specifiable location at a specific point in time in the manner described or it did not. Forensic truth allows us to judge such a case. The term forensic, after all, means simply analogous to court proceedings, and it is thus a truth inextricably linked to the faculty of judgment. In short, then, forensic truth seeks to answer the question: what happened? The proper mode of interpretation in this context is analytic.

On the other hand, if we *listen* to testimony, thereby forging an attentive relationship with the speaker, we are connecting with what might be termed 'experiential truth'. Because listening is an inherently inter-subjective activity, the truth that it generates is necessarily the subjective truth of the interlocutors. Since testimony is not dialogic but necessarily monologic, at least for the historian, the subjective truth in this instance is simply that of the witness.[24] It is the truth of his or her state of mind, the truth of what he felt or she experienced, of how a person is in the world and how he or she responds to that condition. This is a more complicated truth than forensic truth because it is not so directly connected to judgment and either/or propositions. It is, rather, a yes/but truth. Yes, that is true for you, but it is not necessarily true for everyone. As such, it is also a non-falsifiable truth. If I say I am feeling sad or had a happy childhood, how can anyone verify or refute those statements? In short, experiential truth seeks to answer the question: what does what happened mean to the person to whom it happened? The mode of interpretation in this case is hermeneutic.[25]

Clearly, testimony is capable of generating both kinds of truth and indeed usually does. It can contain both statements of fact and statements of subjective experience. As Robert Eaglestone has noted, 'specific memories and accounts also function as "counters" or evidence in traditional history: but they are not only this – they open up a world that is not ours'.[26] As historians, then, when approaching testimony, it is important to both hear it and listen to it but also to remember the difference between the two. Otherwise, we are likely to either miss half of what is being said in testimony or to confuse one kind of truth for another, with serious and adverse consequences for our analysis of the past.

So now the question becomes one of technique or method. How do we hear? How do we listen? What kinds of interpretive strategies or research methods do we apply? To answer such questions, it is best to offer some concrete examples to illustrate some of the salient features of hearing and listening to testimony.

## Hearing and listening

On July 27, 1964, the witness Simon Gotland testified in the Frankfurt Auschwitz Trial. Regarding the defendant Stefan Baretzki, an SS non-commissioned officer who had worked as a 'block leader' in Auschwitz, Gotland testified:

> I know Baretzki as well as I know my own heart. Everywhere where he was sent, he appeared like a tiger. In the camp, one heard repeatedly, 'There goes Baretzki! Get out of his way!' I saw Baretzki several times on the Ramp. He went to the ramp on foot like a tiger. He always had a club in his hand. With

respect to the unloading of the train wagons, he had a say. He always yelled at the Kapos and at the others who drove the people out of the wagons. It had to go quickly because usually a new transport was expected. He was very active, so active that one can't really describe it.[27]

First, let's *hear* this testimony. What are the factual claims in this testimony? That Baretzki went to the Ramp, that he was an active and eager participant in the unloading of the arriving trains and that he carried a club, implicitly threatening the prisoners with grave violence. These are significant forensic claims. During the trial, Baretzki had denied in his opening deposition that he had participated in the ramp selections.

[Judge]: Who conducted the selections?
[Baretzki]: The officers.
[Judge]: Not you?
[Baretzki]: No, only officers, not even noncoms. Your Honour, the commission was made up largely of officers. How do you think they would have liked it if a noncom had run around among them.[28]

Here we have an either/or proposition. Either Baretzki or Gotland was lying. How do we decide between the two? Sir William Hamilton, who provided our initial definition of testimony, proposed that its validity could be gauged by, first, 'the subjective trustworthiness of the witness' and, second, by 'the objective probability of the fact itself'.[29] In other words, who seems more personally reliable, Gotland or Baretzki? And, based on other sources of information, whose claims seem more plausible? At first glance, one would be inclined to say that Gotland was the more subjectively trustworthy, since he had less incentive to lie, while Baretzki's claim may have been more objectively plausible, given the military hierarchy of the SS. The situation, however, is actually much more complicated than this.

In terms of objective plausibility, it is true, on the one hand, that the SS was organized on military lines, with a fairly strict chain of command and and at least nominally rigorous division of labor.[30] So perhaps officers would have objected to overly zealous activity by a noncom. Ultimately, though, this seems unlikely. It is clear that in the concentration camps, SS military discipline was often quite lax and even low-ranking SS men had considerable leeway in their treatment of prisoners and their degree of active participation in atrocities.[31] While it is true that medical personnel, including dentists and pharmacists, as well as doctors, were directly responsible for ramp selections in Auschwitz, lower-ranking personnel often played crucial roles in the collective supervision of the arriving transports. On objective grounds, then, there is no reason *per se* to doubt Gotland's testimony. It might well be true. Consequently, the validity of Gotland's forensic claims can only be decisively judged on subjective grounds.

As far as trustworthiness goes, Baretzki was on trial and faced a possible life sentence for his crimes in Auschwitz, giving him every incentive to lie. This is particularly true because German law distinguishes perpetrators from accomplices in part based on how eagerly they participated in their crimes.[32] Since perpetrators were generally punished much more severely than accomplices in Nazi cases, it would very much have been in Baretzki's interest to deny active participation in ramp selections. This assumption, that in criminal trials at least, perpetrators have a standing inclination to lie has led Daniel Goldhagen to argue that their testimony cannot be taken seriously, at least whenever it is in the least bit self-exculpatory.[33] In a similar vein, other historians such as Jan Gross have made parallel arguments for treating victim testimony as *prima facie* true:

> By accepting what we read in a particular account [by a victim] as fact *until we find persuasive arguments to the contrary*, we would avoid more mistakes than we are likely to commit by adopting the opposite approach, which calls for cautious skepticism toward any testimony *until an independent confirmation of this content has been found.* The greater the catastrophe, the fewer the survivors. We must be capable of listening to lonely voices reaching us from the abyss . . .[34]

Both of these propositions, that perpetrators always lie and that victims can never be mistaken, are overstated and overly simplistic. Perpetrators sometimes tell the truth and victims occasionally make mistakes. The question is how to tell when this is the case.

Here, it is a good idea to hear as much testimony as possible, to approach it, as Christopher Browning has put it, 'in the individual plural, not collective memory but rather collected memories'.[35] Browning and Goldhagen have been explicitly critical of each other's use of testimony. Goldhagen rejects out of hand all exculpatory perpetrator testimony as dishonest, while Browning insists that carefully collated perpetrator testimony can reveal important truths, even when it is exculpatory.[36] According to Browning, it is perfectly possible to reconstruct historical events using even the 'variety of different, often conflicting and contradictory, in some cases clearly mistaken, memories and testimonies'.[37] Contrary to Jan Gross, however, Browning insists that relying on the testimony of a single person sets 'too low an evidentiary threshold', that one must always compare as broad a range of testimony as possible in order to detect 'tendencies and recurring patterns', what he terms a 'firm core of shared memory'.[38]

This is particularly true because, although perpetrators may have greater incentive to lie than victims, outright fraud on the part of purported victims is not unheard of, as the unfortunate case of Binjamin Wilkomirski's fake memoirs show.[39] Wilkomirski's 'memoir' of his alleged childhood in German extermination camps, initially published in German in 1995 to great acclaim, turned out to have been completely made up. Wilkomirski was in fact one Bruno Grosjean, born and raised in Switzerland, and had never been in a concentration camp at all. Ultimately then, Browning's rule of thumb that it is necessary to collate and cross-check as much witness testimony as possible, for both perpetrators and victims, seems most persuasive here. Shared memory can be treated as very likely true, precisely because it is independently verified by a large number of different witnesses.

However, to truly understand why both Goldhagen and Gross are mistaken, it is necessary to revisit Gotland's testimony and *listen* to it. What do we learn of Gotland's experience, his state of mind? The first thing to note in this regard is that Gotland claimed to know Baretzki as well as he knew his own heart. This was simultaneously an emotional and a self-reflexive claim; knowledge of the dangerous other had become, for Gotland, a form of self-knowledge. He remained what he had been in the camp, a product of his tormenters, as well as of himself. As a result, his knowledge of himself became a form of knowledge of the perpetrators as well. The other striking experiential truth that emerges in Gotland's testimony is his repeated emphasis that Baretzki was like a tiger. Baretzki appears here as a figure of pure terror, a club-bearing predator, to be avoided at all costs. The dominant experiential truth here is fear.

So far, hearing and listening may seem more straightforward than they in fact are. Nor is it yet clear exactly how the experiential truth of Gotland's testimony impacts on its forensic truth, for we have not yet heard all that he had to say, or rather could not say. Gotland spoke in a broken mix of French, Polish and Yiddish. He spoke no German and struggled to make himself understood by the court. Here it is worthwhile quoting a journalistic description of his testimony at some length.

> His hands gripping the arms of his chair, the heavy-set man sits facing the court as if he needs to be ready to jump up and flee at any moment. He looks helplessly from side to side. He obviously does not understand most of the questions put to him in well-chosen words by the numerous men in black robes. He sometimes starts in shock when his own words come back to him magnified three-fold from the loudspeakers. And the more intensely the memories pour forth from him, the less the remaining trial participants can understand him. It is as if he were surrounded by a wall.[40]

Gotland's testimony, which seems so articulate in the trial transcript, was anything but when he delivered it. He was a broken man, stammering, trying to articulate what he himself could barely stand to recall. Had we been able to hear Gotland in person, to listen to his broken efforts to articulate meaning, we might have known better than to assume either task would be easy. Part of the lesson here is simply that testimony always loses something in translation to the printed page and it is important to be aware of that. But we also begin to learn something about the different methods for hearing and listening.

Gotland's inarticulateness may call into question the forensic value of his testimony, and thus call into question Gross's assertion that a single witness is sufficient to reconstruct forensic truth. If we merely hear him, without also listening, what we now hear is inarticulate stammering. This is what prompted the Frankfurt court to reject Gotland's testimony in its final verdict as juridically worthless. Since the court did not even deign to consider Gotland's testimony in its final verdict, it is necessary to get a sense why they rejected such testimony from their evaluation of another witness, Czeław Głowacki, who testified against the defendant Klaus Dylewski. The court noted that Głowacki, who had worked carrying corpses to the crematoria while in Auschwitz, 'still suffered a great deal emotionally from those bloody events. They were obviously still on his mind, with all their attendant terrible side-effects, during his testimony.'[41] As a consequence, the court rejected Głowacki's testimony. In effect, the court felt that overt exhibitions of traumatic symptoms rendered witnesses unreliable. The emotionalism that renders testimony valuable as evidence of experiential truth may undermine its forensic value – and, one could add, though a court of law would not – that the reverse is true as well. A purely factual statement may tell us nothing about the experience of the witness. Those who would always reject perpetrator testimony and always accept victim testimony would do well to remember this interplay between forensic and experiential truth, between hearing and listening.

In effect, the Frankfurt court privileged hearing to the exclusion of listening. It followed the forensic impulse to its logical conclusion, rejecting all obviously traumatized testimony. Of course, it thereby excluded one of the central experiential truths of the Holocaust – that all Holocaust experience was traumatic. This tendency to privilege forensic hearing over experiential listening is hardly surprising in a court, but it is not inevitable. Nor need historians follow the Frankfurt court's lead in this regard. In the trial of Adolf Eichmann, for instance, the lead prosecutor Gideon Hausner sought in ways that went well beyond anything that happened in the Auschwitz trial to stress the essential Jewishness of the Holocaust and in so doing tried to privilege listening over hearing.[42] In his opening speech, he proclaimed: 'When I stand before you here, Judges of Israel, to lead the Prosecution of Adolf Eichmann, I am not standing alone. With me are six million accusers ... I will be their spokesman and in their name I will unfold the awesome indictment.'[43] Hausner, in other words, claimed not to be speaking for the state of Israel or even for justice, much less the law. He claimed to be speaking for the Jews of the world, those who were murdered in the Holocaust, those still alive, and even those of the past, noting that 'The history of the Jewish people is steeped in suffering and tears. "In thy blood, live!" (Ezekiel 16:6) is the imperative that has confronted this nation ever since it made its first appearance on the stage of history.'[44]

Thus, for Hausner, the Eichmann trial was at its core not just about the recollection of Jewish catastrophe, but also the imperative of Jewish survival. In short, Hausner embraced the narrative character of intentional evidence that so troubled Bloch and turned it to redemptive political ends. (This is, of course, precisely what Hannah Arendt found so appalling about the prosecution's approach in this case.)[45] For all the limitations of this narrative approach from a forensic point of view, it meant certain dimensions of the trauma of the Holocaust were acknowledged in the Eichmann trial which had remained submerged in the Auschwitz trial, most especially that it was not just Jews who perished, it was Jewish culture and Jewish life as it had existed.[46] Hausner's approach to listening to testimony was particularly good at eliciting the communal dimensions of Jewish experience, something Nazi sources rarely acknowledge.

This emerges quite clearly in the kinds of seemingly extraneous testimony that Hausner elicited; these were of little forensic value but of tremendous experiential interest. For instance, on May 3, 1961, Rahel Auerbach from Yad Vashem, a survivor of the Warsaw ghetto, testified about the Holocaust in Warsaw. At the start of her testimony, however, Hausner asked her for 'a general description, and a very concise one, of Warsaw as it was, from the Jewish point of view, before the outbreak of the War?' To which Auerbach responded:

> I would want to speak mainly about Warsaw from the spiritual aspect, about the cultural world of Jewish Warsaw. When I came to Warsaw for the first time . . . I was astonished at the intensity of the Jewish life. It was especially the Orthodox Jews who made an impression on me . . . this Jewry, Orthodox Jewry, was the great reservoir of Jewish life. Jews from modern social strata, the intellectual elite, all the time were leaving Jewish life, but these Orthodox Jews remained and they continually produced new strata of cultural creation. There was a complete Jewish state there.[47]

What emerges in this testimony, then, is a fuller sense of what was lost in the Holocaust: not just Jews but Jewishness was murdered, a point Auerbach made clear when she asserted that:

> [i]t was known that the enemy wanted to destroy us also from the spiritual point of view; this was also a prelude to physical destruction, to humiliate us and to convince their own people and the world at large that this was a nation of parasites who were not fit to live in the world, that they were a kind of gypsies.[48]

She went on then to describe the incredible efforts made by Jews in the Warsaw ghetto to preserve their cultural and educational institutions in the face of German hostility and about various efforts at Jewish self-help in the ghetto. Aside from the unfortunate racism implicit in her reference to the gypsies, what is most telling about Auerbach's testimony is the way that, in contrast to Simon Gotland, hers is a testimony not about personal trauma, not about self-knowledge, but about the character of Jewish life in Warsaw before and even during the ghetto.

Auerbach's testimony thus tells us much about the experiential truth of both pre- and postwar Jewish life as well as the connections between them. This is a particularly important point. For survivors, the Holocaust was only one part of their life. It may have been – and frequently was – a moment which defined all others. But it was nonetheless an experience that had meaning not solely in its own terms but also in relation to the rest of their lives. That aspect of the Holocaust is impossible to recover without listening carefully to what survivors have to say.

The Zionist implications of Auerbach's testimony could hardly be clearer. And that is how we can know that this is not simply a forensic claim about prewar Jewish life but an experiential claim about the character of the Jewish community as Auerbach experienced it. On a forensic level, Auerbach was right that the Jewish community had considerable autonomy before the war, but she also underplays the assimilationist tendencies among Warsaw's Jews.[49] This raises the important question of how one can verify experiential claims. On the one hand, such claims are, by their nature, self-validating. We cannot read people's states of being, and so must take their self-reported emotions more or less at face value.

There is, however, a fundamental difficulty with testimony such as Auerbach's in this regard. She was testifying in the 1960s about the 1930s and 1940s. However honest her testimony may have been, it was mediated by twenty years of postwar experience. There was, in effect, a temporal filter in place between her past experience and the moment of her testimony. She had no capacity to recover past states of being except as seen through the lens of subsequent experience. So, when she emphasized the state-like character of Jewish life in prewar Warsaw, might she not have been, perhaps unintentionally, assimilating that memory to her experience of an actual Jewish state after the war? How could we tell?

On the one hand, it should be noted, that this may not matter. As long as we are aware that her testimony may tell us more about the 1960s than it does about the 1930s, this temporal filter may be irrelevant. However, if we really need to recover the 1930s and 1940s, we ought, at a minimum, to cross-check Auerbach's testimony against more immediate sources. These too can take the form of intentional testimony. Although very little of it survives, some testimony given by Jews at the time of the Holocaust itself remains.

Leib Langfuss, for example, worked in the Jewish Sonderkommando in the gas chambers of Auschwitz, whose gruesome job it was to accompany victims to the gas chambers, gather their belongings, remove their hair and gold fillings, and cremate their corpses.[50] Prior to his execution in November 1944, he kept a diary which he buried in the vicinity of crematorium 2 in Auschwitz-Birkenau. As a contemporary document, the testimonies recorded in Langfuss's diary do not suffer from the temporal filtering of Auerbach's testimony. One entry, in particular, is of relevance. On Passover 1944 a transport arrived from France, bringing with it, among others, Rabbi Moshe Friedman of Bayon. According to Langfuss, Friedman addressed himself to the Germans as he was being led naked into the gas chamber, still clinging to his clothing:

> 'You, cruel murderers, human scum, do not think that you will succeed in destroying the Jewish people. The Jewish people will live forever and will not vanish from the stage of history . . .' He spoke with great emotion and great strength. Then, when he had finished, he put on his hat and in great excitement called out 'Shema Israel', and all the Jews faithfully responded with him 'Shema Israel' out of a sense of profound faith which had surrounded them all in the last moments of their lives. It was a moment of supreme elevation, such as may be encountered but once in a lifetime, proving the eternal nature of Jewish spiritual resistance.[51]

Although more overtly religious than Auerbach's testimony (Langfuss was himself a rabbinical judge), this account strongly confirms Auerbach's communal sensibilities. Clearly, for some Jews at least, one of the central experiential truths of the Holocaust was communal solidarity, a sense of shared suffering and hence, shared identity, whether religious or political.

This raises a final point to consider when listening to testimony for its experiential truth. Experience is always personal and idiosyncratic. No two people experience the same event in the same way. If, for Langfuss, the ultimate meaning of his impending death in Auschwitz was that of 'Jewish spiritual resistance', one of his colleagues in the Sonderkommando, Zalman Loewenthal, noted in his own buried manuscript, that many found the price of survival very high indeed.

> . . . why do you do [such] unsuitable labor, how do you live, what is the purpose of your life, what is your will - - - what more do you want to achieve in your life - - - here hides the weak point - - - from our commando, which I do not intend to defend at all. But I must state the truth, that more than one of them lost his human image in the passage of time; you become ashamed of yourself; they have simply forgotten what they do, the nature of their work. [In the course of time] they adapted, until you become filled with wonder - - - at the sound of weeping, until - - - normal, average - - - simple, modest people - - - without realizing, it has become routine; one gets used to everything, and whatever happens no longer makes an impression; someone screams, people look on indifferently, as at an everyday matter, how tens of thousands of people are being wiped out.[52]

Loewenthal's account is vastly more pessimistic than either Langfuss's or Auerbach's. The price of survival, usually only temporary for those in the Sonderkommando, was not only a coerced complicity in Nazi murder, it was also frequently the loss of one's own ability to even lament that price. When considering the experiential truth of Auschwitz, one must keep both Langfuss's and Loewenthal's perspective in mind. Both are true. Neither is the whole truth.

## Conclusion

In the best case, of course, historians should always both hear and listen to testimony. Only rarely is testimony purely of either forensic or experiential value. It is a matter of delicate historical judgment to discern the precise admixture of both in any given testimony. On this issue, there is no substitute for experience and sensitivity. It will of course matter a great deal what exactly the historian is trying to achieve with his or her research. The project will in important respects dictate the method. Still, almost no project is so one-sided as to not benefit from approaching testimony with an ear for its complexity and range of usefulness.

A careful historian, then, will develop the distinct analytical skills to both hear and listen to testimony. Hearing requires both broad and deep historical knowledge to situate what one hears meaningfully, to cross-check one witness against others and against other kinds of sources, to notice minor and major errors and to evaluate both the subjective trustworthiness and objective plausibility of any given witness. Listening requires an intuitive sympathy, as well as an analytical awareness of the limits of such sympathy. Above all, it takes a willingness to take another person's experience seriously, to remember that it is not just evidence, but that it is a recounting of a human life. One cannot truly listen if one does not hear the humanity of one's witnesses.

## Notes

1  P. Levi, *Survival in Auschwitz*, trans. S. Woolf, New York: Collier Books, 1960, p. 27.
2  For an excellent historical overview, see A. Wieviorka, *The Era of the Witness*, Ithaca: Cornell University Press, 2006.
3  H. White, *Metahistories: The Historical Imagination in Nineteenth Century Europe*, Baltimore: Johns Hopkins University Press, 1975 and H. White, *The Content of the Form: Narrative Discourse and Historical Representation*, Baltimore: Johns Hopkins University Press, 1987.
4  M. Bloch, *The Historian's Craft*, Manchester: University of Manchester Press, 1954, pp. 60–61.
5  On the origins of 'scientific' history, see G.G. Iggers, *The German Conception of History: The National Tradition of Historical Thought from Herder to the Present*, Middletown, Conn.: Wesleyan University Press, 1968.
6  Bloch, *Historian's Craft*, p. 62.
7  See D.H. Fischer, *Historians' Fallacies: Toward a Logic of Historical Thought*, New York: Harper & Row, 1970, pp. 132–140.
8  This is a point that historians of gender have particularly stressed in recent decades by pointing to the ways in which gender norms are silent, taken for granted, in a wide variety of historical sources. See for instance J.W. Scott, 'Gender: A Useful Category of Historical Analysis', *AHR* 91 (1986), 1053–1075, 1070.
9  G. Reitlinger, *The Final Solution: The Attempt to Exterminate the Jews of Europe, 1939–1945*, New York: Beechhurst Press, 1953.
10 For correctives to this trend, see S. Friedländer, *Nazi Germany and the Jews*, vol. 1, *The Years of Persecution, 1933–1939*, New York: Harper Collins, 1997, and I. Gutman, *Resistance: The Warsaw Ghetto Uprising*, New York: Houghton Mifflin, 1994.
11 P. Gourevitch, *We Wish to Inform You that Tomorrow We Will be Killed with our Families: Stories from Rwanda*, New York: Picador, 1998, p. 201.
12 Bloch, *Historian's Craft*, p. 64.
13 Sir W. Hamilton, *Lectures on Metaphysics and Logic*, vol. 2, *Logic*, Boston: Gould and Lincoln, 1860, p. 459.
14 'Only in Israel and nowhere else is the injunction to remember felt as a religious imperative to an entire people.' Y.H. Yerushalmi, *Zakhor: Jewish History and Jewish Memory*, Seattle: University of Washington Press, 1982, p. 9.
15 See for example, D.K. Dunaway and W.K. Baum, *Oral History: An Interdisciplinary Anthology*, 2nd edn, Walnut Creek, Calif.: Altamira Press, 1996, or D.A. Ritchie, *Doing Oral History*, New York: Twayne Publishers, 1995.
16 See my analysis of these matters in D.O. Pendas, *The Frankfurt Auschwitz Trial, 1963–1965: Genocide, History and the Limits of the Law*, Cambridge: Cambridge University Press, 2006, pp. 161–168.
17 In general, see R.I. Rotberg and D. Thompson, *Truth v. Justice: The Morality of Truth Commissions*, Princeton: Princeton University Press, 2000, and P.B. Hayner, *Unspeakable Truths: Facing the Challenge of Truth Commissions*, New York: Routledge, 2002.
18 On the better atmosphere for victims in Truth Commissions, see M. Minow, *Between Vengeance and Forgiveness: Facing History after Genocide and Mass Violence*, Boston: Beacon Press, 1998, pp. 61–74.
19 For the German expellees, see T. Schieder (ed.), *Dokumentation der Vertreibung der Deutschen aus Ost Mitteleuropa*, 8 vols, Munich: DTV, 2004 [1954–61]. On the history of these volumes, see M. Beer, 'Die Dokumentation der Vertreibung der Deutschen aus

Ost-Mitteleuropa: Hintergründe—Entstehung—Wirkung', *Geschichte in Wissenschaft und Unterricht* 50 (1999), 99–117. On the Veterans History Project, see http://www.loc. gov/vets/ [accessed on September 20, 2007].

20 For the Fortunoff Archive, see http://www.library.yale.edu/testimonies/ [accessed on September 20, 2007]. For the Shoah Foundation, see http://www.usc.edu/schools/ college/vhi/ [accessed on September 20, 2007].

21 See for example J. Barton (ed.), *Turkish Atrocities: Statements of American Missionaries on the Destruction of Christian Communities in Ottoman Turkey, 1915–1917*, Ann Arbor, Mich.: Gomidas Institute, 1998, or J. Lepsius, *Der Todesgang des armenischen Volkes: Bericht über das Schicksal des armenischen Volkes in der Türkei während des Weltkrieges*, Potsdam: Tempelverlag, 1919. For a recent compilation, see D.E. Miller and L.T. Miller, *Survivors: An Oral History of the Armenian Genocide*, Berkeley: University of California Press, 1993.

22 *Oxford English Dictionary*, online ed., s.v. 'hear'.

23 Ibid., s.v. 'listen'.

24 For this distinction, see M.M. Bakhtin, *The Dialogic Imagination: Four Essays*, Austin: University of Texas Press, 1981.

25 See e.g. H. Greenspan, *On Listening to Holocaust Survivors: Recounting and Life History*, Westport, Conn.: Praeger, 1998.

26 R. Eaglestone, *The Holocaust and the Postmodern*, Oxford: Oxford University Press, 2004, p. 158.

27 Fritz Bauer Institut and State Museum Auschwitz-Birkenau (eds), *Der Auschwitz-Prozeß: Tobandmitschnitte, Protokolle, Dokumente*, DVD-Rom, Berlin: Directmedia Publishing, 2004. Das Verfahren: 70 Verhandlungstag, p. 13403.

28 B. Naumann, *Auschwitz: A Report on the Proceedings against Robert Karl Ludwig Mulka and Others Before the Court at Frankfurt*, trans. J. Steinberg, London: Pall Mall, 1966, p. 56.

29 Hamilton, *Lectures on Metaphysics and Logic*, p. 457.

30 Though both older, the standard histories of the SS remain: H. Höhne, *The Order of the Death's Head: The Story of Hitler's SS*, trans. R. Barry, New York: Coward-McCann, 1970, and G. Reitlinger, *The SS: Alibi of a Nation, 1922–1945*, New York: Viking Press, 1957.

31 See for example R. Zürcher, '*Wir machten die schwarze Arbeit des Holocaust': Das Personal der Massenvernichtungsanlagen von Auschwitz*, Nordhausen: Verlag Traugott Bautz, pp. 191–94 and K. Orth, *Die Konzentrationslager-SS: Sozialstrukturelle Analysen und biographische Studien*, Göttingen: Wallstein, 2000, pp. 201–203.

32 The details are complicated. See Pendas, *The Frankfurt Auschwitz Trial*, pp. 61–71.

33 D.J. Goldhagen, *Hitler's Willing Executioners: Ordinary Germans and the Holocaust*, New York: Knopf, 1996, pp. 467–468.

34 J.T. Gross, *Neighbors: The Destruction of the Jewish Community in Jedwabne, Poland 1941*, New York: Penguin, 2001, p. 92.

35 C. Browning, *Collected Memories: Holocaust History and Postwar Testimony*, Madison: University of Wisconsin Press, 2003, p. 39.

36 See for example Goldhagen's critiques of Browning in *Hitler's Willing Executioners* and Browning's response in C. Browning, 'Afterword' in Browning, *Ordinary Men: Reserve Police Battalion 101 and the Final Solution in Poland*, New York: Harper Perennial, 1998 [1992], pp. 191–223.

37 Browning, *Collected Memories*, p. 39.

38 Ibid., pp. 43, 46.

39 The 'memoir' is B. Wilkomirski, *Fragments: Memories of a Childhood*, trans. C. Brown Janeway, New York: Schocken, 1996. For the best account of the affair, see S. Maechler, *The Wilkomirski Affair: A Study in Biographical Truth*, trans. J.E. Woods, New York: Schocken, 2001.

40 'Die Sprache die niemand versteht', *Frankfurter Neue Presse,* July 28, 1964.

41  F.-M. Balzer and W. Renz (eds), *Das Urteil im Frankfurter Auschwitz-Prozess, 1963–1965*, Bonn: Pahl-Rugenstein, 2004, p. 207.
42  On Hausner's strategy, see L. Douglas, *The Memory of Judgment: Making Law and History in the Trials of the Holocaust*, New Haven: Yale University Press, pp. 123–149.
43  Attorney Gen. of Israel *v.* Eichmann, 36 I.L.R. 5. http://www.vex.net/~nizkor/ hweb/people/e/eichmann-adolf/transcripts/Sessions/Session-006-007-008-01.html. [Accessed on May 12, 2007].
44  Ibid.
45  H. Arendt, *Eichmann in Jerusalem: A Report on the Banality of Evil*, rev. edn, New York: Penguin, 1964.
46  For an important reflection on the Holocaust as the murder of European Jewish culture, see M. Postone, 'Anti-Semitism and National Socialism', in A. Rabinbach and J. Zipes (eds), *Germans and Jews since the Holocaust: The Changing Situation in West Germany*, New York: Holmes & Meier, 1986, pp. 302–314, p. 314.
47  Attorney Gen. of Israel *v.* Eichmann, 36 I.L.R. 5. http://www.vex.net/~nizkor/hweb/ people/e/eichmann-adolf/transcripts/Sessions/Session-026-01.html.
48  Ibid.
49  W. Bartoszewski and A. Polonsky (eds), *The Jews in Warsaw: A History*, Oxford: Basil Blackwell, 1991.
50  For the definitive account, see Eric Friedler, Babara Siebert and Andreas Kilian, *Zeugen aus der Todeszone: Das jüdische Sonderkommando in Auschwitz*, Lüneberg: zu Klampen Verlag, 2002.
51  B. Mark, *The Scrolls of Auschwitz*, Tel Aviv: Am Oved Publishers, 1985, pp. 159–160, quote p. 208.
52  Ibid., p.221. Loewenthal's manuscript was recovered in 1962 and was heavily damaged by humidity. The dashes represents illegible words in the original.

## Select bibliography

Browning, C., *Ordinary Men: Reserve Police Battalion 101 and the Final Solution in Poland*, New York: Harper Perennial, 1998 [1992].

Browning, C., *Collected Memories: Holocaust History and Postwar Testimony,* Madison: University of Wisconsin Press, 2003.

Friedlander, S. (ed.), *Probing the Limits of Representation: Nazism and the 'Final Solution'*, Cambridge, Mass.: Harvard University Press, 1992.

Goldhagen D. J., *Hitler's Willing Executioners: Ordinary Germans and the Holocaust*, New York: Knopf, 1996.

Greenspan, H., *On Listening to Holocaust Survivors: Recounting and Life History*, Westport, Conn.: Praeger, 1998.

Gross, J.T., *Neighbors: The Destruction of the Jewish Community in Jedwabne, Poland*, New York: Penguin, 2001.

Hilberg, Raul, *Sources of Holocaust Research. An Analysis*, Chicago: I.R. Dee, 2001.

Langer, L.L., *Holocaust Testimonies: The Ruins of Memory*, New Haven: Yale University Press, 1991.

Mark, B., *The Scrolls of Auschwitz*, Tel Aviv: Am Oved Publishers, 1985,

Wieviorka, A., *The Era of the Witness*, Ithaca: Cornell University Press, 2006.

# Glossary

**Concept**    A word (usually a noun and its related adjectives) which has accumulated not only a set of key and generally accepted meanings, but also a cluster of diverse and sometimes contested connotations over time. Concepts are thus an important element in the social and political semantics of a society. The history of concepts, or *Begriffsgeschichte* in German, is an interpretative approach developed by historians such as Quentin Skinner and Reinhart Koselleck which seeks to trace the evolution of these meanings over time. 'Freedom', 'Liberalism', 'Modern' and 'Modernisation' and 'Terror' are examples of important political concepts.

**Discourse**    From the Latin *discurrere*, meaning 'running back and forth'. Traditionally, discourse either meant a treatise on an intellectual subject (as in René Descartes, *Discours de la méthode*, 1637) or the reasoned dialogue between different speakers. In the wake of the linguistic turn, the term discourse has acquired a distinctively different meaning. The term now denotes a body of assertions and utterances which are related to a certain topic and follow a certain set of rules. Discourse analysis is thus the attempt to reconstruct the rules according to which these assertions or enunciations (in French: *énoncés*) are created. Discourse history follows the changes of these rules over long periods of time. Discourse analysis differs from a history of concepts or *Begriffsgeschichte*, because it extends the object of analysis beyond the level of terms or sentences to the level of whole texts. With the history of concepts and other forms of enquiry inspired by the linguistic turn it shares the focus on the surface and materiality of the text and the rejection of the hermeneutical idea to search for intentions or interests 'behind' the text.

**Deconstruction**    An approach to textual interpretation developed by the French philosopher Jacques Derrida (1930–2004). Deconstruction relates the meaning of a text not to the identity of a stable subject or author (as in hermeneutics), but rather to the instability of differences between terms and concepts in the text which constitute that meaning. Deconstructing a text means to unearth the hidden oppositions and contradictory connotations which constitute the meaning of a text, without being fully visible in it. A text might for instance comment on the possibility of openly admitting homosexuals to a career in the armed forces, and the problems that might create. A deconstruction of such a text would look out for the *différance* (shifting difference) between homosexuality and heterosexuality, and would ask if and how the meaning of that text is constituted by the (implicit) assumption that these categories are fixed opposites, rather than alternatives with fluid boundaries.

**Emplotment**    The narrative structure or plot of a text determines the order of appearance, the nature and the significance of events which are included in a story. The relationship between the 'hero' of a story and the wider world is another important aspect of emplotment. In his critical analysis of nineteenth-century historiography, the philosopher Hayden White has posited romance, comedy, tragedy, satire as the four basic forms of emplotment. In the context of primary source interpretation, attention to the mode of emplotment points to the importance of the narrative structure for the overall message or 'morale' of a text.

**Hermeneutics**    From the Greek *hermeneuein*, meaning 'to interpret'. In a more narrow sense, the term refers to techniques of textual interpretation which have been practised in classical philology, Protestant theology and jurisprudence since the sixteenth century. In a wider sense, the nineteenth-century tradition of philosophical hermeneutics, developed by authors such as Friedrich Schleiermacher, Johann Gustav Droysen and Wilhelm Dilthey, which sees the 'objectivity' of research in the humanities based on the understanding of 'subjectivity'. Historical research in this tradition is thus partly a reconstruction and re-enactment of and partly a dialogue with subjects in the past, and with the overarching 'spirit' (*Geist*) which formed the context of their actions. Hermeneutical interpretation of texts and other cultural artefacts from the past aims to reconstruct the meaning subjects have invested in them.

**Historicism**    Name for a nineteenth-century intellectual current on the continent, particularly in German-speaking Central Europe. In a more narrow usage, the term denotes research-based academic historiography which rests on the hermeneutical 'understanding' of the past, as it had been developed by Ranke, Droysen and other authors since 1800. In a wider usage, the term denotes the genuinely historical orientation of all humanities in the nineteenth century. Around 1900, controversies about historicism affected Protestant theology, economics and philosophy, when the alleged relativistic consequences of this historical orientation for moral values and for the concept of 'truth' came under attack. Critics argued that the notion of historicity would not allow the upholding of 'eternal' values.

**Linguistic turn**    A line of reasoning in the humanities that refers back to the linguistics of Ferdinand de Saussure (1857–1913), but that has only fully come to the fore since the late 1960s in the writings of Roland Barthes, Jacques Derrida, Michel Foucault and other French post-structuralist thinkers. The proponents of the linguistic turn do not deny the existence of a physical reality outside language and texts (of which they have sometimes been accused). They do, however, reject the older, representational understanding of the nature of language, according to which language and its basic elements, signs, are a mere representation or reflection of objective reality. For the post-structuralists, language can never be a neutral medium. Following de Saussure, they point to the arbitrary nature of the connection between the word (the signifier) and the idea or object to which it refers (the signified). Because of its arbitrary nature, this connection evolves over time, meaning it is never fixed. Proponents of the linguistic turn believe that the attempt to stabilise the meaning of signifiers is one of the key operations which constitutes culture and society. At the level of tropes and emplotment, the 'linguistic turn' implies that the strict distinction between a 'literal' and a 'figurative' use of language is problematic, or even fundamentally flawed.

**Metaphor** From the Greek *meta-pherein*, meaning 'carrying over'. This is the most widely used trope. In tune with the literal meaning, a metaphor carries meaning from one semantic field into another. At least three different functions of metaphors in texts can be distinguished: in their *illustrative* function, they are meant to increase the plausibility of an argument; in their *heuristic* function, they offer a new perspective on a well-known topic; in their *constitutive* function, they substantiate a fundamentally new understanding of a certain topic.

**Semantics** In literary studies a sub-discipline which studies the meaning of words. Those interested in historical semantics study the repertoire of key concepts which provided a set of shared assumptions and expectations at a given moment in the past. A wide usage of semantics sees it as an equivalent of culture, i.e. the web of meanings that is framing our interpretation of the social world.

**Signs** A wide definition of signs includes words, images, sounds, graphic symbols, gestures and so on, and sees them as means of communication. According to Ferdinand de Saussure (1857–1913), a sign is defined as the difference between the form or *signifier* (i.e. the word or symbol) and the content or *signified* (the object or idea to which it refers). In the wake of the linguistic turn, literary scholars tended to reject the idea that signifiers simply reflect the signified objects, but rather posit that language is based on the infinite possible relations between signifiers.

**Text** Usually a written statement of varying length. In discourse theory, the term denotes a sequence of utterances or signs which show a connection with regard to their meaning, or, in other words, a semantic structure. Thus, also a series of photos, the questionnaire of an opinion poll or a statistical tabulation can be interpreted as a text.

**Trope** The figurative use of expressions, i.e. a figure of speech. The four basic tropes are irony, metaphor, metonymy, and synecdoche.

# Index

# The Modern Historiography Reader
## Western Sources
### *Edited by Adam Budd*

Historiography – the history of historical writing – is one of the most important and basic areas of study for all historians. Yet in such a broad and expanding field, how should students find their way through it?

In *The Modern Historiography Reader: Western Sources*, Adam Budd guides readers through European and North American developments in history-writing since the eighteenth century. Starting with Enlightenment history and moving through subjects such as moral history, national history, the emergence of history as a profession, and the impact of scientific principles on history, he then looks at some of the most important developments in twentieth-century historiography such as social history, traumatic memory, postcolonialism, gender history, postmodernism, and the history of material objects.

This is the only book that brings together historiographical writing from anthropology, literary theory, philosophy, psychology, and sociology as well as history. Each of the thirteen thematic sections begins with a clear introduction that familiarizes readers with the topics and articles, setting them in their wider contexts. They explain what historiography is, how historians' perspectives and sources determine the kinds of questions they ask, and discuss how social and ideological developments have shaped historical writing over the past three centuries.

With a glossary of critical terms and reading lists for each section, *The Modern Historiography Reader: Western Sources* is the perfect introduction to modern historiography.

Hb: 978–0–415–45886-3   Pb: 978–0–415–45887–0

For ordering and further information please visit:
www.routledge.com

# Routledge History

## History Beyond the Text
## A Student's Guide to Approaching Alternative Sources
### *Edited by Sarah Barber and Corina Peniston-Bird*

Over the past few years the question of 'what is a historical source' has become an increasingly prominent concern. In *History Beyond the Text*, Sarah Barber and Corinna Peniston-Bird open up the discussion on sources to those beyond the 'traditional' ones.

Across ten chapters different historians look at a variety of alternative sources: visual – fine art, cartoons, photography, film and television; aural – music and oral testimony; and physical – ephemera, architecture, and landscape, as well as virtual space. While the sources discussed are 'interdisciplinary', each contributor examines how the source can be approached from an historical perspective. Each chapter introduces the reader to the source, suggests the methodological and theoretical questions that historians should keep in mind when using it, and provides empirical examples of approaches to the source. Pulling these disparate sources together, the introduction discusses the nature of historical sources and those factors which are unique to, or shared by, the sources covered throughout the book.

Taking examples of sources from around the globe, this is the ideal companion for every student of history who wants to engage with sources.

Hb: 978–0–415–42961–0   Pb: 978–0–415–42962–7

For ordering and further information please visit:
www.routledge.com

Lightning Source UK Ltd.
Milton Keynes UK
UKOW06f0743200516

274638UK00008B/144/P